NEW RULES OF GLOBAL TRADE

A Guide to the World Trade Organization

Jeffrey S. Thomas
Michael A. Meyer

CARSWELL
Thomson Professional Publishing

Canadian Cataloguing in Publication Data
Thomas, Jeffrey S.
The new rules of global trade: a guide to the World Trade Organization
Includes bibliographical references and index.
ISBN 0-459-25452-9

1. Agreement Establishing the World Trade Organization (1994).
2. World Trade Organization.   3. Foreign trade regulations.
4. International trade.   I. Meyer, Michael A. (Michael Andrew), 1965- .
II. Title.

K4600.T46 1997   341,7'54   C97-932135-2

CARSWELL
Thomson Professional Publishing

One Corporate Plaza, 2075 Kennedy Road, Scarborough, Ontario M1T 3V4
Customer service:
Toronto 1-416-609-3800
Elsewhere in Canada/U.S. 1-800-387-5164
Fax 1-416-298-5094

Scribimus indocti doctique

From JST

To Caroline and Matti

"[it was] a long pull, and a strong pull,
and a pull altogether . . ."

From MAM

To my parents, Frank and Patricia Meyer,
whose hard work, dedication and
encouragement made this book and all of
my accomplishments possible.

Foreword

After eight years of often punishing negotiations, the World Trade Organization Agreement came into effect on January 1, 1995. This book is an attempt at a relatively comprehensive guide to the new rules of global trade and the overseeing organization introduced with the coming into force of this Agreement. In our view, it is difficult to over-estimate the importance of this Agreement to all WTO Member countries. With this in mind, we have been guided by an overriding principle in producing this text—it should be aimed at, and accessible to, as wide a readership as possible. Guided by this principle, we have attempted to provide value for both student and expert. While generally keeping explanations as simple as possible, we have not avoided areas of complexity in the Agreement. It is perhaps inevitable that complex ideas cannot always be simply explained, and therefore there are parts of the volume that some may find opaque. We have attempted to keep these to a minimum.

In addition, while co-written by a Canadian and an American, we have attempted to avoid nationalistic approaches to description and discussion. We do not dwell on obligations or issues of particular relevance to our respective countries. Our approach has been that of an impartial international observer. In our view, readers from all WTO Member countries should find equal value in the discussion.

We commenced work on the manuscript in March of 1995 and it has taken over two years to complete. While other work pressures were in part responsible for this delay in completion, the complexity of the Agreement and the rate at which it continues to evolve were also responsible. A number of developments which have occurred since January 1, 1995 meant that many parts of the manuscript required re-working. One advantage of this has been that we have been able to increase the value of the text by including some important recent developments, including a discussion of the first WTO Ministerial Meeting that was held in December of 1996. Consequently, the commentary can be considered up-to-date as of September 1, 1997.

Contents

List of Abbreviations

AMS	Aggregate Measurement of Support
ATC	Agreement on Textiles and Clothing
BISD	Basic Instruments and Selected Documents
CCC	Customs Co-operation Council
CG-18	Consultative Group of Eighteen
DSB	Dispute Settlement Body
DSU	*Understanding on Rules and Procedures Governing the Settlement of Disputes*
EC	European Communities
EU	European Union
EEC	European Economic Community
FIRA	Foreign Investment Review Agency
FOGS	Functioning of the GATT System
GATS	*General Agreement on Trade in Services*
GATT	*General Agreement on Trade and Tariffs*
GNG	Negotiating Group on Trade in Goods
GNS	Negotiating Group on Trade in Services
HS	Harmonized Commodity Description and Coding System
IASC	International Accounting Standards Committee
ICITO	Interim Commission for the International Trade Organization
IFAC	International Federation of Accountants
ILO	International Labour Organization
IMF	International Monetary Fund
IOSCO	International Organization of Securities Commissions
IPIC Treaty	Treaty on Intellectual Property in Respect of Integrated Circuits
ITO	International Trade Organization

ITU	International Telecommunications Union
LLDCs	Least-developed countries
MERCOSUR	Mercado Comun del Sur (the Southern Cone Common Market)
MFA	Multi-Fibre Arrangement (known more formally as *Arrangement Regarding International Trade in Textiles*)
MFN	Most-Favoured Nation
MLATs	Mutual Legal Assistance Treaties
MOU	Memorandum of Understanding
MTN	Multilateral Trade Negotiations
MTO	Multilateral Trade Organization
NAFTA	North American Free Trade Agreement
NGBT	Negotiating Group on Basic Telecommunications
NGMTS	Negotiating Group on Maritime Transport Services
OECD	Organization for Economic Co-operation and Development
OTC	Organization for Trade Co-operation
PGE	Permanent Group of Experts
PPA	Protocol of Provisional Application
SDRs	Special Drawing Rights
SG and A	Selling, General & Administrative (Costs)
SPSMs	Sanitary and Phytosanitary Measures
TBT	Technical Barriers to Trade
TMB	Textiles Monitoring Body
TNC	Trade Negotiations Committee
Total AMS	Total Aggregate Measure of Support
TPRB	Trade Policy Review Body
TPRM	Trade Policy Review Mechanism
TRIMs	Trade-Related Investment Measures
TRIPS	Trade-Related Aspects of Intellectual Property Rights
TSB	Textile Surveillance Body
UN	United Nations
UNCTAD	United Nations Conference on Trade and Development
VER	Voluntary Export Restraint

WIPO   World Intellectual Property Organization

World Bank   International Bank for Reconstruction and Development

WTO   World Trade Organization

1

A Brief History of the GATT/WTO System and the Uruguay Round Negotiations

1. INTRODUCTION

While it is certainly possible to review any international agreement in some detail without a discussion of the rationale behind its creation, a review of an agreement's historical context can add considerably to the depth of understanding. This is particularly true in the case of the WTO Agreement which is a massive and complex document. In many cases an understanding of specific rules requires interpretive background. And, while historical context is important for interpretive purposes, it also serves to highlight the fundamental significance of the Agreement and the reforms it has introduced to the world trading system. With these benefits in mind, this chapter provides an overview of the historical development of the GATT/WTO system, commencing with certain pre-World War II developments that led to the eventual negotiation of the GATT in 1946, and then concluding with the entry into force of the WTO Agreement on January 1, 1995. This overview is then expanded upon in some important areas in the subject-specific chapters that follow.

2. THE BIRTH OF THE GATT SYSTEM

International cooperation on trade matters did not begin with the negotiation of the *General Agreement on Tariffs and Trade* (or the "GATT") in 1946. International trade and, consequently, international cooperation on trade matters, has been present in various forms for hundreds of years. More recently, prior to the establishment of the United Nations, its predecessor, the League of Nations, made various unsuccessful attempts to formalize multilateral rules on trade and other economic issues. The GATT, negotiated in 1946, was significantly influenced by this long history of cooperation on trade matters.

The specific origins of the GATT/WTO system can, however, be more directly traced back to the period between the two World Wars and the "Great Depression" of the 1930s. One notable aspect of the Depression was a substantial reduction in global trade. This reduction was due primarily to increased tariffs and other trade restrictions, as many countries adopted "beggar-thy-neighbour" polices in attempts to improve their own economies by restricting imports. These attempts, however, had the opposite effect and were generally considered to have aggravated and prolonged the Depression.

U.S. President Franklin D. Roosevelt came to power in 1933, at the height of the Great Depression. Among his many proposed policy reforms, President Roosevelt (and his Secretary of State, Cordell Hull) advocated a reduction of U.S. tariffs, on a reciprocal basis, and a general liberalization of trade as a method of improving the U.S. and global economies, and thus overcoming the Depression. The United States Congress subsequently passed the *Reciprocal Trade Agreements Act of 1934*, granting to the President the authority to negotiate a reduction of U.S. tariffs in exchange for the reciprocal reductions in the tariffs of U.S. trading partners. Under the *Reciprocal Trade Agreements*

Act and its various extensions, the U.S. then negotiated bilateral trade agreements with over 20 countries prior to the start of World War II in 1939.

With the outbreak of the War, trade again became governed by national security concerns rather than bilateral or multilateral rules. In spite of the national security concerns of the time, the Allies began considering post-war economic issues as early as 1941, primarily at the urging of the United States. Commitments concerning the creation of a post-war trading system were included in the 1941 *Atlantic Charter*—an agreement between the United States and the U.K.—and in the lend/lease arrangements between the United States and a number of other countries. These basic commitments were then further pursued by the United States and the U.K. through a series of informal meetings during the War, between 1943 and 1945. Developments on the trade side were mirrored by developments on the monetary/financial side, where, at the Bretton Woods Conference in 1944, the Allies drafted charters for two other post-war international economic institutions, the International Monetary Fund ("IMF") and the International Bank for Reconstruction and Development (now known as the "World Bank").

Based on U.S. pre-war bilateral agreements and wartime discussions, the United States and the U.K. then issued their *Proposals for Expansion of World Trade and Employment* in late 1945. Based on a belief that economic problems were one of the primary causes of the War, the Proposals called for the negotiation of an international trade agreement based on the principle of non-discrimination and the establishment of an International Trade Organization (or "ITO") to oversee and administer the new agreement. The agreement was to be negotiated within the context of a proposed United Nations Conference on Trade and Employment. In order to "jump-start" the process of trade liberalization, the Proposals also called for a separate and prior set of tariff negotiations amongst a smaller number of countries, the results of which could then be rolled into the results of the ITO negotiations once they had been completed and the ITO had become operational.

The Proposals were accepted by the United Nations Economic and Social Council in February 1946. A United Nations Conference on Trade and Employment was planned and a Preparatory Committee, comprised of 18 countries, immediately commenced work on a draft charter for presentation to the Conference, to be held in Havana, Cuba in November of 1947. A number of preparatory sessions then took place during 1946 and 1947. As envisaged in the Proposals, concurrently with the second preparatory meeting held in Geneva in April to August of 1947, a group of 23 countries met to negotiate a series of preliminary tariff reductions and draft a temporary agreement that would govern these reductions, to be called the *General Agreement on Tariffs and Trade,* or the "GATT".

In developing this temporary GATT, the 23 participating countries drew the essential elements from the draft ITO Charter as it then existed — in particular, the Charter's existing chapter on "Commercial Policy".[1] In determining what obligations were to be included within the GATT, the negotiators were guided by two primary considerations. First, the GATT was to be a temporary agreement only, to be rolled into the ITO Charter. It was not considered necessary to repeat much of what would eventually be found in the Charter itself. The Agreement could thereby be kept brief and relatively simple. Second, the negotiators were also limited by a desire of the United States to restrict the GATT's obligations to those that the U.S. Administration would be able to implement without requiring any further Congressional approval. Therefore no "new" obligations, other than further tariff reductions, could be included within the GATT. This result was then further assured by the negotiation of an additional Protocol of Provisional Application (or "PPA"), which provided that the GATT would not come definitively into force, but would only come into effect "provisionally" — that is, only on a temporary basis and to the extent that it did not conflict with any pre-existing inconsistent legislation. This meant that the new GATT obligations would only apply to future legislation and participating countries would not be required to amend any existing mandatory legislation in order to bring their obligations into effect. At the time, the PPA and its effects were not considered to be of much long-term import, as the ITO Charter, with all of its more substantive and definitive obligations, was to follow shortly. The GATT and its accompanying PPA were signed on October 30, 1946 and came into effect on January 1, 1947. And, while the GATT contained no specific expiry date, it was clearly understood by the participants that the GATT was to be a temporary agreement, to remain in force only until such time as the ITO become effective.

While the GATT was being negotiated, further negotiations on the draft ITO Charter continued. The UN Conference on Trade and Employment was convened as planned in Havana, Cuba in November of 1947 and, with the notable absence of the USSR, was attended by over 57 UN Members. The Conference completed its work in March of 1948 and the Havana Charter was signed by 53 of the 57 participating countries on March 24, 1948.

In spite of the long process of consensus-building and preparatory work that had gone into the preparation of the Charter, it was immediately subject to

---

[1]The Charter's Commercial Policy provisions were themselves based substantially on the Proposals and the main obligations of the pre-war U.S. bilateral agreements. The Charter as it then existed, and as finally approved, was comprised of five substantive parts: the Commercial Policy part, dealing with trade in goods; a section concerning Employment and Economic Activity, which addressed certain issues relating to employment policies; a part which addressed economic development and reconstruction; a part concerned with restrictive business practices; and a section addressing inter-governmental commodity agreements. A final part provided for the establishment and operation of the ITO and the settlement of disputes through the Organization. The fact that only one of the Havana Charter's five substantive parts found its way into the GATT led the *Economist* magazine to observe that the GATT had been "four-fifths throttled at birth".

intense criticism, particularly within the United States. The compromises necessary to achieve a broad agreement amongst 53 countries resulted in criticisms from both sides of the trade-policy debate. On the one hand, many of those favouring freer trade considered that the Charter was worse than the present situation in that it legitimized much existing discrimination and it did not go far enough to ensure a non-discriminatory international trading regime. On the other hand, most protectionists felt that the Charter went too far and would significantly limit U.S. sovereignty. Criticism in the United Sates was compounded by a growing suspicion of international institutions generally, this suspicion being initiated by the developing Cold War between the United States and the USSR, and the apparent ineffectiveness of the UN. In December of 1950 the Truman Administration in the U.S. quietly dropped approval of the Havana Charter from its legislative agenda. Up to that time, few other countries had ratified the Charter, most preferring to await the outcome of the ratification debate in the United States. The U.S. decision to remove ratification from the legislative agenda thus effectively killed any chance that the Charter would ever come into force.

While a number of attempts were subsequently made to either revive the Charter or establish an organization similar to the proposed ITO, all would prove unsuccessful. Instead, the global trading regime was to develop in a much more *ad hoc*, piecemeal fashion over the next 40 years. With the failure of the ITO, the GATT remained, by default, the sole multilateral agreement then in place to deal with global trade issues, a role which it had never been designed to play. In spite of this history, the GATT proved to be a very adaptable and malleable agreement in many respects, particularly when it came to producing reductions in tariffs, which had been its original mandate.

3. PRIOR ROUNDS OF GATT NEGOTIATIONS

With the apparent death of the ITO, and the failure of subsequent attempts to develop any replacement regime, the GATT was forced to take on the role as the primary multilateral trade agreement. While, contrary to popular perception, the GATT never was a formal international organization, the General Agreement did serve as the framework for a series of negotiations on trade issues. These negotiations were usually conducted within the context of formal negotiating sessions, or "Rounds", held over the course of several months or years. There have been seven such Rounds held under the auspices of the GATT prior to the Uruguay Round. These Rounds were:

- 1946—Geneva, Switzerland (in parallel with negotiation of the Agreement);
- 1949—Annecy, France;
- 1950-51—Torquay, England;

- 1955-56—Geneva, Switzerland;
- 1960-61—the "Dillon Round" in Geneva, Switzerland;
- 1964-67—the "Kennedy Round" in Geneva, Switzerland; and
- 1973-79—the "Tokyo Round" in Geneva, Switzerland.

Prior to the Tokyo Round of 1973-79, GATT negotiations had been almost exclusively focused on achieving tariff reductions. Of the initial five Rounds, the most successful in this respect was the first, held in conjunction with the negotiation of the Agreement itself. The Annecy, Torquay and Geneva Rounds which followed did not produce significant multilateral tariff reductions, as these Rounds were largely dedicated to negotiating the accession of new members, or "contracting parties", to the Agreement. The Dillon Round of 1960-61 also did not produce significant reductions as its focus was on negotiating compensation for the introduction of the so-called "Common External Tariff" by the then newly-created European Economic Community.

The 1964-67 Kennedy Round was relatively more successful in terms of multilateral tariff reductions. This Round was also notable in a number of other aspects, which served to distinguish it from all previous Rounds. First, some of the tariff negotiations took place on a "linear basis" for the first time, as opposed to the "item-by-item basis" which had been employed in all previous GATT tariff negotiations.[2] Second, some discussions addressed trade issues beyond tariffs on a sectoral basis (such as aluminum, steel and textiles) for the first time. Although no substantive sectoral agreements were reached as a result, these sectoral discussions did set a negotiating precedent that was to be followed in future Rounds. Third, for the first time issues concerning non-tariff barriers were specifically negotiated, resulting in GATT's first agreement on non-tariff issues, the "Anti-dumping Code".[3] Finally, prior Rounds had been dominated by negotiations amongst developed countries. The Kennedy Round was the first time that developing countries played a significant role in GATT negotiations.

4. TRADE IN TEXTILES

It is necessary at this point in GATT history to deviate somewhat and discuss contemporaneous developments relating to one specific sector —

---

[2] Tariff negotiations had previously been conducted on a bilateral item-by-item basis, whereby in a series of bilateral negotiations one country would request the reduction of another's tariffs, on specific products. This would then be matched by counter-requests by the other country. This method of tariff negotiation became increasingly complex as the number of contracting parties grew, thereby requiring an ever-increasing series of bilateral negotiations. In linear negotiations, participating countries, as a group, agreed to reduce their tariffs on a particular type of product by a set amount. Thus, tariff negotiations could be greatly simplified as only one larger negotiation was required.

[3] *Agreement on Implementation of Article VI of the Agreement on Tariffs and Trade*, GATT, BISD 15S/24.

textiles.[4] Problems concerning the international trade of textiles dates back to at least the early 1950s. During this period some developing countries were becoming increasingly competitive in many aspects of textile and clothing manufacturing. Some developed countries became concerned that inexpensive cotton textiles manufactured in these developing countries would flood their domestic markets, causing damage to domestic producers, significant market disruption and concomitant political problems. These developed countries began to demand that the newly-competitive textile-exporting countries enter into special "voluntary" bilateral export restraint arrangements which would provide for the imposition of quantitative restrictions on cotton textile exports, and thereby prevent further market disruption. Several such agreements were negotiated during the late 1950s. In 1961, these bilateral agreements were then brought within the scope of a formal agreement entered into under the GATT framework, designed to provide for greater multilateral oversight to trade in cotton fabrics — the *Short-Term Arrangement* regarding cotton textiles.[5] The *Short-Term Arrangement* was, in essence, a negotiated derogation from the then-existing GATT rules applicable to cotton fabrics. It was initially intended to be in effect for one year only, during which time a long-term solution was to be achieved. However, the *Short-Term Arrangement* was then replaced the following year by the *Long-Term Arrangement Regarding International Trade in Cotton Textiles,*[6] which, while long on procedural oversight, essentially continued the negotiated derogation for trade in cotton textiles that had been the primary feature of the *Short Term Arrangement.* Upon the expiry of the *Long-Term Arrangement* in 1973, it was subsequently replaced by the *Multi-Fibre Arrangement* (or "MFA").[7] The MFA not only extended the ability of developed countries to impose quantitative restrictions on cotton textiles, but it also extended the product coverage far beyond cotton, to include almost all types of fabrics and clothing. The MFA was itself extended in 1978, 1981, 1986, 1991, 1992 and 1993. The primary result of these special arrangements was to substantially exclude trade in clothing and textiles from the basic GATT obligations for over 40 years.

---

[4] Additional historical background concerning trade in textiles is provided in chapter 3, Part C. See pages 95-104.

[5] See "Arrangements Regarding International Trade", BISD, 10S/18. The *Short Term Arrangement* is found at 19.

[6] BISD, 11S/25.

[7] The MFA is known more formally as the *Arrangement Regarding International Trade in Textiles*, BISD 21S/3. Like the two textile arrangements which preceded it, the MFA was not formally part of the GATT, but operated within the GATT framework. There were many GATT contracting parties that were not MFA signatories and there were some MFA signatories that were not GATT contracting parties.

5. THE TOKYO ROUND

The Kennedy Round of 1964 to 1967 had been a major undertaking, both because of the number of countries involved and the significance of the resulting tariff reductions. Although another GATT round was not foreseen for some time, there was a growing appreciation that a number of problems in the international trading system remained unresolved. There was also a recognition that tariffs were no longer the only international trade issue that GATT should be addressing. As tariffs were being substantially reduced, other "nontariff" barriers to trade were gaining in importance. As a result of this growing concern, immediately following the formal completion of the Kennedy Round, the GATT Contracting Parties adopted a revised "Programme of Work", aimed at ensuring the full implementation of the Kennedy Round and preparing the ground work for the next Round of GATT negotiations.[8] Part of the Work Programme provided for the development of an inventory of nontariff and para-tariff barriers then affecting international trade. With the notable exception of the Kennedy Round's Anti-dumping Code, the new Work Programme was the first tentative step in the expansion of the GATT beyond its traditional focus of tariff barriers to trade in goods.

In spite of the general trade negotiation fatigue resulting from the Kennedy Round, it was not long after its conclusion that the United States began pressing for a new round of GATT negotiations. This renewed pressure came primarily as a result of a balance-of-payments problem in the United States and its resulting monetary pressures. In August of 1971, due to its balance-of-payments problem, the United States imposed a 10 percent surcharge on approximately one-half of all U.S. imports, and introduced new fiscal incentives to encourage U.S. exports. In the eyes of some in the United States, the balance-of-payments problem was directly related to foreign barriers to U.S. exports. The argument was that the U.S. market was substantially more open to imports than the markets of its major trading partners. The U.S. was thus importing more than it was able to export, resulting in greater financial outflows than inflows, and the consequential balance-of-payments problem. One way to address these foreign barriers to U.S. exports was through a new Round of GATT negotiations. The U.S. therefore demanded support for a new Round as a condition for the removal of its 10 percent import surcharge. Most developed countries agreed to this condition in the "Smithsonian Agreement" of December 1971, under which the United States dollar was devalued, the import surcharge was eliminated, and the European Community ("EC"), Japan and Canada agreed to support "urgent" GATT negotiations to address

---

[8]"Programme of Work of the Contracting Parties", GATT, BISD 15S/67. A work programme entitled "GATT Programme for Expansion of International Trade" had first been adopted by the Contracting Parties in 1958. In addition to new work in the area of non-tariff barriers, the new Work Programme continued many aspects of the pre-existing Programme.

non-tariff barriers to trade. The Smithsonian Agreement was then followed by discussions between the United States, the EC and Japan in February of 1972. The GATT Council subsequently established a Preparatory Committee in November of 1972 with the purpose of completing preparatory work for a new Round by the fall of 1973.[9]

The "Tokyo Round" was subsequently officially launched at a GATT Ministerial Meeting held in Tokyo, Japan in September, 1973. Reflecting the novel nature of the preparatory work that had been done to date and the U.S. concern over non-tariff barriers, the Ministerial Declaration commencing the Round provided that negotiations would not address just the traditional issue of tariffs, but would go beyond tariffs to include, among other issues: (i) new disciplines on non-tariff measures; (ii) the adequacy of GATT's existing so-called "safeguard" mechanism; and (iii) issues specifically relating to agriculture.[10]

While Ministers declared the intention to conclude the negotiations in 1975, formal negotiations did not even commence until the U.S. Administration received its formal negotiating authority from the U.S. Congress in January of 1975. Once negotiations commenced in earnest, a stalemate quickly developed over issues relating to agriculture and the formula for negotiating tariff reductions. It was not until the United States abandoned its objectives concerning reforms to trade in agriculture in July of 1977 that the negotiations entered an intensive final phase. The negotiations were then substantially finished in the spring of 1979, although they were not formally concluded until July 1, 1979.

The Tokyo Round achieved some important advances, but there were also some notable deficiencies. With respect to advances, significant tariff reductions were again negotiated. However, the focus of the Tokyo Round had been non-tariff barriers. In this area the results were more equivocal. Several agreements or "Codes" concerning non-tariff barriers were negotiated. These Codes were:

- a **"Subsidies Code"**,[11] which attempted to provide a series of rules concerning the use of government subsidies and remedies available to offset the injurious effects of such subsidies, including countervailing duties;
- an **"Anti-dumping Code"**,[12] which modified the pre-existing Kennedy Round Code and set out disciplines on determinations of "dumping" in international trade and the use of the remedy of anti-dumping duties;

---

[9] See "Programme of Work of the Contracting Parties", BISD 19S/12.

[10] "Declaration of Ministers Approved at Tokyo on 14 September 1973", BISD 20S/19.

[11] Formally known as the *Agreement on Interpretation and Application of Articles VI, XVI and XXIII of the General Agreement on Tariffs and Trade.* See BISD 26S/56.

[12] Formally known as the *Agreement on Implementation of Article VI of the General Agreement on Tariffs and Trade.* See BISD 26S/171.

- a "**Customs Valuation Code**",[13] which attempted to establish standard procedures for the determination of value of imported goods for customs purposes;

- an "**Import Licensing Code**",[14] which attempted to standardize the manner in which import licences, when required, were issued;

- a "**Standards Code**",[15] which provided a series of obligations relating to the establishment and application of domestic product standards to imported products; and

- a "**Government Procurement Code**",[16] which provided basic transparency requirements and non-discriminatory obligations applicable to national government procurement of certain goods over certain value thresholds.

In addition to these Codes, three sectoral agreements were also completed,[17] as well as a number of other arrangements and agreements negotiated under the Round's "Framework for the Conduct of International Trade". These additional "Framework" arrangements include the so-called "Enabling Clause" concerning developing countries,[18] a decision concerning balance-of-

---

[13] Formally known as the *Agreement on Implementation of Article VII of the General Agreement on Tariffs and Trade.* See BISD 26S/116.

[14] Formally known as the *Agreement on Import Licensing Procedures.* See BISD 26S/154.

[15] Formally known as the *Agreement on Technical Barriers to Trade.* See BISD 26S/8.

[16] Formally known as the *Agreement on Government Procurement.* See BISD 26S/33.

[17] The three sectoral agreements were:

- the *Agreement on Trade in Civil Aircraft*—a substantive agreement among a group of developed countries which provided for tariff elimination on trade in civil aircraft and parts therefor, as well as for new disciplines on governmental measures relating to aircraft production;

- the *International Dairy Arrangement*—an agreement that built on pre-existing arrangements in the dairy sector, providing for certain controls on export prices and consultative mechanisms; and

- the *Arrangement Regarding Bovine Meat*—essentially a consultative arrangement relating to trade in beef.

[18] The Enabling Clause (known more formally as *Differential and More Favourable Treatment, Reciprocity and Fuller Participation of Developing Countries,* BISD 26S/203) was part of a group of major concessions obtained at the last minute by developing countries under a threat of leaving the negotiations. Among other things, the Enabling Clause allows developed countries to extend special and differential treatment to developing countries notwithstanding GATT's MFN obligations of Articles I and II, and allows developing countries to enter into tariff reduction agreements amongst themselves without requiring strict compliance with GATT Article XXIV.

payments measures,[19] and an understanding on dispute settlement procedures.[20]

While some of these Tokyo Round Codes (such as the Government Procurement and Customs Valuation Codes) were successful in bringing increased clarity and discipline to areas that were previously without sufficient multilateral discipline, most of these Codes were not entirely successful. The Subsidies Code, for example, while long on new procedural requirements for countervailing duty investigations, imposed very few new substantive disciplines on the use of government subsidies, particularly in the area of export subsidies on agricultural products. Perhaps more importantly, unlike the agreements negotiated as part of the Framework, membership in the Codes was optional. Consequently, not all contracting parties became signatories to the Codes. Some, mainly developed countries, signed all. Others signed one or two. Many signed none at all. As had been the case with the *Multi-Fibre Arrangement*, these Codes therefore were not an integral part of the GATT and consequently did not amend the General Agreement nor did they, strictly speaking, legally operate within the GATT system.

Moreover, the Codes raised an important new legal issue related to GATT's unconditional most-favoured-nation (or "MFN") obligation. Did the existing MFN obligation mean that Code signatories were required to extend the benefits of the Codes to all GATT contracting parties regardless of whether those contracting parties were also Code signatories? This issue was substantially settled by a Decision of the Contracting Parties which reiterated that a contracting party's rights under the MFN obligation remained unaffected by the new Codes.[21] In the end, there was a perception among some contracting parties that the structure of the GATT system had become overly and unnecessarily complex, and it now allowed some countries to "free ride" on the system by obtaining all the benefits of the Codes (through the operation of the MFN obligation) without requiring them to undertake any of the corresponding Code obligations. This view would come to play a major role in determining the structure of the Uruguay Round negotiations and the implementation of its subsequent results.

Other major areas where the Tokyo Round was considered to have failed included textiles and clothing and agriculture. With respect to textiles and

---

[19] *Declaration on Trade Measures Taken for Balance-of-Payments Purposes*, BISD 26S/205. The Declaration provides for increased disciplines and oversight on measures taken for balance-of-payments reasons.

[20] The *Understanding Regarding Notification, Consultation, Dispute Settlement and Surveillance*, BISD 26S/210. This Understanding formalized certain customary practices and introduced certain procedural improvements to GATT's existing dispute settlement process under Articles XXII and XXIII.

[21] See "Action by the Contracting Parties on the Multilateral Trade Negotiations", BISD 26S/201.

clothing, the *Multi-Fibre Arrangement* remained in place, generally un-affected by the Round. With respect to agriculture, the United States had abandoned its demands for substantial reform in the area in July of 1977 and, for the most part, agricultural issues also remained unaffected by the Round. While two sectoral agreements noted above were concluded, these agreement were essentially consultative in nature and purpose.[22]

The final area where the Tokyo Round was considered to have failed was that of safeguards. While negotiations were extensively pursued on the issue during the Round, participants were unable to reach any agreement on the issues of selective use of the safeguard remedy or on the treatment of so-called voluntary export restraints (or "VERs"). As a result, no "safeguard code" could be produced and participants could only agree to continue negotiations on the issue after the Round concluded. In the end, nothing substantive resulted from these further negotiations.[23]

In summary, while bold in its original concept, the Tokyo Round was generally considered to have resulted in limited success. Although substantial tariff reductions had been negotiated, and significant new disciplines intro-duced in some important areas such as customs valuation, the Round had failed to introduce any advancements in many areas of long-standing diffi-culty. The *Multi-Fibre Arrangement*, restricting trade in textiles and clothing, remained in place. No progress had been achieved in agricultural trade, particularly in the areas of non-tariff barriers and subsidization. No agreement had been reached in safeguards and VERs remained undisciplined. And, while some improvements had been introduced to dispute settlement, no improve-ments had been made to the GATT as an institution.

6. FROM TOKYO ROUND TO URUGUAY ROUND

Most of the contracting parties accepted that the Tokyo Round had been of limited success in some respects and many of the problem areas identified above were immediately targeted for further work in a new and even more ambitious Work Programme, adopted immediately following the formal con-clusion of the Tokyo Round in November of 1979.[24] Unfortunately for the results of the Round and the new Work Programme, the conclusion of the Round coincided with the second oil crisis, a serious global recession, rising inflation, high interest rates and a subsequent developing-country debt crisis. These economic problems both dampened any remaining enthusiasm for the

---

[22] The history of problems in international agricultural trade and attempts to remedy them are discussed in greater depth in chapter 3, Part B. See pages 71-74.

[23] Problems relating to the safeguard remedy and attempts to resolve them are discussed in greater depth in chapter 3, Part G.

[24] GATT Work Programme, BISD 26S/219.

Work Programme and substantially increased pressure on the new GATT system that had emerged from the Tokyo Round. By early 1982, no progress was being made on any of the major items of business in the Work Programme.

In an attempt to re-start the stalled Work Programme, the United States called for a GATT Ministerial Meeting for November of 1982, hoping that it could build sufficient support during such a meeting for a commitment to launch a new round of GATT negotiations in the near future.[25] The U.S. was unable to find sufficient support during the meeting for its proposal. In fact, the meeting verged on total collapse. In the end, Ministers were able to cobble together a closing declaration only marginally acceptable to most participants. It was still considered too early for a new round and the U.S. proposal was rejected.[26] Instead, Ministers agreed to substantially revise the 1979 Work Programme and they issued a new Declaration setting out the new work plan for the next few years. Once complete, the results of this new work plan could then provide a substantial basis for the next round of negotiations.[27] The areas identified in the Declaration for work included a number of areas of continuing concern (including safeguards, dispute settlement, agriculture, textiles and clothing, tariff and non-tariff barriers). Largely at the insistence of the United States, and in the face of extensive reluctance from many developing countries, the Declaration also provided for limited work in some important new subject areas that had not previously been discussed in the GATT context, including trade in counterfeit goods and trade in services.

As part of the effort to build consensus toward the initiation of a new Round, and with the support of a number of contracting parties, in November of 1983 the then Director-General of the GATT, Arthur Dunkel, announced that seven "eminent" persons had been asked and had agreed to serve as an independent group to study and report on the problems facing the international trading system.[28] The Group, chaired by Dr. Fritz Leutwiler of Switzerland,

---

[25] The GATT contained no specific provisions concerning regular Ministerial meetings of its contracting parties, and, consequently, such high-level meetings were rarely held. The last Ministerial meeting prior to 1982 had been held in 1973 to officially launch the Tokyo Round. Thus, the U.S. call for such a Ministerial meeting perhaps brought with it unrealistically high expectations as to its potential results.

[26] It is interesting to note that one consequence of this 1982 rejection was that the United States then determined that it must chart a new trade policy course, away from exclusive reliance on the GATT and multilateral trade negotiations. It then began to consider the option of negotiating bilateral or regional agreements with other interested countries. This change in policy would eventually lead to the negotiation of the *U.S.-Israel Free Trade Agreement*, the *Canada-U.S. Free Trade Agreement* and the *North American Free Trade Agreement*.

[27] See "Ministerial Declaration" of 29 November 1982, BISD 29S/9.

[28] The seven persons were Dr. Fritz Leutwiler (Chairman, Swiss National Bank and Presi-

produced a unaminous report in 1985 entitled *Trade Policies for a Better Future: Proposals for Action.*[29] The Group made 15 specific recommendations concerning the international trading system, including:

- trade in agricultural goods and textiles and clothing needed to be brought within basic GATT rules;
- all voluntary export restraints should be eliminated and prohibited, and the rules concerning safeguards improved and followed;
- rules concerning subsidies needed to be improved;
- the existing Tokyo Round Codes needed to be improved;
- disciplines concerning customs unions and free trade areas needed to be revised and improved;
- new rules concerning trade in services should be explored;
- rules concerning dispute settlement needed to be strengthened;
- a new and permanent Ministerial-level body needed to be established; and
- a new round of multilateral trade negotiations should be launched to address these outstanding issues.

The Leutwiler Report played a pivotal role in moving the process forward and, in the end, almost all the Group's recommendations found their way onto the Uruguay Round's negotiating agenda.

While the Leutwiler Report was being researched and written, the United States and a number of other developed countries continued to try on other fronts to build consensus towards the initiation of a new Round. In 1984, the U.S., Japan and Canada jointly called for a new Round, but still found insufficient support. The issue was again discussed in 1985 at both the "Quadrilateral meeting of Trade Ministers" in Tokyo[30] and the G7 Summit[31]

---

dent, Bank of International Settlements), Senator Bill Bradley (U.S. Senator, Member of the Senate Finance Committee), Dr. Pehr Gyllenhammer (Chairman AB Volvo), Dr. Guy Ladreit de Lacharrière (Vice-President, International Court of Justice), Dr. I.G. Patel (Director of the London School of Economics and former Governor of the Reserve Bank of India), Professor Mario Henrique Simonsen (former Brazilian Minister of Finance), and Dr. Sumitro Djojohadikusumo (former Indonesian Minister of Finance and Trade, and Industry). The establishment of such a group, was, in part, based on past experience. An equally eminent group of economists had been called together in the mid-1950s, and in 1958 produced an influential report, *Trends in International Trade.*

[29] GATT, 1985. The Group's report has since become better known as the "Leutwiler Report".

[30] The Quadrilateral or "Quad" is a Ministerial-level group comprised of the trade ministers from the United States, Canada, Japan and the EU. It meets regularly to consult on trade issues.

[31] The G7 is a group of developed countries comprised of the world's seven largest economies and includes the United States, Canada, Japan, Britain, France, Germany and Italy. Leaders of the G7 meet at least yearly to consult and coordinate policy in a number of areas of mutual interest, including trade.

in Bonn. At a further Quad meeting in July 1985 a decision was made amongst the U.S., the EC, Japan and Canada to attempt an all-out push to initiate a new Round.

A GATT Council meeting in June of 1985 then saw another full debate on the issue of a new Round. A group of developing countries, led by India, continued to soundly reject any idea of a new Round, particularly because of the proposed negotiation of rules to govern a number of so-called "new" issues for the GATT, including services, intellectual property and investment. Most developing countries had significant concerns over such proposed negotiations and they remained convinced that the outstanding issues of concern to them, such as trade in textiles and agriculture, should be addressed first, before the GATT attempted any work in new areas.

The EC subsequently proposed a high-level meeting to commence planning for a new Round, but a group of developing countries blocked any consensus on this proposal by refusing to participate in any such meeting.[32] Becoming increasingly frustrated, the United States chose to force the issue by requesting that a special "Session of the Contracting Parties" be held, with the intention that a formal vote would be called on the initiation of a new Round.[33] The special Session was then held in late September and early October of 1985 and, while there was some prospect that the meeting might collapse in disaster, in the end no formal vote was required and a consensus was finally reached on the initiation of a new Round. The Session concluded with an announcement that "a preparatory process on the proposed new Round of multilateral trade negotiations has now been initiated".[34] A Preparatory Committee, open to all contracting parties, was subsequently established at the regular annual session of the GATT Contracting Parties in November 1985. The Preparatory Committee was charged with preparing negotiating recommendations which could then be adopted into a formal negotiating agenda at a Ministerial Meeting to be held in September of 1986.

For a number of reasons the negotiation and drafting of the agenda by the Preparatory Committee proved difficult. Some issues were new to the GATT and therefore the negotiating mandates had to be carefully considered. GATT

---

[32] The provisions of the GATT did not require that all decisions of the Contracting Parties be taken by consensus. In fact, GATT Article XXV permitted certain decisions to be taken with only a two-thirds majority of votes cast. However, over the previous 40 years a practice had developed that the GATT did take all decisions by consensus.

[33] In the almost 40 years of the GATT up to that time, only three such special Sessions had been called. The calling of a special Session required the same two-thirds majority that the initiation of a new Round would require. Thus, once sufficient support was given to the calling of such a special Session, it was virtually assured that if a formal vote were to be called on the issue there would have been sufficient support for the initiation of a new Round.

[34] "Contracting Parties—Decision Adopted at Their Fourth Special Session", BISD 32S/9.

membership had now grown to over 90 countries and therefore sheer numbers made consensus difficult. Finally, many countries had only reluctantly supported the new Round and therefore continued to fight a rear-guard action in an attempt to limit the scope of the negotiations and pre-determine outcomes by manipulating the draft agenda. In particular, issues concerning the new subjects of services, intellectual property and investment continued to prove difficult. Consensus within the Preparatory Committee on a draft Ministerial declaration could not be achieved in time for the scheduled Ministerial meeting in late September 1986. Instead, three different draft agendas, each prepared by a different group of countries, were forwarded to Ministers for consideration at their meeting to be held in Punta del Este, Uruguay. At the meeting, the draft agenda prepared by Switzerland and Columbia quickly became the text of choice and negotiations almost immediately focused on this proposed agenda. After protracted negotiations on agriculture, investment, services and intellectual property, Ministers were finally able to issue their Declaration on September 20, officially launching the new Round of multilateral trade negotiations, from that time forward to be known as the "Uruguay Round".[35]

7. THE PUNTA DEL ESTE DECLARATION

The Punta del Este Declaration is an important document as the negotiating agenda included as part of it established the form, content and structure of the Round. One of the more important features of the Declaration is its treatment of the so-called "new issues". In part, consensus had been reached on the inclusion of new issues in the Round by structuring the negotiations to address the concerns of certain developing countries. With respect to services, this was accomplished by formally separating the trade-in-goods negotiations from those concerning trade in services. The first part of the Declaration, addressing trade in goods, placed these negotiations clearly within the GATT framework. This part of the Declaration was adopted by Ministers in their capacity as representatives of the GATT contracting parties. Part II of the Declaration, concerning services, established a separate, but concurrent negotiating framework for services. While it provided that usual GATT procedures would apply, this portion of the Declaration was adopted by Ministers acting, not as GATT contracting parties, but more generally as representatives of their respective governments.

---

[35] "Ministerial Declaration on the Uruguay Round', BISD 33S/19. The Uruguay Round was, in fact, the first GATT Round to have such an official title. The names that had been used to connote almost all previous GATT Rounds had never been officially sanctioned. The fact that the Ministerial Meeting launching the Round was held in Uruguay, a developing country, and that the Round bore the name of a developing country, was intended to symbolize the importance placed on the participation of all developing countries in the negotiations.

With respect to the other new issues of intellectual property and invest-ment, they were placed in Part I of the Declaration, but with an understanding that issues and concessions rising in these areas would not be directly linked to other traditional trade-in-goods issues. This understanding remained gener-ally effective up until the final push to conclude the Round.

The Declaration established three formal bodies: a Group of Negotiations on Goods; a Group of Negotiations on Services; and, to oversee these two Groups, a Trade Negotiations Committee (the names of these three groups were quickly shortened to "GNG", "GNS" and "TNC", respectively). Within the GNG, the Declaration established 14 separate issue-specific nego-tiating groups. These groups, in their respective negotiation agendas, were as follows:

- **Tariffs Group** — negotiations aimed at the traditional GATT issue of tariff reductions;

- **Non-Tariff Measures Group** — negotiations aimed at the reduction and elimination of non-tariff measures, including quantitative restric-tions;

- **Tropical Products** — negotiations aimed at the liberalization of trade in tropical products;

- **Natural Resource-Based Products Group** — negotiations aimed at the liberalization of trade in natural resource-based products;

- **Textiles and Clothing Group** — negotiations aimed at integrating trade in textiles and clothing into the GATT;

- **Agriculture** — negotiations aimed at liberalizing trade in agricultural products by bringing such trade within the scope of improved GATT rules and disciplines;

- **GATT Articles Group** — to review existing GATT articles and negoti-ate any necessary improvements;

- **Safeguards Group** — negotiations to improve the rules on the use of safeguards based on existing GATT principles;

- **Multilateral Trade Negotiations ("MTN") Agreements and Arrange-ments Group** — to review and improve, to the extent necessary, those agreements and arrangements negotiated as part of the Tokyo Round MTN;

- **Subsidies and Countervailing Measures Group** — to review and improve upon existing disciplines concerning subsidies and counter-vailing measures;

- **Dispute Settlement Group** — negotiations to improve rules relating to dispute settlement in the GATT context;

- **Trade-Related Aspects of Intellectual Property ("TRIPS") Group** — negotiations to clarify existing rules concerning trade-related aspects of intellectual property and elaborate, as appropriate, new rules and disciplines;

- **Trade-Related Investment Measures ("TRIMs") Group** — negotiations to review existing GATT disciplines relating to such measures, and elaborate, as appropriate, further provisions; and

- **Functioning of the GATT System ("FOGS") Group** — negotiations aimed at enhancing the surveillance function of the GATT, improving GATT as an institution, and increasing participation of the GATT in global economic policy coherence.

In addition to the formal structure and an initial negotiating agenda for each group, the Declaration set out a series of broad objectives, general guiding principles governing the negotiations, and provisions concerning a standstill and rollback. With respect to general principles, these included, most notably, that the launching, conduct and implementation of the outcome of the negotiations were to be treated as a "single undertaking". A number of principles concerning the participation of developing countries in the negotiations were also provided, drawn substantially from the existing provisions of the Enabling Clause. Participation in the negotiations generally was stated to be open to all contracting parties, all provisional contracting parties, all countries applying GATT on a *de facto* basis and intending to accede to the GATT, and certain other countries wishing to accede to the General Agreement.

With respect to the standstill and rollback, participants agreed that until formal negotiations had been completed they would not take any trade restrictive or distorting measure inconsistent with their existing GATT obligations, or otherwise take any trade measure so as to improve their negotiating position. A "Surveillance Body" was established to oversee this stand-still commitment. Figure 1, below, provides an overview of the structure of the negotiating framework.

The Declaration ambitiously stated that the Uruguay Round "will be completed within four years". The Negotiating Group on Tariffs was the first group to commence formal work, meeting on February 10, 1987. All remaining groups formally commenced their work soon after.

Figure 1 — Structure of Uruguay Round

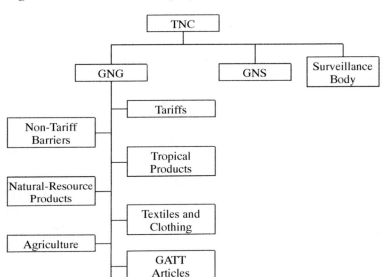

8. FROM PUNTA DEL ESTE TO MARRAKESH[36]

In an attempt to ensure that negotiations progressed apace, the first milestone established by the TNC was a proposed mid-term meeting, to be held at the Ministerial level, set for Montreal in early December 1988. The purpose of this meeting would be to assess the negotiating progress, provide further guidance where necessary and, to the extent possible, allow for an "early harvest" of any preliminary results. During the initial two years of the

---

[36] This part of chapter 1 only provides a general overview of the Uruguay Round negotiations. More specific details concerning individual negotiating groups can be found within the issue-specific chapters that follow.

Round prior to the Montreal Meeting a number of the negotiating groups made adequate progress. As a result, in four subject areas an early harvest appeared possible. This included:

- a liberalization agreement concerning trade in tropical products;
- an agreement on certain improvements to GATT's dispute settlement process which could be implemented on a trial basis immediately; and
- the introduction, on a trial basis, of a Trade Policy Review Mechanism (or "TPRM") whereby the GATT secretariat would undertake periodic reviews of the trade policies of all contracting parties.

In some other groups work had not progressed satisfactorily. In particular, agriculture, textiles and clothing, safeguards and intellectual property were areas where little progress had been made during the previous two years, and where Ministerial attention would be substantially directed during the Montreal Meeting. By the conclusion of the Meeting, no substantive progress had been made in these four areas. In particular, the issue of agriculture showed no signs of solution. Neither of the two main participants, the EC and the U.S., were prepared to move from their completely opposing positions. In light of this apparently intractable problem, some suggested that agriculture should be left out of the Montreal Declaration and that Ministers should agree on those items where agreement was possible. This proposal was completely unacceptable to a group of Latin American agricultural exporting countries. If agreement could not be reached on agriculture they would accept no agreements elsewhere.

Accordingly, Ministers were forced to formally suspend the Uruguay Round for four months while solutions were found in the four problem areas. Ministers directed the TNC to meet again in April 1989 to review the situation. In the interim, informal meetings were held in Geneva in an attempt to overcome the problems. Agreements in all four areas were eventually achieved, and on April 8, 1989, the TNC, meeting in Geneva, adopted the Montreal Mid-Term Declaration (which included the early harvest provisions).[37] The Declaration set the agenda for the second half of the Uruguay Round. Substantive negotiations were then re-commenced.

Following the April 1989 TNC meeting, the GATT Director-General Arthur Dunkel proposed a three-phase approach to the conclusion of the negotiations. The first phase, to be completed by the end of 1989, would see all participants complete work on their national positions and table these positions in each negotiating group. The objective of the second phase, to be completed by August of 1990, was to see broad agreement reached in all negotiating areas. The final phase, to be completed prior to the Brussels

---

[37] See GATT *Focus Newsletter*, No. 61, May 1989.

Ministerial Meeting planned for the end of 1990, would be used to finalize all agreements and polish a complete text for tabling to Ministers. The TNC adopted Dunkel's proposal at its July 1989 meeting.

Work then continued in all negotiating groups following the adopted timetable. The first phase was completed largely within the planned timeframe. By April 1990, however, concern was being raised in some negotiating groups that the timetable for the second phase could not be met. As the Brussels Ministerial Meeting approached, it became clear that it would not be possible to table a complete draft agreement for Ministers' consideration. Some groups had made substantial progress and had reached agreement on comprehensive texts. Other groups had reached broad agreement, but certain issues prevented a completed text of an agreement from being tabled. However, other, more problematic groups, could not even table proposed texts. These groups included Anti-dumping (MTN Arrangements), Agriculture and TRIMs Groups. In some cases, all that could be prepared for Ministers to consider was a list of basic questions or issues that could not be resolved by the Group.

What had been accepted to-date was compiled into a "first approximation of the Final Act Embodying the Results of the Uruguay Round of Multilateral Trade Negotiations".[38] In light of the status of many of the negotiating groups, the contents of this "first approximation", and the number of issues that still remained outstanding, expectations for the outcome of the Brussels Meeting were not exceedingly high.

The meeting commenced in Brussels as planned on December 3, 1990. While negotiations did progress in some areas, agriculture would again become the crucial subject. As had been the case at Montreal in 1988, and for perhaps the first time in GATT negotiations, it was a group of developing countries that demanded progress on agriculture and that were prepared to veto any package that did not include such progress. It was not long after the Agricultural Negotiating Group commenced its work in Brussels that it reached a stalemate. This was followed, as had been the case in Montreal, by the withdrawal from the negotiations by a group of Latin American agricultural exporters. What was to have been the final concluding meeting of the Uruguay Round then quickly collapsed.

With the collapse, Ministers could only announce that the Round would have to be prolonged beyond its planned deadline. Director-General Dunkel was asked to engage in intensive consultations with all participants and to call a meeting of the TNC when he considered a re-commencement of the negotiations was appropriate. No official negotiating sessions or meetings took place for over three months. In February of 1991, the EC finally agreed

---

[38] GATT Doc. MTN.TNC/W/35, 26 November 1990.

that a successful conclusion to the Round would require it to accept some significant concessions in agriculture. This acceptance, combined with further agreements in a number of other problem areas, then allowed Director-General Dunkel to formally re-commence negotiations in late February of 1991.

The negotiating structure was substantially altered in an attempt to accelerate progress. Groups that had effectively completed their work were disbanded or combined with others. Fourteen negotiating groups were thereby reduced to six: one each for the difficult areas of textiles, agriculture and TRIPS; one each for market access issues and rule making (which included anti-dumping and safeguards); and one for institutional issues.

Negotiations commenced on this basis in June 1991, with the new goal of completion by the end of that year. As late December approached, negotiations were ongoing almost continuously. A successful conclusion appeared within reach. Director-General Dunkel asked the chairs of all negotiating groups to provide him with consensus texts for incorporation into a Draft Final Act. In those areas where consensus had not been reached within the group or was not possible, the chairs of the group were asked to apply their knowledge of the issues and the national positions gained during the negotiations, to develop and provide balanced "arbitrated" provisions or texts. The Secretariat staff then compiled all these texts into the next version of the Draft Final Act.

On December 20, 1991, the TNC met to receive the completed Draft Final Act.[39] The Director-General's hope was that, as a consolidated text, participants would be able to see a positive balance of concessions across the entire range of agreements for the first time. This, it was thought, might then persuade all participants to accept the Draft Final Act without alterations and conclude the Round, even though they may continue to be displeased with certain individual provisions. The TNC was then adjourned to allow participants time to consider their national positions and review the Draft Final Act. It was not long thereafter that agriculture again proved to be the most difficult barrier to a successful conclusion of the Round. The proposed agricultural text was almost immediately rejected by the EC as being unacceptable. This was then quickly followed by complaints from a number of other participants concerning the total unacceptability of numerous other provisions.

While not completely acceptable, in a January 1992 meeting of the TNC, the main participants in the Round agreed that the Dunkel Draft provided an acceptable basis for "final" negotiations. Out of this TNC meeting also came

---

[39] *Draft Final Act Embodying the Results of the Uruguay Round of Multilateral Trade Negotiations*, GATT Doc. MTN.TNC/W/FA, 20 December 1991. This version of the Draft Final Act quickly became known as the "Dunkel Draft".

the new plan for the final negotiating phase. A four-track format was adopted. The final market access negotiations concerning goods and services would proceed down tracks one and two respectively. Track three would involve non-substantive or mere technical rectification and correction of the Dunkel Draft text. Track four, to be followed by the TNC itself, was to address proposed substantive changes to the Dunkel Draft. While some progress initially occurred on tracks one, two and three, no effective progress occurred on track four for over 10 months, due primarily to the inability of the United States and the EC to reach a compromise on agricultural issues.

The agricultural impasse finally appeared to be breached on November 20, 1992, when representatives of the United States and the EC met at "Blair House" in Washington, D.C., and subsequently announced that they had reached a compromise on a number of agricultural issues. In particular, the United States had agreed to support a number of EC proposed changes to the Dunkel Draft's agricultural provisions. The TNC met three days later and agreed to re-commence negotiations immediately, with the goal of concluding them by the end of 1992.

This initial burst of optimism again quickly faded. After reviewing its contents, France announced that it could not accept the substance of the Blair House Accord. The United States for its part, having apparently finalized agricultural issues, then turned its attention to other areas of the Dunkel Draft where it wanted changes to be made. These included provisions in the anti-dumping agreement, the TRIPS text, and the complete abandonment of the proposed institutional body, the proposed Multilateral Trade Organization (or "MTO").

While the United States was roundly criticized for these proposed changes, the TNC again agreed to a short recess, with negotiations to re-commence in January 1993. However, instead of commencing in January as planned, a series of intervening events meant that no further negotiations could be held until the middle of July. These intervening events included the inauguration of President Clinton in January in the United States (and a subsequent granting of an extension of negotiating authority to the new U.S. Administration), a French national election in which agricultural trade policy played a central role, and a change in the GATT's Director-General. Arthur Dunkel retired as Director-General after serving in that position for 13 years and was replaced by Peter Sutherland, former Irish Attorney General and EC Commissioner. Once appointed, Sutherland immediately called for a meeting of the TNC and a re-launch of negotiations as of the middle of July. He then established critical paths for the final negotiations, aiming for a conclusion by a new deadline of December 15, 1993.[40] In the end, Sutherland's work and his deadline, real or artificial, had the desired effect and gave the participants the sense of urgency required to finally conclude the negotiations.

As December 15th fast approached, negotiations accelerated and finally entered the so-called "end game". At the last minute, the EC and the United States were finally able to reach agreement on a number of outstanding issues, including those remaining in the agriculture area. This then cleared the way for numerous other agreements and compromises, including some changes in the anti-dumping, TRIPS and services areas. It was then agreed that several difficult service sectors would be left out of the final results, either completely, or with negotiations to re-commence shortly after formal completion of the Round. It was also agreed that the name of the proposed multilateral trade organization would be changed to the "World Trade Organization" (or "WTO"). With these final changes, there was consensus on all major aspects of the Final Act and substantive negotiations could finally be concluded. At 7:30 PM on December 15, 1993, Peter Sutherland brought his gavel down and, after over seven years, substantive negotiations could be formally and finally concluded.

With the formal negotiations concluded, the emphasis shifted to implementation. There was still much work to be done before the results could be brought into force. The Final Act had to be completely reviewed to ensure legal correctness and internal consistency. All final market access negotiations had to be completed, with all resulting schedules of concessions finalized and verified. All this labour-intensive work had to be completed prior to the scheduled final Ministerial Meeting to be held in Marrakesh, Morocco in April 1994.

At the Marrakesh meeting in April, the Final Act and all of its finalized schedules of concessions, some 26,000 pages in total, were signed by the over 100 participating countries. A decision was also taken shortly following the Marrakesh meeting to accelerate the implementation of the Final Act. The Final Act had originally set July 1, 1995 as the planned date for implementation of the results and the entry into force of the WTO. It was soon agreed, however, that implementation should be brought forward six months, to January 1, 1995.

In the period between the Marrakesh meeting and January 1, 1995, much ground work had to be done by the Preparatory Committee (established by

---

[40] Some participants suggested that this was not a "real" deadline, but an artificial one, driven by the U.S. expiry of its own negotiating authority, which, these critics claimed, could be extended again if need be. Others rejected this view by saying the deadline requested by the U.S. Administration had been chosen after consultation with other participants in the negotiations and it was not likely to be extended again by Congress. It was considered by some that the Round needed something such as the expiration of U.S. negotiating authority to provide a sense of urgency in order to bring it to a successful conclusion.

Ministers at Marrakesh and chaired by Director-General Sutherland) in order to prepare for the transition from the GATT to the WTO. In addition, all participants had to pursue their various national implementing processes. In this regard, most anxiously awaited was the vote on the implementing legislation in the United States. Passage of the U.S. legislation by Congress was far from assured. After much debate and considerable uncertainty, Congress passed the U.S. implementing legislation in late December of 1994, thereby assuring that the WTO would come into force on January 1, 1995 as planned. With the last uncertainty removed, the global trading system was about to be fundamentally transformed.

9. CONCLUSION

There is no doubt that 26,000 pages of text are a testament to the complexity of the WTO Agreement (this complexity is often confirmed in the chapters that follow). It is not possible, however, to fully appreciate the fundamental significance of the WTO Agreement without being somewhat cognizant of the historical context which gave rise to it. The stated goals of the Uruguay Round were exceedingly ambitious. The Round was, in essence, established to solve all the fundamental problems of the GATT/MTN regime — problems which, in some cases, had bedeviled international trade for over 40 years. As if this goal was, by itself, somehow immodest, the Round was also to craft entirely new rules addressing subject areas not previously falling within the GATT system. Many times it appeared as though the negotiations were doomed. This agenda was perhaps too ambitious. Yet, after seven years of negotiations, and in spite of all the problems encountered along the way, the final results came close to meeting even the most extravagant of expectations.

2

The Structure and Operation of the World Trade Organization

1. INTRODUCTION

The establishment of the new international organization — the WTO is generally considered to be one of the most important accomplishments of the Uruguay Round. For the first time in the history of global trade rules, there is now a formal multilateral organization with the power to oversee the implementation and application of those rules and settle disputes relating thereto. And yet, this important accomplishment occurred almost as an afterthought. The possible creation of a new international trade organization was not even referred to in the negotiating agenda of the Uruguay Round. Perhaps more importantly, if the 1990 Brussels Ministerial Meeting (which was to have concluded the Round) had not collapsed over agricultural issues, there may never have been a WTO. In this respect, the delay occasioned by the collapse in Brussels probably resulted in a significantly better global trading regime than might otherwise have been the case.

This chapter reviews the structure and organization of the new WTO through an analysis of its charter document, the *Marrakesh Agreement Establishing the World Trade Organization* (now more commonly referred to as the "WTO Agreement"). Section 2, below, briefly provides some historical context and reviews some of the more important developments of the Uruguay Round negotiations as they relate to the creation of the WTO. Section 3 of the chapter then reviews the WTO Agreement in depth.

2. PRE-WTO PROCEDURES AND THE URUGUAY ROUND NEGOTIATIONS

As noted in chapter 1, the GATT never was, and never was intended to be, a formal international organization. The GATT was to be a temporary agreement only, to remain in force only until such time as the International Trade Organization became effective. This negotiating consideration, combined with U.S. concerns over its own negotiating authority, meant that during the negotiations, the GATT was purged of any provisions which had any "institutional" flavour to them. In an effort to ensure that the GATT could not be characterized as being anything more than a basic tariff-reduction agreement, among other changes, all references to an "Interim Tariff Committee" were deleted, and the term for signatories to the Agreement was modified to "contracting parties" (with all signatories acting as a group then simply being referred to as the capitalized "CONTRACTING PARTIES"). In other words, GATT was to be little more than an international contract.

While not necessarily an immediate concern, the lack of specific institutional support in the GATT gradually came to cause increasing difficulty, eventually resulting in the ad hoc creation of a quasi-formal international body that could, at times, be ineffective and unwieldy to manage. Among the problems which became evident over time were the following:

- there developed some uncertainty as to the decision-making powers of the Contracting Parties in some areas of the Agreement;
- lack of formal international status for the Contracting Parties or the GATT as an organization hindered its operation and effectiveness;
- there was no formal provision or status for a secretariat to assist the Contracting Parties;
- increasing problems developed relating to dispute settlement and the lack of ability of the GATT to enforce its obligations and decisions, which, in part, could be related back to the lack of a formal institutional structure;
- it proved very difficult to amend the Agreement, resulting in assorted attempts to avoid the formal amendment procedures and, eventually, in the fragmentation of the GATT system through the adoption of the "à la carte" approach employed during the Tokyo Round;
- there was no clear ability for the Contracting Parties to negotiate rules in new areas beyond trade in goods; and
- the lack of a formal structure meant that management of the organization could only proceed on an ad hoc basis, with decisions and improvements occurring only gradually and only after considerable negotiation and consensus-building.

While many of these problems took some time to become evident, it was not long after the failure of the ITO that the Contracting Parties began to realize that improvements were necessary in order to formalize the GATT's organizational structure. For example, as part of a comprehensive review of the GATT undertaken during 1954 and 1955, the GATT Working Party on Organizational and Functional Questions proposed the establishment of a formal Organization for Trade Co-operation (or "OTC")[1] and drafted a proposed agreement to establish such an organization.[2] This proposed OTC would have been governed by an Assembly, with a managing Executive Committee composed of thirteen elected and five permanent member countries. The Agreement was finalized and opened for signature. While it was accepted by some contracting parties, it never received the requisite number of signatures to enter into force.

Faced with this lack of formal structure the GATT evolved independently, over time, to have many of the attributes of an international organization. The only formalized organizational structure found in the GATT 1947 was Article XXV, which provided that the Contracting Parties were to meet from time to

---

[1] See, for example, the Report of the Working Party on Organizational and Functional Questions, adopted on February 28, March 5 and 7, 1955, at GATT, BISD 3S/231.

[2] The text of the proposed Agreement is in GATT, BISD Volume I.

time, and act "jointly" to give effect to the Agreement. Based in this authority to act jointly and in attempts to improve the administration of the Agreement, the Contracting Parties adopted a number of practices in the years prior to the commencement of the Uruguay Round. These included:

- While the GATT 1947 contained rules governing voting, since the late 1950s all important decisions were taken by consensus without a formal vote (with the exception of waiver and accession decisions, which were regularly voted upon).

- There was no provision in the GATT for a secretariat to provide support to the Contracting Parties. Since January 1, 1951, the Secretariat of the Interim Commission for the International Trade Organization (the "ICITO") (which had been established in 1948 to prepare for the implementation of the ITO) began to work exclusively for the Contracting Parties and from that time forward effectively formed a GATT Secretariat.

- In 1960, the Contracting Parties established a Council of Representatives (more commonly, the "GATT Council") to assist in the day-to-day operations of the Agreement between meetings of the Contracting Parties.[3]

- The GATT did not originally provide for the position of a "Director-General", as the ITO had, but instead for an "Executive Secretary". The position of GATT Director-General was created in 1965, although no formal amendment was ever made to the Agreement. As with the Secretariat, the Director-General was under the employ of the ICITO.[4]

- Over time the Contracting Parties established an extensive group of Councils, Committees, Working Parties and other types of groups to assist in the operation and administration of the Agreement.[5] Nowhere did the Agreement actually provide for the establishment of these groups and, consequently, they performed their work through the delegated authority of the Contracting Parties.

- In an attempt to improve administration of the Agreement, and to provide a smaller executive group of representative countries, the

---

[3] See GATT, BISD 9S/8.

[4] See GATT, BISD 13S/19. By the time of the commencement of the Uruguay Round, the GATT had only had three Directors-General or Executive Secretaries. The first Executive Secretary was Eric (later Sir Eric) Wyndham White, who held the position for over 20 years until his retirement in 1968. He was succeeded in 1969 by Olivier Long of Switzerland. Long was succeeded in 1980 by another Swiss, Arthur Dunkel. Dunkel oversaw the commencement of the Uruguay Round, but retired prior to the completion of the negotiations, being succeeded by Peter Sutherland of Ireland in 1993.

[5] The Committees, for example, came to include the Committee on Trade and Development; the Committee on Balance of Payments Restrictions; the Committee on Tariff Concessions; and the Committee on Budget, Finance and Administration.

Consultative Group of 18 (or "CG-18") was formed in 1975, initially on a temporary basis. The Group's mandate was subsequently made permanent. Although it never did develop into a functioning executive-type body, it did assist during the Tokyo Round and in the planning stages for the Uruguay Round.[6]

Notwithstanding these developments and improvements, the GATT continued to suffer from many of its original defects. Yet, in spite of these institutional problems, concerns over the underlying substantive rules dominated the debate leading up to the development of the Uruguay Round agenda. For example, the Leutwiler Report of 1985 made only three recommendations indirectly related to institutional improvement to the GATT, one directed at improving overall transparency,[7] one concerning the establishment of a Ministerial-level body within the GATT,[8] and the third relating to greater international policy coordination.[9]

In light of the apparent pre-occupation with the much larger and seemingly intractable problems then plaguing the world trading system, it is not surprising that institutional issues received limited attention during the development of the Uruguay Round negotiating agenda. Without much of the debate that surrounded some of the other potential agenda items, under the heading of "Functioning of the GATT System" and following substantially the recommendations of the Leutwiler Report, three institutional negotiating items were identified in the Uruguay Round's Ministerial Declaration:

   (i) to enhance the surveillance in the GATT to enable regular monitoring of trade policies and practices of contracting parties and their impact on the functioning of the multilateral trading system;

  (ii) to improve the overall effectiveness and decision-making of the GATT as an institution, including, *inter alia*, through the involvement of Ministers;

---

[6] See GATT, BISD 22S/15. The membership of the Group was made up of Argentina, Australia, Brazil, Canada, Egypt, the EC, India, Japan, Malaysia (for the ASEAN countries), Nigeria, Norway (for the Nordic countries), Pakistan, Peru, Poland, Spain, Switzerland, the United States and Zaire.

[7] In this respect the Leutwiler Report recommended that: "At the international level, trade policy and the functioning of the trading system should be made more open. Countries should be subject to regular oversight or surveillance of their policies and actions, about which the GATT Secretariat should collect and publish information."

[8] In this respect the Leutwiler Report recommended that: "To ensure continuous high-level attention to the problems in international trade policy, and to encourage prompt negotiation of solutions of them, a permanent Ministerial-level body should be established in GATT."

[9] In this respect the Leutwiler Report recommended that: "The health and even the maintenance of the trading system, and the stability of the financial system, are linked to a satisfactory resolution of the world debt problem, adequate flows of development finance, better international co-ordination of macroeconomic policies, and greater consistency between trade and financial problems."

(iii) to increase the contribution of the GATT to achieving greater coherence in global economic policy-making through strengthening its relationship with other international organizations responsible for monetary and financial matters.[10]

Interesting to note is the lack of any specific mention of the establishment of a formal international organization, although item (ii) could be interpreted quite broadly to provide, at least, a mandate for such a development.

Negotiations on institutional issues initially took place within the FOGS Negotiating Group. In spite of a potentially broad interpretation of the Group's negotiating agenda, the initial negotiating proposals tabled within the Group were quite limited. It quickly became apparent that there was relatively broad support for increased Ministerial participation in the GATT and for increased policy coordination amongst the major international economic institutions. Negotiations therefore tended to focus on the remaining agenda item, that of some form of enhanced surveillance function to be performed by the GATT. Here again there was general acceptance of such a surveillance mechanism, and negotiations therefore almost immediately focused more on the structure of the proposed mechanism, rather than the underlying need for it in the first instance. By the time of the Montreal Mid-term Meeting in late 1988 there was already wide-spread agreement on the implementation of a new Trade Policy Review Mechanism (or "TPRM") which would see the GATT Secretariat undertake regular reviews of the trade policies of all contracting parties. This TPRM was then one of the improvements adopted on a provisional basis following the Montreal Mid-term Meeting.[11] Ministers then asked the FOGS Group to reassess the TPRM prior to the completion of the Round, as well as continue work on the other two negotiating issues.

Following the Montreal Meeting, many in the Group considered that their work had largely been completed and it only remained to fine tune the TPRM and the agreements reached in other areas of the Group's mandate. This view was only slightly disturbed when in February 1990 then-Italian Trade Minister Renato Ruggiero informally proposed that a new international body should be created to oversee the implementation and operation of all the agreements that would result from the Uruguay Round. This informal suggestion was followed by a more formal proposal made by Canada's Minister of International Trade, John Crosbie, in mid-1990.

Response to these proposals was initially minimal, and mixed. Some, such as the United States, rejected the proposals completely, arguing that they

---

[10] Ministerial Declaration on the Uruguay Round, GATT, BISD 33S/19 at 26.

[11] See "Decisions Adopted at the Mid-Term Review of the Uruguay Round", GATT Focus, No. 61, May 1989. The TPRM, along with two other decisions concerning Ministerial participation and increasing global policy coherence, were adopted and implemented on a temporary basis by the GATT Council through a decision of 12 April 1989. See GATT, BISD 36S/403.

came too close to the scheduled end of the Round. Much more important work was left to be done and any attempt to negotiate the terms for such an organization at such a late date would divert attention and effort away from the more important business at hand. Others thought the proposals were worth pursuing, but still shared the United States' view that it was too late in the day to commence serious negotiations. Much better to place the issue on the agenda for further negotiations which could be commenced once the Round had been completed.

By late 1990, there was general agreement on the three main negotiating issues that had been presented to the Group. More importantly, there was now a growing appreciation that some form of institutional improvements would have to be introduced as a result of the implementation of the results of the Uruguay Round. There was, however, no consensus on what form this institutional improvement should take. Some, such as the EC and Canada, remained of the view that this improvement should take the form of a new international organization. Others were not yet convinced that a new international organization was the preferred route. The first approximation of the Draft Final Act, produced for the 1990 Brussels Ministerial Meeting, did not attempt to finally resolve this issue.[12] Rather, it only provided for further negotiations on the issue once the Round had been formally concluded. The collapse of the Ministerial Meeting over agricultural issues meant that no substantive discussions took place on institutional issues in Brussels. However, the delay resulting from the Brussels collapse did provide additional time for the negotiation and resolution of many of the questions concerning institutional improvements. A post-Brussels change in the negotiating structure resulted in the FOGS Group being rolled into the newly-created "Institutions" Negotiating Group. While U.S. support for a new institution still was not certain, by the time the "Dunkel Draft" was prepared in late 1991, a draft agreement on a new "Multilateral Trade Organization" had been completed and, with the consensus of the Institutions Group, was included as Annex IV to the Dunkel Draft when it was released to participants on December 20, 1991.[13]

While the idea of a new MTO had by then firmly taken hold among most participants, the draft "Agreement Establishing the Multilateral Trade Organization" included in the Dunkel Draft had been hurriedly prepared and many of its specific aspects were found to be controversial. These included the draft Agreement's provisions on voting, amendments and membership. As the negotiations continued, acceptable resolutions were eventually found to many of these problems. As late as November of 1993 the United States, fearing a domestic political backlash, was still not convinced of the necessity or politi-

---

[12] GATT Doc. MTN.TNC/W/35.

[13] GATT Doc. MTN.TNC/W/FA.

cal acceptability of the proposed Organization. It proposed instead that the MTO be abandoned and suggested in its place a substantially less formal institutional structure, which would be overseen by Ministers. Whether serious or simply negotiating tactics, the United States was eventually persuaded to accept the proposed institution late in the negotiations.[14] The final change to the draft agreement was made when the United States proposed that the name of the new organization be changed from the Multilateral Trade Organization to the World Trade Organization. With this change the *Marrakesh Agreement Establishing the World Trade Organization* was finalized and then included as the "crowning achievement" of the Uruguay Round's Final Act.

With the signing of the WTO Agreement in Marrakesh, attention then shifted to implementation issues. The first issue to be addressed was the date of the Agreement's entry into force. That date had specifically been left unspecified during the negotiations because a realistic implementation date could not be ascertained at that time. The second and perhaps more important transitional issue related to the inter-relationship between the new WTO legal regime and the old GATT/MTN regime. The continued existence of both regimes had the potential to cause significant conflict due to the operation of the most-favoured nation clause of the GATT 1947 and the substantively different obligations between the two regimes.

In December 1994, the so-called WTO "Implementation Conference" convened in Geneva to resolve these and other related implementation issues. The Conference first concluded that sufficient domestic ratifications had by then occurred and that the implementation date could be set as January 1, 1995. With respect to the other transitional issues, the Conference decided that the GATT 1947 and the WTO would co-exist for one year to allow for proper transition, but that the GATT 1947 would then be terminated as of December 31, 1995, leaving only the WTO regime in place thereafter. Similar decisions were taken with respect to the Tokyo Round's Anti-dumping Code and Subsidies Code. It was also agreed that all assets, liabilities, records and staff of the GATT and the ICITO would eventually be transferred to or be assumed by the WTO.

3. THE MARRAKESH AGREEMENT ESTABLISHING THE WORLD TRADE ORGANIZATION

(a) Introduction

The preamble to the WTO Agreement summarizes the intention of the Agreement when it provides that the WTO Members have resolved thereby to:

---

[14] It should be noted that the creation of the new WTO, and the resulting concerns over sovereignty, did in fact make passage of the WTO Agreement through the U.S. Congress much more difficult than otherwise would have been the case.

. . . develop an *integrated*, more viable and durable multilateral trading system *encompassing* the General Agreement on Tariffs and Trade, the *results of past liberalization efforts*, and *all of the results* of the Uruguay Round of Multilateral Trade Negotiations. [emphasis added]

The WTO system is "integrated" in that it substantially fulfils the "single undertaking" vision of the Punta del Este Declaration. Gone is the "à la carte" approach of the Tokyo Round. This newly-integrated system overseen by the WTO encompasses not only the GATT 1994, but the "results" of past liberalization efforts (and not necessarily a past agreement) as well as "all of the results" of the Uruguay Round within the framework and oversight of one international organization.

(b) Establishment, Scope and Functions of the Organization

The Organization is established under Article I of the Agreement, while its scope and coverage is determined under Article II. The purpose of the WTO is to provide a common institutional framework for the conduct of trade relations among its Members in matters relating to the agreements and legal instruments which were accepted as part of the Uruguay Round. Paragraph 2 provides that all the agreements and legal instruments included within Annexes 1,[15] 2[16] and 3[17] to the Agreement (collectively referred to as the "Multilateral Trade Agreements") are an integral part of the WTO Agreement. In addition, in a significant advancement on multilateral trade system as it emerged from the Tokyo Round, and important in ensuring the overall consistency of WTO rights and obligations, all of the Multilateral Trade Agreements are binding on all Members. Gone is the "à la carte" approach of the Tokyo Round, under which Members could choose which obligations they were prepared to accept. WTO membership now means that a Member must accept all the obligations of all the Multilateral Trade Agreements.

In contrast to the Multilateral Trade Agreements, four other agreements, referred to in paragraph 3 of Article II as the "Plurilateral Trade Agreements" (set out in Annex 4[18]) are also included as part of the WTO Agreement, but

---

[15] Annex 1 to the WTO Agreement includes many of the important Uruguay Round agreements, such as all the Multilateral Agreements on Trade in Goods (including the GATT 1994), the *General Agreement on Trade in Services*, and the *Agreement on Trade-related Aspects of Intellectual Property Rights*.

[16] Annex 2 to the WTO Agreement is the *Understanding on Rules and Procedures Governing the Settlement of Disputes*.

[17] Annex 3 to the WTO Agreement provides the WTO's Trade Policy Review Mechanism, discussed below at pages 43-44.

[18] The four agreements included within Annex 4 are: the *Agreement on Trade in Civil Aircraft*; the *Agreement on Government Procurement*; the *International Dairy Agreement*; and the *International Bovine Meat Agreement*. These four agreements, which were not formally part of the Punta del Este Declaration or the Uruguay Round negotiations, are discussed below in chapter 6.

only for those Members that have accepted them and are binding only on those accepting Members. These agreements do not create rights or obligations for Members who have not signed them.

The final paragraph of Article II clarifies the legal status of the GATT 1994 as compared to the original GATT, now known as the GATT 1947. While the two agreements are substantially similar in many respects, GATT 1994 is stated to be legally distinct from GATT 1947. Among other things, this means that being a signatory to the GATT 1947 does not, in and of itself, bestow rights and obligations on a country under GATT 1994. Separate membership in and ratification of GATT 1994 is necessary.[19]

Among others, the functions of the Organization are stated in Article III to be to:

- facilitate the implementation, administration, and operations, and further the objectives of the WTO Agreement and the Multilateral Trade Agreements;
- provide a forum for negotiations among Members on trade matters;
- administer the Dispute Settlement Understanding (or "DSU") of Annex 2;
- administer the Trade Policy Review Mechanism (or "TPRM") of Annex 3; and
- cooperate, as appropriate, with the IMF and the World Bank and other intergovernmental organizations with responsibilities related to those of the WTO.[20]

(c) Structure and Operations of the Organization

Structural and organizational provisions of the WTO are set out in Articles IV through VIII of the WTO Agreement. With respect to structure of the Organization, the highest level body of the WTO is the Ministerial Conference, composed of representatives of all Members. The Conference is

---

[19] See further discussion of this issue in chapter 3 at pages 52-54.

[20] This cooperative responsibility was then further reinforced by the Ministerial *Declaration on the Contribution of the World Trade Organization to Achieving Greater Coherence in Global Economic Policymaking*, agreed to by Ministers as part of the Uruguay Round final package. The Declaration further calls on the WTO to cooperate with the IMF and the World Bank with the goal of achieving greater coherence in global economic policymaking. Pursuant to this mandate, in late 1996, the WTO signed cooperation agreements with both the IMF and the World Bank. Among other things, these agreements establish formal consultative processes; grant observer status to staff of each organization thereby allowing such staff to attend and observe formal meetings of the other organizations; and provide for greater information exchange among the organizations to facilitate decision-making and avoid duplication.

to meet every two years,[21] and is to take all actions necessary to carry out the functions of the WTO. Between meetings of the Ministerial Conference, the day-to-day operations of the Organization are conducted by a number of other subsidiary bodies. The first such body is the General Council, also comprised of representatives of all Members, which is to meet as appropriate. The General Council may also convene as the Dispute Settlement Body (or "DSB") or as the Trade Policy Review Body, to discharge the responsibilities of those Bodies as provided for under the DSU and the TPRM respectively.

Below the General Council level are three sector-specific councils: the Council for Trade in Goods; the Council for Trade in Services; and the Council for Trade-Related Aspects of Intellectual Property Rights. Membership in these Councils is also open to representatives of all Members. The Councils are to meet as necessary to carry out the functions assigned to them under the relevant Multilateral Trade Agreements of Annex 1 to the WTO Agreement. These Councils may also establish any additional subsidiary bodies that they may consider necessary, and many such subsidiary bodies have already been established.

The General Council has also established five additional subsidiary bodies with more specific mandates. Three of these bodies—the Committees on Trade and Development, Balance-of-Payments Restrictions, and Budget, Finance and Administration—were established by the Ministerial Council pursuant to Article IV:7 of the WTO Agreement, and they report to the General Council. The General Council also established the Committee on Trade and the Environment[22] in January 1995 and the Committee on Regional Trade Agreements in February 1996.[23] The four Plurilateral Agreements also provide for governing bodies which report to the General Council. Table 1 provides a graphic representation of the WTO's institutional structure.

---

[21] The first meeting of the Ministerial Conference took place in December of 1996 in Singapore. See pages 337-338 for a discussion of this meeting. The next meeting of the Conference is scheduled to be held in Germany on May 18-20, 1998.

[22] The Committee on Trade and the Environment was established pursuant to the Decision on Trade and Environment, one of the decisions agreed to as part of the Uruguay Round final package. The mandate of the Committee is, among other things, to investigate the linkages between trade and environmental regulation. The extensive work of this Committee is discussed briefly in chapter 8, pages 338-340.

[23] The Committee on Regional Trade Agreements was established by the General Council to replace the working party process that had been used in the past to review regional trade arrangements that had been notified to the GATT or to the WTO. At the time of its establishment in February 1996, 24 such working groups were active, each reviewing one arrangement. The terms of reference for the Committee include, not only the review function previously served by the working parties, but also the review of broader issues relating to regional trading arrangements such as consideration of the systemic implications of such arrangements for the multilateral trading system.

TABLE 1

WTO Structure

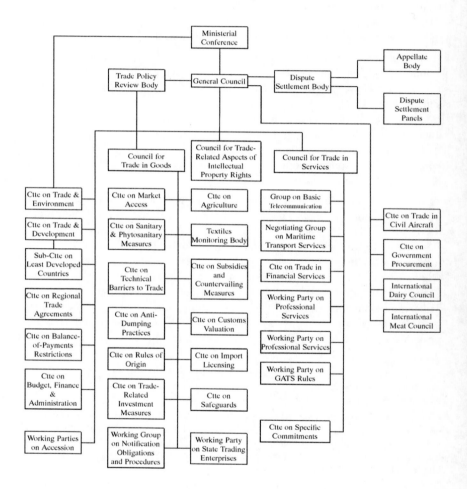

Source: WTO Focus Newsletter, No. 13, October-November 1996, at 3.

The bodies of the WTO are assisted by the staff of the WTO Secretariat, provided for under Article VI. The Secretariat is headed by the Director-General, who is appointed by the Ministerial Conference.[24] The Director-General has the power to appoint all other members of the Secretariat staff and determine their duties and conditions of service according to any regulations that may be adopted by the Ministerial Conference.[25] The Director-General is currently assisted by four Deputy-Directors General and a staff of approximately 450.

Budgetary issues of the Organization are addressed in Article VII. The Committee on Budget, Finance and Administration was required to propose financial regulations concerning Members' contributions to the Organization's annual budget. These regulations were to be based, so far as practical, on the financial regulations previously used under the GATT 1947. Consistent with that direction, financial regulations were adopted by the General Council whereby individual contributions to the WTO's annual budget are based on each Member's respective share of total trade.

The Director-General presents an annual budget and financial statement to the Committee for review. The Committee reviews the budget and the statement and makes recommendations thereon to the General Council. The annual budget is then subject to the approval of the General Council.[26] Members are expected to promptly contribute their respective shares of the budget once approved by the Council.

The international status of the Organization is provided for under Article VIII. The WTO has a legal personality and in this regard is permitted to conclude so-called "headquarters" agreements.[27] Members are required to accord to the WTO such legal capacity, privileges and immunities as may be necessary for it to carry out it functions. Similarly, Members must accord to WTO officials and other Members' representatives such privileges and immunities as may be necessary for them to carry out their functions.

---

[24] The first, and current, Director-General of the WTO is Mr. Renato Ruggiero. Among his many other trade-related postings, Mr. Ruggiero is a former Italian Minister of Foreign Trade.

[25] Article XVI:2 provides that to the extent practical, the GATT Secretariat shall become the WTO Secretariat. Thus the WTO essentially inherited the staff of the ICITO/GATT Secretariat. Secretariat staff are considered to be international civil servants, and, in order to ensure their continued respectability and objectivity, are not to seek or accept any instructions from any government or authority external to the WTO. Moreover, Members are expected to respect this objectivity and they are not to attempt to influence Secretariat staff in the discharge of their duties.

[26] The current operating budget of the Organization is approximately (US) $80 million.

[27] In June 1995, the WTO signed a Headquarters and Infrastructure Agreement with the Swiss Confederation. Negotiations with Switzerland commenced after the GATT Contracting Parties had selected Geneva as the site for the WTO's headquarters. This Agreement addresses two basic issues, the provision of physical facilities to the Organization, and the privileges and immunities to be accorded to the Organization, its missions and related staff.

(d) Decision-making Functions of the Organization

The rules concerning the decision-making functions of the Organization are provided for in Article IX of the Agreement. Generally speaking, the WTO is to continue the practice of decision-making by consensus which had previously been the basic feature of decision-making under the GATT 1947.[28] Except as otherwise provided in the Agreement, if consensus cannot be reached, the matter at issue will be decided by voting, based on the principle of "one-country-one-vote". And, again, except as otherwise provided, decisions are to be taken by a simple majority of votes cast. Decisions under the Plurilateral Agreements are governed by the terms of those Agreements.

While the general rule is consensus, the WTO Agreement specifically anticipates voting in four circumstances. First, the Ministerial Conference and the General Council have the exclusive authority to adopt "interpretations" of the WTO Agreement and the Multilateral Trade Agreements. Formal votes on such interpretations must achieve a three-fourths majority in order to be adopted. Second, in exceptional circumstances the Ministerial Conference may decide to "waive" a Member's obligation. In most cases such waiver decisions also require a three-fourths majority vote.[29] The Agreement's provisions concerning amendments and the admission of new Members, as discussed below, also provide for special majority votes.

Article X provides extensive rules concerning amendments to the WTO Agreement and the Multilateral Trade Agreements. Proposals for amendment may be submitted to the Ministerial Conference by the WTO's Councils or by Members themselves. Such proposals may be adopted either by unanimity or by two-thirds majority depending upon the provisions at issue. Proposed amendments to five specified provisions require unanimity.[30]

---

[28] "Consensus", for the purposes of this provision, has now been specifically defined for the first time to mean that no Member, present at the meeting where the decision is to be taken, formally objects to the proposed decision.

[29] Article IX provides special rules concerning requests for waivers. A request for a waiver of an obligation imposed under the WTO Agreement must first be submitted to the Ministerial Conference for consideration by the normal consensus practice. If consensus is not reached within 90 days, or such shorter period as may be determined by the Conference, then a vote is to be held, subject to a three-fourths majority required to grant the waiver. A request for a waiver of an obligation imposed under one of the Multilateral Trade Agreements must first be submitted to the relevant Council for consideration. After consideration, that Council is to submit a report to the Conference. Any decision by the Conference to grant a waiver must set out the special circumstances giving rise to the waiver, any special terms and conditions, and its termination date. Waivers granted for more than one year are subject to annual review and may be extended, modified or terminated as part of each such review.

[30] These five provisions are: Article IX of the WTO Agreement (concerning decision-making of the WTO); Article X of the WTO Agreement (setting out the amendments procedures

Proposed amendments to most other provisions of the WTO Agreement or the Multilateral Trade Agreements (other than those of Annexes 2 and 3) which would alter the rights and obligations of Members require a two-thirds majority to be approved, and those amendments will only apply to Members specifically accepting them.[31] Proposed amendments to other provisions of those Agreements which will not alter the rights and obligations of Members generally take effect for all Members upon acceptance by a two-thirds majority. Amendments to the TRIPS Agreement meeting the requirements of Article 71(2) of that Agreement are to be adopted by the Ministerial Conference without further formal acceptance process.[32]

Any Member may propose amendments to the Dispute Settlement Understanding and the Trade Policy Review Mechanism. Decisions concerning a proposed amendment to the DSU may only be made by consensus and will take effect for all Members upon approval by the Ministerial Conference. Decisions to approve amendments to the TPRM will also take effect for all Members upon approval by the Conference.

With respect to the Plurilateral Agreements of Annex 4, amendments to those Agreements will be governed by the terms of the Agreements themselves. Members may also request additional agreements be added to or deleted from Annex 4. Decisions for additions to the Annex must be by consensus.

(e) Membership, Accession and Non-application

The original membership of the WTO and the accession procedures for new Members are set out in Articles XI and XII of the Agreement. For purposes of accession, the Agreement draws a distinction between the original Members and those countries that may join later. The original WTO Members are those countries or customs territories (and the EC) which, as of January 1, 1995, were contracting parties to the GATT 1947 and which had accepted the

---

themselves); Articles I and II of the GATT 1994 (concerning the most-favoured-national ("MFN") obligation as it applies to trade in goods); Article II:1 of the General Agreement on Trade in Services ("GATS") (concerning the MFN obligation as it applies to trade in services); and Article 4 of the TRIPS Agreement (concerning the MFN obligation as it applies to intellectual property).

[31] The Ministerial Conference may decide that an amendment is too important to permit such "opting-out". Such a decision must then be made by a three-fourths majority, at which time Members that still wish to reject the amendment may withdraw from the Organization.

[32] Article 71(2) of the TRIPS Agreement concerns amendments which adjust to higher levels of protection that have already been achieved and have entered into force in another international agreement and have already been accepted by all Members under that other agreement. In such cases, the TRIPS Council may submit a request for the proposed amendment to the Ministerial Conference on the basis of a consensus proposal.

WTO Agreement and had annexed their required Schedules to the WTO Agreement. The original Members need only accept the WTO Agreement. Most former GATT contracting parties thus became original WTO Members on January 1, 1995. (Some contracting parties did not complete their domestic ratification processes until later in 1995, or had not yet completed their respective Schedules by January 1, 1995, and therefore did not become Members until sometime after January 1, 1995, but they are still considered to be original Members.) WTO Membership as of September 6, 1997 is set out in Annex 1 to this chapter.

The negotiated accession of all other countries or customs territories to the Agreement is provided for in Article XII. Any state or separate customs territory possessing full autonomy in the conduct of its external commercial and trading relations may accede to the WTO Agreement and the Multilateral Trade Agreements on such terms as may be agreed to between it and the WTO.[33] Any decisions concerning accessions are to be taken by the Ministerial Conference by a two-thirds majority vote of all Members. Accession to the Plurilateral Agreements is governed by the terms of those Agreements. A list of those states that as of May 1, 1997, were in the process of negotiating accession under Article XII is found in Annex 2 to this chapter.

Article XIII deals with the non-application of the Agreements between Members. In some cases countries may not maintain diplomatic or commercial relations with one another. Article XIII thus permits such countries to still become WTO Members without requiring them to apply the WTO Agreement vis-à-vis one another. This provision can only be invoked by the original WTO Members against one another if there was an existing invocation of the similar right under GATT 1947 Article XXXV. Article XIII may be invoked against new Members acceding under Article XII upon notification to the Ministerial Conference prior to approval of the accession of the new Member by the Conference.

---

[33] WTO accession substantially follows the process that had developed for accession to the GATT 1947. The process commences with a formal application from the interested state. This is then followed by the filing of an extensive memorandum by the state which details its legal framework in all areas that may be affected by the WTO Agreement. This memorandum provides the basis for an extensive review of the state's laws and their consistency with the WTO by the working party struck to oversee the accession process. Simultaneous with this review, the state engages in bilateral market access negotiations with most WTO Members in both the goods and services areas. Once the legal review and the market access negotiations are concluded, the basic accession agreement is drafted by the working party. The working party will then table a report to the Ministerial Conference for decision, attaching the draft protocol of accession and the state's schedules of concessions and commitments. Once accepted by the Conference, the state is free to sign the WTO Agreement and become a WTO Member, subject to its own domestic ratification procedures.

(f) Acceptance, Withdrawal and Other Provisions

Under Article XIV, the WTO Agreement was stated to come into force on a date to be determined by Ministers. As noted above, January 1, 1995 was subsequently agreed to. Under Article XV, any Member is permitted to withdraw from the Agreement, with such withdrawal to take effect six months from the date written notice of the withdrawal was provided to the Director-General.

Article XVI provides a number of important miscellaneous provisions. Paragraph 1 states that except as otherwise provided, the WTO is to be guided by decisions, procedures and customary practices of the GATT 1947 and bodies established within the GATT framework. Paragraph 3 provides that in the event of a conflict between a provision of the WTO Agreement and a provision of any other of the Multilateral Trade Agreements, the provision of the WTO Agreement shall prevail to the extent of the inconsistency. Each Member is required to ensure it is in conformity with the Agreement. No reservations may be made with respect to any of the provisions of the WTO Agreement. Reservations are permitted concerning the Multilateral Trade Agreements only to the extent provided in those Agreements.

4. THE TRADE POLICY REVIEW MECHANISM

The Trade Policy Review Mechanism (or "TPRM"), which had first been provisionally agreed to as part of the Montreal Mid-Term Review, was definitively adopted as part of the Final Act and included as Annex 3 to the WTO Agreement. Until the adoption of the TPRM there had been little multilateral systematic review of countries' trade policies. The purpose of the TPRM is to improve adherence to the new rules of the WTO Agreement by improving the transparency and understanding of all Members' trade policies. This is to be accomplished by the regular review and evaluation of the full range of Members' trade policies. The reviews are intended to be transparency enhancing only, and are not to judge the consistency of Members' measures with their WTO obligations in any way.

The Trade Policy Review Body is established under Annex 3 to carry out the trade policy review function. The frequency of review under the TPRM is dependent on each Member's importance in global trade terms. The four most important entities (the United States, the EC (counted as one) Japan and Canada) are subject to review every two years. The next 16 Members are subject to review every four years, while all other Members are subject to review every six years (subject to additional extensions granted to least-developed countries on a case-by-case basis).

Individual TPRM reviews are based primarily on two documents: a report that has been prepared by the Member which is the subject of the review, and a second report and analysis prepared by the WTO Secretariat. These two reports, plus the minutes of the meeting of the Trade Policy Review Body at which the reports are discussed, are then published by the WTO following the meeting.

The Trade Policy Review Body is to review the operation of the TPRM within five years and present its report to the Ministerial Conference. In addition, the Body is also to undertake an annual review of developments in the international trading environment generally.

5. CONCLUSIONS

It is difficult to conceive of the results of the Uruguay Round without the new WTO. In this respect, a new international organization may have been an inevitable consequence of the ambitious scope of the Punta del Este Declaration. While not specifically mentioned in the Declaration, once the sweeping nature of the results of the Round became more apparent and attention began to turn to implementation, it was perhaps obvious that the existing GATT 1947 framework was simply no longer up to the institutional challenge. Aware of the existing defects in the GATT, the lessons of the "à la carte" approach adopted at the conclusion of the Tokyo Round, and the "single undertaking" approach that had guided the Uruguay Round negotiations, any failure to take the opportunity to establish an international organization to oversee the implementation and operation of the Uruguay Round agreements would have dealt a serious blow to the newly integrated global trading system.

Having commented on the importance of the Organization to the entire Round, it must also be noted that the WTO is not without its problems. Already proposals are being made to streamline decision-making within the Organization. With 132 Members, many with divergent views and interests, consensus is often a long and difficult process. Some suggest that some form of executive committee, perhaps similar to the GATT's CG-18, should be introduced to allow for better and more efficient administration. Others, particularly some developing countries, reject such proposals because they see them as an attempt to marginalize their existing influence. This issue is likely to fester as WTO Membership continues to expand.

Another challenge for the Organization is the effective performance of its mandate. The GATT Secretariat had developed a well-deserved reputation for being lean, yet very effective by international standards. While the mandate of the new WTO is significantly broader than that of the GATT, Members have been reluctant to allow the WTO Secretariat to expand too quickly, fearing, perhaps, that the new Organization may lose the efficiency of its predecessor. The WTO Secretariat has therefore been asked to do much more with essentially the same resources. If this trend continues, it may undermine many of the other important substantive achievements of the Round.

ANNEX 1

WTO MEMBERSHIP AS OF SEPTEMBER 6, 1997

As of September 6, 1997, the following 132 governments had accepted the *Marrakesh Agreement Establishing the World Trade Organization*, effective as noted:

1.	Angola	23 November 1996
2.	Antigua and Barbuda	1 January 1995
3.	Argentina	1 January 1995
4.	Australia	1 January 1995
5.	Austria	1 January 1995
6.	Bahrain	1 January 1995
7.	Bangladesh	1 January 1995
8.	Barbados	1 January 1995
9.	Belgium	1 January 1995
10.	Belize	1 January 1995
11.	Benin	22 February 1996
12.	Bolivia	13 September 1995
13.	Botswana	31 May 1995
14.	Brazil	1 January 1995
15.	Brunei Darussalam	1 January 1995
16.	Bulgaria	1 December 1996
17.	Burkina Faso	3 June 1995
18.	Burundi	23 July 1995
19.	Cameroon	13 December 1995
20.	Canada	1 January 1995
21.	Central African Republic	31 May 1995
22.	Chad	19 October 1996
23.	Chile	1 January 1995
24.	Colombia	30 April 1995
25.	Congo	27 March 1997
26.	Costa Rica	1 January 1995
27.	Côte d'Ivoire	1 January 1995
28.	Cuba	20 April 1995
29.	Cyprus	30 July 1995
30.	Czech Republic	1 January 1995
31.	Democratic Republic of the Congo	1 January 1997
32.	Denmark	1 January 1995

33.	Djibouti	31 May 1995
34.	Dominica	1 January 1995
35.	Dominican Republic	9 March 1995
36.	Ecuador	21 January 1996
37.	Egypt	30 June 1995
38.	El Salvador	7 May 1995
39.	European Communities	1 January 1995
40.	Fiji	14 January 1996
41.	Finland	1 January 1995
42.	France	1 January 1995
43.	Gabon	1 January 1995
44.	Gambia	23 October 1996
45.	Germany	1 January 1995
46.	Ghana	1 January 1995
47.	Greece	1 January 1995
48.	Grenada	22 February 1996
49.	Guatemala	21 July 1995
50.	Guinea Bissau	31 May 1995
51.	Guinea, Republic of	25 October 1995
52.	Guyana	1 January 1995
53.	Haiti	30 January 1996
54.	Honduras	1 January 1995
55.	Hong Kong	1 January 1995
56.	Hungary	1 January 1995
57.	Iceland	1 January 1995
58.	India	1 January 1995
59.	Indonesia	1 January 1995
60.	Ireland	1 January 1995
61.	Israel	21 April 1995
62.	Italy	1 January 1995
63.	Jamaica	9 March 1995
64.	Japan	1 January 1995
65.	Kenya	1 January 1995
66.	Korea	1 January 1995
67.	Kuwait	1 January 1995
68.	Lesotho	31 May 1995
69.	Liechtenstein	1 September 1995

70.	Luxembourg	1 January 1995
71.	Macau	1 January 1995
72.	Madagascar	17 November 1995
73.	Malawi	31 May 1995
74.	Malaysia	1 January 1995
75.	Maldives	31 May 1995
76.	Mali	31 May 1995
77.	Malta	1 January 1995
78.	Mauritania	31 May 1995
79.	Mauritius	1 January 1995
80.	Mexico	1 January 1995
81.	Mongolia	29 January 1997
82.	Morocco	1 January 1995
83.	Mozambique	26 August 1995
84.	Myanmar	1 January 1995
85.	Namibia	1 January 1995
86.	Netherlands	1 January 1995
87.	New Zealand	1 January 1995
88.	Nicaragua	3 September 1995
89.	Niger	13 December 1996
90.	Nigeria	1 January 1995
91.	Norway	1 January 1995
92.	Pakistan	1 January 1995
93.	Panama	6 September 1997
94.	Papua New Guinea	9 June 1996
95.	Paraguay	1 January 1995
96.	Peru	1 January 1995
97.	Philippines	1 January 1995
98.	Poland	1 July 1995
99.	Portugal	1 January 1995
100.	Qatar	13 January 1996
101.	Romania	1 January 1995
102.	Rwanda	22 May 1996
103.	Saint Kitts and Nevis	21 February 1996
104.	Saint Lucia	1 January 1995
105.	Saint Vincent & the Grenadines	1 January 1995
106.	Senegal	1 January 1995

107.	Sierra Leone	23 July 1995
108.	Singapore	1 January 1995
109.	Slovak Republic	1 January 1995
110.	Slovenia	30 July 1995
111.	Solomon Islands	26 July 1996
112.	South Africa	1 January 1995
113.	Spain	1 January 1995
114.	Sri Lanka	1 January 1995
115.	Suriname	1 January 1995
116.	Swaziland	1 January 1995
117.	Sweden	1 January 1995
118.	Switzerland	1 July 1995
119.	Tanzania	1 January 1995
120.	Thailand	1 January 1995
121.	Togo	31 May 1995
122.	Trinidad and Tobago	1 March 1995
123.	Tunisia	29 March 1995
124.	Turkey	26 March 1995
125.	Uganda	1 January 1995
126.	United Arab Emirates	10 April 1996
127.	United Kingdom	1 January 1995
128.	United States	1 January 1995
129.	Uruguay	1 January 1995
130.	Venezuela	1 January 1995
131.	Zambia	1 January 1995
132.	Zimbabwe	3 March 1995

ANNEX 2

ACCESSION NEGOTIATIONS

The following 29 governments were in the process of negotiating accession to the WTO as of September 6, 1997, and have been granted observer status pending their accession.

1. Albania
2. Algeria
3. Armenia
4. Azerbaijan
5. Belarus

6. Cambodia
7. People's Republic of China
8. Chinese Taipei
9. Croatia
10. Estonia
11. Georgia
12. Jordan
13. Kazakhstan
14. Kirgyz Republic
15. Latvia
16. Lithuania
17. Former Yugoslav Republic of Macedonia
18. Moldova
19. Nepal
20. Russian Federation
21. Saudi Arabia
22. Seychelles
23. Sudan
24. Sultanate of Oman
25. Tonga
26. Ukraine
27. Uzbekistan
28. Vanuatu
29. Vietnam

3

Multilateral Agreements Concerning Trade in Goods

This chapter, comprised of nine parts, reviews the WTO Agreement's provisions relating to trade in goods. Part A reviews the primary agreement relating to trade in goods, the *General Agreement on Tariffs and Trade 1994* ("GATT 1994"), and its related Understandings. Parts B through I then discuss a number of additional WTO agreements which further elaborate upon, interpret, and, in some cases, amend the provisions of GATT 1994. Two of these parts are specific to certain sectors—Part B, Agriculture and Sanitary and Phytosanitary Measures; and Part C, Textiles and Clothing. Certain customs issues are addressed in Part D. The next three parts address trade remedies—Part E, Anti-dumping; Part F, Countervailing Duties; and Part G, Safeguards. Finally, the two horizontal issues of Technical Barriers to Trade and Trade-related Investment Measures are reviewed in Parts H and I respectively.

Part A:

The GATT 1994 and Related Understandings

1. INTRODUCTION

The GATT 1994 contains the WTO Agreement's primary obligations concerning trade in goods.[1] Concerning GATT 1994, it is important to bear in mind that the original *General Agreement on Tariffs and Trade* is now referred to as "GATT 1947". And, while it is substantially similar to the new GATT 1994, these are two separate and legally distinct agreements.[2] This subtle distinction means that being a contracting party to the GATT 1947, in and of itself, carries with it no legal implications so far as GATT 1994 is concerned. Being legally distinct, separate membership in and ratification of the WTO Agreement is required before a former GATT contracting party obtains any rights or obligations under the GATT 1994.[3]

GATT 1994 is the combination of most of the important elements of the GATT 1947, plus a number of other provisions, including many additional "understandings" that were negotiated and accepted as part of the Uruguay Round. GATT 1994, as it appears in Annex 1A to the WTO Agreement, is comprised of only three articles. The first and most important article sets out

---

[1] GATT 1994 is included within Annex 1A (Multilateral Agreements on Trade in Goods) to the WTO Agreement.

[2] Article II:4 of the WTO Agreement, as discussed above at page 36, provides that GATT 1994 "is legally distinct" from GATT 1947.

[3] The GATT 1947 and the GATT 1994 did co-exist from January 1, 1995 to December 31, 1995 in order to allow the GATT contracting parties adequate time to accede to the new WTO Agreement. As of December 31, 1995, the GATT 1947 then ceased to exist.

the scope of the Agreement primarily by the incorporation of a number of other provisions by reference. Article 1 provides that GATT 1994 consists of four main elements:

(a) the provisions of GATT 1947, including all amendments that had entered into force prior to January 1, 1995,[4] but excluding the Protocol of Provisional Application;[5]

(b) the provisions of certain specified legal instruments that had entered into force under GATT 1947, including all previous tariff protocols, protocols of accession,[6] waivers granted under GATT Article XXV that were still in force on January 1, 1995, and other decisions;

(c) six Understandings reached during the Uruguay Round which further elaborate upon certain provisions of GATT 1994; and

(d) the results of the Uruguay Round's tariff negotiations as set out in the "Marrakesh Protocol".

These provisions are discussed, in turn, below.

One of the changes to GATT 1947 introduced under the WTO Agreement is the use of somewhat different terms in some circumstances. Thus, paragraphs (a) and (b) of Article 2 of GATT 1994 provide a series of explanatory provisions designed to clarify the use of certain of these altered terms. All references to "contracting parties" in the provisions of GATT 1994 will now be deemed to read "Members" instead. References to "less developed contracting party" and "developed contracting party" will be read as "develop-

---

[4] It is important to note that only the "provisions" of GATT 1947 have been incorporated into the new Agreement, and not the 1947 Agreement itself. These two agreements, though substantially similar, remain legally distinct.

[5] It is a little-known fact that the GATT 1947 never definitively entered into force. It was a provisional agreement only, which was applied by its signatories under the terms of another agreement, the Protocol of Provisional Application. Under this Protocol the original signatories to the GATT 1947 agreed to give effect to the terms of the Agreement, but only to the extent that it was not inconsistent with then-existing legislation. This allowed the contracting parties to bring the Agreement into effect without having to obtain formal domestic approval or amend any existing inconsistent domestic legislation. All such inconsistent legislation which was in force at the time the GATT 1947 came into effect remained "grandfathered" under the Protocol. New contracting parties which thereafter acceded to the Agreement were then extended similar benefits under their respective protocols of accession. A number of GATT disputes have turned on whether the inconsistent measure at issue was grandfathered under the terms of the Protocol of Provisional Application or similar protocols of accession. The Protocol of Provisional Application has specifically not been incorporated into the GATT 1994, meaning that unless otherwise exempted, all inconsistent measures which had been grandfathered under the Protocol had to be brought into consistency with the obligations of GATT 1994 as of January 1, 1995.

[6] The incorporation of the provisions of protocols of accession has specifically excluded any provisions of those protocols concerning provisional application, thereby having the same effect of the exclusion of the Protocol of Provisional Application.

ing country Member" and "developed country Member". References to the "Executive Secretary" are to be read as the "Director-General of the WTO". References to the "CONTRACTING PARTIES" acting jointly under certain GATT articles are to be read as a reference to the WTO. Other functions assigned to the CONTRACTING PARTIES acting jointly are to be considered to be assigned to the WTO's Ministerial Conference. Paragraph (c) of Article 2 then addresses certain langauge issues. The English, French and Spanish texts of GATT 1994 are all considered to be equally authentic. The paragraph also identifies where the authentic French and Spanish texts are to be found.

Article 3 of GATT 1994 provides a limited exemption directed primarily at certain provisions of the *Jones Act*[7] of the United States. Dating back to 1920, the *Jones Act* generally restricts maritime cabotage within the U.S. to vessels built, owned and registered in the U.S., and staffed by U.S. citizens. It is generally considered that some aspects of the *Jones Act* were inconsistent with the GATT. However, as the measure pre-dated the GATT 1947, these inconsistencies were considered to be grandfathered under the Protocol of Provisional Application. The elimination of the Protocol under GATT 1994 then meant that the United States would lose the protection of the Protocol and would be required to bring the measure into consistency with the new Agreement. A *de facto* continuation of the Protocol to protect the *Jones Act* was therefore requested and obtained by the United States, subject to ongoing reporting and review requirements.

2. OVERVIEW OF THE MAJOR PROVISIONS OF GATT 1994

As noted, Article 1(a) of GATT 1994 incorporates the provisions of GATT 1947 into the new Agreement by reference, along with a number of related understandings that were agreed to as part of the Uruguay Round final package. These provisions are discussed below.

Article I: General Most-favoured-Nation Treatment

Article I:1 is considered to be one of the cornerstones of the world trading system as it sets out the Agreement's unconditional most-favoured-nation ("MFN") obligation. Subject to certain exceptions, this MFN obligation prohibits Members from discriminating among the products of other Members. Any favour, privilege or immunity that a Member grants to a product of another Member must be extended automatically and unconditionally to the like product of all other Members. The MFN obligation applies generally, to all customs duties, other import or export charges, to all rules concerning

---

[7]The *Jones Act* is known more formally as the *Merchant Marine Act, 1920,* and the provisions at issue are found in section 27 of that Act.

imports or exports, and to all internal regulations and taxation measures related to goods.[8]

Article II: Schedules of Concessions

Most early GATT negotiations focused almost exclusively on tariff reductions. The results of these tariff negotiations, or "concessions" as they are referred to, would then be summarized by each contracting party in their own "Schedule of Concessions". These Schedules are then incorporated into the Agreement.[9] Article II deals with some of the more important aspects of these Schedules and the application of tariffs generally. First, paragraph 1 of Article II specifically applies the unconditional MFN obligation to tariff concessions contained in these Tariff Schedules. Subject to some exceptions, in applying its import duties a Member must treat imports from all other Members in a non-discriminatory fashion, meaning that a product imported from one Member must be charged a duty which is no less favourable than that charged on like imports from any other Member. Paragraph 1 also "binds" tariff concessions that have been agreed to and included within a Schedule, meaning that those bound tariffs cannot be subsequently increased above the bound rate except in certain specified circumstances. This paragraph also provides that a Member is not permitted to impose any customs duty or any "other duties or charges" on imported products that are in excess of the applicable bound rate or charge set out in the Member's Schedule.[10]

Members are permitted to impose additional charges or avoid the MFN obligation of Article II in a number of specified circumstances. Paragraph 2 sets out some of these circumstances. First, a Member is free to impose charges at the border which are equivalent to internal taxes imposed on like domestically-produced products (sales or consumption taxes, for example). Second, Members are able to impose anti-dumping or countervailing duties on imported products, provided such duties are determined and applied in a

---

[8] Paragraphs 2, 3, and 4 of Article I provide certain exceptions from the MFN obligation for preferences required to be extended under other international agreements which pre-dated the original GATT 1947.

[9] GATT Article II:7 provides that the tariff schedules annexed to the Agreement are an integral part of Part I of the Agreement. By virtue of Article 1(b) of GATT 1994 all tariff concessions that had been accepted in previous rounds of GATT negotiations have been incorporated into GATT 1994.

[10] With respect to "other duties or charges" Members have entered into an understanding as part of the Uruguay Round's final package to further clarify and ensure compliance with the obligations of Article II—the *Understanding on Interpretation of Article II:1(b) of the General Agreement on Tariffs and Trade 1994*. Among other things, the Understanding provides that all such applicable "other duties or charges" imposed by a Member must be recorded in that Member's Schedule to GATT 1994, thereby increasing transparency and making the relevant obligations of Article II specifically applicable to those additional charges.

manner that is otherwise consistent with the Agreement. Finally Members may charge additional "service fees" on imports provided those fees are commensurate with the cost of the services being provided.

Article III: National Treatment

While the MFN obligation of Articles I and II prohibit a Member from discriminating among other Members, Article III imposes another type of non-discriminatory obligation—that of "national treatment". Subject to certain exceptions, the national treatment obligation of Article III prohibits Members from discriminating between like imported and domestically-produced products. This non-discriminatory obligation is applied broadly by the various paragraphs of Article III to cover all internal taxes and charges, and all laws, regulations, and requirements affecting the internal sale, offering for sale, purchase, distribution or use of a product. Specifically exempted from the national treatment obligation are non-commercial government procurement practices and domestic subsidies, meaning that a Member will not violate Article III by preferring to procure local over imported goods, or by granting subsidies only to domestic producers.

Article IV: Cinematograph Films

At the time of the original GATT negotiations there was special concern over trade in cinematograph films, not unlike the current debate in international trade concerning cultural protection. Article IV is a special provision directed at such cinematograph films which allows Members to impose internal quantitative restrictions on imported films, in the form of screen quotas, whereby domestically-produced films may be granted a certain minimum proportion of screen time. But for Article IV, such discriminatory internal quantitative regulations likely would conflict with the national treatment obligations of Article III.

Article V: Freedom of Transit

Goods and their means of transit often pass through one country on their way to their final destination in another country. Article V deals with these situations, and, subject to reasonable regulations, generally requires freedom of transit across or through the territory of one Member to a final destination in another Member. Specifically, Members are not permitted to impose any customs duties or charges on such transiting goods, except those for transportation or commensurate with the cost of other services that may be rendered.

Article VI: Anti-dumping and Countervailing Duties

Article VI deals with two types of duty-based "trade remedies"—that of anti-dumping and countervailing duties. These remedies are intended to offset the negative effects of what are generally considered to be unfair trade practices.

Generally speaking, "dumping" is the selling of a product in an export market for a price that is less than that charged for the same product in the domestic market of the seller. While many consider this form of international price discrimination to be unfair, Article VI does not prohibit it outright. The article only provides that dumping is to be "condemned" if it causes or threatens to cause material injury to the domestic industry of another Member. More importantly, under certain circumstances Article VI allows for the imposition at the border of a special anti-dumping duty, in order to offset the margin of dumping. Anti-dumping duties may not be imposed under Article VI unless it has been determined that the effect of the dumping is such as to cause or threaten material injury to the relevant domestic industry of the importing Member. While the obligations of Article VI as they apply to dumping are quite vague, they have been substantially elaborated upon by the *Agreement on Implementation of Article VI of the General Agreement on Tariffs and Trade 1994*, discussed below in Part E.[11]

Article VI also provides for the application of another similar duty-based remedy—that of the "countervailing duty". This remedy may be used to offset the government subsidization of exported products in certain circumstances. Article VI defines a countervailing duty as a special duty levied for the purpose of offsetting any bounty or subsidy bestowed, directly or indirectly, upon the manufacture, production or export of any merchandise. Like the anti-dumping duty, a countervailing duty may only be imposed if the effect of the subsidization of the product is such as to cause or threaten material injury to the relevant domestic industry of the importing Member. The duty cannot be in excess of the amount of subsidization that has been determined to exist. As is the case with the anti-dumping duty, the provisions of Article VI applicable to countervailing duties are quite vague and have also been substantially elaborated upon by another WTO agreement, the *Agreement on Subsidies and Countervailing Measures*, discussed below in Part F.[12]

Article VII: Valuation for Customs Purposes

Most customs duties that Members apply to imported goods are referred to as *ad valorem* duties—that is, the determination of the amount of duty that is payable is based upon a percentage of the value of the imported good. As a result, the method by which the value of the imported good is determined for duty purposes is crucial. Article VII sets out certain obligations that must be met in determining such product values for customs purposes.

---

[11] See pages 131-149.

[12] See pages 150-176.

Generally speaking, under Article VII value for customs purposes of imported goods must be based on the "actual value" of the imported good and not on the value of a like domestically-produced good, or some other arbitrary or fictitious value. Actual value in these circumstances should be the price at which the good is sold for export in the ordinary course of trade under fully competitive conditions. If these conditions are not present and such an actual value cannot be ascertained, value should then be based on the nearest ascertainable value.

Directly related to valuation, prices for goods in international trade are often expressed in foreign currency. Article VII therefore also sets out rules that must be observed in converting foreign currency based prices into the currency of the importing country. Generally, for freely-trading currencies, Members must use a conversion rate that effectively reflects the current value of the currencies in commercial transactions.

These obligations, particularly those concerning the use of "actual value" and alternative methods of valuation, have being substantially elaborated upon by another WTO agreement, the *Agreement on Implementation of Article VII of the General Agreement on Tariffs and Trade 1994*, discussed below in Part D.[13]

Article VIII: Fees and Formalities Connected with Importation and Exportation

Article VIII provides additional disciplines applicable to fees and other formalities connected with importation or exportation. Among other obligations, Article VIII provides that any fees or charges (other than duties and domestic taxes) imposed on or in connection with importation or exportation must be limited in amount to the approximate cost of the services being rendered, and must not represent indirect protection for domestic products or a form of revenue generation. The obligations of Article VIII apply to any fees, charges, formalities or requirements relating to consular services, quantitative restrictions, licensing, exchange controls, inspections and quarantine, sanitation and fumigation.

Article IX: Marks of Origin

Article IX sets out certain obligations applicable to origin marking—that is, a requirement that imported products bear a mark or indication of where the product was manufactured. Such requirements have been used for protectionist purposes in the past. Members recognize that such requirements should be reduced to a minimum, with due regard being given to the protection of

---

[13] See pages 107-116.

consumers from fraudulent or misleading indications of origin. Any such requirements that are imposed must be done so on an MFN basis, and must permit compliance so as not to seriously damage the products, materially reduce their value, or unreasonably increase their cost. Members should permit marking at the time of importation whenever practical, and no special duty or penalty should be imposed for a failure to mark any goods prior to importation. In addition, Article IX also requires Members to cooperate with each other to prevent the use of trade names which misrepresent the true origin of products to the detriment of distinctive regional or geographical names.[14]

Article X: Publication and Administration of Trade Regulations

Article X, dealing with the publication and administration of trade regulations, incorporates certain basic transparency and due process obligations into the Agreement. First, with respect to transparency, all laws, regulations, judicial and administrative rules and inter-governmental agreements relating to certain aspects of the importation, exportation and sale of goods must be promptly published. With respect to due process, each Member is required to administer its relevant laws in a uniform, impartial and reasonable manner. In addition, Members are generally required to maintain independent judicial, administrative or arbitral tribunals or procedures that allow for the prompt review or appeal of administrative actions relating to customs matters.

Article XI: General Elimination of Quantitative Restrictions

Tariffs are not the only measures that can act to restrict trade. Non-tariff import and export restrictions (such as quotas and prohibitions) can also be used to restrict both imports and exports. Note that the GATT 1994 does not prohibit tariffs. Rather, it calls for their gradual elimination through negotiation. In contrast, subject to certain limited exceptions, Article XI prohibits outright all non-tariff import or export restrictions, whether made effective through quotas, import or export licences, or other measures.

Some of the more important exceptions to this general prohibition are found in paragraph 2 of Article XI. For example, a Member may temporarily impose export restrictions on essential products in order to prevent or relieve critical domestic shortages. It is also worth noting that subparagraph (c) previously allowed Members to impose import restrictions on agricultural or food products in certain circumstances. The exceptions set out in subpara-

---

[14]This last obligation has been substantially strengthened by certain obligations concerning "geographical indications" found in the *Agreement on Trade-Related Aspects of Intellectual Property Rights*. This Agreement is discussed in depth in chapter 5. See pages 252-295.

graph (c) have been substantially altered by certain obligations of the WTO's *Agreement on Agriculture*, discussed below in Part B.[15]

Article XII: Restrictions to Safeguard to Balance of Payments

Another exception to the basic prohibition on quantitative restrictions is provided under Article XII. In some cases, the total value of a country's imports can be greater than the value of its exports, creating what is referred to as a "balance of payments" problem. Article XII permits certain actions to be taken so as to avoid such problems, while attempting to ensure that such restrictive actions are not subject to abuse. Notwithstanding the prohibition in Article XI:1, Members are permitted to impose import restrictions or quotas in order to safeguard their external financial positions and balance of payments. Use of the Article XII exception is subject to a number of requirements and limitations, including an obligation to report the imposition of any new measures and a requirement to consult in certain situations.

The obligations of Article XII have been further elaborated upon by the *Understanding on the Balance-of-Payments Provisions of the General Agreement on Tariffs and Trade 1994*, part of the final Uruguay Round package.[16] Under this Understanding, Members have affirmed their commitment to publicly announce time-schedules for the elimination of balance-of-payments measures, and to give preference to the least trade-disruptive measures, such as price-based import surcharges. In addition, Members are to seek to avoid the imposition of new quantitative restrictions for balance-of-payments purposes. In any case, balance-of-payments measures are to be administered in a transparent manner. The Understanding also establishes the Committee on Balance-of-Payments Restrictions and imposes additional consultative obligations on Members imposing balance-of-payments measures.

Article XIII: Non-discriminatory Administration of Quantitative Restrictions

Articles XI and XII both provide certain exceptions to the general prohibition of Article XI:1, meaning that in certain circumstances non-tariff import

---

[15] See pages 70-88. Note that the potential for conflicts between a provision of GATT 1994, such as Article XI:2(c), and that of another agreement found in Annex 1A, has been addressed by a General Interpretative Note to Annex 1A. This Note provides that in the event of a conflict between a provision of GATT 1994 and a provision in another agreement in Annex 1A, the provision in the other agreement prevails. Thus, in the case of import restrictions on agricultural products, the obligations of the *Agreement on Agriculture* will prevail over those of GATT Article XI:2(c).

[16] Article XII also remains subject to the 1979 *Declaration on Trade Measures Taken for Balance-of-Payments Purposes* (adopted 28 November 1979, BISD 26S/205) incorporated into the GATT 1994 by virtue of Article 1(b).

or export restrictions may be imposed in a GATT-consistent fashion. The purpose of Article XIII is to ensure that any such restrictions are employed in a non-discriminatory basis by specifically applying the MFN obligation to all such measures. Paragraph 1 of Article XIII provides that no import or export prohibition or restriction may be applied against the imports from or exports to any one Member unless imports from or exports to all other countries are similarly prohibited or restricted. The remaining provisions of Article XIII provide procedural guidance as to how this MFN obligation is to be applied in certain circumstances.

Article XIV: Exceptions to the Rule of Non-discrimination

Article XIV sets out a number of exceptions to the MFN obligation of Article XIII. In certain very limited and specified cases Members may avoid the obligations of Article XIII and impose discriminatory restrictions.

Article XV: Exchange Arrangements

Prior to the Second World War countries occasionally attempted to manipulate their currency exchange rates in order to affect their terms of trade. While such manipulation was substantially addressed in the negotiation of the *Articles of Agreement of the International Monetary Fund* (the "IMF"), which took place in 1944, the original GATT negotiators still considered that additional disciplines on currency manipulation should be included in the GATT, and that these GATT obligations should be specifically linked with those of the IMF. Article XV serves this purpose. Among other obligations, the article requires a degree of cooperation between the two groups, with the IMF having the lead on monetary matters. Members are generally prohibited from frustrating the intent of the GATT through the use of exchange actions, although nothing in the GATT 1994 precludes the use of exchange controls in accordance with the IMF. Article XV also includes special arrangements to address those Members that are not signatories to the IMF.

Article XVI: Subsidies

Governmental subsidies are the subject of Article XVI. What is somewhat curious about the provisions of Article XVI is that while they impose some limited disciplines on the use of subsidies, the term "subsidy" is never defined. This remained the case until the negotiation of the WTO's *Agreement on Subsidies and Countervailing Measures*, which includes, for the first time, an agreed definition of what constitutes a subsidy. It should be noted that the obligations of Article XVI have been substantially amended and reinforced by the *Agreement on Subsidies and Countervailing Measures* and the *Agreement on Agriculture*, discussed below in Parts F[17] and B[18] respectively.

---

[17] See pages 150-176.

[18] See pages 70-88.

Article XVI is divided into two parts: Part A, which applies to all subsidies, and Part B, which only applies to export subsidies. Part A requires a Member to notify the WTO of any subsidy that it grants which acts to increase exports from or decrease imports into its territory. Consultations are provided for in certain circumstances. The obligations of Part B of Article XVI are divided between primary products and other, or industrial, products. Paragraph 3 of Article XVI originally required that contracting parties only "seek to avoid" the use of export subsidies on the export of primary products. With respect to non-primary products contracting parties were prohibited from granting export subsidies on such products where such a subsidy resulted in a sale for export at a price that was lower than the domestic price of the product. As noted, these very limited disciplines have been substantially altered and strengthened by both the *Agreement on Subsidies and Countervailing Measures* and the *Agreement on Agriculture*.

Article XVII: State Trading Enterprises

Article XVII imposes certain obligations on Members concerning enterprises that are owned or controlled by government. While the GATT 1994 does not generally attempt to regulate the behaviour of individual commercial actors, such as corporations or other forms of commercial enterprises, state enterprises are considered to be an exception. In many cases state enterprises are simply the form through which governments intervene in the economy. Thus, if the actions of such enterprises were not subject to some discipline Members might attempt to avoid their GATT obligations by employing state-owned or controlled corporations rather than by directly adopting GATT-inconsistent measures.

Paragraph 1 of Article XVII imposes a general obligation of non-discriminatory treatment. Any state enterprise is required to act in a manner consistent with the general principles of non-discriminatory treatment in its commercial purchases or sales. This means that such enterprises must make their purchases or sales solely in accordance with commercial considerations, such as price, quality and availability. It is important to note that these obligations do not apply to imports for governmental consumption, or what is more commonly referred to as government procurement.[19]

In order to increase transparency in the area of state-trading enterprises, the obligations of Article XVII have been further reinforced by the *Understanding on the Interpretation of Article XVII of the General Agreement on Tariffs and Trade 1994*, part of the final Uruguay Round package. This Understanding requires Members to notify the Council for Trade in Goods of

---

[19] Government procurement by some Members is subject to the obligations of the *Agreement on Government Procurement*. This agreement is discussed in chapter 6 below. See pages 300-303.

all such enterprises that fall within the scope of Article XVII. These notifications are then to be reviewed by the Working Party on State Enterprises which is established under the Understanding.

Article XVIII: Governmental Assistance to Economic Development

Article XVIII provides a number of special exceptions designed to enable developing countries to avoid certain obligations of the Agreement in order to assist them in achieving economic development. (The exceptions of Article XVIII should be read in conjunction with Part IV of the Agreement, discussed below.)

Article XVIII is divided into four sections, A through D. Section A addresses tariff concessions, allowing certain developing country Members to withdraw a previously bound tariff concession in order to promote the establishment of a particular industry. Section B addresses balance-of-payments issues, allowing certain developing country Members to take measures for balance-of-payments reasons and imposing less onerous obligations on developing country Members than those found in GATT Article XII. Sections C and D provide for the imposition of other measures relating to imports that are considered necessary in order to promote the establishment of a particular industry.

Article XIX: Emergency Action on Imports of Particular Products

Article XIX provides for the imposition of special border measures that would otherwise be in violation of Articles II or XI in certain emergency situations. If, as a result of unforeseen developments, a product is being imported in such increased quantities as to cause or threaten serious injury to the domestic producers of the like product, then, subject to certain obligations, Members are permitted to impose a quantitative restriction, or impose or increase a tariff so as to prevent or remedy such injury. The obligations of Article XIX have been substantially elaborated upon and clarified by the *Agreement on Safeguards*, discussed below in Part G.[20]

Article XX: General Exceptions

Article XX sets out a number of general exceptions applicable to all the obligations of the Agreement. Subject to the requirement that measures are not applied in a manner that would constitute a means of arbitrary or unjustifiable discrimination between countries, or a disguised restriction on trade, nothing in the Agreement is to be construed to prevent the adoption or enforcement by

---

[20] See pages 176-184.

a Member of certain specified types of measures. Such measures include those necessary to protect human, animal or plant life or health, and those necessary to secure compliance with other laws which are themselves consistent with the Agreement.

Article XXI: Security Exceptions

Further to the exceptions of Article XX, Article XXI provides three additional exceptions based on national security concerns. For example, nothing in the Agreement is to be construed as preventing a Member from taking any action that it considers necessary for the protection of its national security interests relating to certain issues, including fissionable materials, or taken in a time of war or other emergency in international relations. In addition, nothing in the Agreement prevents a Member from taking any action pursuant to its obligations under the United Nations Charter.

Article XXII: Consultations

Article XXII requires Members to consult with and accord sympathetic consideration to any other Member with respect to any matter affecting the operation of the Agreement.

Article XXIII: Nullification and Impairment

While entitled "nullification and impairment" Article XXIII is essentially the Agreement's dispute settlement provision. Paragraph 1 sets out the basis upon which a Member may initiate the Agreement's dispute settlement procedures. A Member is able to initiate the dispute settlement process whenever it considers that any benefit accruing to it directly or indirectly under the Agreement is being nullified or impaired by:

(a) the failure of another Member to carry out its obligations under the Agreement;

(b) the application by another Member of any measure, whether or not it conflicts with the provisions of the Agreement; or

(c) the existence of any other situation.

The first step under paragraph 1 is a written representation to the other Member or Members involved. Any Member so approached is to give sympathetic consideration to such representations. If no satisfactory solution is reached within a reasonable period of time, the matter may be referred to the WTO. These consultative and dispute settlement provisions of both Article XXII and XXIII are then substantially elaborated upon by the *Understanding on Rules and Procedures Governing the Settlement of Disputes* (or "DSU"), discussed below in chapter 7.[21]

---

[21] See pages 308-327.

Article XXIV: Territorial Application, Frontier Traffic, Customs Unions and Free-Trade Areas

Article XXIV contains a number of disparate obligations. The first type, found in paragraph 2, addresses the territorial application of the Agreement. Generally speaking, the Agreement applies to the customs territories of its Members. The second type of obligation, found in paragraph 3, permits Members to extend special advantages to adjacent countries in order to facilitate frontier traffic.

A third type of obligation concerns the application of the Agreement to sub-national governments of Members. Paragraph 12 of Article XXIV requires Members to take such reasonable measures as may be available to them to ensure that their regional and local governments comply with the Agreement. Due to some uncertainty concerning the obligations of paragraph 12, this paragraph was further clarified and reinforced by certain provisions of the *Understanding on the Interpretation of Article XXIV of the General Agreement on Tariffs and Trade 1994*, part of the Uruguay Round final package. Paragraphs 13 through 15 of this Understanding address Article XXIV:12. Each Member is stated to be fully responsible under GATT 1994 for the observance of all of its provisions, and must take all reasonable measures as may be available to it so as to ensure such observance by its regional and local governments. Moreover Articles XXII and XXIII, as applied and elaborated upon by the DSU, may be invoked concerning the measures of sub-national governments. If the Dispute Settlement Body makes a determination that the measure of a sub-national government is inconsistent with a GATT obligation, the responsible Member is required to take all reasonable measures in order to ensure compliance by the sub-national government. However, due to the Member's internal constitutional rules it may not be possible in all cases to ensure such compliance. If this situation arises, the WTO's provisions concerning compensation and suspension of concessions will then become applicable.[22]

The final type of provision found in Article XXIV concerns the establishment of customs unions and free trade areas. Two of the distinguishing features of customs unions and free trade agreements is that while they liberalize trade among signatory countries, they generally do not extend the same privileges to non-signatories. Thus, such arrangements would be contrary to the Agreement's non-discriminatory obligations unless they are otherwise exempted from those obligations. This is the effect of paragraphs 4 through 10 of Article XXIV. The Agreement does not prevent the establishment of customs unions and free trade areas provided a number of specified conditions are met. These conditions include requirements that duties and

---

[22] See Article 22 of the DSU in this regard, as discussed below in chapter 7, pages 324-325.

other barriers to trade should be eliminated on substantially all trade among the signatory countries, and barriers to trade with non-signatories should not be increased. Signatories are also required to notify the WTO of the arrangement and to provide it with any required information.

Due to some dissatisfaction and uncertainty concerning these provisions, paragraphs 4 through 10 of Article XXIV were also clarified and further supplemented by paragraphs 1 through 11 of the *Understanding on Article XXIV*. Among other things, these provisions clarify how certain calculations are to be undertaken and reaffirm the process that must be followed when a Member forming part of a customs union proposes to increase otherwise bound tariffs. In addition, the Understanding also provides improved notification procedures and allows for more substantive review of proposed customs unions and free trade areas.[23]

Article XXV: Joint Action

Article XXV of GATT 1947 dealt with certain actions of the Contracting Parties acting jointly. Under the article, each contracting party was entitled to one vote at meetings and, except as otherwise provided in the Agreement, decisions were to be taken by a majority of votes cast. While these obligations have been continued in GATT 1994, they have largely been replaced by the applicable obligations of the WTO Agreement discussed above in chapter 2.[24]

Paragraph 5 of Article XXV of GATT 1947 provided that in exceptional circumstances, and subject to certain requirements, the Contracting Parties, acting jointly, were permitted to waive any GATT obligation imposed on any contracting party. Such waiver decisions required a two-thirds majority of the votes cast, with the majority accounting for more than one-half of all contracting parties.[25] All WTO waiver decisions, including those concerning GATT 1994 obligations, are now governed by the more onerous obligations of Article IX:3 of the *WTO Agreement*, as discussed above in chapter 2.[26]

Waivers that had previously been granted under GATT Article XXV:5 and that were still in force as of the entry into force of the WTO Agreement

---

[23] In addition to this Understanding, in February 1996, the WTO's General Council agreed to establish a permanent Committee on Regional Trade Agreements, which then replaced a number of *ad hoc* working parties that had been reviewing such agreements on a case-by-case basis. In addition to assuming the work of all ongoing reviews and having responsibility for any new reviews, this Committee is also expected to develop improved review procedures and possibly make recommendations to the General Council as to whether and how the provisions of Article XXIV might be improved. See *WTO Focus*, No. 8, January-February 1996, at 4.

[24] See pages 28-49.

[25] As of April 1, 1994, 113 original waiver decisions had been taken under Article XXV:5, and apparently in only two cases were waiver requests denied. See the *Guide to GATT Law and Practice*, at 823.

[26] See pages 40-41.

are subject to the *Understanding in Respect of Waivers of Obligations under the General Agreement on Tariffs and Trade 1994*, part of the Uruguay Round final package.[27] Paragraph 2 of that Understanding provides that any waiver that was in force as of January 1, 1995 will terminate on the earlier of January 1, 1997 or the waiver's stated expiry date, unless the waiver is extended in accordance with the procedures of the Understanding and Article IX of the *WTO Agreement*. The Understanding also clarifies that any Member that considers a benefit accruing to it under GATT 1994 as being nullified or impaired as a result of another Member's measure imposed under cover of a waiver still has access to GATT Article XXIII as elaborated and applied by the DSU.

Article XXVI: Acceptance, Entry into Force and Registration

Article XXVI contains a number of provisions related to entry into force, authentic texts, acceptance of the Agreement and territorial coverage, which have all been superseded by the relevant provisions of the WTO Agreement, discussed above in chapter 2.[28]

Article XXVII: Withholding or Withdrawal of Concessions

Article XXVII provides that a Member is free to withhold or withdraw any tariff concession if that Member determines that the concession was originally negotiated with a country which has not become or ceases to be a Member. Any Member taking such action is to provide notification and must consult with other Members which have a substantial interest in the product.

Article XXVIII: Modification of Schedules

A Member's tariff concessions are set out in its Schedule of Concessions, which is a part of the GATT 1994. Article XXVIII sets out two circumstances under which a Member may be permitted to modify its Schedule, and, as a result, will then be free to increase a previously bound tariff. First, once every three years Members have the opportunity to modify their Schedules through negotiation. If an agreement cannot be reached on adequate compensation for such modifications, the Member remains free to modify its Schedule as proposed, but substantially equivalent concessions may be withdrawn by other Members in return, subject to receiving approval for such action from the WTO. Procedures for negotiation and implementation of the provisions of Article XXVIII have been further elaborated upon by the *Understanding on*

---

[27] Note that Article 1(b)(iii) incorporates certain waiver decisions made under GATT 1947 into GATT 1994.

[28] See pages 28-49.

the Interpretation of Article XXVIII of the General Agreement on Tariffs and Trade 1994, part of the Uruguay Round final package.[29]

Second, the WTO may at any time, in special circumstances, permit a Member to enter into negotiations for the modification or withdrawal of a concession, subject to similar requirements concerning compensation and authorized retaliation, as outlined above.

Article XXVIII *bis*: Tariff Negotiations

The eventual elimination of tariffs through negotiation has always been one of the primary goals of the GATT. Article XXVIII *bis* specifies this goal and generally establishes the procedures for its attainment. The article notes that duties often constitute serious obstacles to trade. Negotiations to reduce them, on a reciprocal and mutually advantageous basis, are "of great importance" to the expansion of world trade. Members are therefore encouraged to sponsor such negotiations from time to time, to be conducted according to agreed procedures.

Article XXIX: The Relation of this Agreement with the Havana Charter

The drafters of the original GATT 1947 had intended the Agreement to be a temporary one, to be in effect only until such time as the much more comprehensive Havana Charter entered into force. Consequently Article XXIX was necessary to address the relationship between the two agreements. Due to problems concerning the ratification of the Havana Charter, it never entered into force. It was then decided that the GATT would remain in effect subject to some amendments. As a result, much of Article XXIX then became irrelevant. This is with the exception of paragraph 1, which provides that the contracting parties have undertaken to observe to the fullest extent possible under existing legislation certain provisions of the Havana Charter. With the incorporation of Article XXIX into the GATT 1994, it appears that this obligation continues to apply, subject to it being in conflict with another WTO obligation.

Articles XXX through XXXV: Amendments, Withdrawal, Contracting Parties, Accession, Annexes and Non-application

Articles XXX through XXXV, dealing with procedural issues such as amendment, withdrawal and accession, are largely irrelevant, having been superseded by the equivalent procedural provisions of the WTO Agreement, Articles X through XV, discussed above in chapter 2.[30] An exception is Article

---

[29] In addition, the "Procedures for Negotiations under Article XXVIII", adopted in 1980 (BISD 27S/26-28), also remain applicable to proposed modifications under Article XXVIII.

[30] See pages 40-42.

XXXIV, which provides that the annexes to the Agreement (including, most importantly, Annex I: Notes and Supplementary Provisions) are an integral part of the Agreement.

Articles XXXVI through XXXVIII: Trade and Development

Articles XXXVI through XXXVIII of the GATT comprise what is known as Part IV of the Agreement, subtitled "Trade and Development". The addition of Part IV to the GATT in 1964-65 was the only other major change to be made to the Agreement since a number of changes were made following a major review in 1954-55. The purpose of Part IV is to assist developing countries to attain their development goals. Article XXXVI sets out a number of principles and objectives, such as a need to increase market access for the products of developing countries and for the WTO to work closely with other inter-governmental agencies and international lending agencies. (Article XXXVIII provides that Members shall collaborate jointly within the framework of Article XXXVI and a number of other fora to further these objectives.) In addition, paragraph 8 of Article XXXVI notes that developed country Members do not expect reciprocity from developing country Members for commitments made by developed countries during trade negotiations.

Article XXXVII then sets out a number of specific, though largely hortatory commitments applicable to developed country Members, including giving high priority to the elimination of barriers on the products of export interest to developing country Members. The article also provides for consultation if a developing country Member considers that these obligations are not being met.

The obligations of Part IV have been directly and indirectly supplemented by a number of other provisions of the Uruguay Round's final package, including, for example, the "Decision on Measures in Favour of Least-Developed Countries", the "Decision on Measures Concerning the Possible Negative Effects of the Reform Programme on Least-Developed and Net Food-Importing Developing Countries", and special and differential treatment extended to developing country Members under a number of the WTO Agreements.

3. THE MARRAKESH PROTOCOL TO THE GENERAL AGREEMENT ON TARIFFS AND TRADE 1994

As was the case with all previous rounds of GATT negotiations, the results of the tariff negotiations and certain other explanatory provisions have been appended to the GATT 1994 by way of an additional protocol to the Agreement—the Marrakesh Protocol. Among other provisions, the Protocol first provides that all the tariff schedules appended to it become Schedules to the GATT 1994, and are thereby integrated into the Agreement. The Protocol also notes that all tariff reductions agreed to by the Members are to be implemented in five equal reductions, unless otherwise specified in a Member's Schedule. The first such reduction occurred on January 1, 1995, with all further annual reductions also occurring on January 1 of subsequent years. Tariff reductions for agricultural products will be implemented as negotiated under the *Agreement on Agriculture* and as specified in the Members' Schedules. Finally, the Protocol addresses procedural issues concerning modification and adjustment of concessions in certain circumstances.

Part B:

Agriculture and Sanitary and Phytosanitary Measures

1. INTRODUCTION

This Part of chapter 3 addresses the WTO's two sector-specific agreements relating to agriculture found in Annex 1A, the *Agreement on Agriculture* and the *Agreement on Application of Sanitary and Phytosanitary Measures*. The Uruguay Round certainly was not the first time agricultural-related issues were negotiated within the GATT. But, without question, the Uruguay Round was the most successful agricultural negotiation in the history of the General Agreement. While the WTO's *Agreement on Agriculture* will not immediately improve market access for agricultural trade to a significant degree, where the *Agreement on Agriculture* has succeeded is in introducing sweeping reform to the international rules governing agricultural trade. As a result of these reforms trade friction will be reduced, the trading environment will become more predictable, and future improvement to market access will be easier to negotiate and achieve. The improvements to market access generated by the *Agreement on Agriculture* have then been reinforced by the *Agreement on Application of Sanitary and Phytosanitary Measures*, which will act to ensure that technical standards in the agriculture and food areas will be developed, implemented and enforced in a non-discriminatory and non-protectionist fashion.

In order to appreciate the nature of the change that has now been introduced, and to place these agreements in their proper context, it is first necessary to briefly discuss those previously-existing GATT rules governing agriculture that have now been substantially altered. In addition, because of their importance to the Round generally, the negotiations leading up to the *Agreement on Agriculture* are briefly summarized. The agreements themselves are then reviewed in depth.

2. THE PRE-WTO GATT RULES GOVERNING AGRICULTURAL TRADE

Most commentators agree that in spite of its dubious birth, in many ways the GATT 1947 proved to be a remarkably resilient and flexible agreement. A quick review of pre-WTO trade disputes, however, shows a clear and unfortunate pattern—about 70 percent of GATT disputes were related to agricultural or food products.[31] In light of continuing problems in agricultural trade, perhaps a more accurate assessment of the success of the GATT 1947 would be that, with respect to industrial products, the Agreement was very successful in reducing barriers and increasing global trade. In contrast, in the area of agricultural products, GATT's performance has never proved as effective. Why such a difference between these two? The many problems that have bedevilled global agricultural trade over the past 40 years can be attributed largely to one source, that being the extraordinary status granted to agriculture during the original GATT negotiations. This special treatment essentially remained unchanged until the Uruguay Round.

The special treatment accorded to agriculture within the GATT 1947 was focused primarily in two areas: the rules governing restrictions on imports, and the rules concerning the use of export subsidies. With respect to restrictions on imports, as noted above, GATT Article XI:1 provided that all non-tariff barriers or restrictions on imports were prohibited. With respect to agriculture, however, a special exemption from this general prohibition was provided in Article XI:2(c), permitting import restrictions to be imposed on agricultural products where the government also had in place a programme of supply management that limited or controlled domestic production of that same product.[32]

With respect to export subsidies, the rules, as they eventually evolved and were applied by developed countries, prohibited the granting of export sub-

---

[31] Consider, for example, some of the more recent Canada-U.S. bilateral disputes. The majority have been agriculture or food related—including products such as wheat, sugar, beer, wine, dairy and poultry products.

[32] One further developmental point worth noting relates to the GATT Article XI:2(c) exemption for import restrictions. It was not long after the GATT came into force that the Article XI:2(c) exemption proved to be insufficient for U.S. purposes. Following World War II, many agricultural import restrictions were imposed by the U.S. President under authority of section 22 of the *Agricultural Adjustment Act of 1933*. Unlike GATT Article XI:2(c), section 22 did not require that these import restrictions be imposed in conjunction with domestic supply or production restrictions. Any use by the President of section 22 would therefore be inconsistent with U.S. GATT obligations under Article XI:2(c). In 1955, the U.S. Administration sought and obtained an Article XXV waiver for section 22. This waiver, granted by the GATT on a non-expiring basis, generally meant that the U.S. was free to invoke section 22 and impose import restrictions on, among other products, sugar, wheat, peanuts and dairy products, in situations where such restrictions normally would be in violation of GATT Article XI.

sidies on the export of industrial goods. However, the subsidization of exports of primary agricultural products continued to be generally permitted, subject only to some vague and largely ineffective disciplines.

As is discussed below, much of the Uruguay Round agriculture negotiations were directed at eliminating these special rules and attempting to bring global agricultural trade within the same general rules that applied to industrial goods.

3. HISTORY OF THE ROUND'S AGRICULTURE NEGOTIATIONS

As noted, the Uruguay Round was not the first time agricultural issues were negotiated at the GATT. Issues relating to agriculture were on the negotiating agenda of most GATT Rounds, including the Kennedy Round (1964 to 1967) and the Tokyo Round (1973 to 1979). While the Tokyo Round, in particular, produced some substantive improvements to the GATT system, the basic exceptional rules applicable to agricultural products generally were not affected by the results of that Round. Indeed, the completion of the Round failed to introduce much optimism into the world trading community generally. Many GATT contracting parties remained of the view that the Round had failed to address adequately a whole host of issues, including those relating to agriculture, which would continue, and, in fact did continue, to plague the GATT trading system.

In light of these continuing concerns, the Thirty-Eighth Session of the Contracting Parties held in November of 1982 was held at the Ministerial level for the first time since 1973. While the U.S. proposed that the next round of multilateral trade negotiations should be commenced immediately, it could not gain sufficient support for this proposal. Instead, Ministers agreed to undertake a number of initiatives, under the "Ministerial Work Programme", directed at preparing for the next round of negotiations which could then begin once all the necessary preparatory work had been completed. One of these initiatives was the establishment of a Committee on Trade in Agriculture, comprised of interested GATT members, which, among other things, was directed to examine trade measures then affecting agricultural trade and to make recommendations to the GATT Council as to how the existing GATT rules might be improved.[33]

The Agriculture Committee presented its recommendations to the GATT Council in 1984, and, among other things, recommended that all quantitative restrictions and related measures affecting imports and exports, and all subsidies affecting trade in agriculture, including export subsidies and other forms of export assistance, be brought within the purview of strengthened and

---

[33] See Ministerial Declaration of the Thirty-Eighth Session of the GATT Contracting Parties, GATT, BISD 29S/9 at 16-17.

more operationally effective GATT rules and disciplines. In other words, the Committee's general recommendation was that the special treatment then accorded to agricultural goods under the GATT be terminated and that trade in such goods be subjected to the same rules generally applicable to trade in industrial goods.[34]

With the preparatory work by then largely complete, the U.S. again proposed a new round of GATT negotiations to the GATT Council meeting in 1985. This time the suggestion had much broader, though, surprisingly, not unanimous support. In spite of the continuing reluctance of some countries, on September 20, 1986 the Uruguay Round of GATT negotiations was officially commenced. One of the issues specifically highlighted for negotiation in the Ministerial Declaration launching the Round was agriculture.[35] Ministers agreed that there was an urgent need to bring increased discipline and predictability to world agricultural trade. Based on the preparatory work of the Agriculture Committee, the Ministerial Declaration noted that the negotiations were to aim to achieve greater liberalization of trade in agriculture and bring all measures affecting import access and export competition under "strengthened and more operationally effective GATT rules and disciplines", by reducing import barriers and increasing disciplines on the use of all direct and indirect subsidies. At the time of its initiation, the Round was originally scheduled to be completed within four years—that is, by the end of 1990.

While the negotiating agenda appeared clear, almost no substantive progress was made during the first four years of the agricultural negotiations. One suggested reason for this initial lack of progress was that some negotiators did not wish any substantive progress to be made and were hoping that history would repeat itself. If no ongoing progress could be made during the negotiations, agriculture would be taken off the table at the last minute and an agreement would be concluded that did not cover agricultural trade. This time, however, many countries simply were not prepared to conclude any agreement that did not address the fundamental problems troubling world agricultural trade.

In Brussels, in December of 1990, Ministers met for what was to be the triumphant concluding meeting of the Uruguay Round. However, by this time there still had been no substantive progress on agriculture as the EC had refused to negotiate on the basis of a proposal that was generally acceptable to all other participants. The EC continued to hold this position throughout the Brussels meeting, prompting a number of countries to walk out and the negotiations collapsed.

---

[34] The Contracting Parties adopted the Committee's recommendations at their Fortieth Session, in November of 1984. See GATT, BISD 31S/10, where the recommendations are reprinted.

[35] See Ministerial Declaration on the Uruguay Round, BISD 33S/19 at 24.

While the future of the Round was uncertain at this point, informal discussions began almost immediately after a brief "cooling-off period". These discussions eventually led to an official re-commencement of negotiations in early 1991. Yet, by December of 1991, almost no progress had been made in the area of agriculture. This stalemate prompted Mr. Arthur Dunkel, then GATT Secretary-General, to issue his own *Draft Final Act*, designed to bring the negotiations to a conclusion.[36] The draft agreement, which then became known as the "Dunkel Draft", reflected areas of agreement, and, in those areas where agreement had not yet been possible, proposed compromise solutions.

The EC rejected the *Draft Final Act*'s provisions applicable to agriculture. The EC's concerns were numerous, related to, among other things, a failure to properly account for its new system of compensation payments, the size of the export subsidy reductions that would be required, and the lack of a re-balancing provision that would allow increased barriers on some products provided that overall reduction commitments were still met.

After numerous attempts at addressing these issues in the multilateral forum, the EC and the U.S. met at Blair House in Washington, D.C. in November of 1992, in an attempt to break the impasse. The agreement that was eventually reached, since known as the Blair House Agreement, addressed many of the EC problems with the Dunkel Draft. The U.S. agreed to support both modifications to the treatment of EC compensation payments and a reduction in the size of required, volume-based export subsidy reductions. Still, this compromise did not meet with unanimous approval within the EC and it subsequently had to be renegotiated in part in December of 1993. The revised agreement then finally met with unanimous approval within the EC and this acceptance then paved the way for unanimous agreement on the final text of the *Agreement on Agriculture*. Once the agricultural issues were concluded, most of the other problems that had been delaying the Round's conclusion were resolved.

4. THE *AGREEMENT ON AGRICULTURE*

The *Agreement on Agriculture* is comprised of 21 Articles (divided into 13 Parts) and 5 Annexes. In addition, many other provisions relevant to the Agreement's implementation are to be found in the draft Agreement on Agriculture that had been included as part of the Dunkel Draft. As discussed below, while individual countries calculated their own offers and reduction commitments on the basis of these rules, once these commitments were set out in Members' Schedules to the Agreement, it was not considered necessary to incorporate the underlying calculation rules into the final Agreement.

---

[36] *Draft Final Act Embodying the Results of the Uruguay Round of Multilateral Trade Negotiations*, GATT Doc. MTN.TNC/W/FA, 20 December 1991.

(a) Scope and Coverage of the Agreement

Articles 1 and 2 and Annex 1 establish the scope and coverage of the Agreement. The Agreement applies to substantially all agricultural products, as found in Chapters 1 through 24 of the Harmonized System,[37] as well as certain non-edible animal and agricultural products such as furs, skins, flax and hemp. Fish and fish products have been specifically excluded from the Agreement.

(b) Implementation Period and Term of the Agreement

The Agreement did not become immediately effective upon general implementation of the WTO Agreement. Instead it is generally to be phased-in over a six-year "implementation period" commencing in the "year" 1995. "Year" as it is used in this context has been defined to mean the calendar, financial or marketing year for individual products as is specified in each Member's Schedule.[38] This means that the implementation date and term of the Agreement varies somewhat depending upon the product and the Member at issue.

As will be seen, even once the Agreement has been fully implemented, it will produce only minor reforms in some areas. As a result, in order to continue the reform process beyond the initial six-year term of the Agreement, under Article 20 the Members have already committed to commence further negotiations at least one year prior to the end of the implementation period in order to continue the reform process.

(c) Market Access

One of the three main issues that was to be addressed during the negotiations were those trade measures that affected market access for agricultural products—that is, tariffs and non-tariff import barriers which act to limit or prohibit the importation of agricultural products. Article 4 of the Agreement and its related Annexes and obligations set out the Agreement's market access obligations and address tariff and non-tariff measures applied by Members.

---

[37] The Harmonized System, or, more properly, the Harmonized Commodity Description and Coding System (or HS), negotiated under the auspices of the Customs Co-ordination Council (now called the World Customs Council), is a customs nomenclature used to classify or categorize imported goods for customs and statistical purposes. The HS came into effect on January 1, 1987 and the GATT officially converted to the HS in 1992 (see the *Geneva Protocol to the General Agreement on Tariffs and Trade*, BISD 39S/3).

[38] The term "Schedules" as used throughout the Agreement are listings of each Member's specific commitments required under the Agreement. As noted, this format of general rules and specific commitments set out in attached schedules has been widely used by the GATT since its inception.

These provisions themselves are brief and provide little guidance as to what a Member's specific market access commitments might be. Instead, the specific commitments made by each Member relating to market access are contained in each Member's Schedule. And, while the Schedules themselves set out the specific market access commitments that have been agreed to, they provide little guidance as to how those commitments were initially calculated and determined. One must look to the *Draft Final Act* for this information as the market access commitments that have been accepted by each Member were calculated largely on the basis of rules and requirements set out in the previous draft of the Agreement.[39] Once individual Members had calculated their initial commitments in accordance with these rules, they were then subject to review by other Members and, in some cases, further negotiation. Generally speaking, it is these commitments made by each Member and contained in each Member's Schedule that are the Agreement's essential obligations with respect to market access.

With respect to non-tariff border measures, the Agreement was one of the first international trade agreements to employ the concept of "tariffication" on a large scale, whereby non-tariff barriers such as quotas were converted to tariffs.[40] There were two steps involved in the tariffication process under the Agreement. First, Members were required to convert all their existing non-tariff border measures applicable to agricultural imports to an appropriate tariff equivalent. The second step involved providing a certain minimum degree of market access through the application of a low or zero tariff to a pre-determined quantity of imports. The combination of these two measures creates what is referred to as a "tariff-rate quota".

The types of border measures that were subject to tariffication under the Agreement included all quantitative import restrictions, variable import levies, discretionary import licensing, non-tariff barriers maintained through state-trading operations and voluntary export restraints. The tariff equivalents of these types of measures were calculated using a price-based formula that

---

[39] Specifically, rules and requirements applicable to market access are found in the *Agreement on Modalities for the Establishment of Specific Binding Commitments under the Reform Process*, which is Part B of the *Draft Final Act*'s Text on Agriculture.

[40] There are a number of reasons as to why tariffs are generally to be preferred over non-tariff measures. Assuming that the same level of protection will still be afforded to the relevant domestic industry, a tariff is considered to be more transparent and less market distorting. And, generally speaking, it is easier to negotiate the reduction or elimination of a tariff than it is a non-tariff measure. As the goal of future negotiations will be to improve market access through further reductions in import barriers, the conversion of non-tariff barriers to tariffs should make that goal somewhat easier to achieve.

was designed to produce a tariff with a protective effect generally equivalent to the non-tariff barrier it was replacing.[41]

Each Member was then required to commit to reduce both their pre-existing agricultural tariffs and all new tariffs that resulted from the tariffication exercise by an overall simple average of 36 percent over the six years of the implementation period, with an absolute minimum reduction for each tariff line of 15 percent.[42] Products that were already freely imported at a zero tariff rate were to be unaffected by the tariffication exercise. In order to ensure the integrity of tariffication and the tariff reduction commitments that had been agreed to, Article 4(2) of the Agreement then provides that subject to certain exceptions, Members are prohibited from maintaining, introducing or re-introducing any non-tariff measures of the type that had been subject to tariffication.

In addition to converting existing non-tariff measures to tariffs, Members were required to combine these new tariffs with a minimum degree of market access under which a specified amount of a given product can be imported at a low or zero tariff rate. Again, as was the case with the tariffication, the rules and requirements concerning these minimum market access commitments are not found in the Agreement itself, but in the *Draft Final Act*.[43]

The rules concerning minimum market access were as follows. Where there previously had been no significant imports of the relevant product, Members were required to permit a minimum level of imports of at least 3 percent of domestic consumption, increasing to 5 percent over the implementation period. Any pre-existing market access could not be reduced as a result of the tariffication exercise. Thus, where existing imports already equalled or exceeded 5 percent of domestic consumption, Members were required to maintain this degree of market access over the implementation period. The combination of this "minimum import opportunity" as it is known, and the newly introduced tariff equivalent, results in a tariff-rate quota. Under such a

---

[41] Annex 3 to Part B of the *Draft Final Act*'s Text on Agriculture provided the "modalities of conversion and related provisions". The Annex stipulated that the tariff equivalent for any specific product was to be calculated using the actual difference between internal and external prices for that product. In general, the external price for the product was to be the actual average c.i.f. unit value of that product for the importing country, or a calculated equivalent. The internal price was to be a representative wholesale price as found for the product in the internal market. These two representative prices were then compared and the resulting difference was converted to either a specific tariff (for example, X dollars per kilogram) or an *ad valorem* tariff (for example, X percent of each unit's value for duty).

[42] Reduction commitments for developing countries were limited to a simple average of 24 percent, with a minimum reduction of 10 percent for each tariff line.

[43] The specific rules concerning minimum market access are found in paragraphs 5, 6 and 7 and Annex 3 of the *Agreement on Modalities for the Establishment of Specific Binding Commitments Under the Reform Programme*, which is Part B of the *Draft Final Act*'s Text on Agriculture.

tariff-rate quota, the required minimum amount of imports will be permitted entry at a low or zero duty rate (the "within-access base rate"). Any imports of the product above that minimum amount will be subject to duty at a higher rate (or the "over-access base rate").

Article 4(2) and Annex 5 of the Agreement then provide a limited special treatment provision applicable to the tariffication and minimum access obligations. In certain specified circumstances, Annex 5 allows a Member to continue to maintain a measure that otherwise would be subject to tariffication (such as a quota) until the very end of the implementation period. Section A of Annex 5 applies to developed countries, while Section B applies to developing countries. Under Section A, in exchange for this special treatment, any Member employing the exception must provide an initial market access of at least 4 percent of the base period domestic consumption for the relevant product, increasing to 8 percent over the implementation period.[44]

(d) The Special Safeguard Provision

Because of the political sensitivity of the agriculture sector generally, Members had to be satisfied that tariffication and subsequent tariff reductions would not produce a flood of previously-restricted products into their territories, causing uncontrollable injury to their domestic agricultural industries. In order to ensure that this would not be the case, Article 5 of the Agreement provides two special tariff-based safeguard provisions. These provisions do not apply to agricultural products generally, but can only be invoked and applied against those agricultural products that were formerly subjected to non-tariff barriers which a Member was required to tariffy under the Agreement.

One safeguard, based on volume, allows an additional duty to be applied whenever total import volumes meet a certain trigger point. The second safeguard is a price-based mechanism under which an additional duty can be applied against any individual import shipment when its price is below a certain point. Paragraphs 1 and 8 of Article 5 ensure that a Member can only apply one of the special safeguards on any product at one time, and also cannot employ both a special safeguard and a safeguard action under GATT Article XIX against the same product simultaneously.

With respect to the volume-based safeguard, the volume trigger is to be established on the basis of the minimum access opportunity for the product. Where the minimum access is less than 10 percent, the volume trigger cannot be less than 125 percent of the actual opportunity level.[45] The additional duty

---

[44] Japan, for example, has claimed the benefit of Annex 5 for rice, and, as a result has not yet tariffied its import restriction on rice, but has greatly enhanced its market access for imported rice.

[45] For example, if the minimum access opportunity for a given product in a given year is 4 percent of domestic consumption, actual imports must reach at least 5 percent of domestic consumption before the volume safeguard can be invoked. Article 5(4) provides the calculation method that must be used to determine domestic consumption and import penetration.

that may be applied under this safeguard cannot exceed an additional one-third of the level of the ordinary duty in effect when the action is taken, and can only be applied until the end of the year in which it was imposed. In addition, the volume-based safeguard cannot be applied against any imports that are subject to the within-access tariff rate.

With respect to the price-based safeguard, the trigger price is based on the average price for the commodity in question during the 1986-88 base period. The duty that may be applied to any particular shipment depends upon the difference between the trigger price and the shipment's price. For example, if the difference between the import price and the trigger price is between 10 and 40 percent of the trigger price, the additional duty that may be applied must be no more than 30 percent of the amount by which the difference exceeds 10 percent of the trigger price. As is the case with the volume-based safeguard, the price-based safeguard cannot be applied against those imports that are subject to the within-access tariff rate.

(e) Domestic Support

The second issue subject to negotiation and reform was market-distorting domestic support. This type of support is to be distinguished from export subsidies, which are treated differently under the Agreement. The obligations applicable to domestic support are found in Articles 3, 6, and 7 and their related Annexes.

The applicable obligations differentiate between those domestic support programmes that can distort trade and those that do not. Domestic support programmes that do not distort trade have become known under a traffic-light analogy as "green box" programmes, because Members generally remain free to employ such programmes. With respect to those programmes that do distort trade, each Member was required to calculate the total of all its trade-distorting domestic support for agriculture (as it existed during the 1986-88 base period), measured on a national basis by the "Total Aggregate Measure of Support" (or "Total AMS"). Determining the Total AMS was a complex calculation. Generally speaking, it is the total of all product-specific support for all agricultural products (at both the national and sub-national levels), plus all non-specific support to agriculture in general (again, at both the national and sub-national levels).[46] Excluded from the Total AMS calculation are non-

---

[46] Article 1 defines the Total AMS as "... the sum of all domestic support provided in favour of agricultural producers, calculated as the sum of all aggregate measurements of support for basic agricultural products, all non-product-specific aggregate measurements of support and all equivalent measurements of support for agricultural products ..." Annexes 3 and 4 then provide detailed rules for calculating the AMS.

distorting domestic programmes, certain *de minimus* subsidies,[47] and certain direct payments to producers under production-limiting programmes.[48]

As was the case with the tariff reduction and market access commitments discussed above, based on certain obligations found in the *Draft Final Act*, each Member was required to determine Total AMS and then undertake certain reduction commitments based on this amount.[49] These specific reduction commitments were then set out in each Member's Schedule to the Agreement.[50] The basic reduction commitment required of each Member was to take the Total AMS as it existed during the base period of 1986-88, and then reduce that amount by 20 percent, in equal steps, over the implementation period. This reduction commitment is applicable to total agricultural support, not commodity-by-commodity support. As a result, each Member is free to determine how it will meet its reduction commitment. Under the requirements of Articles 3(2) and 6(3) of the Agreement in any given year of the implementation period, a Member's Total AMS cannot be more than the commitment applicable for that year.

It is generally considered that this reduction commitment will have very little immediate effect as most Members, including Canada and the United States, had already reduced their levels of domestic support by more than 20 percent from their 1986-88 levels prior to the implementation of the Agreement. The Agreement will, however, prevent future increases in trade-distorting domestic support.

---

[47] Article 6:4(a) permits a Member to exclude from its Total AMS any product-specific domestic support where that support does not exceed five percent of the Member's total value of production of that basic agricultural product during the relevant year.

[48] Article 6:5 provides an exception for direct payments to producers under production limiting programmes provided those payments are based on fixed area and yields, are made on 85 percent or less of the base level of production, or, in the case of livestock payments, are made on a fixed number of heads. The U.S. is apparently of the view that this provision excludes from its Total AMS calculation those deficiency payments made under the *Food, Agriculture, Conservation, and Trade Act of 1990* and also EC direct payments made under the 1992 reform of its Common Agricultural Policy. These programmes have become known as "blue box" programmes because, strictly speaking, they do not fall within the green box, but are still exempt from the reduction commitment. This exception was one that was agreed to as part of the Blair House Agreement between the U.S. and the EC.

[49] The modalities for establishing a Member's commitments concerning Total AMS are found in the *Draft Final Act*'s Text on Agriculture, Part B (Agreement on Modalities for the Establishment of Specific Binding Commitments Under the Reform Programme) at paragraphs 8, 9 and 10, and in Annexes 5 and 6 to Part B.

[50] Paragraph 1 of Article 6 provides that the domestic support reduction commitments of Members are to be contained in Part IV of their Schedules and apply to all domestic support to agricultural producers, with the exception of those green and blue box programmes. These commitments are expressed in Members' Schedules in terms of Total AMS and "Annual and Final Bound Commitment Levels".

It is essential to note the types of non-distorting domestic support measures which, by virtue of Article 6(1), are excluded from the Total AMS and thus are exempt from a Member's domestic support reduction commitment. The provisions applicable to these "green-box" programmes are found in Annex 2 to the Agreement. Generally speaking, exempt support programmes are permitted to have, at most, minimal trade-distorting effects or effects on production. They must also meet two additional criteria in order to be excluded from the Total AMS calculation: they must be government, rather than consumer financed, and they cannot be in the form of a price support to producers.

A number of specific types of programmes which take the form of direct payments to producers will be excluded if they meet certain additional criteria. Generally speaking, these criteria involve a decoupling of the financial or other support being provided to the producer from commodity prices or production levels. For example, farm income support will fall within the green-box category if, among other things, the payment amounts are not related to, or based on, the type, volume, or price of the production undertaken by the producer during any year after the base period. Other types of green-box programmes can include general governmental services (such as training, infrastructure, and inspection services), research, natural disaster relief (including crop insurance), regional assistance programmes, and structural adjustment assistance such as producer and resource retirement programmes, provided they meet the conditions for exclusion specified in Annex 2.

(f) Export Subsidy Commitments

The third issue subject to negotiation was export subsidies. An export subsidy is generally considered to be any form of subsidy that is paid or granted to a producer or exporter made contingent on the export of that product.[51] While export subsidies granted to industrial products have been subject to increasing discipline, export subsidies being granted to agricultural products have never before been subject to any substantive multilateral discipline. The Agreement will, for the first time, begin to impose restraints on this type of subsidization.

The essential obligation concerning export subsidies is found in Article 8 of the Agreement, which provides that Members are not permitted to grant any form of export subsidy to agricultural products except in conformity with the

---

[51] For purposes of the Agreement, "export subsidy" is defined in Article 1 as referring to ". . . subsidies contingent upon export performance, including the export subsidies listed in Article 9 . . ." Article 9 then lists six specific types of export subsides that are subject to reduction commitments under the Agreement, including programmes such as direct export subsidies, internal transport subsidies granted to export shipments, marketing subsidies, below market price disposal programmes, and producer-financed export subsidies.

Agreement and the export subsidy commitments contained in each Member's Schedule. This obligation is reinforced by Article 3(3), which provides that, subject to certain exceptions, Members are not permitted to grant export subsidies in excess of their budgetary outlay and quantity commitments contained in their respective Schedules. Members are not permitted to grant export subsidies to any agricultural product that is not listed in their Schedules, meaning that Members are not permitted to provide new export subsidies where none had been previously granted.

In developing their basic export subsidy reduction commitments Members are again guided by rules and requirements found in the *Draft Final Act*.[52] Over the implementation period Members are required to reduce export subsidies by 36 percent in monetary or budgetary terms, and by 21 percent in volume terms.[53] Generally speaking, the base level for these export subsidy reductions is the average levels that existed during the 1986 to 1990 period. As required by Article 9(2)(a), each Member's Schedule then sets out the maximum budgetary and volume amounts for every product group for each year of the implementation period. Members are still permitted to grant export subsidies under existing programmes provided they do not exceed the specific commitments set out in their Schedules.[54] Once the maximum annual monetary or volume commitments for a product are reached, the Member cannot grant any further export subsidies on that product for the rest of that year. If the export of a product is not currently being subsidized, the Agreement effectively precludes the granting of any new export subsidies on that product.

The export reduction commitments are reinforced by the provisions of Articles 10 and 11. Article 10, an anti-circumvention provision, prevents

---

[52] The modalities for establishing a Member's export subsidy commitments are found in the Draft Final Act's Text on Agriculture, Part B (Agreement on Modalities for the Establishment of Specific Binding Commitments Under the Reform Programme) at paragraphs 11 and 12, and Annexes 7 and 8 to Part B.

[53] The combination of both budgetary and volume reduction commitments is intended to ensure that the commitments will be effective notwithstanding the state of the world price for the commodity in question. For example, although both disciplines are likely to work in conjunction, if the world price for a commodity is close to a Member's domestic price, the volume commitment will be the more effective discipline. If the domestic price is much higher than the world price, the budgetary limitation will likely be the more effective discipline.

[54] For example, pursuant to its reduction commitments, Canada has committed to reduce the export subsidies granted to wheat exports through the *Western Grain Transportation Act* and export subsidies granted to dairy products by the Canadian Dairy Commission. On wheat and wheat flour, Canada's maximum export subsidy expenditure level will be reduced from (CDN) $326,861,000 in the 1995-96 crop year, to (CDN) $199,061,000 in the 2000-01 crop year. Its maximum volume level will be reduced from 13,590,251 tonnes in 1995-96 to 8,851,788 tonnes in 2000-01.

The U.S. Schedule lists reductions in the Export Enhancement Program, the Dairy Export Incentive Program and CCC Dairy Export sales.

Members from applying subsidies in a manner that would have the effect of avoiding their export subsidy commitments. In addition, Members agree to work toward a set of internationally agreed disciplines governing export credits and insurance programmes (which can act as export subsidies in certain circumstances) and once such disciplines have been developed, to provide such programmes only in accordance with the disciplines. With respect to food aid, Article 10(4) requires Members to provide such aid only in accordance with certain agreed to principles, and to ensure that such aid is not, directly or indirectly, tied to commercial exports of agricultural products.

Article 11 ensures that Members cannot avoid their export subsidy commitments by incorporating primary commodities into further processed products. In no case may the per-unit subsidy paid on an incorporated primary product exceed the per-unit export subsidy that could have been payable on the export of the primary product if it had been exported in its primary form and not incorporated into the further processed product.

(g) Disciplines on Export Prohibitions and Restrictions

While import restrictions were considered to be the more important issue, restrictions on the exportation of agricultural products were also discussed and additional disciplines on the use of such measures were agreed to.[55] Much like Article XI:2(c), which provides an exemption for certain agricultural import restrictions, GATT Article XI:2(a) provides an agricultural-related exemption for certain export restrictions or prohibitions temporarily applied to relieve or prevent critical shortages of food stuffs. Generally speaking, this exemption has not been subject to wide misuse or abuse. The new obligations of Article 12 attempt to ensure this exception will not be subject to any such misuse or abuse. Where, in reliance on GATT Article XI:2(a), a Member introduces a new export restriction or prohibition, the Member is required to give notice of the measure to the Committee on Agriculture,[56] consult with any other interested Member, and take into account the effect of the measure on any importing Member's food security. Generally speaking, under paragraph 2 these additional disciplines will only apply to developing country Members in certain circumstances.

(h) Due Restraint (or the "Peace Clause")

While entitled "Due Restraint", Article 13 has become widely-known as the "Peace Clause", as it sets out a peace agreement relating to domestic and

---

[55] It bears repeating that the prohibition on quantitative restrictions found in GATT Article XI:1 applies equally to both import and export restrictions.

[56] The Committee on Agriculture is established under Article 17 of the Agreement.

international challenges to Members' agricultural subsidy programmes which will remain in force during the implementation period. For example, during the implementation period, green-box programmes cannot be countervailed (that is to say, they are exempt from actions under Part III of the *Agreement on Subsidies and Countervailing Measures*[57]), and are also exempt from actions based on nullification and impairment under GATT 1994 Article XXIII:1(b). While other domestic support measures and export subsidies that are being applied in a manner consistent with a Member's obligations under the Agreement may still be countervailed, under certain specified conditions they will be exempt from certain other types of complaint procedures under the *Subsidies Agreement* and the GATT 1994.

(i) Sanitary and Phytosanitary Measures

Article 14 provides that Members will give effect to the *Agreement on the Application of Sanitary and Phytosanitary Measures*, an agreement largely applicable to agricultural production, also found in Annex 1A to the WTO Agreement and discussed below.[58]

(j) Special and Differential Treatment for Developing Countries

Article 15 notes that differential and more favourable treatment for developing country Members was an integral part of the agricultural negotiations leading to the Agreement. This special and differential treatment is reflected in a number of provisions of the text and the modalities that were employed by developing countries' Members in establishing their specific reduction commitments under the Agreement. Generally, the reduction commitments of developing country Members were limited to two-thirds of those applicable to developed country Members and are to be implemented over a longer period of time. For example, with respect to market access, the reduction commitment for agricultural tariffs of developing country Members was limited to a simple average of 24 percent, with a minimum reduction of 10 percent for each tariff line (as opposed to 35 and 15 percent for developed country Members). With respect to domestic support, the *de minimus* level for developing country Members is 10 percent (as opposed to 5 percent for developed country Members). With respect to export subsidies, developing country Members' reduction commitments were limited to 24 percent in budgetary terms and 14 percent in volume terms (as opposed to 36 and 21 percent respectively for developed country Members).

Finally, Article 15(2) notes that developing country Members may extend implementation of their reduction commitments over 10 years, as compared to

---

[57] See pages 157-159 for a discussion of actions under Part II of the *Agreement on Subsidies and Countervailing Measures.*

[58] See pages 88-95.

six years for developed country Members. In addition, least-developed country Members are not subject to any of the reduction commitments, although they were still required to bind their existing levels of agricultural tariffs, domestic support and export subsidies.

(k) Least-developed and Net Food-importing Developing Countries

Many of the least-developed country Members and other net food-importing Members were concerned that the reduction commitments provided for under the Agreement would mean that they would no longer have access to sufficient supplies of low-cost imported agricultural products. For example, export subsidy reductions will likely mean that the world price for grain will increase. As importing developing country Members had been the main beneficiaries of these export subsidies, their reduction and subsequent increases in prices could have a disproportionately negative effect on those Members that could least afford these higher costs. So as to ensure that these concerns were addressed, as part of the Uruguay Round final package Ministers adopted the "Decision on Measures Concerning the Possible Negative Effects of the Reform Programme on Least-developed and Net Food-importing Developing Countries". In summary, Members have agreed to adopt appropriate mechanisms, primarily within the context of the *Food Aid Convention* of 1986, to ensure that implementation of the WTO Agreement does not adversely affect the level of available food aid. Additional financing is to be made available through appropriate international financial institutions to meet any additional need for short-term credit that might be induced by the implementation of the Agreement. Under Article 16(2), the Committee on Agriculture is to monitor the follow-up to the Decision.

(l) Review and Implementation of Commitments

Article 18 of the Agreement provides certain obligations governing its continuing review and implementation. First, the Committee on Agriculture is to review Members' implementations of the Agreement. This review is to be undertaken on the basis of notifications provided by Members. The review process must permit Members to raise any matter relevant to implementation of commitments under the Agreement.

In addition to notifications concerning implementation, Members are also required to notify the Committee of any new support measure or modification of an existing support measure which the Member claims to be exempt from the domestic support reduction commitment. This notification must include details as to its conformity with the applicable criteria for exemption.

(m) Consultation and Dispute Settlement

Article 19 provides that any dispute that arises under the Agreement is to be subject to settlement in accordance with Articles XXII and XXIII of GATT 1994, as elaborated upon by the DSU.[59]

(n) Continuation of the Reform Process

Article 20 provides for the initiation of further negotiations at least one year prior to the end of the implementation period. These further negotiations are to take into account a number of specific factors, including any experience to-date from implementation of the Agreement and what further commitments might be necessary to achieve long-term objectives, including the establishment of a fair and market-oriented agricultural trading system.

(o) Final Provisions

Article 21(1) provides that all the provisions of GATT 1994 and the other WTO agreements found in Annex 1A will also apply to agricultural products, subject to the terms of the Agriculture Agreement itself. Paragraph 2 provides that the Agreement's five Annexes are an integral part of the Agreement.

5. SANITARY AND PHYTOSANITARY MEASURES

In most countries agricultural and food production is controlled by a complex system of measures which regulate every phase of the production process. Among other things, these measures dictate how and where food may be produced, what can be added to it, how plants and animals are to be cared for, and, most often, subject all imported food products to identical requirements. These technical standards are generally adopted to protect human, animal or plant life or health and have become known as sanitary and phytosanitary measures (or "SPSMs"). The *Agreement on the Application of Sanitary and Phytosanitary Measures* was designed to impose certain disciplines on the development and implementation of SPSMs so as to ensure that these measure can continue to be properly employed to protect human, animal or plant life or health, but cannot be employed as unjustifiable non-tariff barriers, protecting domestic production from import competition.

6. PRE-URUGUAY ROUND DISCIPLINES ON SPSMs

SPSMs were already subject to a number of obligations prior to the commencement of the Uruguay Round. For example, many obligations of GATT 1947 were generally applicable to SPSMs, including the national

---

[59] See chapter 7, pages 308-327 for a discussion of the DSU.

treatment obligation of Article III, and the prohibition on non-tariff barriers found in Article XI. In addition, GATT Article XX(b) provided a limited exception applicable to such measures in some circumstances. Subject to certain disciplines, the Article XX(b) exception permitted contracting parties to take measures "necessary to protect human, animal or plant life or health". Thus, in the application of their SPSMs, contracting parties were able to violate GATT Articles III and XI and restrict imported plant, animal and food products provided they met the other requirements of Article XX(b).

During the 1970s there developed a general recognition that the applicable provisions of GATT 1947 could be subject to abuse, and technical standards could be and often were adopted as disguised restrictions on trade. As a result of this general view, all forms of technical standards, including SPSMs, were the subject of negotiations during the GATT's Tokyo Round. These negotiations produced the *Agreement on Technical Barriers to Trade* (also known as the "Technical Standards Code").[60] While the Code was considered to be an improvement on the pre-existing situation, generally speaking it did little more than elaborate on the existing GATT obligations applicable to technical standards and failed to impose any new substantive disciplines on the development and implementation of technical standards generally, or SPSMs in particular.

By the time discussions were underway on developing the negotiating agenda for the Uruguay Round, there was a general consensus among GATT members that the rules applicable to SPSMs should be improved. Many GATT members were also of the view that a reduction in tariff and non-tariff barriers to trade in agricultural products which the Round would hopefully produce, likely would increase the pressure on governments to adopt new SPSMs for protectionist purposes. Thus, increased disciplines on the development and implementation of SPSMs were required to ensure that what was given with one hand was not taken back by the other. The Ministerial Declaration on the Uruguay Round therefore specifically addressed the issue of SPSMs, providing that the negotiations should attempt to liberalize agricultural trade by, among other things:

> . . . minimizing the adverse effects that sanitary and phytosanitary regulations and barriers can have on trade in agriculture, taking into account the relevant international agreements.[61]

While the negotiations initially focused only on proposed amendments to GATT Article XX(b), it was soon recognized that a broader agreement would be necessary. By the time of the Brussels Ministerial meeting in November of 1990, the initial proposals for amending GATT Article XX(b) had developed

---

[60] GATT, BISD 26S/8.

[61] Ministerial Declaration on the Uruguay Round, GATT, BISD 33S/19, at 24.

into a significant agreement modelled after the Technical Standards Code. It is interesting to note that, in contrast to the agriculture negotiations, which caused the collapse of the Ministerial meeting, by November of 1990 the SPSM negotiations had produced an essentially complete and largely uncontroversial text.

7. THE *AGREEMENT ON THE APPLICATION OF SANITARY AND PHYTOSANITARY MEASURES*

(a) General Provisions

Article 1 sets out a number of general provisions. Most importantly, the scope and coverage of the Agreement is established under paragraph 1, which provides that the Agreement is to apply to all SPSMs which may, directly or indirectly, affect international trade. The term "SPSMs" is then defined in Annex A to the Agreement as including a number of different types of measures directed at protecting human, animal or plant life or health.[62] It is important to note that the definition of SPSMs limits the scope of such measures to those that apply to or concern, human, animal or plant life or health within the territory of a Member. All measures which fall within the definition of SPSMs must be developed and applied in accordance with the obligations of the Agreement.[63]

(b) Basic Rights and Obligations

It is important to note that the Agreement does not deal with any specific SPSMs. Rather it provides general disciplines that apply to the development

---

[62] The phrase SPSMs is defined broadly to include a number of different types of measures concerning health and safety of animals and food products, such as:

  (a) those to protect animals or plants from the entry, establishment or spread of pests, diseases and similar problems;

  (b) those to protect humans and animals from food additives and contaminants;

  (c) those to protect humans and animals from diseases carried by animals or plants; and

  (d) those to prevent or limit the damage that might be caused by the spread of pests.

Thus, among other things, the definition of SPSMs will include measures such as food process and production methods, measures concerning the use of food additives, packaging and labelling requirements for food products, measures relating to the use of pesticides, herbicides and fertilizers, and rules relating to animal husbandry.

[63] Paragraph 4 of Article 1 clarifies the relationship between the Agreement and the *Agreement on Technical Barriers to Trade*, another WTO agreement found in Annex 1A. Generally speaking, if a standards-related measure does not fall within the definition of an SPSM, it will be subject to the obligations of the *Agreement on Technical Barriers to Trade*. Similarly, Article 1(5) of the *Agreement on Technical Barriers to Trade* states that the Agreement does not to apply to SPSMs.

and application of all SPSMs. Members remain free to develop and implement their own specific measures subject to these disciplines. Article 2 sets out the Agreement's four basic obligations. First, paragraph 1 confirms that Members retain the right to take SPSMs necessary to protect human, animal or plant life or health, provided those measures are consistent with the Agreement. Second, Members must ensure that all their SPSMs are applied only to the extent necessary, that they are based on scientific principles, and, subject to a limited exception, that they are not maintained without sufficient scientific evidence.[64] Third, repeating one of the basic obligations of GATT Article XX, Members must ensure that their SPSMs do not arbitrarily or unjustifiably discriminate between Members where identical or similar conditions prevail. In addition, such measures must not be applied in a manner that constitutes a disguised restriction on trade. Finally, under paragraph 4, any SPSM that complies with the relevant obligations of the Agreement will be deemed to be consistent with a Member's relevant obligations under GATT 1994, including those under Article XX(b).

(c) Harmonization

As noted, the Agreement does not address any specific SPSM. Rather it sets out general rules for their development and application. One way to attempt to ensure that SPSMs are not being used as barriers to trade is to have all Members adopt identical measures and apply them in the same manner—in other words harmonize all Members' SPSMs. This is the ultimate goal of Article 3.

Paragraph 1 provides the starting point. So as to permit harmonization to occur on as wide a scope as possible, Members are to base their SPSMs on international standards, guidelines or recommendations where they exist.[65] In addition, Members are required, to the limit of their resources, to participate in the international bodies which develop such standards.

Under paragraph 2, there is significant benefit in basing an SPSM on such an international standard, because where an SPSM conforms with the appro-

---

[64] As neither "scientific principles" nor "scientific evidence" are defined in the Agreement there is some uncertainty as to the actual scope of these obligations. In the view of the U.S., for example, the use of the terms "scientific principles" rather than the "best science", and "scientific evidence" rather than the "weight of scientific evidence" is a recognition that scientific certainty is rarely possible, and in the face of such uncertainty it is up to the individual Member to determine whether the measure is called for.

[65] The phrase "international standards, guidelines and recommendations" is specifically defined in Annex A to include the standards, guidelines and recommendations developed by certain pre-existing international bodies with recognized expertise in the SPSMs-related areas, including the Codex Alimentarius Commission, the International Office of Epizootics and the Secretariat of the International Plant Protection Convention.

priate international standard, it will be deemed to be necessary, and in compliance with the applicable obligations of both the Agreement and GATT 1994.

While existing international standards are considered to be the benchmark, paragraph 3 provides that a Member may introduce or maintain an SPSM which results in a higher level of protection than that provided by the applicable international standard under certain circumstances. Such circumstances include where there is sufficient scientific justification for the higher standard or where a Member has undertaken a risk assessment and determined the higher standard to be appropriate.

Finally, under paragraph 5, the Committee on Sanitary and Phytosanitary Measures[66] is to develop its own internal procedures in order to monitor and coordinate the process of international harmonization that may be ongoing within the relevant international organizations.

(d) Equivalence

While harmonization constitutes a movement towards identical measures, equivalence is the acceptance that formally different measures still provide, in effect, substantially similar levels of protection. Under paragraph 1 of Article 4, Members must accept the SPSMs of other Members as being equivalent to their own, even if such measures are formally different, if the other Member is able to objectively demonstrate that its measure achieves the same level of protection. In addition, with the goal of achieving bilateral or multilateral agreements on recognition of equivalency, on request, Members are required to enter into consultations on such agreements.

(e) Risk Assessments and Appropriate Levels of Protection

Members are required to ensure that all SPSMs are based on an appropriate assessment of the risks to human, animal or plant life or health.[67] In assessing such risks, Members are required to take a number of factors into account, including the available scientific evidence, testing methods, environmental conditions, the existence of disease- and pest-free areas, and quarantine and other treatments.

Members are also required to take into account a number of economic factors when assessing risk and determining the type of measure and level of protection applicable to animals or plants. These factors include the potential

---

[66] The Committee on Sanitary and Phytosanitary Measures (the "SPSM Committee") is established under Article 12 of the Agreement.

[67] While Article 5 does not require that any specific type of "risk assessment" be undertaken, the phrase is defined generally in Annex A.

for financial loss, the costs of control or eradication, and relative cost-effectiveness of the various potential approaches. Minimizing any potential negative trade effects is also a consideration which Members should take into account when establishing the level of protection.

Members are also required to avoid arbitrary or unjustifiable distinctions in the levels of protection that they consider appropriate, if such distinctions result in discrimination or a disguised restriction on trade. For example, a Member should not establish a high level of protection for one type of food additive, but a lower level for another equally dangerous additive, if such a distinction is unjustifiable and acts to restrict trade. Members are to work within the SPSM Committee to develop guidelines for the application of this obligation, taking into account all relevant factors including the fact that humans often voluntarily expose themselves to a number of health risks.[68]

Under paragraph 6, when establishing or maintaining a measure to achieve an appropriate level of protection, Members are required to ensure that the measure is no more trade restricting than required, taking into account technical and economic feasibility.[69] Under paragraph 7, in cases where the scientific evidence is insufficient a Member is permitted to adopt temporarily an SPSM on the basis of available evidence, provided that within a reasonable time the Member attempts to obtain the necessary additional information and then conduct a review of the provisional measure.

Where a Member believes that an SPSM of another Member is not based on the appropriate international standard and is restricting or has the potential to restrict trade, it may request that the Member imposing the measure provide an explanation for the measure.

(f) Adaptation to Regional Conditions

Article 6 concerns regional conditions in the application of SPSMs. Pests and disease are often localized within the territory of a country and often do not present a problem in many other regions. Thus, what might be an appropriate response to imports from one region may be inappropriate for imports from another. Article 6 requires Members to take such factors into account.

---

[68] Humans often voluntarily expose themselves to health risks through, for example, smoking or the consumption of alcohol. However, paragraph 5 distinguishes between these voluntary cases and involuntary exposures. This permits a Member also to distinguish between these situations, thereby allowing it, for example, to prohibit the use of a food additive that may pose a slight risk to health, while at the same time continuing to allow the sale of unpasteurized cheese, which might present a greater health risk.

[69] A footnote to paragraph 6 indicates that a measure is not to be considered to be more trade restrictive than required unless, taking into account technical and economic feasibility, there is another measure reasonably available to the Member that achieves the same level of protection, but is significantly less trade restrictive.

Members are required to ensure that their SPSMs are adapted to the characteristics of the region from where the product at issue is being imported, whether the region is an entire country, part of a country, or many countries. Members are required to take into account a number of factors when assessing the characteristics of the relevant region, including the level of specific diseases or pest, the existence of control programmes, and any relevant international guidelines. In particular, Members are required to recognize the concept of disease- or pest-free areas. However, the onus falls on the exporting Member to demonstrate that such unaffected areas exist. Exporting Members which consider that they have such areas within their territories are to provide the importing Member with the evidence necessary to demonstrate that such areas do exist and that they are likely to remain disease or pest free.

(g) Transparency

Article 7 addresses the issue of transparency. Members are required to notify any changes to their SPSMs and provide information in accordance with Annex B to the Agreement. Annex B establishes a number of specific obligations applicable to the publication of regulations, the establishment of enquiry points, and certain notification procedures.

With respect to the publication of regulations, Members are required to ensure that all sanitary and phytosanitary regulations that have been adopted are published promptly. Generally speaking, Members are to provide a reasonable period between the publication of a regulation and its entry into force so as to permit producers to adjust their processes or products to meet the new standard.

With respect to enquiry points, Members are required to provide one enquiry point that is able to answer Members' questions and provide relevant documents concerning the Member's SPSMs and other related issues.

With respect to notification procedures, the obligations are primarily aimed at those situations where a Member is adopting an SPSM in an area where an international standard does not yet exist or where the measure being adopted does not substantially conform with that standard. In such a case, the Member is required, among other things, to: publish a notice of the proposed measure; provide early notification to other Members of the proposed measure and include relevant information such as the products covered and the rationale for the measure; on request, provide Members with copies of the proposed measure; allow reasonable time for Members to comment, discuss these comments on request; and take the comments and discussions into account. In cases of urgency a Member is not required to follow these procedures prior to implementing the measure, and may immediately adopt an SPSM, provided that, among other things, the Member immediately notifies other Members of the measure, the products covered and the rationale for the measure, and consults with the other Members on request.

(h) Control, Inspection and Approval Procedures

Article 8 addresses issues concerning control, inspection and approval procedures. These procedures are used to ensure compliance with the relevant SPSM, but can often result in delays upon importation and consequent restrictions on trade. Members are required to observe the obligations of Annex C with respect to the operation of control, inspection and approval procedures, including national systems for approving the use of additives in food. With respect to procedures to check and ensure compliance with any SPSM, Members are required to meet a number of obligations, including ensuring that: such procedures are undertaken without undue delay; procedures meet certain basic due-process requirements; information requirements are limited to those necessary; confidentiality is protected; any fees payable are equitable; and a procedure exists to review complaints concerning the operation of such procedures.

(i) Technical Assistance

Under Article 9 Members have agreed to assist in the provision of technical assistance in a number of areas relating to sanitary and phytosanitary standards, including areas such as infrastructure and research. This assistance may take the form of advice or financial grants or credits. Particular emphasis is to be given to assisting developing country Members. In some cases, a standard imposed by an importing Member may require the exporting Member to undertake substantial new investment in order to meet the standard. Where such significant financial investment is required to be made by a developing country Member, the importing Member is to consider providing assistance so that the developing country Member is still able to maintain and expand its market access for the product at issue.

(j) Special and Differential Treatment

Special and differential treatment for developing country Members is provided for under Article 10, in addition to certain provisions of Article 14, discussed below. Generally, Members are required to take into account the special needs of developing country Members in the preparation and application of their SPSMs. When new SPSMs can be phased-in over time, longer phase-in periods should be accorded to products of interest to developing country Members so that such Members will have additional time in which to bring their products into compliance.

With respect to meeting their obligations under the Agreement generally, the SPSM Committee may, upon request, grant developing country Members additional time to bring themselves into compliance with the Agreement. However, Article 14 does provide for delayed implementation which does not require Committee approval. Least-developed country Members are permitted to delay application of most of the Agreement's obligations until January 1, 2000. All other developing country Members were permitted to delay implementation of most obligations until January 1, 1997, but only where such a delay was necessitated by a lack of technical expertise, infrastructure or resources.

(k) Consultations and Dispute Settlement

Article 11 provides the Agreement's dispute settlement provisions. Generally speaking, GATT 1994 Articles XXII and XXIII, as elaborated upon by the DSU, apply to the settlement of any disputes that may arise under the Agreement. Article 11 also sets out certain additional obligations applicable to disputes under the Agreement. If a dispute arises concerning scientific or technical issues, the panel hearing the dispute is expected to seek the advice of experts in the relevant area, chosen by the panel in consultation with the disputing Members. A panel may, when it considers appropriate, establish a technical advisory group to assist it. In addition, panels may also consult with a relevant international organization, either on its own initiative or when requested by one of the disputing Members.

The rights set out in the Agreement are considered to be an addition to those rights that may already exist under other international agreements in the area of SPSMs. Therefore, nothing in the Agreement is to be interpreted as impairing the rights that Members may have under such other international agreements in the area, including the right to invoke the dispute settlement provisions of other agreements or international organizations.

(l) Administration of the Agreement

The SPSM Committee is established under Article 12 to carry out certain administrative functions and to provide a forum for regular consultations on SPSM-related issues. Notably, in carrying out its specified functions it is required to take all decisions by consensus.

Article 12 sets out a number of specific functions the Committee is to serve. First, it is generally to encourage the use of appropriate international standards and encourage and facilitate consultations and negotiations among Members on SPSM issues. In particular, the Committee is to sponsor technical study of certain issues related to food additives and contaminants. Second, the Committee is to maintain close contacts with the relevant international organizations in the SPSM area so as to secure the best information available and avoid an unnecessary duplication of effort. Third, the Committee is to develop internal procedures so as to ensure proper monitoring of international harmonization of SPSMs and use of international standards. At a minimum, the

Committee is expected to develop a list of those international standards that it considers to have a major trade impact. This list should also indicate which Members apply the relevant standard as a condition of import. Where the applicable international standard is not applied, the Member should indicate why the standard is not applied. If a Member subsequently modifies its standard it should provide an explanation for the modification. Finally, the Committee is to review the operation and implementation of the Agreement by January 1, 1998 and thereafter as necessary. The Committee is permitted to submit proposals for amendment of the Agreement to the Council for Trade in Goods, if and when the Committee considers it necessary.

(m) Implementation

Article 13 specifies that Members are fully responsible for observing all the obligations of the Agreement. Sub-national governments, such as those of states and provinces, are bound by the Agreement. Members are required to formulate and implement positive mechanisms to support the observance of the Agreement by such governments. Members are required to take all reasonable measures to ensure compliance with the Agreement by non-governmental entities. In addition, Members are not permitted to take measures which have the direct or indirect effect of requiring that sub-national governments or non-governmental entities violate the Agreement. Members are only permitted to rely on non-governmental entities to assist in the implementation of SPSMs where those entities comply with the Agreement.

Part C:

Textiles and Clothing

1. INTRODUCTION

As discussed in chapter 1, trade in textiles and clothing has taken place largely outside the basic rules of the GATT system for a number of years.[70] Since 1961, textiles trade has been governed by a series of "temporary" agreements which provided for the imposition of quantitative import restraints that would otherwise have been inconsistent with some basic GATT obligations: the *Short-Term Arrangement* (1961-1962); the *Long-Term Arrangement Regarding Trade in Cotton Textiles* (1962-1974); and the *Arrangement Regarding International Trade in Textiles* (1974-1995), better known as the *Multi-Fibre Arrangement* or the "MFA".[71] The overriding purpose of the

---

[70] See above at pages 6-7.

[71] The MFA was extended and modified six times prior to being carried over into the WTO Agreement through the *Agreement on Textiles and Clothing*.

textile and clothing provisions of the WTO Agreement is to re-integrate these products fully into the revised GATT system over a specified transitional period.

2. THE PRE-WTO RULES AND URUGUAY ROUND NEGOTIATIONS

The MFA was, in essence, a managed trading arrangement between developed importing countries and developing exporting countries that covered virtually all cotton, wool and man-made fibre textiles. The Arrangement was not a GATT agreement, but rather a "negotiated derogation" from the GATT under which the MFA signatories agreed that the basic GATT obligations would not apply to textiles trade.[72] While the Arrangement did not impose specific quantitative restraints itself, it did establish a framework under which individual, primarily developed countries were able restrict imported textiles and clothing in certain situations. For example, in order to ensure "the orderly and equitable development" of textile trade, the MFA provided a special sectoral safeguard measure that was only to be used in "exceptional circumstances" to assist in the adjustment to textile trade liberalization.[73] The MFA also provided that participating countries could enter into bilateral agreements to eliminate "real risks of market disruption".[74] Unfortunately, for a number of political and economic reasons the use of quantitative restrictions under the MFA, particularly bilateral restraint agreements, became the rule rather than the exception.[75]

Recognizing the failure of the MFA to liberalize textiles trade, many GATT contracting parties sought to eliminate the MFA and fully re-integrate

---

[72] The relationship between the two agreements is somewhat more complex in that, although not formally a GATT agreement, the MFA was negotiated under the auspices of the GATT and the MFA's Textiles Surveillance Body reported to the GATT Textiles Committee and to the GATT Council. Thus, practically speaking, there was extensive interplay between the two agreements.

[73] Under MFA Article 3, an importing country was permitted to establish import levels or limit annual growth rates for quotas if it determined that its market was being disrupted by imported textile products. If the importing and exporting countries failed to agree on an appropriate safeguard measure during a 60-day consultation period, the importing country was permitted to unilaterally impose import restrictions no lower than the level of actual imports that had taken place during a previous representative period.

[74] While this provision, found in Article 4 of the MFA, required that these bilateral agreements be more liberal than Article 3 safeguards, the term "real risk" was not defined in the MFA and was generally viewed as a less demanding standard than the market disruption standard of Article 3.

[75] For example, as of 1993 the United States had bilateral agreements with 41 countries negotiated under Article 4 of the MFA, governing approximately 70 percent of its clothing imports. See United States International Trade Commission, *Potential Impact on the US Economy and Industries of the Uruguay Round Agreements*, Publication No. 2790 (USITC: Washington, 1994) at IV-15. The coverage of Canada's bilateral agreements was substantially similar.

textiles and clothing trade into the GATT system.[76] For example, in 1981 many developing countries only reluctantly accepted another extension of the MFA until 1986. Renewed pressure to eliminate the MFA surfaced once again during the 1982 GATT Ministerial Meeting. As a result of this developing-country pressure trade ministers resolved during the meeting to begin to examine the ways and means of eliminating the MFA and integrating textiles and clothing back into the GATT system. Further evidence of the lack of support for the MFA and pressure for its elimination came in 1985, when the Leutwiler Report stated that:

> No clearer example exists of the mistakes made in deviating from the essential principles of the multilateral system than the Multifibre Arrangement... Sectoral and discriminatory in nature, directed against developing countries as a whole, and inimical to the operation of comparative advantage even among developing countries, it should be brought to an end.[77]

The Report went on to recommend that "trade in textiles and clothing should be fully subject to the ordinary rules of the GATT".[78] This call to action was warmly received by many developing countries, but not so by most developed countries, many of which remained exceedingly reluctant to eliminate the quantitative restrictions imposed on textiles and clothing imports under cover of the MFA, along with the flexibility to impose even greater restrictions if necessary.

This basic debate continued within the context of the Uruguay Round's Preparatory Committee which, as of January 1986, had begun to draft the Round's negotiating agenda. Developing countries insisted on the inclusion of the MFA on that agenda for the new Round. Primarily as a result of the many concessions developing countries made in other areas of the negotiating agenda, the Committee eventually agreed to the inclusion of textiles and clothing in the negotiations. The Punta Del Este Declaration formally commencing the negotiations subsequently provided that:

> Negotiations in the area of textiles and clothing shall aim to formulate modalities that would permit the eventual integration of this sector into GATT on the basis of strengthened GATT rules and disciplines, thereby also contributing to the objective of further liberalization of trade.[79]

---

[76] The wish to "integrate" textiles and clothing trade into the GATT is generally considered to mean subjecting such trade to the basic GATT rules that then applied to other non-agricultural products, including: MFN treatment under GATT Article I; the prohibition on quantitative restrictions under GATT Article XI; the binding of tariffs under GATT Article II; and, in specified circumstances, the use of safeguard remedies under GATT Article XIX.

[77] GATT, *Trade Policies for a Better Future* (GATT: Geneva, 1985) at 39.

[78] *Ibid.*

[79] GATT, BISD, 33S/19, at 23.

The Declaration also provided for the establishment of a separate and distinct Textiles and Clothing Negotiating Group that would undertake the negotiations in the area.

While agreement had been reached on inclusion of the issue on the agenda, the basic disagreement concerning the elimination of the MFA which had previously divided developing and developed countries continued on in the Textiles and Clothing Negotiating Group. By the time of the Montreal Mid-term Meeting in late 1988, after almost two years of negotiations, essentially no progress had been made by the Group. In fact, disagreement on textiles and clothing was one of the reasons the Mid-term Review could not be completed as planned during its December meeting, but had to be continued until April of 1989 in Geneva. Ministers were eventually able to agree that:

(a) substantive negotiations will begin in April 1989 in order to reach agreement within the time-frame of the Uruguay Round on modalities for the integration of this sector into GATT, in accordance with the negotiating objective;

(b) such modalities for the process of integration into GATT on the basis of strengthened GATT rules and disciplines should *inter alia* cover the phasing out of restrictions under the Multi-fibre Arrangement and other restrictions on textiles and clothing not consistent with GATT rules and disciplines, the time span for such a process of integration, and the progressive character of this process which should commence following the conclusion of the negotiations in 1990 . . .[80]

While the Mid-term Review had provided a basic road map for the Textiles and Clothing Negotiating Group, basic differences still continued in a number of areas. These outstanding differences included: (i) the modalities of integration—on what basis was integration to be achieved; (ii) the length of the transition period—how long would full integration be permitted to take; (iii) the scope of transition—which products would be covered by the integration, when and on what basis; and (iv) other linkages to the basic GATT obligations—would trade remedies and safeguard actions still be available, for example. By the time of the Brussels Meeting in late 1990 the basic modalities of integration had been agreed to, but the specifics of integration still had not. For example, while it had been accepted that integration would take place over four separate stages, the length of time for each stage had not finally been settled. Seven other major issues which remained outstanding in the Negotiating Group at this time included: the product coverage of any agreement; growth rates in those quotas that would still be maintained during any transition period; whether a special sectoral safeguard mechanism was necessary during the transition period; and would recourse to safeguard actions

[80] GATT, "Decisions Adopted at the Mid-Term Review of the Uruguay Round", *GATT Focus*, No. 61, May 1989. Reprinted in 28 I.L.M. 1023 (1989) at 1026.

under GATT Article XIX still be permitted during and after the transition period. While these issues appeared large in number, the Negotiating Group had, in fact, come some way since the Montreal Mid-term Meeting in late 1988 and had reached agreement on many of the modalities of integration. As a result, it is likely that the Ministers would have been able to reach agreement on the remaining specific issues of integration had the Brussels Meeting not collapsed over agricultural issues.

While further work on the remaining issues continued once negotiations resumed again in Geneva in early 1991, most of the issues were not fully and finally resolved until Arthur Dunkel tabled his *Draft Final Act* in late December 1991.[81] The provisions of the *Draft Final Act* concerning textiles and clothing generally were met with the reluctant acceptance of most participants. And, while there was some pressure very late in the negotiations to re-open important elements of the finalized draft textile agreement, in the end these changes were successfully resisted and the Dunkel Draft's agreement on textiles and clothing was essentially carried over unaltered into the WTO Agreement's Annex 1A as the *Agreement on Textiles and Clothing*.

3. THE *AGREEMENT ON TEXTILES AND CLOTHING*

The *Agreement on Textiles and Clothing* attempts to achieve full integration of textiles and clothing into the GATT system over a 10-year period, during which all MFA restrictions will be phased-out in four stages and all WTO Members will institute plans to eliminate all non-tariff barriers to trade in textiles and clothing. By January 1, 2005, all non-tariff barriers to textile and textiles trade will be removed, those products will be treated as any other industrial product under the WTO Agreement and the *Agreement on Textiles and Clothing*, as a transitional agreement only, will cease to exist.

(a) Integration of Pre-existing MFA Restrictions

The first step of the integration process brings all MFA restrictions under the control of the *Agreement on Textiles and Clothing*. Under Article 2, by early March of 1995, all Members were required to have fully reported their then-existing MFA quantitative restrictions to the Textiles Monitoring Body (or "TMB"), a textiles review board established under Article 8 of the Agreement.[82] The MFA restrictions reported under Article 2 are then deemed to have been the totality of MFA restrictions to be integrated into GATT 1994.

---

[81] *Draft Final Act Embodying the Results of the Uruguay Round of Multilateral Trade Negotiations*, GATT Doc. MTN.TNC/W/FA, 20 December 1991.

[82] Notifications were filed under this provision by Canada, the EC, Norway and the United States.

Any other restrictions not properly reported to the TMB by that time were to have been terminated immediately, and no new restrictions on textile trade may be implemented, unless otherwise authorized under the Agreement or the GATT 1994.

Paragraph 5 of Article 2 then addresses certain transitional issues. Any unilateral measure taken under MFA Article 3 prior to January 1, 1995 may remain in effect for its stated duration (in no case longer than 12 months) provided it has been reviewed by the MFA's Textiles Surveillance Body (or "TSB"). If such a unilateral measure has not been reviewed by the TSB, the measure will be reviewed by the WTO's TMB, but under the rules and procedures of the MFA. Likewise, if the MFA's TSB has not reviewed an MFA Article 4 agreement that becomes the subject of a dispute, the WTO's TMB will review that agreement as well, again under the terms and procedures of the MFA.

Once properly reported to the TMB, integration of pre-existing restrictions into the GATT 1994 will occur in four stages over a 10-year period, with much of the integration to occur in the final year of the Agreement. Under paragraph 6 of Article 2, the first stage of integration took place on January 1, 1995, the date of entry into force of the WTO Agreement. In this stage, every WTO Member was required to integrate at least 16 percent of the total volume of the textile products covered by the Agreement that were imported by the Member in 1990.[83] That is to say, each WTO Member was required to remove all MFA restrictions on a group of textile products that accounted for at least 16 percent of the total volume of the Member's 1990 imports of those products. The full details of these actions were then to have been notified to all other Members in accordance with Article 2(7).[84]

Under subparagraph 8(a) of Article 2, the second stage of integration, to occur on January 1, 1998, requires Members to integrate an additional group of products accounting for at least a further 17 percent of the total volume of the Members' 1990 imports of the products. The third stage of integration, to occur on January 1, 2002 under subparagraph 8(b), requires the integration of products accounting for an additional 18 percent of the total volume of the Members' 1990 imports of those products. Finally, under subparagraph 8(c), the last stage of integration of MFA restricted products into GATT 1994 will take place on January 1, 2005. By that date all remaining MFA restrictions, which could account for approximately 49 percent of a Member's textile imports in 1990, must be removed, and all MFA restrictions will then cease to exist.

---

[83] Product coverage under the Agreement is established under Article 1(7) and the Annex to the Agreement, and essentially includes all textile and clothing products included within Chapters 50 to 63 of the Harmonized System.

[84] As of December 1995 the WTO had received notifications from 32 of the 37 former MFA signatories and from four Members that were not MFA signatories.

In order to continue the integration process in interim periods between each reduction stage and to lessen the sudden effect of the staged elimination of restrictions, WTO Members are also required to increase annually the level of imports permitted under those restrictions that remain in place between specified reductions. After the initial reduction (that is, between January 1, 1995 and December 31, 1997) WTO Members must increase the level of quantitative restrictions annually by not less than the growth rate established for the respective restrictions plus an additional 16 percent. Article 2(14) provides that after the second reduction (January 1, 1998 to December 31, 2001), restrictions must be increased annually by the established growth rate plus 25 percent, and following the third reduction (January 1, 2002 to December 31, 2004) restrictions must be increased annually by the established growth rate, plus an additional 27 percent.

There are two additional characteristics of the integration process for MFA restrictions that are worth note. First, the Agreement does not specify which products Members must integrate in each stage of the process. Members are therefore free to integrate whichever products they choose during whichever stage they choose, provided that the products integrated in each stage of the process encompass all four of the following product groups: tops and yarns, fabrics, made-up textile products and clothing. The second important characteristic of the integration process is the deferral of nearly half of the integration process to the final stage of integration. The combination of these characteristics should permit policy makers to delay the integration of the most import-sensitive products for a full 10 years.

(b) Integration of Non-MFA Restrictions

Article 3 of the Agreement requires that textile products subject to non-MFA restrictions also be integrated into GATT 1994. By early March of 1995, WTO Members were to have notified the TMB of all such other non-MFA restrictions on textile trade that they maintained.[85] Under the terms of Article 3, Members must either bring such restrictions into conformity with GATT 1994 by January 1, 1996 (that is, remove all restrictions that are not justified under the GATT 1994), or phase out those barriers during the 10-year integration period. Members choosing the latter option were required to have submitted an integration programme to the TMB by June 1, 1995. While the TMB may make recommendations to Members regarding their integration programmes, the TMB is not authorized to dictate how or when products should be integrated into GATT 1994. Again, the Agreement leaves it to each Member to determine how and when to remove barriers to textile trade, so long as the integration process is completed by January 1, 2005.

---

[85] The WTO received notifications from 27 Members under this provision.

(c) Anti-circumvention Provisions

Article 5 of the Agreement addresses attempts to circumvent any remaining import restrictions by, for example, transhipment or misstating the country of origin of imported products. Because restrictions imposed under cover of the MFA were not applied on an MFN basis, the attempted circumvention of quota restrictions was a persistent problem under the Arrangement. Under the Agreement, Members are expected to establish domestic anti-circumvention measures and then take the necessary action consistent with those measures to prevent or stop circumvention from occurring. A Member may request consultations if it suspects that circumvention is occurring and that inadequate action is being taken by another Member to prevent or stop it. Members are also given the ability to take unilateral action in some cases. If a Member has sufficient evidence that circumvention is occurring, it may prohibit entry of the relevant imported goods or it may adjust the relevant quota accordingly. Somewhat different procedures apply in cases of false declarations of fibre content.

(d) Transitional Safeguard Measures

Article 6 of the Agreement contains a special sectoral safeguard mechanism that is to be used "as sparingly as possible" during the Agreement's 10-year transition period. The safeguard is only available for use against those products set out in the Annex that have not yet been integrated into the GATT 1994 under Article 2 and products that are not already under restraint. These restrictions on the application of the transitional safeguard remedy essentially limit its use to those Members that had not been applying import restraints under the MFA. Members wishing to reserve their right to use the transitional safeguard remedy were generally to have notified the TMB by early March 1995.[86]

Once a product has been integrated into the GATT 1994, Members may only resort to the GATT 1994's general safeguard provisions of Article XIX, or other unfair trade remedies provided under the GATT 1994.

A transitional safeguard, or quota, may be applied when it is demonstrated that a particular product is being imported in such increased quantities as to cause serious damage, or actual threat thereof, to the domestic industry producing a like and/or directly competitive product. A safeguard may only be introduced when such serious damage is demonstrably being caused by the increased quantities of imports and not by other factors such as technological advances or changes in consumer preferences. The determination of serious

---

[86] By late 1995, the TMB had received a total of 55 notifications under this provision, 37 from former MFA signatories and 18 from non-signatories. Under these notifications, all but six Members reserved their right to use the transitional safeguard mechanism.

damage must include an examination of the condition of the industry as reflected by changes in "relevant economic variables" such as output, productivity, capacity utilization, inventories, market share, exports, wages, employment, domestic prices, profit and investment.

In contrast to Article XIX of GATT 1994 (which provides that safeguard measures must generally be applied on an MFN basis, not just against selected export sources), transitional safeguards under the Agreement must be applied on a Member-by-Member basis. Accordingly, under paragraph 4 of Article 6, in determining serious damage, Members seeking to implement a safeguard measure must first demonstrate a sharp and substantial increase in imports from individual sources on the basis of the level of imports compared to imports from other sources, market share, and domestic and import prices.

Under Article 6(7), a Member seeking safeguard protection must, prior to its implementation, request consultations with other Members that would be affected by the proposed measure. If, during the 60-day consultation period, the Members involved agree that a safeguard measure is appropriate, paragraph 8 permits a level of restraint to be imposed that is no lower than the level of exports from the Member concerned during a previous representative period. Paragraph 9 then requires that details of any agreed restraint must be reported to the TMB, which will determine whether the restraints are justified in accordance with the terms of the Agreement.

Under paragraph 10 of Article 6, if the Members concerned do not agree that the safeguard measure is appropriate in the circumstances, the Member seeking safeguard protection may impose restraints and refer the matter to the TMB. The TMB will review the matter, make a determination concerning serious damage and the causes thereof, and make recommendations to the Members involved.

Under paragraphs 12 and 13 of Article 6, transitional safeguard measures may only be imposed for a period of up to three years without extension, or until the subject product is integrated into GATT 1994, whichever is earlier. If a safeguard measure is imposed for a period longer than one year, the amount of permitted imports under the restraint must be increased by 6 percent per year in each subsequent year.

(e) Market Access

Article 7, addressing certain market-access-related issues, requires Members to take action necessary to meet their other obligations under the GATT 1994 concerning tariff reductions, facilitation of customs, administrative and licensing procedures, trade remedy laws and intellectual property as they may relate to textiles and clothing. Where a Member considers that another Member is not meeting its obligations in this regard and the balance of rights and obligations under the Agreement are thereby being upset, that Member is able to bring the matter before the relevant WTO bodies and to inform the TMB under Article 8.

(f) The Textiles Monitoring Body

The TMB is established under Article 8, to supervise the Agreement's implementation, to examine all measures taken under it, and to take certain other specified actions. The TMB consists of a Chair and 10 members, who act in their personal capacity.[87] Membership of the Body is to be balanced and broadly representative of the Members. All decisions of the Body are taken by consensus. In the case of an unresolved issue, consensus does not require the concurrence of members of the Body whose countries are involved in the dispute at issue. At the request of any Member, the Body is to promptly review any matter under the Agreement where consultations have failed to resolve the matter and then produce its observations and recommendations on the matter. Once such recommendations have been issued, the relevant Members are expected to endeavour to accept them in full. If a Member considers that it is unable to do so, it must provide the TSB with appropriate reasons for non-compliance. The TSB is to review these reasons and issue any further recommendations that it considers appropriate. If the matter remains unresolved, either Member may bring the matter before the WTO's Dispute Settlement Body under GATT Article XXIII:2 and the other appropriate provisions of the Dispute Settlement Understanding.

(g) Termination of the Agreement

The Agreement is a temporary transitional arrangement only, through which textile and clothing trade may be fully integrated into the GATT 1994. As such, Article 9 provides for termination of the Agreement on January 1, 2005, the date on which all textiles are scheduled to be re-integrated into the GATT system. The Agreement explicitly states that "[t]here shall be no extension of this Agreement".

Part D:

Customs Issues

1. INTRODUCTION

It has long been recognized that the administrative formalities relating to the import and export of goods (commonly referred to as "customs laws")

---

[87] The membership of the Body for its initial three years (1995-1997) was decided by the WTO's General Council in January of 1995.

can, in themselves, constitute barriers to trade. The WTO Agreement includes four Agreements related to these customs issues: the *Agreement on Implementation of Article VII of the General Agreement on Tariffs and Trade* (addressing custom valuation issues); the *Agreement on Preshipment Inspection*; the *Agreement on Rules of Origin*; and the *Agreement on Import Licensing Procedures*. All four of these Agreements appear in Annex 1A to the WTO Agreement and are therefore considered part of the Multilateral Agreements on Trade in Goods. After a brief historical introduction, this Part of chapter 3 discusses each of these customs-related Agreements in depth. While section 3, below, briefly outlines negotiations in the customs area, negotiating issues relevant to specific Agreements are also addressed in the sections discussing each Agreement.

2. THE PRE-WTO CUSTOMS OBLIGATIONS

Due to concerns over their protectionist effects, governments have long sought multilateral cooperation in customs matters, as evidenced by several Agreements designed to publicize and harmonize customs formalities. One of the first multilateral agreements concerning customs issues, the *International Convention Concerning the Creation of an International Union for the Publication of Customs Tariffs*, came into force over 100 years ago.

The drafters of the Havana Charter and the GATT 1947 were also aware of the trade-restricting potential of customs formalities. The GATT 1947 contained a number of obligations relevant to customs issues. These include, among others:[88]

- **Article VII: Valuation for Customs Purposes**—provides certain general obligations concerning the use of "actual value" for customs valuation purposes;

- **Article VIII: Fees and Formalities Connected with Importation and Exportation**—sets out certain basic obligations respecting customs procedures;

- **Article X: Publication and Administration of Trade Regulations**—imposes certain transparency and due process obligations that apply to customs procedures; and

- **Article XI: General Elimination of Quantitative Restrictions**—prohibits the imposition of prohibitions and restrictions on imports and exports, whether made effective through quotas, import or export licences, or other measures.

These provisions remained substantially unaltered until the Tokyo Round of 1973-1979, when two customs-related "Codes" were concluded, the *Agree-*

---

[88] These GATT obligations are discussed in greater depth above at pages 57-60.

ment on Implementation of Article VII[89] and the *Agreement on Import Licensing Procedures.*[90] The overriding goal of the Tokyo Round had been to address the trade-restricting effects of non-tariff barriers. At the time there was a general recognition, at least among developed countries, that due to weaknesses in the underlying GATT rules, customs valuation and import licensing procedures had become major barriers to trade. While these Codes subsequently did improve the administration of customs laws in many developed GATT countries, most developing countries never accepted these two Codes, meaning that ambiguous valuation methodologies and burdensome licensing requirements continued to cause serious problems in many countries.

In addition to incorporating the Tokyo Round Customs Valuation Code nearly verbatim into the WTO Agreement through the *Agreement on Implementation of Article VII of the General Agreement on Tariffs and Trade 1994*, and amending the Tokyo Round Import Licensing Code through the *Agreement on Import Licensing Procedures*, the Uruguay Round negotiations produced two additional agreements which address certain other trade-restrictive effects of customs administration: the *Agreement on Preshipment Inspection*, and the *Agreement on Rules of Origin*. The introduction of additional detailed rules relating to customs procedures has been further reinforced by the mandatory acceptance of these agreements by all WTO Members through the single undertaking requirement.

3. THE URUGUAY ROUND NEGOTIATIONS ON CUSTOMS ISSUES

The Ministerial Declaration on the Uruguay Round did not specifically identify customs issues as a separate topic for negotiation. The Declaration did, however, identify non-tariff barriers generally as a negotiating area, as well as contemplating improvements to the existing Tokyo Round Agreements and Arrangements. With respect to non-tariff measures, these fell within the mandate of the Negotiating Group on Market Access. The negotiating plan gave this Group wide latitude to initially identify all relevant non-tariff barriers and negotiate as appropriate. With respect to the Tokyo Round Agreements and Arrangements, the Negotiating Group on MTN Agreements and Arrangements was instructed to identify those Tokyo Round Agreements and Arrangements which required improvement, and negotiate as appropriate. The negotiations on customs issues were undertaken primarily within these two Groups. Pre-shipment inspection and rules of origin were identified by the Market Access Group relatively early in the negotiations as potential non-

---

[89] GATT, BISD 26S/116. As noted, GATT Article VII concerns customs valuation, and consequently this Agreement became better known as the "Customs Valuation Code".

[90] GATT, BISD 26S/154, better known as the "Import Licensing Code".

tariff barriers where improved disciplines might be in order. The Tokyo Round Codes addressing customs valuation and import licensing were also quickly identified by the MTN Group as potentially in need of improvement.

Substantive negotiations in all four of these areas did not begin until after the Montreal Mid-term Meeting in late 1988. In fact, it was not until early 1990 that the negotiations entered a critical phase. Generally speaking, customs issues were relatively uncontroversial and therefore this late start was not a significant barrier to progress. Negotiations generally proceeded smoothly and in all cases substantially complete draft texts could be and were prepared for the Brussels Ministerial Meeting in December 1990. In most cases, those few issues which still required further work were agreed to in Brussels prior to the Meeting's collapse. In stark contrast to most other topic areas of the Round, therefore, the negotiations on customs issues met the original deadline for the Uruguay Round of December 1990.

4. THE *AGREEMENT ON IMPLEMENTATION OF ARTICLE VII* (CUSTOMS VALUATION)

The customs requirements of many, if not all, WTO Members rely in large part on the "value" of goods as the basis for assessing the applicable customs duties payable on importation.[91] As a result, the determination of the "value" of the imported goods is a fundamental part of the duty assessment process. Ambiguous or arbitrary valuation methodologies can therefore easily be used to overstate the value of imported goods, thereby increasing the amount of duties that are payable. Such actions can seriously impede the free flow of goods across borders and act to undermine the value of negotiated tariff concessions.

Negotiations on customs valuation were aimed primarily at refining the Tokyo Round Customs Valuation Code. It was generally considered that the Code had worked reasonably well, but was hampered by its limited application. The Code had reinforced the obligations of GATT Article VII by establishing the mandatory presumption that customs valuation should be based on the amount actually paid by the importer for the goods—known under the Code as the "transaction value". Most developing countries were unwilling to accept this obligation (and therefore refused to become signato-

---

[91] There are generally considered to be two types of import duties, "*ad valorem*" and "specific". *Ad valorem* duties are those duties which are based on the value of the imported good and are often expressed as a percentage of that value. Specific duties are those duties which are based on the volume or quantity of the good and are often unrelated to the good's value. In some cases, both types can be combined. For example, there could be a specific duty set at $1 per tonne, with an additional *ad valorem* duty also being assessed at 10 percent of the good's value. *Ad valorem* duties are, by far, the most common type of import duty assessed and therefore valuation is critical in determining that actual amount of duty payable.

ries to the Code) because it was widely believed that importers often misstated customs values either to avoid payment of duties (through under-valuation) or to avoid currency restrictions (through over-valuation).

The Uruguay Round negotiations therefore sought to expand application of the Code through addressing these concerns by providing enough flexibility to use alternative valuation methods if fraud was suspected. Negotiations on a revised agreement within the MTN Agreements and Arrangements Group did not commence in substance until early 1990. By the summer of 1990, a revised text and two draft Ministerial decisions had been negotiated which substantially addressed developing countries' concerns. While some further refinements were later made, this, in essence, completed negotiations on the new Agreement.

As stated in its preamble, the *Agreement on Implementation of Article VII* (the "Customs Valuation Agreement") was incorporated into the WTO system to address the need for a fair, uniform and neutral system for the valuation of goods for customs purposes that precludes the use of arbitrary or fictitious customs values. The Agreement consists of four Parts and three Annexes. Generally, the Agreement: (i) establishes a hierarchy of valuation methodologies; (ii) provides detailed rules concerning customs valuation and even more detailed interpretive notes; (iii) creates the Committee on Customs Valuation to oversee the Agreement and a Technical Committee on Customs Valuation to assist in the implementation of the Agreement and the settlement of disputes; and (v) encourages special treatment for developing countries.[92]

(a) Part I: Rules on Customs Valuation

Part I of the Agreement creates a strict and detailed hierarchy of valuation methodologies. Articles 1 through 7 of the Agreement define the methods for determination of customs value in a sequential order of application. Article 1 defines the primary method of valuation, which must be used whenever the conditions of Article 1 are met. When the conditions of Article 1 are not met, customs value will be determined by proceeding sequentially through the succeeding Articles to the first Article under which customs value can be determined. Except as provided in Article 4, it is only after the customs value cannot be determined under a particular Article that the provisions of the next Article are to be used.[93]

---

[92] Article 14 provides that the Annexes form an integral part of the Agreement and that the articles of the Agreement should be read in conjunction with their respective (and extensive) notes in Annex I. These Annexes are discussed where appropriate.

[93] Article 4 provides that upon request of the importer, the application of Articles 5 and 6 will be reversed. However, if the importer does not request that the order be reversed, these Articles will be considered in their natural sequence. If the importer does request that the order be reversed, but customs value cannot be determined under Article 6, customs value will be determined under Article 5, if possible.

Article 1 establishes the fundamental rule that the customs value of an imported good is to be the "transaction value" of that good—that is, the price actually paid or payable for the goods when sold for export to the country of importation. However, this so-called transaction value will be deemed an appropriate measure of customs value only under certain conditions, these being where:

(a) there are no restrictions on the disposition or use of the goods by their buyer, other than restrictions which are imposed by law, that limit the geographical area in which the goods are sold, or do not substantially affect the value of the products;

(b) the sale price is not subject to some condition or consideration for which a value cannot be determined;

(c) no part of the proceeds from the subsequent resale of the product accrues to the seller without adjustment to the transaction value; and, perhaps most importantly,

(d) the buyer and seller are not related.[94]

Notwithstanding that parties may be deemed to be related under the Agreement, paragraph 2 of Article 1 cautions that the fact that the buyer and the seller are related is not in itself grounds for considering the transaction value to be unacceptable. When a buyer and a seller are related, the customs officials are required to examine the circumstances of the sale and must use the transaction value as the customs value when the relationship does not affect the price paid or payable.[95] The transaction value between related parties must be accepted whenever the importer can demonstrate that the value closely approximates the transaction value of sales to unrelated buyers

---

[94] Article 15 provides the rules for determining if persons are related for purposes of the Agreement. It provides that persons will be deemed to be related only if:

(a) they are officers or directors of one another's businesses;

(b) they are legally recognized business partners;

(c) they are employer and employee;

(d) any person directly or indirectly owns, controls or holds 5 percent or more of the outstanding voting stock or shares of both persons;

(e) one person directly or indirectly controls the other;

(f) both persons are directly or indirectly controlled by a third person; or

(g) they are members of the same family.

[95] As stated in the notes in Annex I, this provision is not intended to mandate an examination of the circumstances surrounding all sales involving related buyers. Customs officials should only conduct such an examination when there are doubts about the acceptability of the price. When such doubts exist, customs officials must give the importer an opportunity to supply relevant information.

of identical or similar goods for export to the same country of importation or the customs value determined under Articles 5 and 6 of the Agreement (discussed below).

Article 8 then lists certain adjustments that must be made to the transaction value. Generally, Article 8 recognizes that there are a number of other costs incurred by a buyer which have the effect of increasing the overall value of an imported good but, for a number of reasons, these costs may not be fully reflected in the price paid or payable by the buyer. The adjustments permitted under Article 8 will therefore tend to increase the customs value for an imported good by adjusting for these additional off-price values.

Article 8 first requires the addition, to the transaction value, for the amounts of certain commissions, brokerage, the cost of containers that are treated as one with the goods, and the cost of packing labour and materials, to the extent that these costs are incurred by the buyer but are not included in the actual price paid or payable for the goods. Article 8 also requires an addition to the transaction value for the amounts of certain other items (often referred to as "assists") to the extent that such items are supplied by the buyer free of charge or at a reduced price in connection with the production and sale of the goods, and when such value has not been included in the sale price. These items include materials and parts incorporated in the imported goods, materials consumed in the production of the imported goods, and engineering, development, plans and sketches necessary to the production of the imported goods. Finally, Article 8 requires the addition of royalties and licence fees that the buyer must pay and the value of any part of the proceeds of the resale of the product that accrues to the seller, to the extent that such values are not already included in the price paid or payable by the buyer.

Certain additional adjustments to the transaction value may be made under paragraph 2 of Article 8, but are not required. In any case, however, Members are required to expressly provide for the inclusion in or the exclusion from the customs value of these additional adjustments in their relevant implementing legislation. These permissible adjustments include transportation costs, loading, unloading and handling charges, and the cost of insurance. Regardless of whether such adjustments are mandatory or permissible, all adjustments must be made on the basis of objective and quantifiable data.

Finally, in order to reinforce the other obligations of Article 8, paragraph 4 provides that no additions may be made to the price actually paid or payable except those expressly permitted under Article 8 itself.

When the transaction value for a good is not the appropriate measure of customs value because it cannot meet the requirements of Article 1, Article 2 of the Agreement then provides that the customs value shall be the transaction value of identical goods sold for export to the same country of importation and exported at or about the same time as the goods being valued. The term "identical goods" is defined in Article 15 to mean "goods which are the same in all respects, including physical characteristics, quality and reputation". However, minor differences in appearance should not preclude otherwise identical goods from being treated as identical.

When customs value cannot be determined under either Article 1 or Article 2, the Agreement provides in Article 3 that the customs value shall then be the transaction value of similar goods sold for export to the same country of importation and exported at or about the same time as the goods being valued. Article 15 then defines "similar goods" to mean "goods which, although not alike in all respects, have like characteristics and like component materials which enable them to perform the same functions and to be commercially interchangeable".[96]

The alternative values provided for in Articles 2 and 3 require that customs officials use a transaction value of identical goods or similar goods, as the case may be, at the same commercial level and in the same quantity as the goods being valued. When such a transaction is not available, customs officials may rely upon the transaction value of goods at different commercial levels or in different quantities, if appropriate adjustments are made to that value to take such differences into account.[97] Such adjustments may result in either an increase or decrease in the customs value. However, if a Member's domestic legislation authorizes any of the permissive adjustments listed in paragraph 2 of Article 8, the adjustment must take into account any significant differences in the costs between the imported goods and the identical or similar goods. Finally, if more than one transaction value for identical or similar goods is found under the respective methodologies, the lowest value must be used to determine the customs value.

In cases where the customs value cannot be determined under Article 1, 2 or 3, the next level of the valuation hierarchy is set forth in Article 5. Under Article 5, the customs value is the unit price of the imported goods or identical or similar goods sold in the largest aggregate quantity at or about the time of importation of the goods being valued, provided that the imported goods are

---

[96] Article 15 also provides that goods will not be considered as either "identical" or "similar" if they are not produced in the same country as the goods being valued. Moreover, goods produced by a different person may only be used when there are no identical or similar goods produced by the same person as the goods being valued.

[97] In these circumstances, the notes to Annex I state that three sales situations are acceptable: (a) a sale at the same commercial level but in different quantities; (b) a sale at a different commercial level but in substantially the same quantities; and (c) a sale at a different commercial level and in different quantities. These situations would require the following adjustments, respectively: (a) quantity factors only; (b) commercial level factors only; and (c) both commercial level and quantity factors.

sold in the condition as imported.[98] This value is subject to deductions for commissions usually paid or additions usually made for profits and general expenses, transportation and insurance costs incurred within the country of importation, customs duties and national taxes and, where appropriate, the costs set forth in paragraph 2 of Article 8.[99]

If the imported goods, identical or similar goods are not sold in the country of importation in the condition as imported, the importer may request that the customs value be based upon the unit price at which the further processed goods are sold in the greatest aggregate quantity to unrelated purchasers. Adjustments must be made for value added by the further processing and deductions for commissions usually paid or additions usually made for profits and general expenses, transportation and insurance costs incurred within the country of importation, customs duties and national taxes, and, where appropriate, the costs set forth in paragraph 2 of Article 8.

The valuation methodology of Article 6 is based upon a computed value for the goods at issue, consisting of the sum of the cost of materials and fabrication of the imported goods, profit and general expenses usually reflected in sales of the same class or kind of goods, and the cost of other expenses necessary to reflect the permissive adjustments adopted by that Member under paragraph 2 of Article 8. Customs officials may not compel any person to produce or allow access to documents for determining the computed value. On the other hand, information provided by the producer may be verified in another country with the agreement of the producer and the government of the other country involved.

Finally, Article 7 provides for cases where the customs value cannot be ascertained under any of Articles 1 through 6 of the Agreement. In such circumstances, customs value will be determined using reasonable means consistent with the principles and general provisions of the Agreement and of GATT Article VII, and on the basis of data available in the country of importation.[100] This broad discretion is tempered by a number of limitations which provide that the customs value may not be determined on the basis of: (i) the selling price in the country of importation of goods produced in that country; (ii) a system that accepts the higher of two alternative values; (iii) the

---

[98] Article 5 continues on to note that if the imported goods, identical goods or similar goods are not sold at or about the time of importation of the goods being valued, the customs value will be based upon the price of the imported goods, identical goods or similar goods sold at the earliest date after importation, but in no case after 90 days from the date of importation.

[99] The notes in Annex I require that the figure for profits and general expenses be determined from information provided by the importer, unless that information is inconsistent with information obtained on sales in the country of importation of imported goods of the same class or kind.

[100] The notes in Annex I encourage the use of previously determined customs values to the greatest extent possible when customs value is determined under Article 7.

price of goods sold in the country of exportation; (iv) the cost of production other than the value computed under Article 6; (v) the price of the goods for export to a third country; (vi) minimum customs values; and (vii) arbitrary or fictitious values. Upon request, an importer must be informed in writing of the value determined under Article 7 and the method used to derive that value.[101]

The Agreement also establishes certain procedural requirements associated with the valuation process. Article 10 provides that customs officials must maintain the strict confidentiality of all information that has been submitted on a confidential basis. Confidential data may not be disclosed without the permission of the submitting party.

Articles 11 and 12 require Members to provide a right of appeal to the importer or any other person liable for payment of the duty of a valuation determination. Although Members may provide for an initial right of appeal to the customs administration or an independent body, all Members must provide a further right of appeal to a judicial authority. In addition, all laws, regulations and judicial determinations relating to customs valuation must be published by the importing country in accordance with GATT Article X.

In cases where the final determination of the customs value is delayed, Article 13 provides that importers shall have the right to withdraw the merchandise from customs control. However, Members may require that importers post some form of guarantee, such as a surety or a deposit, to cover the customs duties which may, upon final determination, be determined to be applicable to the goods.

(b) Part II: Administration, Consultations and Dispute Settlement

Part II of the Agreement provides the administrative structure and dispute settlement procedures for matters involving customs valuation. Article 18 establishes the Committee on Customs Valuation, comprised of representatives of all Members. The Committee is intended to provide Members with a forum to consult on matters relating to the administration of the Agreement and to carry out any other responsibilities assigned to it by Members. Members are also required under Article 22 to inform the Committee of any changes in their laws and regulations relating to the Agreement. Article 23 requires the Committee to conduct an annual review of the operation of the Agreement and to inform the WTO's Council for Trade in Goods of any developments in the area. The WTO Secretariat is to serve as the secretariat for the Committee.

Part II and Annex II of the Agreement then create the Technical Committee on Customs Valuation ("Technical Committee") under the auspices of the

---

[101] Article 17 then provides that upon written request, an importer is entitled to a written explanation of how the customs value was determined.

multilateral Customs Co-operation Council ("CCC").[102] The Technical Committee has been established to ensure, at a technical level, that there is uniformity in interpretation and application of the Agreement amongst Members. Each Member has the right to be represented on the Technical Committee and may nominate one delegate and one or more alternates as its representative. Any participants in the CCC that are not WTO Members may also be represented on the Technical Committee by one delegate and one or more alternates, but such delegates may attend Technical Committee meetings as observers only.

Annex II of the Customs Valuation Agreement charges the Technical Committee with the following responsibilities:

(a) examining and giving advisory opinions concerning specific technical problems arising in the day-to-day administration of the customs valuation system;

(b) studying and preparing reports concerning valuation laws, procedures and practices;

(c) preparing annual reports on the technical aspects of the operation of the Agreement;

(d) furnishing information and advice on valuation matters;

(e) facilitating technical assistance to Members; and

(f) examining matters referred to it by a dispute resolution panel.

The Technical Committee is to meet at CCC headquarters in Brussels, as necessary, but at least twice annually. All decisions of the Technical Committee are made by a two-thirds majority of the Members present, with a simple majority of the Technical Committee members constituting a quorum.

Article 19, dealing with consultation and dispute settlement, provides that the WTO's Dispute Settlement Understanding applies to disputes arising under the Customs Valuation Agreement. The Article also provides that the Technical Committee may provide, upon request, advice and assistance to Members engaged in consultations. The Technical Committee is also authorized, upon request of a dispute settlement panel, to examine any technical question before the panel. Dispute settlement panels that request the assistance of the Technical Committee are to set the terms of reference for the Technical Committee's review, and the panel is then required to take the Technical Committee's report into account in rendering its decision on the issue before it.

---

[102] The Customs Co-operation Council is a multilateral organization established in 1950 to address, in multilateral forum, a number of customs-related matters. In June 1994, the Council adopted the informal working name the "World Customs Organization". The Convention that established the Council has not been amended and therefore the Customs Co-operation Council remains its formal name.

(c) Part III: Special and Differential Treatment

It is generally considered that the adoption of the requirements of the Agreement may impose significant additional burdens on some Members. As a result, under Article 20, developing country Members that were not signatories to the Tokyo Round Customs Valuation Code have until January 1, 2000 to bring their customs valuation laws and practices into conformity with the Agreement. In addition, those Members have been granted a further three years to bring their laws and practices concerning computed value (under paragraph 2(b)(iii) of Article 1 and Article 6) into conformity with the Agreement. Certain additional provisions concerning developing country Members are found in Annex III to the Agreement.

Article 20 also requires developed country Members to provide technical assistance to developing country Members upon request. Developed country Members are to establish technical assistance programmes including training, assistance in implementation, access to customs valuation information, and advice on the application of the Agreement.

These provisions concerning special and differential treatment have been reinforced by two Ministerial Decisions accepted as part of the final Uruguay Round package. The first, the "Decision Regarding Cases Where Customs Administrations Have Reasons to Doubt the Truth or Accuracy of the Declared Value", was adopted to specifically address developing country concerns respecting the potential for fraud. The decision invited the Customs Valuation Committee to take its own decision respecting the matter, which thereby allows a customs administration to request further information where it has reason to doubt the truth or accuracy of a valuation declaration. If, after receiving a response to its inquiry (or no response), it still has reasonable doubts about the truth or accuracy of the declared value, it is permitted to deem the application of Article 1 of the Agreement inappropriate.

The second decision, the "Decision on Texts Relating to Minimum Values and Imports by Sole Agents, Sole Distributors, and Sole Concessionaires", provides for certain reservations that may be exercised by developing country Members relating to established minimum import values. The Decision also suggests that, during the five-year implementation period extended to developing country Members under Article 20 of the Agreement, they undertake appropriate studies into the potential problems related to imports by sole agents, distributors and concessionaires.

(d) Part IV: Final Provisions

Like all of the multilateral agreements under the WTO umbrella, Members may not enter reservations with respect to any of the provisions of the Agreement without the consent of the Members. Finally, Article 22 provides a general obligation that, subject to Article 20, each Member is required to bring its laws, regulations and procedures into conformity with the Agreement no later than the date of entry into force of the Agreement for that Member.

5. THE *AGREEMENT ON PRE-SHIPMENT INSPECTION*

Pre-shipment inspection is a process by which the quantity, quality and customs value of exported goods are examined, usually by private entities acting on behalf of the government of the importing country or a party to the transaction, prior to exportation of the goods. Pre-shipment inspection regimes are used primarily by developing countries in Africa, Latin America and Asia. These regimes are used as a means of controlling imports, prices and the release of foreign exchange, and to prevent fraud. Many of these countries do not have adequate customs facilities or staff in their own countries that are necessary to conduct these inspections. Pre-shipment inspection thereby allows them to ensure their customs rules are being met and their controls are effective without requiring extensive expenditures on such staff and facilities. Although pre-shipment inspection requirements date back to the 1800s, most regimes, particularly those in Latin America, were not implemented until the late 1970s and the 1980s. The relatively recent adoption of these practices generally explains the lack of a Tokyo Round Code dedicated to the issue.

During the mid-1980s, developed countries began to complain that these inspection systems were acting as a non-tariff barrier in contravention of the Tokyo Round Customs Valuation Code (which most developing countries had not signed), and the issue was therefore examined by the Customs Valuation Committee. Developed countries especially complained of the delays in shipments and increased administrative costs associated with these inspection regimes. In addition, some cited the lack of transparency in the price-verification process, failures to protect confidential business information and the lack of appeal or dispute settlement as further evidence of the trade restrictive nature of many pre-shipment inspection regimes.

While not a specific item on the Uruguay Round negotiating agenda, in February 1988 Indonesia (a country which employed pre-shipment inspection) first proposed that pre-shipment inspection be addressed in a separate agreement under the GATT, recognizing that the issues associated with pre-shipment inspection were broader than those being discussed in the Customs Valuation negotiations. Other developing countries complained that pre-shipment inspection should not be a topic of negotiations, primarily because such measures, rather than being non-tariff barriers to trade, were a legitimate means for developing countries to deter fraud and prevent capital flight. In the end, it was agreed that negotiations would be undertaken, but would not be aimed at the elimination of pre-shipment inspection. Instead they would attempt to establish sufficient disciplines on pre-shipment inspection practices so as to ensure that they did not come to constitute non-tariff barriers.

Unlike many other areas, the pre-shipment inspection negotiations were concluded relatively quickly. Negotiations did not commence in earnest until early 1990. The United States submitted a proposal in January of that year that was to become the basis for the draft Agreement. Following additional proposals from the European Communities, Zaire, Switzerland, and the Nordic countries, the first draft Agreement on Pre-shipment Inspection was released in July 1990. Almost all outstanding issues were then resolved prior to the Brussels Meeting in December 1990. And, again in a notable exception to most other aspects of the Round, these remaining issues were resolved at Brussels prior to the Meeting's collapse. This basically concluded negotiations on the topic.

The resulting Pre-shipment Inspection Agreement recognizes both the need of developing countries to use pre-shipment inspection and the need to establish an international framework that defines the rights and obligations of user Members and exporter Members.

The Agreement applies to all pre-shipment inspection activities carried out on the territory of Members whether contracted or mandated by a Member government. Pre-shipment inspection is defined for this purpose in Article 1 as

> all activities relating to the verification of the quality, the quantity, the price, including currency exchange rate and financial terms, and/or the customs classification of goods to be exported to the territory of the user Member.

While not formally divided into separate parts, functionally the Agreement is comprised of four separate elements: (i) those obligations applicable to user Members; (ii) those obligations applicable to exporter Members; (iii) an independent review procedure; and (iv) final consultative and dispute settlement provisions.

(a) Obligations Applicable to User Members

The most important obligations of the Agreement are those applicable to "user Members"[103] as set forth in Article 2 of the Agreement. As with almost all WTO Agreements, the primary obligation of user Members under the Agreement is that of non-discrimination. User Members are required to ensure that all pre-shipment activities are carried out in a non-discriminatory manner using objective criteria applied equally to all exporters. User Members must also ensure that entities contracted or mandated by them to perform pre-shipment activities carry out their work in a uniform manner and in accordance with the standards defined by the buyer and the seller. If no such standards are specified, international standards will apply.[104]

---

[103] The term "user Member" is defined in paragraph 1 of Article 1 to mean a Member that contracts for or mandates the use of pre-shipment inspection activities.

[104] The only limitation on the use of international standards in the Agreement is that such standards must be relevant. However, the Agreement defines an international standard as a standard adopted by a governmental or non-governmental body whose membership is open to all Members, one of whose recognized activities is in the field of standardization.

In a further reinforcement of the basic non-discrimination obligation, the Agreement specifically applies the national treatment provisions of GATT Article III:4 to pre-shipment inspection laws, regulations and requirements. These provisions require treatment for imports that is no less favourable than treatment given to products of national origin with respect to laws and regulations affecting their internal sale, transportation, purchase, distribution or use.

Article 2 also requires that all pre-shipment inspection activities be conducted in the customs territory of the relevant exporting Member. If the inspection cannot occur in the customs territory of the exporting Member as a result of the complex nature of the products in question, the pre-shipment inspection activities may be conducted in the customs territory in which the products were manufactured.

One of the key aspects of the Agreement, and an important overall goal of the negotiations, is the requirement that pre-shipment inspection activities be transparent. Under the Agreement, user Members are required to ensure that their inspection entities provide exporters with a list of all of the information that the exporters will need to provide in order to comply with the inspection requirements as well as the procedures and criteria that will be used in the inspection process. This information must be made available to exporters in a "convenient manner" and must be accompanied by references to the relevant laws and regulations of the Member. User Members must also publish their laws and regulations relating to pre-shipment inspection activities and notify the WTO Secretariat of such laws and regulations. Amendments to these laws and regulations may not be enforced before they have been officially published.

Another frequently complained of aspect of pre-shipment inspection activities was the failure of inspection entities to protect confidential business information. The Agreement addresses this problem by mandating confidential treatment of all information that is not already published, generally available to third parties or otherwise in the public domain. Toward this end, user Members are responsible for ensuring that their inspection entities do not release confidential business information to any third parties. However, the Agreement does allow inspection entities to disclose confidential information to the user Member to the extent necessary for forms of payment, or for customs, import licensing or exchange control purposes.

Paragraph 12 of Article 2 further protects confidential information by prohibiting inspection entities from requesting certain types of confidential information. This includes information relating to: manufacturing data concerning patented, licensed or undisclosed processes; unpublished technical data other than that necessary to demonstrate compliance with technical standards; internal pricing and manufacturing costs; profits; and contract terms.

The Agreement contemplates that conflicts of interest may arise between inspection entities and entities whose shipments the inspection entity must examine (where, for example, the two entities have a financial or commercial interest in one another). In order to promote the objectivity of the pre-shipment inspection process, user Members are required to maintain procedures to ensure that such conflicts of interest do not arise.

The most frequently expressed concern over pre-shipment inspection is the delays caused by such requirements. In response to this concern, the Agreement requires user Members to ensure that pre-shipment inspection entities employed by them avoid unreasonable delays in inspection of shipments. When inspectors and exporters agree on an inspection date, the inspection must occur on that date unless otherwise agreed by the parties, or inspection is prevented by a *force majeure*. Within five business days of the completion of the inspection and receipt of all documentation, the inspectors must issue a so-called "Clean Report of Findings" or a written explanation as to why such a Report was not issued. In the case of non-issuance, the inspection entity must provide exporters with the opportunity to respond in writing and to receive re-inspection at the earliest convenient date. Exporters also have the right, upon request, to a preliminary verification of the price and exchange rate prior to the physical inspection of the merchandise. Preliminary determinations of price and exchange rates shall not be withdrawn as long as the goods conform to the submitted documentation.

The Agreement also imposes disciplines on the price verification process. Under paragraph 20 of Article 2, a user Member may only reject an agreed contract price between an exporter and an importer if a price verification process was undertaken in accordance with the criteria established under paragraph 20 of Article 2. These criteria include:

(a) the inspection entity must base its price comparison on the price of identical or similar goods exported from the same country at or about the same time and under competitive and comparable conditions of sale;

(b) the inspection entity must make appropriate allowances for the terms of sale of the contract and adjusting factors including commercial level, quantity, delivery periods, price escalation clauses, quality specifications, special features, packing, seasonal influences, *etc.*;

(c) transportation charges must relate only to the agreed price of the mode of transportation in the export country as agreed in the contract; and

(d) the selling price in the country of importation, the price of goods for export from a third country, cost of production and arbitrary or fictitious prices may not be used for price verification purposes.

User Members must also establish procedures that allow exporters to raise grievances arising from the pre-shipment inspection process. Inspection entities are to designate one or more officials who will be available during normal business hours to receive, consider and render decisions on an exporter's grievance. They must also afford exporters the opportunity to submit in writing the facts, the nature of the grievance and a proposed solution. The designated officials must give sympathetic consideration to exporters' grievances and must to render their decisions as soon as possible after receipt of the necessary documentation.

Finally, user Members who establish a minimum value under which merchandise will not be inspected must ensure that shipments under that value are not inspected. The minimum value information must be made available to exporters along with the information requirements discussed above.

(b) Obligations Applicable to Exporter Members

Although the Agreement establishes far fewer obligations applicable to exporter Members than it does with respect to user Members, the obligations on exporter Members are important to the effective operation of the Agreement. Under Article 3, exporter Members must ensure that their laws and regulations pertaining to pre-shipment inspection are applied in a non-discriminatory manner and must publish such laws in a manner that will enable governments and traders to become acquainted with them. In addition, exporter Members must provide technical assistance to user Members, upon request, in order to further promote the objectives of the Agreement.

(c) Independent Review Procedures

When exporters and inspectors are unable to resolve disputes by mutual agreement, the Agreement provides a process for independent review of the dispute by a panel of experts. The independent review procedures are administered by the so-called "Independent Entity" jointly constituted by representatives of inspection entities and representatives of exporters.[105] The Independent Entity has established three lists of experts comprised, respectively, of members nominated by inspection entities, members nominated by exporters and independent trade experts nominated by the Independent Entity. The lists of experts are required to have broad geographical distribution to ensure the expeditious resolution of disputes, and they must be publicly available and notified to the WTO Secretariat and circulated to all Members.

---

[105] The Independent Entity became operational on May 1, 1996. It was constituted by the International Chamber of Commerce, on behalf of exporters, and the Federation of Inspection Agencies, on behalf of inspection entities. Its operation is overseen by the WTO and it is considered to be a subsidiary body of the WTO's Council for Trade in Goods.

An inspector or exporter seeking to raise a dispute will first formally notify the Independent Entity of its request for the formation of a panel. The Independent Entity will then establish a panel of three members, one chosen from each of the three lists of experts. The panelist chosen from the list of independent trade experts appointed by the Independent Entity will serve as the chair of the panel. Upon agreement of the parties to the dispute, the dispute may be reviewed by a single panelist selected from the list established by the Independent Entity. Panelists are chosen in a manner that will avoid unnecessary costs and delays, and no objections may be made to the selection of panelists.

The purpose of the review is to ensure compliance with the Agreement. Parties to the dispute are afforded an opportunity to present their views to the panel in person or in writing, and all procedures are to be expeditious.[106] Panels are to render their determinations within eight business days of the request for independent review, unless the parties to the dispute agree to extend the deadline. Panel determinations are binding on the parties to the dispute.

(d) Consultation, Dispute Settlement and Final Provisions

Articles 7 and 8 provide that the consultative provisions of GATT Article XXII and the dispute settlement provisions of GATT Article XXIII, as elaborated and applied by the Dispute Settlement Understanding, apply to the Preshipment Inspection Agreement.

The final provisions under the Agreement include a requirement for Members to take all necessary measures to implement the Agreement, ensure consistency with the Agreement and to submit to the WTO Secretariat copies of their laws and regulations by which they have brought the Agreement into force domestically. The Agreement is also to be reviewed periodically, and may be amended as experience dictates.

6. THE *AGREEMENT ON RULES OF ORIGIN*

Rules of origin are rules used to determine the country of origin of imported products. When a product is wholly produced in a single country, unprocessed agricultural products for example, the determination of the country of origin of the product is relatively straightforward and certain. However,

---

[106] The WTO's General Council has adopted two sets of rules concerning the Independent Entity, one concerning the structure and operation of the Independent Entity itself, and the second set providing the rules of procedure for the independent reviews (including rules concerning panel appointments, procedures before the panel, rules of evidence and timing of the process). See "Operation of the Independent Entity Established under Article 4 of the Agreement on Preshipment Inspection", General Council Decision of December 13, 1995.

sophisticated manufactured goods that are comprised of materials from several countries, and may be assembled or further processed in a number of countries, require special and complex rules to determine a single country of origin.

When an importing country applies different tariff rates to imports from different countries, or where a country allocates specific import quotas to imports from different countries, the country of origin of an imported good is critical to proper customs administration. While imports by WTO Members from other WTO Members are, at a minimum, to receive the most-favoured-nation (or "MFN") tariff rate that the importing country grants to all WTO Members, imports from non-WTO Member countries are frequently subjected to much higher rates of duty. Thus, rules of origin are used to determine if a good qualifies for this better MFN treatment. Perhaps more importantly, the applicable GATT rules do allow Members to extend better-than MFN, or "preferential", tariff treatment to imports in many cases, and rules of origin are often used to determine eligibility for such preferential treatment.[107]

Somewhat curiously, the GATT 1947 contained no provisions governing the determination of origin for imported goods, and there were no internationally accepted standards prior to the entry into force of the WTO Agreement. As a result, the rules of origin in force around the world have taken on many forms, and individual countries often apply several different rules of origin depending on the nature of the product, the country of export, and what type of preferential treatment is being sought. In spite of this overall complexity, there are two basic types of rules of origin:

(1) goods that are wholly produced in a given country are accorded the origin of that country; and

(2) goods that undergo substantial transformation in a given country are accorded the origin of the last country in which the substantial transformation occurs.

While the first basic rule is straightforward, "substantial transformation" under the second basic rule can be, and is, defined in several ways. A product may be considered substantially transformed in the country where a specified manufacturing process takes place, where a specified amount of value is added, or where a product undergoes a change in character sufficient to alter its tariff classification. In fact, many importing countries define substantial

---

[107] For example, eligibility of imports for the preferential tariff benefits of the *North American Free Trade Agreement* is determined by a comprehensive and complex set of rules of origin found in Chapter Four of that Agreement. Other important preferential arrangements which require rules of origin to determine their applicability include the General Preferential Tariff Programme of Canada, the Generalized System of Preferences and the Caribbean Basin Initiative of the United States and the European Free Trade Agreement and the Lome Convention of the European Union.

transformation differently depending on the products involved and the circumstances of the transaction.

With so many different rules of origin in use, several contracting parties to the GATT pressed for the inclusion of standardized rules of origin as part of the Uruguay Round agenda. In the words of the United States delegation, "rules of origin had become the source of trade tensions over the years and had the potential to become a major non-tariff measure if they were not subjected to GATT disciplines".[108] There was agreement in 1988 within the Market Access Negotiating Group that the Group would review the issue of rules of origin as part of the negotiations.

While there was some agreement among the negotiators that rules of origin might be harmonized (as the GATT's adopted tariff classification system had been harmonized in 1988), the negotiators split on two main issues.

First, there was considerable disagreement amongst the negotiators as to whether the GATT was even the appropriate forum for a discussion concerning the harmonization of rules of origin. Because of the highly technical nature of rules of origin, several participants, including the EC, felt that a more technical body (such as the CCC) would be the more appropriate forum for such negotiations. Others, including the United States and Japan, recognizing the trade distorting potential of rules of origin, argued for GATT leadership in the harmonization process with the technical assistance of the CCC.

Second, the negotiators disagreed as to whether the harmonization process should cover rules of origin for both preferential and non-preferential arrangements. The EC proposed that the negotiations only work towards establishing harmonized rules of origin for non-preferential arrangements. Rules applicable to preferential trading arrangements such as NAFTA would therefore be exempted from the new disciplines. The United States and others sought the broadest possible application for the harmonized rules, including their application to preferential arrangements.

By February 1990, there was general agreement that the Group should develop a series of obligations, but no agreement on their potential scope. A first draft agreement was completed by July 1990. By the time of the Brussels Meeting in December 1990, most issues had been resolved, with the exception of whether the new obligations should apply to rules of origin applied in preferential trading arrangements. Like the *Agreement on Pre-shipment Inspection*, all outstanding rule of origin issues were resolved in Brussels prior to the Meeting's collapse, and the text remained basically unchanged from that time forward.

In sum, the resulting *Agreement on Rules of Origin* provides for further negotiations to harmonize rules of origin with the assistance of the CCC. A set

---

[108] Note by the Secretariat, GATT Doc. No. MTN.GNG/NG2/12 (October 18, 1989) at 2.

of transitional disciplines applicable in the interim to rules of origin was also agreed to. While preferential arrangements are generally excluded from some of the more important obligations of the Agreement, Annex II of the Agreement does impose certain disciplines on the rules of origin applicable in preferential arrangements. The Agreement consists of four parts, discussed below.

(a) Part I: Definitions and Coverage

Article 1 of the Agreement defines rules of origin as the laws, regulations and administrative determinations of general application that are applied by Members to determine the country of origin of goods. Article 1 expressly excludes rules of origin "related to contractual or autonomous trade regimes leading to the granting of tariff preferences" from the scope of the Agreement. However, the Agreement expressly covers rules of origin used in commercial policy instruments, such as determinations of MFN treatment, anti-dumping and countervailing duty programmes, safeguard measures, origin marking requirements, quantitative restrictions or tariff quotas, and government procurement and trade statistics purposes.

(b) Part II: Disciplines Governing the Application of Rules of Origin

The Agreement establishes two sets of disciplines on the application of rules of origin: one during the period of transition to harmonized rules and one following implementation of these harmonized rules. During the transition period, 11 rules apply:

(1) When issuing administrative determinations of general application, Members must clearly define the requirements to be fulfilled, including specific headings and subheadings when change in tariff classification is used, calculation methods when an *ad valorem* percentage method is used, and specification of the process that confers origin when a manufacturing process is used to determine origin;

(2) rules of origin may not be used directly or indirectly to pursue trade objectives—that is, they are not to be used to influence trade flows;

(3) rules of origin must not create restrictive, distorting or disruptive effects on international trade;

(4) rules of origin applied to imports may not be more restrictive than the rules to determine whether a product is a domestic product and may not discriminate between Members;

(5) Members must administer rules of origin in a consistent, uniform, impartial and reasonable manner;

(6) rules of origin must express a positive standard—that is, they must state what confers origin, not what does not confer origin, unless this is done to clarify a positive standard;

(7) Members must publish their laws, regulations administrative and judicial determinations relating to rules of origin;

(8) upon the request of an interested party, Members must assess the origin that they would confer upon a product no later than 150 days after a request; such assessment must remain in effect for three years as long as the facts remain comparable;

(9) changes in rules of origin cannot be applied retroactively;

(10) Members must provide prompt review of origin determinations by independent judicial, arbitral or administrative tribunals; and

(11) confidential information may not be disclosed except with the permission of the person or entity that furnished the information.[109]

Upon completion of the harmonization process, nine rules will govern the application of rules of origin. In addition to rules 4, 5, and 7 through 11 listed above as applicable during the transition period, the following additional rules will apply after implementation of the harmonized rules:

- Members must apply rules of origin equally for all purposes; and

- country of origin must be either the country where the product is wholly obtained or the country where the last substantial transformation takes place.

(c) Part III: Procedural Arrangements on Notification, Review, Consultation and Dispute Settlement

Article 4 of the Agreement creates two institutions to administer the provisions of the Agreement. The first is the Committee on Rules of Origin, comprised of representatives of all Members. The Committee, which is to meet at least once a year, is designed to provide a forum for the Members to consult on matters affecting the operation of the Agreement. The Committee is also charged with the annual review of the implementation and operation of Parts II and III of the Agreement, and is to report its findings to the WTO's Council for Trade in Goods. The Committee may also propose amendments to Parts I, II and III of the Agreement that it considers necessary to reflect the results of the harmonization process and, with the assistance of the Technical Committee discussed below, may propose amendments to the harmonization process. The WTO Secretariat serves as the secretariat for the Committee.

---

[109] The disciplines on rules of origin applicable to preferential arrangements set forth in Annex II are identical to Rules 1, and 6 through 11.

The second institution established under Article 4 and Annex I of the Agreement is the Technical Committee on Rules of Origin. The Technical Committee is established under the auspices of the CCC. Each Member has the right to be represented on the Technical Committee and may nominate one delegate and one or more alternates as its representatives. Participants in the CCC that are not Members may be represented on the Technical Committee by one delegate and one or more alternates, but such representatives are permitted to attend meetings as observers only.

The Technical Committee's primary responsibility is to carry out the technical work for the harmonization of rules of origin set forth in Part IV of the Agreement. The Technical Committee may also give advisory opinions to Members concerning technical problems relating to the day-to-day administration of rules of origin, furnish advice on origin determinations, prepare reports on the technical aspects of the Agreement, and conduct an annual review of the technical aspects of the implementation of Parts II and III of the Agreement.

Article 5 of the Agreement requires each Member to notify the WTO Secretariat of all laws, regulations and rulings relating to rules of origin within 90 days of the entry into force of the WTO Agreement for each Member. During the transition period, Members are required to publish any modifications to their rules of origin, or new rules of origin at least 60 days prior to the effective date of such rules.

The consultation provisions of GATT Article XXII and the dispute settlement provisions of GATT Article XXIII, as implemented by the Dispute Settlement Understanding, apply to the Agreement.

(d) Part IV: Harmonization of Rules of Origin

Article 9 establishes the following principles to govern the planned harmonization of rules of origin under the Agreement:

(1) rules of origin must be applied equally for all purposes;

(2) country of origin must be either the country where a product is wholly obtained or the country where the last substantial transformation occurred;

(3) rules of origin must be objective, understandable and predictable;

(4) rules of origin must not be used directly or indirectly to pursue trade objectives and must not disrupt, distort or restrict trade;

(5) rules of origin must be administrable in a consistent, impartial, uniform and reasonable manner;

(6) rules of origin must be coherent; and

(7) rules of origin must be based on a positive standard; negative standards may only be used to clarify positive standards.

The harmonization process began upon entry into force of the WTO Agreement in 1995 and is scheduled to be completed by 1998. The Committee on Rules of Origin and the Technical Committee are responsible for carrying out the harmonization process. The harmonization process is being conducted on a sector basis as set forth in the Harmonized Tariff System and is divided into three parts: first, the Technical Committee will develop harmonized definitions of products that are considered to be wholly obtained in one country; second, the Technical Committee will development criteria for determining substantial transformation through changes or "shifts" in tariff classification; and finally, the Technical Committee will then develop criteria for determining substantial transformation for products where the use of the Harmonized Tariff nomenclature is inappropriate for the determination of substantial transformation. (These latter criteria may include, for example, *ad valorem* percentages and/or manufacturing processes.)

Upon completion of the harmonization work program, the results must be adopted by the Ministerial Conference of the WTO. The results will be incorporated in an Annex as an integral part of the Agreement on Rules of Origin, and the Ministerial Conference will establish a time period for the entry into force of the Annex.

7. THE *AGREEMENT ON IMPORT LICENSING PROCEDURES*

Many countries require government licensing or import permits before goods may be imported into their territory. Such licensing or permitting systems serve many purposes, such as administration of quota programs, to ensure protection from imported pests and diseases, to control the importation of dangerous or otherwise controlled products, to enforce environmental or endangered species laws, and to gather accurate import statistics. It is also commonly believed, however, that import licensing can also be used as a non-tariff barrier to protect domestic industries and to discourage import trade. Because import licensing programmes frequently involve an application process before one or more government agencies, the costs and delays associated with such programmes have long been recognized as potential non-tariff barriers to trade.

Recognizing the potential trade distorting effects of import licensing, the GATT Contracting Parties negotiated the *Agreement on Import Licensing Procedures*[110] during the Tokyo Round. In the words of the Import Licensing Code itself, its purpose was to simplify, and bring transparency to, the administrative procedures and practices used in international trade, and to ensure the fair and equitable application and administration of such pro-

---

[110] GATT, BISD 26S/154. This Tokyo Round Agreement was more commonly referred to as the "Import Licensing Code".

cedures and practices. The Code established an Import Licensing Code Committee, which was charged with examining the effectiveness of the Code and provided a forum for the discussion of disputes relating to import licensing procedures. Prior to the commencement of the Uruguay Round, the Committee had already discussed a number of possible improvements to the Code.

During the Uruguay Round, several countries within the MTN Agreements and Arrangements Negotiating Group proposed renegotiation of certain aspects of the Import Licensing Code. In 1988, the GATT Secretariat prepared a checklist of import licensing issues that had previously been raised. These issues fell into three general areas concerning: (i) clarification of the Code language; (ii) increased discipline over import licensing; and (iii) expanding the application of the Code to also capture export licensing. The United States took the lead throughout most of the negotiations, urging most of the procedural and substantive changes to the Code.

In September 1989, the United States and Hong Kong proposed a comprehensive revision of the Tokyo Round Code that sought to simplify and clarify licensing procedures, establish fixed time periods for the completion of licensing activities and require notification of import licensing regimes to a Committee on Import Licensing. The U.S.-Hong Kong proposal served as the primary negotiating document for the *Agreement on Import Licensing Procedures*. The debate from that point forward focused on the issues of automatic and non-automatic licensing and the notification requirements. Most issues were settled by February 1990, and a final consensus draft emerged in October 1990. This draft essentially remained unchanged through the rest of the Round.

Substantially based on the Tokyo Round Code, the new WTO *Agreement on Import Licensing Procedures* establishes general rules for import licensing regimes as well as more specific rules aimed at automatic and non-automatic import licensing procedures. In addition, the Agreement contains detailed notification requirements and establishes the Committee on Import Licensing to oversee the operation of the Agreement.

(a) General Provisions

Import licensing is defined in Article 1 of the Agreement as

administrative procedures used for the operation of import licensing regimes requiring the submission of an application or other documentation (other than that required for customs purposes) to the relevant administrative body as a prior condition for importation into the customs territory of the importing Member.

Under the Agreement, Members are obligated to apply neutral, fair and equitable import licensing procedures with the aim of preventing trade distortions. Moreover, Members must publish all information concerning import licensing practices and procedures, including application forms and lists of products subject to import licensing. Whenever practicable, Members must publish changes in their procedures 21 days prior to their effective date.

Application and renewal forms and procedures must be as simple as possible, and only documents that are considered "strictly necessary" to the functioning of the licensing system may be required. Where an application period has a closing date, applicants should have at least 21 days to submit applications. Members may not refuse applications for minor errors, and applicants should not be penalized with more than a warning for omissions or mistakes that clearly were made without fraudulent intent or gross negligence.

An important feature of the general provisions (and a notable improvement upon the Tokyo Round Code) is the requirement that applicants only be required to approach one administrative body in the application process. If the need to approach more than one body is "strictly indispensable", applicants should not be required to approach more than three administrative bodies in the application process. Finally, licensed imports must not be refused for minor variations from the price, quantity or weight on the licence resulting from minor differences consistent with normal commercial practice.

(b) Automatic Import Licensing

Automatic import licensing refers to licensing practices where approval of applications is granted in all cases. Among other purposes, such automatic systems can be used to gather highly accurate and up-to-date import statistics. In addition to the general rules set forth in Article 1 of the Agreement, Article 2 requires that automatic import licensing procedures not have trade restrictive effects. Licensing procedures will be deemed to have trade restrictive effects unless any person fulfilling the legal requirements is equally eligible to apply for and receive import licences, licence applications may be submitted on any business day prior to the customs clearance of the goods, and applications that are submitted in complete form are immediately approved within a maximum of 10 business days. Any developing country Member that was not a signatory to the Tokyo Round Code and has specific difficulty in meeting certain of the obligations under Article 2 may delay application of those obligations for up to two years.

(c) Non-automatic Import Licensing

Non-automatic import licensing is the catch-all term used to refer to all import licensing regimes that do not fall within the Article 2 definition of automatic import licensing systems. In addition to the general rules set forth in Article 1 of the Agreement, Article 3 provides an additional set of rules applicable to all such licensing systems. Non-automatic import licensing systems must not have trade restrictive effects and must be no more burdensome than absolutely necessary to administer the system. Members must publish sufficient information concerning their licensing procedures, including provisions concerning requests for derogations from licensing requirements.

Upon request of any Member, importing Members must provide information concerning licensing restrictions, import licences granted over a recent period, the distribution of licences among supplying countries, and import statistics relating to products subject to import licensing.

Members who administer quotas through import licences must publish overall amounts of quotas by quantity and value and the opening and closing dates of the quotas. If quotas are allocated among supplying countries, Members must inform the countries of their current allocations by quantity and value, and licences must specify the country. If quotas are not allocated, licence-holders are free to determine the source of supply. Members may not prevent importations of licensed products under a quota and must not discourage the full use of the quota.

Licences must be equally available to any person or organization that fulfils the legal requirements, and applicants who are denied a licence must have the right to an explanation of the denial and the right to appeal that denial. The Agreement requires that licence applications be processed in no more than 30 days if applications are considered on a first-come-first-served basis and no longer than 60 days if all applications are considered simultaneously. Finally, licences must be valid for a reasonable period of time, which must not be so short as to preclude imports.

(d) Institutions

Article 4 of the Agreement establishes the WTO's Committee on Import Licensing to oversee the administration of the Agreement. The Committee is comprised of representatives from all Members. The Committee is responsible for reviewing the operation of the Agreement at least every two years. To assist the Committee with this review, the WTO Secretariat will prepare a report based upon an annual questionnaire on import licensing procedures provided to all Members.

(e) Notification

A significant addition to the Agreement not found in the Tokyo Round Code is the addition of the notification requirements of Article 5. Under these provisions, Members must notify the Committee of the institution or amendment of licensing procedures within 60 days of their publication. Notifications must contain information concerning, *inter alia,* the products subject to the licensing procedure; contact points for information; administrative bodies that receive applications; the date and name of the publication where licensing procedures are published; and notification of whether the licence is automatic or non-automatic.

(f) Consultation and Dispute Settlement

Article 6 provides that consultations and dispute settlement are governed by the provisions GATT Articles XXII and XXIII, as elaborated and applied by the WTO's Dispute Settlement Understanding.

Part E:

Agreement on Implementation of Article VI (Anti-dumping)

1. INTRODUCTION

Dumping—the practice of selling a product into a foreign market at a price less than that charged for the product in the exporter's home market— has become an increasingly controversial issue over the past 10 to 15 years. Dumping has been recognized as an unfair trade practice since at least the beginning of this century when Canada implemented the first anti-dumping law in 1904 in an attempt to prevent the dumping of steel rails from the United States. The theory originally supporting anti-dumping law was that foreign producers operating within a closed domestic market are able to use their excessive profits gained in that market to sell their products at an unfairly low price in their export markets, thereby capturing foreign market share and eliminating foreign competition. In other words, anti-dumping laws were originally conceived as predatory pricing laws applied to imports. While current-day anti-dumping practice now bears little resemblance to this original theoretical foundation, anti-dumping laws are still largely defended on this anti-predatory basis.

2. THE PRE-WTO OBLIGATIONS CONCERNING ANTI-DUMPING

While not extensively used, the anti-dumping remedy was already well-known and accepted at the time of the original GATT and ITO negotiations. There was little discussion over the inclusion of an anti-dumping exception in the GATT 1947. The negotiators apparently accepted the view that dumping was a pernicious trade practice and required a corresponding remedy, that being GATT Article VI:1, which provided:

> The Contracting Parties recognize that dumping, by which products of one country are introduced into the commerce of another country at less than the

normal value of the products, is to be condemned if it causes or threatens material injury to an established industry in the territory of a contracting party or materially retards the establishment of a domestic industry.

While condemning (but not prohibiting) injurious dumping, Article VI also sets forth the basic rules for the determination of dumping and authorized the imposition of anti-dumping duties on dumped imports under certain conditions and in an amount no greater than the "margin of dumping" (that is, the difference between normal value and the export price of those imports).[111]

The first substantive review of the anti-dumping practice and GATT Article VI occurred during the Kennedy Round of GATT negotiations (1964-1967). These negotiations resulted in GATT's first anti-dumping Code, amplifying and clarifying the obligations of Article VI by providing more specific rules for the determination of dumping and injury, and establishing requirements for the imposition of provisional and final anti-dumping duties. Interestingly, as part of the negotiations, in 1966 the United States (which was soon to become one of the major anti-dumping proponents) questioned the entire concept of anti-dumping. These first attempts to interject true competition policy concepts into the realm of anti-dumping were effectively rebuffed by the EC.[112]

The Contracting Parties revisited anti-dumping during the Tokyo Round of Multilateral Trade Negotiations, where, in 1979, they concluded a new *Agreement on Implementation of Article VI of the General Agreement on*

---

[111] GATT Article VI:2 defines "normal value" in three ways:

(1) the comparable price, in the ordinary course of trade, for the like product when destined for consumption in the exporting country, or, in the absence of such domestic price,

(2) the highest comparable price for the like product for export to any third country in the ordinary course of trade, or

(3) the cost of production of the product in the country of origin plus a reasonable addition for selling cost and profit.

These alternative forms of normal value are commonly referred to as "home market price", "third country price" and "constructed value", respectively.

[112] In a note circulated as part of the negotiations, the U.S. delegation posed the following questions:

Should anti-dumping measures be limited to prevention of market monopolization by foreign exporters? . . . Should anti-dumping measures permit alignment of exporters' prices to meet competitive prices in the export market? Should such provision be limited to meeting the prices of foreign but not domestic competitors in the export market? . . . Where a seller lowers his price to gain entry, *i.e.*, consumer familiarity and acceptance, into an export market, should anti-dumping measures permit such price discrimination? . . . Where consumers' or competitors' information regarding changes in supply or demand varies in different markets, and price moves up or down in response to those variances, should anti-dumping measures permit such geographic price discrimination?" (See GATT Doc. TN.64/NTB/W/36, 10 January 1966.)

Tariffs and Trade.[113] The Tokyo Round Anti-dumping Code, primarily drafted by the United States and the EC, was substantially similar to the Kennedy Round Code, with the most notable exception being a lessening of the standard for finding injury.[114] The Tokyo Round Anti-dumping Code would remain in force for 15 years until the conclusion of the Uruguay Round, during which time the use of anti-dumping measures increased significantly.[115]

Between 1980 and 1989, GATT contracting parties initiated over 1,400 anti-dumping cases, averaging almost 150 new cases a year.[116] During the four-year period from 1990 to 1993, the number of new anti-dumping investigations totalled over 900, or approximately 227 new cases per year on average and more than 60 percent of the number of cases filed in the previous 10 years.[117] From July 1, 1994 to June 30, 1995, the WTO estimates that there were 160 new anti-dumping investigations initiated by WTO Members.[118]

The proliferation of new anti-dumping investigations under the Anti-dumping Code began to raise serious concerns over the application of , and the rationale behind, anti-dumping measures. Large exporters, in particular, began to complain of being increasingly subjected to anti-dumping investigations and duties abroad, charging that such measures were being used as non-tariff barriers to trade, rather than curbing unfair trade practices. On the other hand, however, certain import-competing industries continued to claim that anti-dumping laws were not strong enough to remedy the full effects of injurious dumping. Rather than questioning the validity of existing anti-dumping laws, many of these industries began to press for changes which would make it easier to obtain anti-dumping relief.

---

[113] GATT, BISD 26S/171. The *Agreement on Implementation of Article VI of the General Agreement on Tariffs and Trade* had been more commonly referred to as the "Anti-dumping Code".

[114] The Kennedy Round Code provided that in order to impose anti-dumping measures, dumped imports had to be the "primary cause" of material injury to a domestic industry. The Tokyo Round Anti-dumping Code, at U.S. insistence, provided a lesser injury standard in that dumped imports only had to be "a cause" of material injury to a domestic industry before anti-dumping duties could be assessed.

[115] The Tokyo Round Anti-dumping Code was formally terminated at the end of 1996, following a two-year transition period.

[116] United States General Accounting Office, *Use of the GATT Antidumping Code,* Pub. No. GAO/NSLAD-90-238FS (1990) at 4.

[117] Calculations by the authors from Semi-annual Reports filed under Article 14:4 of the Anti-dumping Code, GATT Docs. ADP/48/Adds. 2-8, ADP/53/Adds. 2-11, ADP/62/Adds. 2-10, ADP/70/Adds. 2-10, ADP/81/Adds. 2-10, ADP/88/Adds. 2-12, and ADP/102/Adds. 2-11.

[118] *WTO FOCUS,* No. 7, December 1995, at 10. These figures likely under-estimate the actual number of new cases, as 34 Members had not submitted notifications of their anti-dumping activities for the period July 1 to December 31, 1994, and 53 Members had not submitted notifications for the period January 1 to June 30, 1995.

3. THE URUGUAY ROUND ANTI-DUMPING NEGOTIATIONS

It is interesting to note that, despite the growing number of anti-dumping cases in the 1980s and the increasing concern over the use of the remedy, the Punta del Este declaration that launched the Uruguay Round did not specifically mention anti-dumping as a subject for negotiation.[119] Instead, anti-dumping issues would be covered under the generic mandate calling for a review, and, to the extent necessary, improvements to all Agreements and Arrangements negotiated as part of the Tokyo Round. While this appeared to indicate that anti-dumping would have a low priority during the negotiations, in fact it became one of the most contentious issues during the later part of the Round.

During the course of the negotiations, the United States and the EC consistently took the position that dumping was a practice to be deterred and remedied to a greater extent than was the case under the existing Tokyo Round Code. Consequently, these countries called for changes to the Code which would facilitate the use of the remedy and increase the size of resulting duties. Most other countries (Canada, the Nordic countries, Singapore, Hong Kong and Japan, in particular) sought to strengthen the disciplines and to provide greater procedural uniformity and consistency in the application of anti-dumping measures. Such changes would make the remedy more difficult to obtain and would result in lower or no duties in more cases. Some countries went further, calling into question the very need for such rules and proposing that the entire concept of dumping be reviewed to determine whether it continued to be supportable from an economic perspective. As a result of the obvious differences between the parties, it is not surprising that little was accomplished in the anti-dumping negotiations during the first two years. In light of such minimal progress, Ministers at the Montreal Mid-term Meeting in late 1988 could do little more than encourage negotiators to accelerate the pace of their work.

By early 1990, the anti-dumping negotiations had become quite bitter and stayed that way for the remainder of the Round. After several contentious drafts, the negotiations stalled. By mid-1990 it had become apparent that anti-dumping, along with agriculture and services, was now one of the major negotiating issues. The negotiating group was unable to even produce a draft text of an agreement for the Brussels Ministerial Meeting in late 1990, one of only a very few groups unable to do so. Instead, the anti-dumping negotiators could only pose a series of questions to Ministers, the answers to which would have presumably provided the basis of an agreement. While consensus was reached by Ministers on a few of the less controversial questions, the Brussels

---

[119] It is also interesting to note that the "Leutwiler Report" of 1985, which formed the basis of much of the Uruguay Round agenda, also made no specific recommendations concerning anti-dumping rules.

Meeting collapsed over agriculture before any of the much more controversial and important questions could be addressed.

Despite repeated attempts to complete the anti-dumping negotiations following the collapse of the Brussels Meeting, by late 1991 no consensus draft agreement had yet been developed. Consequently, in an attempt to bring the negotiations to a conclusion, Arthur Dunkel called on the Chair of the negotiating group to draft an "arbitrated" rather than a negotiated text, for inclusion in a *Draft Final Act*, hoping that such an arbitrated text would be marginally acceptable to all participants in light of achievement in other areas. This was done and a *Draft Final Act*, including the arbitrated anti-dumping text, was distributed to all participants in late December 1991. Some participants immediately identified the draft anti-dumping agreement as being unacceptable. In particular, the agreement had not sufficiently addressed two issues of importance to the United States—anti-circumvention and the so-called "standard of review" applicable to anti-dumping disputes.

Notwithstanding the importance of anti-dumping and the unacceptability of the draft Agreement, no further substantive negotiations took place on the text for almost a year. Other issues simply took priority. In late 1992 and early 1993, renewed efforts were undertaken in all areas to finalize the results of the Round. In this context, the United States again pressed for fundamental changes to the anti-dumping text. In the closing stages of the negotiations the United States demanded that 11 specific changes be made to the Dunkel Draft text, some uncontroversial, others very controversial. In the end, in exchange for some concessions in other areas, a number of the demanded changes were accepted. While the United States did not obtain all its demands, it did obtain enough to satisfy certain domestic constituencies and could declare itself sufficiently satisfied with the results. The draft Agreement was then finalized, with the deletion of certain provisions concerning anti-circumvention, the inclusion of other provisions addressing standard of review, and the adoption of a number of Ministerial decisions addressing both issues.

4. THE *AGREEMENT ON IMPLEMENTATION OF ARTICLE VI OF THE GENERAL AGREEMENT ON TARIFFS AND TRADE 1994*

While based on the 1979 Anti-dumping Code, the new *Agreement on Implementation of Article VI of the General Agreement on Tariffs and Trade 1994* introduces important changes and new rules in some areas, and is much more detailed and specific in all areas.

(a) Principles

Article 1 of the Agreement establishes the basic principle that Members should apply anti-dumping measures only under the circumstances provided in and pursuant to investigations conducted in accordance with Article VI of GATT 1994 and the Anti-dumping Agreement. Article 1 also provides that the Anti-dumping Agreement governs the application of Article VI of GATT 1994 when actions are taken pursuant to anti-dumping legislation or regulations.

(b) Determination of Dumping

Before a Member can apply anti-dumping duties on an imported good, the Agreement requires the Member to make two separate determinations: (i) a determination that the subject imports are "dumped"; and (ii) a determination that those dumped imports have caused, are causing or are threatening to cause "material injury" to the relevant domestic industry. Article 2 of the Agreement then establishes detailed rules governing the determination of whether imports are "dumped"—that is, introduced into the commerce of another country at less than their normal value. Generally speaking, an imported good is being dumped when its "normal value" exceeds its "export price". Thus, a determination of dumping requires the calculation of two preliminary values, "normal value" and "export price", and then a comparison between these two values.

(i) Normal Value

Article 2.1 sets out the general rule that a product is being dumped "if the export price of the product exported from one country to another is less than the comparable price, in the ordinary course of trade, for the like product[120] when destined for consumption in the exporting country". Under the basic rule of Article 2.1, normal value is first to be considered to be the price charged for the product in the exporter's home market, and a product will be considered dumped when the export price is less than this home market price.

When there are no sales of the like product in the ordinary course of trade in the home market of the exporter or when home market sales do not permit a proper comparison because of the particular market situation or because of the proper comparison because of the particular market situation or because of the low volume of home market sales,[121] Article 2.2 permits the determination of

---

[120] Article 2.6 defines the term "like product" for purposes of the Agreement as meaning "a product that is identical, i.e. alike in all respects to the product under consideration, or in the absence of such a product, another product which, although not alike in all respects, has characteristics closely resembling those of the product under consideration".

[121] A footnote to Article 2 states that home market sales should normally be considered a sufficient quantity for the determination of normal value when home market sales constitute five percent or more of the exported merchandise that is subject to the anti-dumping investigation. Members are admonished that a lower ratio should be considered sufficient when evidence demonstrates that the lower ratio is of sufficient magnitude. This provision is often referred to as the "viability test".

dumping to be made through a comparison of export price to a "third country price" or a "constructed value". For these purposes, a third country price is the comparable price of that product when exported to an "appropriate" third country, as long as that price is representative. A constructed value is the cost of production in the country of origin plus a "reasonable amount" for selling, general and administrative costs (often referred to as "SG and A") and for profit. Article 2.2.2 clarifies the calculation of a reasonable amount of profit and SG and A by requiring that such figures be based upon actual data pertaining to production and sale in the ordinary course of trade of the like product by the exporter under investigation. When profit and SG and A cannot be determined in this manner, an investigating Member may resort to three alternatives: (i) the actual amounts incurred and realized by the same exporter on the same general category of products; (ii) the weighted average actual profit and SG and A incurred and realized on the like product by other exporters subject to investigation; or (iii) "any other reasonable method", as long as profit does not exceed the amount of profit normally realized on the same general category of products by other exporters or producers in the country of origin.[122]

(ii) Sales Below Cost of Production

One of the more contentious issues of the negotiations was the treatment of sales below the cost of production. Under the Tokyo Round Code, most major users of anti-dumping measures disregarded home market or third country below-cost sales as being outside the ordinary course of trade. Because including below cost sales in the calculation of normal value would tend to lower normal value and, consequently, lower dumping margins, the issue of disregarding below cost sales became a politically charged issue between Members seeking stronger anti-dumping rules and those seeking to limit anti-dumping measures.

While the Tokyo Round Code gave no guidance as to when sales below cost could be disregarded, Article 2.2.1 of the Agreement now provides detailed rules defining cost of production and the circumstances when below cost sales may be disregarded. The Agreement first defines cost of production

---

[122] Article 2.2.2 of the Agreement has been viewed by many as an improvement on past practices. For example, the requirement that profit and SG and A be determined based upon actual data is seen as a significant improvement over the past practice of the United States, which had a statutory minimum eight percent profit figure and a minimum 10 percent SG and A figure in its anti-dumping law. Most companies did not consider these minimum figures were commercially reasonable. On the other hand, the requirement that profit and SG and A be calculated based upon sales "in the ordinary course of trade" is seen as validating the practice of the EU of calculating profit based only upon sales made at prices that are above the cost of production. Many consider that a certain amount of sales below the cost of production are often made in the ordinary course of trade, and therefore are relevant to the calculation of overall profit.

as fixed and variable costs of production plus SG and A. Cost of production normally must be calculated based upon the exporter's or producer's records, as long as the costs reasonably reflect the costs associated with the production and sale of the product under investigation and the records are kept in accordance with the generally accepted accounting principles of the exporting country. In addition, the calculation of cost must be adjusted for non-recurring costs and for costs associated with start-up operations. These requirements are generally considered to have brought the definition of cost of production in the anti-dumping context closer to commercial reality.

Home market and third country sales below cost of production may be treated as outside the ordinary course of trade (and may therefore be disregarded) only if the investigating authority determines that such sales are: (i) made within an extended period of time;[123] (ii) in substantial quantities;[124] and (iii) at prices that do not provide for the recovery of all costs within a reasonable period of time. However, sales that are below cost at the time of the sale, but above the weighted average per unit cost for the period under investigation, will be considered to provide for the recovery of costs within a reasonable period of time.

(iii) Export Price

The second preliminary calculation that must be undertaken is that of the product's "export price". The Agreement extends investigating authorities a wide degree of discretion in calculating export price in certain situations where the export price is deemed unreliable because of some association or relationship between the exporter and the importer. In such circumstances, Article 2.3 of the Agreement allows the construction of an export price based upon the price at which the product is sold to the first independent purchaser. If the product is not sold to an independent purchaser, or if the product is not sold in the condition as imported (for example, the product was further manufactured prior to sale), the export price may be calculated "on such reasonable basis as the authorities may determine".

(iv) Fair Comparison of Export Price to Normal Value

Once normal value and export price have been determined, they must then be compared with one another to determine if dumping exists, and, if so,

---

[123] Footnote 4 to the Agreement provides that this is normally to be one year, but in no case less than six months.

[124] Footnote 5 to the Agreement provides that below cost sales are made in substantial quantities when the weighted average selling price of the home market or third country transactions is less than the weighted average per unit costs, or the below cost sales represent 20 percent or more of the home market or third country sales under consideration.

the "margin of dumping". An important achievement of the Agreement is its express requirement in Article 2.4 of a fair comparison between the export price and the normal value. This requirement is important in that, over the history of anti-dumping measures, certain "tilts" began to appear in the calculation of dumping margins. For example, several anti-dumping regimes required the deduction of certain expenses from the export price but denied the same deduction from normal value. The net effect of such requirements was therefore to tilt the comparison calculation in favour of the domestic petitioners by increasing the likelihood that dumping would be found to exist.

To counter such tilts, Article 2.4 requires that the comparison between the export price and the normal value be made at the same level of trade (normally the ex-factory level) using sales made as nearly as possible at the same time. Administering authorities must make due allowance for any differences that affect price comparability, including, but not limited to, differences in the conditions and terms of sale, taxes, levels of trade, quantities, and physical characteristics of the merchandise. If sales are made to affiliates in the export market, allowances for costs incurred between importation and resale to an unaffiliated customer (duties and taxes, for example) and for profits must also be made.

When the comparison of export price to normal value requires a currency conversion, the exchange rate on the date of sale must be used unless the sale of currency on forward markets is directly linked to the export sale, in which case the exchange rate on the forward sale must be used. Exchange rate fluctuations must be ignored, and exporters must be allowed 60 days in which to adjust prices to reflect sustained movements in exchange rates.

Another tilt that was often employed by some Members was to compare export prices in individual sales to a weighted average normal value of all sales, which also tended to result in higher dumping margins.[125] This practice was argued to be necessary to counter so-called "targeted dumping"—that is, dumping aimed at specific customers or regions. The Agreement appears to have struck a balance between these two competing concerns. Article 2.4.2 states that dumping margins must "normally" be calculated on the basis of a comparison of a weighted average normal value with a weighted average export price or by a comparison of normal value and export prices on a

---

[125] The effect of this practice can be seen in the following example. If a foreign producer made three sales in the home market at an ex-factory price of $1, $2 and $3, respectively, and three sales in the export market at the same prices, the weighted average ex-factory sales price in both markets would be $2. If the weighted average price in the export market ($2) is compared to the weighted average price in the home market ($2), no dumping has occurred. However, if the individual export prices ($1, $2 and $3) are compared to the weighted average home market price ($2), the sale at $1 will be considered to be dumped.

transaction-to-transaction basis.[126] However, individual export prices may be compared to a weighted average normal value when the authorities find a pattern of export prices that differ significantly among different purchasers, regions, or time periods. An administering authority employing this methodology must explain why the differences cannot be accounted for through weighted-average-to-weighted-average comparison or a transaction-to-transaction comparison.

(c) Determination of Injury

As noted above, dumping, in and of itself, is insufficient to justify the imposition of an anti-dumping duty. There must be consequential injury resulting from that dumping. Therefore, the second phase of any anti-dumping case is an "injury" investigation. In the anti-dumping context, injury may take one of three forms: material injury to a domestic industry; the threat of material injury to a domestic industry; or the material retardation of the establishment of a domestic industry.[127] Article 3 of the Agreement provides that an injury determination under Article VI of GATT 1994 must be based upon positive evidence of both: (i) the volume of dumped imports and the effect of dumped imports on the prices of the like products in the domestic market; and (ii) the impact of dumped imports on domestic producers of the like product.

(i) Factors to be Taken into Account

With respect to the volume of dumped imports, Members are directed to consider whether there has been a significant increase in such imports. Concerning the effect of dumped imports on prices, Members must consider whether there has been significant price undercutting, price suppression or price depression by the dumped imports. However, no one or several of these factors is decisive.

Regarding the impact of dumped imports on the domestic industry, Article 3.4 requires an evaluation of all relevant factors bearing on the state of the domestic industry, including actual and potential decline in sales, profits,

---

[126] Some Members claim that this provision is limited to anti-dumping investigations only, and does not apply to any subsequent administrative reviews of a dumping margin because the specific language of Article 2.4.2 includes the phrase "during the investigation phase". However, because Article 2.4.2 specifically invokes the fair comparison requirement of Article 2.4, which is not limited to investigations, a strong argument exists that a comparison of individual export transactions to a weighted average normal value in a subsequent review would violate the Agreement to the extent that such a comparison was unfair.

[127] This definition of injury is found in footnote 9 to the Agreement. Throughout this chapter, as in the Agreement itself, the term "injury" will be used to refer to all three types of injury.

output, market share, productivity, return on investments, or utilization of capacity; factors affecting domestic prices; the magnitude of the dumping margin; and negative effects on cash flow, inventories, employment, wages, growth, the ability to raise capital or investments. Again, this list is not intended to be exhaustive and no one or several of these factors should be considered decisive.

(ii) Causation

Article 3.5 of the Agreement requires a link between the dumped imports and the injury being suffered by the domestic industry (referred to as the "causation" required). It must be demonstrated that dumped imports, through the effects of dumping, are causing the claimed injury. This Article directs administering authorities to examine any factors other than the dumped imports that may be causing injury to the domestic industry, and cautions authorities not to attribute the injury being caused by such other factors to the dumped imports. Factors relevant to this inquiry would include the volume and prices of imports not sold at dumped prices, contraction in demand or changes in consumption patterns, trade restrictive practices of and competition between the foreign and domestic products, developments in technology and the export performance and productivity of the domestic industry.

(iii) Cumulation

In some anti-dumping investigations, imports of like products from many countries are subject to investigation at the same time. In these circumstances, Article 3.3 provides that the injury effects of the dumped imports from all sources may be assessed all together, or "cumulatively", but only if the authorities first find that: (a) the dumping margins for the imports from each country under investigation are more than *de minimis;*[128] (b) the volume of imports from each country under investigation is not negligible;[129] and (c) cumulation is appropriate in light of the conditions of competition between the imports and the conditions of competition between the imports and the domestic product.

(iv) Threat of Material Injury

A special situation arises when injury from dumped imports has not yet occurred, but is threatened to occur in the future. Article 3.7 provides that any

---

[128] Dumping margins are considered *de minimis* under Article 5.8 if the margin of dumping is less than two percent, expressed as a percentage of the export price.

[129] Article 5.8 provides that imports from a given country are normally to be considered negligible if imports from that country are less than three percent of all imports of the like product, unless countries which individually account for less than three percent of imports of the like product collectively account for more than seven percent of all imports of the like product.

threat of material injury determination must be based on facts and not merely on allegation, conjecture or remote possibility. In rendering a threat determination, the change in circumstances that would create a situation in which dumping would cause present injury must be foreseen and imminent. The factors to be considered in a threat determination include the rate of increase of dumped imports and the likelihood of increased imports in the future, excess or increased capacity of the foreign producers, the price suppressing or depressing effect of the dumped imports, the likely future demand for such imports and inventories of the product under investigation. These factors taken as a whole must lead to the conclusion that further dumped imports are imminent and, unless protective action is taken, material injury would occur.

(d) Definition of Domestic Industry

In any anti-dumping investigation, an important preliminary issue is what constitutes the "domestic industry". The scope of the domestic industry is important to determine if the requirements for the initiation of an investigation have been met and in making the necessary injury determination. Article 4 defines the domestic industry as the domestic producers of the like product as a whole, or those producers that constitute a major proportion of the total domestic production of the like product.[130]

In some cases, dumping and consequent injury may be occurring only in one region or area of the importing country. Thus, Article 4.1(ii) provides that in exceptional circumstances, the territory of a Member may be divided into two or more competitive markets, and the producers in each market may be considered to be a separate industry for the purposes of an anti-dumping investigation, provided that two pre-conditions are met: (a) the producers in each market sell all or almost all of their production in their respective market; and (b) the demand in a given market is not served to any substantial degree by producers outside of the market. In the case of such "regional markets", injury may be found to exist even where the major portion of the total domestic industry is not being injured, provided that there is a concentration of dumped imports into the isolated regional market, and dumped imports are causing injury to producers of all or almost all production in that market. Under Article 4.2, special rules will then apply to the imposition of any resulting anti-dumping duty.

Under Article 4.3, where two or more countries have formed a customs union, such as the EU, the relevant industry in the entire customs area must be taken to be the domestic industry for anti-dumping purposes, subject to the regional market exception of Article 4.2.

---

[130] Article 4.1(i) provides that domestic producers that are related to exporters or importers or that are themselves importers of the subject merchandise may be excluded from the domestic industry.

(e) Initiation and Subsequent Investigation

The basic rules for the initiation of an anti-dumping investigation and its subsequent conduct are found in Article 5 of the Agreement. Paragraph 1 of Article 5 provides that generally, a dumping investigation can only be initiated upon the written application by or on behalf of a domestic industry.[131] An application for the initiation of an investigation must include evidence of dumping, injury and causation, and may not be based on simple assertion unsubstantiated by any evidence. More specifically, the Agreement requires that the following information be included in any petition for anti-dumping relief:

- the identity of the applicant and the domestic producers of the like product and a description of the volume and value of the domestic production of the like product;
- a description of the allegedly dumped product, the countries of origin in question and the identity of all known foreign producers, exporters and importers;
- information on the normal value and export price of the merchandise in question; and
- information relevant to the injury determination.

Administering authorities must then examine the accuracy and adequacy of the information submitted to determine if there is sufficient evidence to justify the initiation of an investigation.

Under Article 5.4, an anti-dumping investigation must not be initiated unless the administering authority determines, based on an examination of the degree of support for the petition, that the request is filed "by or on behalf of the domestic industry". For this purpose, a petition will be considered to have been filed by or on behalf of a domestic industry only if it is supported by those domestic producers that constitute more than 50 percent of the total production of the like product, produced by that portion of the domestic industry that has expressed an opinion (that is, either support or opposition) on the petition. However, in any case, an investigation cannot be initiated unless the producers expressly supporting the application account for at least 25 percent or more of the total domestic production of the like product.

In order to prevent unnecessary commercial disruption, the administering authority is to avoid any publication of a petition that it has received until it has decided whether to pursue an investigation. Evidence of dumping and

---

[131] Under Article 5.6, Members' administering authorities are permitted to initiate anti-dumping investigations on their own accord, without being requested to do so by the domestic industry, but only if the authority has sufficient evidence of dumping, injury and causation to justify the initiation.

injury is to be considered simultaneously, both when deciding whether to initiate an investigation and during the investigation itself once it has been commenced. Any petition or investigation is to be rejected or terminated as soon as the administering authority is satisfied that there is insufficient evidence. There is also to be immediate termination where the margin of dumping is found to be *de minimis*, or the level of imports negligible.[132] Investigations are normally to be concluded within 12 months, but in no case more than 18 months after their initiation.

Article 6 of the Agreement sets forth certain guidelines concerning the manner and form in which evidence may be submitted and considered during an investigation, including minimum time periods for the submission of information, the opportunity for interested parties to present information, and the protection of confidential information. In addition, Article 6 and Annex I present detailed procedures for on-the-spot verifications of any information that may have been submitted.

(f) Provisional Measures

Preliminary, or so-called "provisional", anti-dumping measures (that is, anti-dumping duties levied while an investigation is ongoing and before a final determination has been made) can be applied by an investigating Member only upon satisfaction of three pre-conditions: (i) an investigation has been initiated in accordance with the Agreement, public notice of the investigation has been given and parties to the investigation have been given adequate opportunity to submit information and comment on the investigation; (ii) the Member has made positive preliminary determinations of both dumping and injury; and (iii) the Member has determined that such provisional measures are necessary to prevent further injury during the ongoing investigation. Provisional measures may not be imposed any earlier than 60 days from the date the investigation was first initiated and should not be in place for more than four months, and in no case longer than six months. If, as part of an investigation, a Member determines a lower duty would be sufficient to offset the injury, these time limits are extended to six and nine months, respectively.

(g) Price Undertakings

In many cases, anti-dumping investigations are terminated without the imposition of provisional or final anti-dumping duties, when the exporters at

---

[132] Recall that dumping margins are to be considered *de minimis* under Article 5.8 if the margin is less than two percent, expressed as a percentage of the export price, and that imports are to be considered negligible if less than three percent of all imports of the like product, unless countries that individually account for less than three percent of all imports of the like product collectively account for more than seven percent of all imports of the like product.

issue agree to adjust their prices to eliminate the margin of dumping, and, as a result, the consequent injury. Article 8 permits such "price undertakings" in certain circumstances. In particular, price undertakings must be given voluntarily and should not be entered into prior to any preliminary determinations of both dumping and injury.

If a price undertaking is entered into, the investigation must be continued at the request of the exporter or upon decision of the authorities. If the subsequent investigation then results in a negative determination of dumping or injury, the undertaking automatically lapses, unless it is determined that the negative determination was the result of the price undertaking. Authorities may require the periodic submission of information to permit verification of the fulfilment of the undertaking. If an undertaking is violated, the administering authority may immediately apply provisional measures using the best information available. Definitive duties also may be applied retroactively on products entered for consumption not more than 90 days prior to the imposition of the provisional duties, but in no case earlier than the violation of the undertaking.

(h) Imposition and Collection of Anti-dumping Duties

A Member that renders definitive positive determinations of both dumping and injury in accordance with the provisions of the Agreement is then permitted to impose anti-dumping duties on the subject imports. The imposition of anti-dumping duties is permissive, and the determination as to whether an anti-dumping duty should be equal to or less than the margin of dumping is left to the discretion of the Member. In no case is the amount of an anti-dumping duty to exceed the margin of dumping that has been determined to exist.

When anti-dumping duties are imposed, they must be assessed on a non-discriminatory basis on imports from all sources that were found to be dumped, except those that have entered into undertakings. For exporters or producers that did not export the product during the period of investigation, but subsequently shipped merchandise to the country applying anti-dumping duties, the authorities must promptly conduct an investigation on an accelerated basis to determine an individual margin for such producers or exporters.

For those Members that assess duties on a retrospective basis[133] (such as the United States), the Member must determine final anti-dumping liability normally within 12 months, and in no case more than 18 months after the date of a request for final assessment. Any refunds normally must be made within 90 days of the determination of final liability.

---

[133] "Retrospective" in this context means that the final liability for anti-dumping duties is not determined until some time after the products have entered the importing country, and liquidation is suspended until such a final determination is made.

Countries assessing anti-dumping duties on a prospective basis[134] (such as Canada and the EU) must, upon request, promptly refund any duties paid in excess of the dumping margin. The decision of whether to grant a refund should be made within 12 months and in no case later than 18 months from the date of the request, and the refund should be paid within 90 days of the decision.

(i) Retroactivity

Generally speaking, provisional duties may only be applied to imports during the course of an anti-dumping investigation once the authorities have made preliminary dumping and injury determinations. Once a final determination is made, duties may then be definitively assessed on all imports of the product that had been subject to such provisional duties. If the definitive duty is determined to be higher than the preliminary duty, the difference cannot be collected on products imported during the period preliminary duties were in effect. If the definitive duty is less, the difference must be refunded.

If only a positive determination of threat of material injury is made, duties may only be applied to goods imported into the country as of the date of that final injury determination. Duties cannot be assessed retroactively on any products imported during the period that provisional duties were in effect (unless there is a finding that injury would have occurred during the preliminary period but for the imposition of the provisional duty) and all duties so collected must be returned. If a final determination is negative, then any duties paid or security posted during the preliminary stage must be returned and no definitive duty may be imposed.

Article 10 does provide, however, that in certain critical circumstances, a retroactive anti-dumping duty may be imposed on products that were imported as early as 90 days before the imposition of provisional duties. The authority must first determine that: (i) there is a history of dumping causing injury, or the importer was or should have been aware that the exporter practised injurious dumping; and (ii) the injury has been caused by massive imports of dumped products and that these products were imported over a relatively short period of time. Under these circumstances, duties may be assessed retroactively, as a form of penalty, if the investigating authority considers them necessary to prevent injury from recurring.

(j) Duration of Anti-dumping Duties and Undertakings

An important achievement of the anti-dumping negotiations is the inclusion of a new "sunset" provision in the Agreement. Article 11 provides that an

---

[134] "Prospective" in this context means that the final anti-dumping duty liability is assessed at the time of actual importation.

anti-dumping duty may remain in force only as long as necessary to counter-act the dumping that is causing injury. Members may review the need for continued anti-dumping duties on their own initiative and, after a reasonable time after the imposition of a duty, must review an anti-dumping measure upon request of an interested party submitting positive evidence substantiating the need for a review. If the authorities determine, as a result of the review, that the duty is no longer warranted, it is to be terminated immediately.

In any case, however, Article 11.3 provides that definitive anti-dumping duties and price undertakings must be terminated no later than five years from the date of their imposition, unless the authorities determine that the expira-tion of the duty or the undertaking would likely lead to the continuation or recurrence of dumping and injury. This "sunset" review must be conducted under the rules of evidence and procedures set out in Article 6.

(k) Public Notice and Explanation of Determinations

Article 12 establishes the requirements for public notification of anti-dumping investigations and determinations. When Members are satisfied that there is sufficient evidence to initiate an investigation, they must provide public notice and must also notify all known interested parties. The public notice must contain the name of the exporting country and the product subject to investigation, the date of initiation of the investigation, the basis upon which dumping and injury are alleged, the address to which representations by interested parties should be directed, and the time limits for the presentation of information.

Public notice must also be given of any preliminary or final determina-tions or the conclusion or termination of undertakings. Such notice must contain adequate explanations on dumping and injury, any margins established and the methodology used to calculate those margins and the main reasons supporting the determination. All public notices must protect confi-dential information. These requirements concerning public notice apply equally to reviews under Article 11 and any decisions to apply duties retroac-tively under Article 10.

(l) Judicial Review

The requirement for the impartial review of certain administrative deci-sions is found in Article 13 of the Agreement. Members must maintain judicial, arbitral or administrative tribunals for the purpose of the prompt review of administrative actions relating to final determinations and reviews of anti-dumping determinations. The review procedures must be independent of the authorities responsible for the determination under review.

(m) Developing Country Members

Like many of the other WTO agreements, the Anti-dumping Agreement encourages special consideration for developing country Members. Under

Article 15, Members are required to take into account the special situation of developing country Members when considering the application of anti-dumping measures, including the consideration of constructive remedies.

(n) Institutions

Part II of the Agreement establishes the Committee on Anti-dumping Practices, composed of representatives from each Member. Members are required to report to the Committee all preliminary and final anti-dumping actions taken by them and must notify the Committee of those authorities charged with the conduct of anti-dumping investigations and their domestic procedures governing such investigations. Under Article 18.5, Members are required to notify the Committee of any changes to their anti-dumping laws. The Committee is further charged with reviewing annually the implementation and operation of the Agreement, and reporting the results to the Council for Trade in Goods.

One additional issue which the Committee has been specifically charged with is that of so-called "anti-circumvention measures". This was done by way of the "Decision on Anti-circumvention" agreed to as part of the Uruguay Round final package. Circumvention, or the practice of making export sales in a manner so as to evade anti-dumping duties, was a difficult issue during the negotiations, and remained unresolved. While the United States pressed for rules to counter circumvention and permit the application of anti-circumvention duties, no specific text could be agreed to. Certain draft provisions that had been included in the Agreement were removed at the last moment due to U.S. dissatisfaction with these proposed provisions. There apparently continue to be significantly differing views on the effect and intent of the Decision on Anti-circumvention and on anti-circumvention measures generally.[135] In any case, the issue has now been referred to the Committee "for resolution".

(o) Dispute Settlement

Article 17 of the Agreement sets forth the special rules for dispute settlement for anti-dumping disputes. The Article first states that the provi-

---

[135] For example, the United States is apparently of the view that "the Ministerial Decision constitutes a recognition of the legitimacy of anti-circumvention measures and does not preclude members [*sic*] from maintaining, modifying or enacting anti-circumvention measures at this time" (U.S. Statement of Administrative Action, at 149). Canada, on the other hand, has stated that "no solution could be found regarding anti-circumvention issues. . . . The absence of such a provision [in the Agreement] may eventually require recourse to the WTO's dispute settlement procedures should Member countries try to extend their anti-dumping measures beyond the bounds of their original investigations" (Canadian Statement on Implementation, at 4900).

sions of the WTO's Dispute Settlement Understanding apply to disputes arising under the Agreement, except as otherwise provided in the Agreement itself. The Agreement requires Members to enter into consultations, and to seek mutually acceptable resolutions to disputes as envisioned in the DSU.

At the insistence of the United States, Article 17.6 provides a more deferential standard of review governing those dispute settlement panels reviewing anti-dumping disputes. During the negotiations, the United States feared that WTO panels would not give appropriate deference to U.S. administering authorities that had rendered anti-dumping determinations. As a result, Article 17.6 requires panels to determine whether the authority's establishment of the facts in the case was proper and whether the evaluation of those facts was unbiased and objective. If a panel finds that the authority's establishment of the facts was proper and the evaluation was unbiased and objective, the panel must uphold the determination even if the panel would have reached a different conclusion. This effectively requires that panels extend some deference to the factual determinations of administering authorities.

With respect to interpretations of the Agreement itself, panels must rely upon customary rules of interpretation of public international law. If the panel finds that a provision is subject to more than one "permissible" interpretation, the panel must uphold the authority's determination if it rests upon one of these permissible interpretations.[136]

(p) Final Provisions

Article 18 presents the final obligations of the Members with respect to the implementation of the Agreement. No specific action against dumped exports from another Member may be taken except in accordance with GATT 1994, as interpreted by the Agreement. No reservations may be entered with respect to the provisions of the Agreement without the consent of the Members. The provisions of the Agreement are made applicable to investigations and reviews initiated after January 1, 1995. Members are required to change their laws and regulations to be in conformity with the Agreement and Members must report all such changes to the Committee.

---

[136] In a further Ministerial decision agreed to as part of the Uruguay Round final package (the "Decision on Review of Article 17.6 of the Agreement on Implementation of Article VI of the General Agreement on Tariffs and Trade 1994"), Members have agreed to review the standard set forth in Article 17.6 with a view to considering whether it is capable of general application.

Part F:

Subsidies and Countervailing Measures

1. INTRODUCTION

The granting of governmental subsidies that distort international trade and efforts to discipline such subsidies have proved to be two of the most intractable problems in the development of international trade law. In simplified terms, the intractability of the problem can be ascribed to two opposing views concerning the use of such subsidies. On the one hand, many countries view the use of economic aid to business to be an important aspect of assisting economic growth and development. On the other hand, other countries consider that granting subsidies to business constitutes an unfair advantage. Their own domestic producers should not be required to compete against the treasuries of foreign governments. This second group therefore considers that there should be strong disciplines on the granting of subsidies which have effects on international trade. In addition, there should be effective remedies, including the countervailing duty, that can be quickly invoked to offset any negative effects that might arise from another government's subsidies. In contrast, the first group generally has been opposed to further disciplines on the use of most types of subsidies and instead hold the view that it is the remedy of the countervailing duty which has distorted trade and needs to be further controlled.

While the GATT has long provided a number of obligations related to subsidization and concomitant remedies (most importantly the countervailing duty), these obligations were considered to be subject to a number of problems, not the least of which was their weak disciplines and legal uncertainty. Inevitably, these deficiencies led to an increasing number of conflicts. The WTO's *Subsidies and Countervailing Measures Agreement* now goes some way to finally bringing more rigorous discipline and clarity to the rules that govern this area.

In order to provide some context, this part of chapter 3 begins with an historical account of rule development in the subsidy and countervailing duty area. The negotiations leading to the Agreement are then discussed. The provisions of the Agreement are then reviewed in detail.

2. THE PRE-WTO OBLIGATIONS CONCERNING SUBSIDIES AND COUNTERVAILING MEASURES

Initially, the only provision in the GATT 1947 governing the use of subsidies by contracting parties was an obligation under Article XVI to notify the GATT of all types of subsidies, both export and domestic,[137] that were being granted, and to consult with other contracting parties on any subsidies that may be causing prejudice to the interests of others.

These obligations comprised the whole of the original GATT 1947 Article XVI (or what is now paragraph A of Article XVI). Article XVI was subsequently amended in 1955 with the addition of what is now paragraph B to that Article. This 1955 addition related only to the use of export subsidies and divided such subsidies into those granted to "primary products"[138] and those bestowed on all other "non-primary products". With respect to export subsidies on primary products, contracting parties were merely required to "seek to avoid" the granting of export subsidies on such primary products, and such subsidies were not to be applied so as to result in a contracting party having "more than an equitable share of the world export trade" in the relevant product.

With respect to export subsidies granted on non-primary products, contracting parties were to seek to grant such subsidies if the subsidy resulted in a sale of the product for export at a price lower than the price charged in the domestic market. No restrictions were imposed on the use of domestic subsidies other than the obligations of notification and consultation found in Article XVI, Paragraph A. The prevailing view at the time was that governments simply could not afford any significant use of subsidies and therefore no further rules-based disciplines would be required.

With respect to the treatment of countervailing duties under the GATT 1947, from the beginning Article VI allowed an importing country to impose a special import tax, or "countervailing duty", to offset the effect of all forms of subsidies, whether direct or indirect, export or domestic, and regardless of whether the subsidy at issue was otherwise permitted under Article XVI. Among other problems, Article VI provided no guidance as to what was to be considered to be a subsidy for countervailing duty purposes nor how the amount of any subsidy was to be measured.

The major limitation placed on the use of the countervailing duty was found in paragraph 6 of Article VI, which required that before a countervail-

---

[137] There has long been a distinction in international trade between subsidies which are made contingent on the export of the product (so-called "export subsidies") and those which are granted regardless of whether a product is exported or consumed domestically (so-called "domestic subsidies").

[138] For the purposes of Article XVI, "primary product" was defined to mean "any product of farm, forest or fishery, or any mineral, in its natural form or which has undergone such processing as is customarily required to prepare it for marketing in substantial volumes in international trade". The most important aspect of this definition is that from this time forward most agricultural products were generally considered to be primary products for purposes of GATT Article XVI.

ing duty could be applied against any imported good, the effect of the subsidization must have been such "as to cause or threaten material injury to an established industry, or is such as to retard materially the establishment of a domestic industry". In other words, before a countervailing duty could be imposed, the foreign subsidies must be having a negative effect on the relevant domestic industry of the importing country. While this could be a significant limitation on the use of the remedy, among other problems, Article VI provided little guidance on how much injury was required nor did it provide any significant indication as to how this injury was to be determined.

The basic problems of GATT Articles VI and XVI were then one of the most important issues raised during the 1973-1979 Tokyo Round GATT negotiations. For many contracting parties, the obligations of GATT Articles VI and XVI were then subsequently elaborated upon by the negotiation of the Tokyo Round's "Subsidies Code".[139] With respect to subsidies, signatories to the Code agreed that export subsidies on non-primary products would be entirely prohibited. And, while no acceptable definition of what constituted an export subsidy could be developed, the signatories were able to agree to an "illustrative list" of those types of subsidies which were considered to fall within the scope of the prohibition. With respect to export subsidies on primary products, the Code essentially repeated the obligation of GATT Article XVI:3, but then attempted to define some of the problematic phrases of that obligation. With respect to "subsidies other than export subsidies", or domestic subsidies, no fundamental change to the provisions of Article XVI were included in the Code. The result was slightly greater disciplines on the use of export subsidies, but no new limitations on the use of domestic subsidies nor on export subsidies for agricultural products.

With respect to countervailing duties, the Code confirmed and elaborated upon the basic material injury requirement. It also provided some elaboration on the "causality" requirement of Article VI by dictating that before subsidized imports could be countervailed, "it must be demonstrated that the subsidized imports are, through the effects of the subsidy, causing injury within the meaning of this Agreement". Finally, the Code provided extensive, mainly procedural, obligations that signatories were required to meet through the provisions of their domestic countervailing duty laws. These procedural requirements included rules governing the manner in which investigations were to be initiated and evaluated, maximum time periods for investigations,

---

[139]The Subsidies Code is known more formally as the *Agreement on Interpretation and Application of Articles VI, XVI and XXIII of the General Agreement on Tariffs and Trade*. See GATT, BISD 26S/56. It is important to note that the obligations of the Subsidies Code were only binding on those contracting parties that were signatories to it. By the end of 1992, only 26, mostly industrialized, contracting parties had become signatories to the Code. These included Canada, the U.S., the EC and Japan. Another 22 contracting parties had non-binding "observer" status.

notice requirements, provisions concerning public notice of the results of investigations, and requirements concerning judicial or equivalent review of any conclusions.

In summary, while long on procedural requirements, the Tokyo Round Subsidies Code remained short on any substantive disciplines on the use of subsidies or countervailing duties. Even as the Tokyo Round was drawing to a close, many had already concluded that the Subsidies Code had essentially failed to introduce any substantive improvement to the basic problems relating to subsidies and countervailing duties. This quickly became evident with the many new disputes that arose in these areas immediately following the conclusion of the Tokyo Round.

By 1985, less than six years after the conclusion of the Tokyo Round, the so-called "Leutweiler Report" could identify subsidies as being "at the root of the most serious and intractable trade disputes that have been brought before the GATT".[140] The Report recommended that GATT's rules concerning subsidies needed to be revised, clarified and made more effective. It is useful to quote at some length from the Leutweiler Report as it is an excellent summary of many of the specific defects in the then-existing international disciplines on subsidies and countervailing duties.

> The present GATT rules on subsidies are far from clear. Moreover, because some of them are incorporated in a separate code negotiated in the Tokyo Round of the 1970s, the same rules do not apply to all GATT members.

> Under the present rules, export subsidies on manufactured products are banned except for developing countries. Export subsidies for primary products are restricted only by the condition that they should not lead to acquisition of "more than an equitable share of world export trade." We believe this concept is economically misconceived, since it implicitly endorses market-sharing. It is also too vague and subjective to permit clear judgment on whether a subsidy is acceptable or not. . . . Although domestic subsidies are permitted, they are subject to retaliation if they damage the trade interests of other countries.

> A better test of legitimacy than that of "equitable shares" is needed for subsidies on primary products; it is not evident to us why such subsidies should be legitimate at all, when those on manufactures are banned. In the case of domestic subsidies, their full effects often emerge only some time after they are granted. If these effects are limited to the country where the subsidy is given, they are solely the affair of its citizens, but if international trade is affected, other countries may be legitimately concerned. In either case, more open procedures for considering subsidies can only be helpful.

> Actions against subsidies must also be brought within clear rules: some measures now being taken against subsidies . . . are illegal and therefore themselves unfair, as are domestic procedures which permit harassment of importers. The rules for

---

[140] *Trade Policies for a Better Future* (GATT: Geneva, 1985) at 39.

defining injury should be clarified, and the type of offsetting procedures and actions permissible more strictly defined. Every effort should be made to bring all GATT members within the scope of the improved subsidy rules.

A country will often retaliate when it feels damaged by another country's subsidy practices: the result is a further deterioration in trade. A clearer GATT definition is needed of what is a subsidy. Tax subsidies? Agricultural price supports? Unless there can be agreement on definition, talk of "subsidy" is useless. Moreover, GATT should be the place where it can be determined what is acceptable under whatever rules are adopted. GATT's complaint procedures for subsidy cases should be broadened and strengthened. Only then will the system be able to determine what is fair and what is not.[141]

The Leutweiler Report was comprehensive in its criticism. There was almost no aspect of GATT's then existing subsidy/countervailing duty regime which escaped unscathed. This was of no real surprise to any GATT contracting party. While they may have differed over what should be done, almost all were well aware that the rules needed to be substantially revised and improved. Therefore there was little disagreement when it was proposed that subsidies and countervailing duties should be included on the negotiating agenda for the Uruguay Round. The Ministerial Declaration which initiated the Uruguay Round then provided that:

Negotiations on subsidies and countervailing measures shall be based on a review of Article VI and XVI and the [Subsidies Code] with the objective of improving GATT disciplines relating to all subsidies and countervailing measures that affect international trade. A negotiating group will be established to deal with these issues.[142]

3. THE URUGUAY ROUND SUBSIDIES NEGOTIATIONS

While the negotiations on subsidies and countervailing duties were difficult and intensive, for the most part they were generally marked by a high degree of participation and cooperation. Unlike many other areas under negotiation, where much of the substantive negotiations took place only among a few dominant countries, many countries were active participants in the subsidies and countervailing duty negotiations.

The early part of the negotiations was marked by a fundamental difference of approach among the participating countries, very similar to the differences in approach which had plagued all previous negotiations in the area. On the one hand, some countries pressed for substantially increased disciplines on all forms of subsidies and they therefore focused their attention on negotiating changes to GATT Article XVI. On the other hand, other

---

[141] *Ibid.* at 39-40.

[142] GATT, BISD 33S/19 at 25.

participants were striving to curb what they saw as abuses of the countervailing duty remedy and therefore were looking to negotiate changes to Article VI.

By the time of the Montreal Mid-term Meeting of December 1988, it had been agreed that the framework for continuing negotiations would be based on a traffic light approach whereby all subsidies could be placed in one of three categories: prohibited (red light); permitted but still actionable (yellow light); and permitted and non-actionable (green light). The framework proved a useful basis for further negotiation and substantially affected the structure of the resulting agreement.

By the time of the Brussels Meeting of December 1990, a draft Agreement had been substantially completed, with few issues being left for top-level political resolution. Had the meeting not collapsed due to differences over agriculture it is likely that Agreement would have been reached on the remaining outstanding issues. This draft text was then substantially incorporated into the Dunkel Draft, and, with the exception of a few issues, met with general acceptance. Once the Dunkel Draft was released, negotiations continued on the draft text so as to reach agreement on the few outstanding issues. This was done and the *Agreement on Subsidies and Countervailing Measures* was included as part of Annex IA to the WTO Agreement.

4. THE *AGREEMENT ON SUBSIDIES AND COUNTERVAILING MEASURES*

The Agreement is comprised of 32 Articles, divided into 11 Parts and seven Annexes. The more important obligations of the Agreement are found in Parts II through V, with Parts II, III and IV addressing subsidy issues, and Part V addressing countervailing duty measures.

(a) Part I: General Provisions

Part I of the Agreement contains a number of general obligations and defines some of the more important terms used throughout the Agreement. Article 1 defines, for the purpose of the entire Agreement, the term "subsidy". This is the first time a consensus has been reached on what is considered to be a "subsidy" for the purpose of international disciplines. The definition is a two-part test under which a subsidy will be deemed to exist if both parts of the test are met.

Under the first part of the test there must be some form of financial contribution by a government or public body. Under the second part of the test a benefit must thereby be bestowed on the recipient of the contribution. With respect to the first part of the test, Article 1 goes into some detail as to the types of governmental financial contributions which are included within the Agreement, including, for example:

(i) direct or potential transfer of funds (such as grants, loans, equity infusions or loan guarantees);

(ii) government revenue that is otherwise due is foregone (such as tax credits);[143]

(iii) the government provides goods or services, other than general infrastructure, or it purchases goods;

(iv) the government directly makes any of the above types of contributions; or

(v) the government provides an income or price support in the sense of GATT Article XVI.[144]

It is important to bear in mind that a subsidy will not be deemed to exist unless both parts of the two-part test are met—that is, a benefit must also be conferred by the financial contribution. In some cases a government will undertake a type of practice considered to constitute a financial contribution, but there will be no benefit conferred thereby (because, for example, a loan being provided is fully repayable at a commercial rate of interest).

Having defined "subsidy", paragraph 2 of Article 1 then introduces a "specificity" requirement into the Agreement. Paragraph 2 notes that subsidies as defined in paragraph 1 will only be subject to Parts II, III and V of the Agreement if the subsidies are "specific" within the meaning of Article 2. In other words, only "specific" subsidies are subject to the Agreement's disciplines. Article 2 then defines the "specific" or "specificity" requirement by providing a number of principles that are to be applied in determining whether a particular subsidy is being bestowed on a specific enterprise, industry, or group of enterprises or industries (referred to in the Agreement as "certain enterprises") within the jurisdiction of the granting authority.

The first principle to be applied concerns what is commonly referred to as *de jure* specificity. *De jure* specificity occurs where the granting authority or the relevant legislation explicitly limits access to the subsidy to only certain enterprises. Where such an express limitation exists, the subsidy will be considered specific. The second principle sets out certain conditions, which, if met, may mean that the subsidy will not be considered specific. These conditions include objective conditions or criteria which are used to determine eligibility for a particular subsidy. The third principle concerns what is

---

[143] This does not include the duty or tax remission schemes whereby duties and taxes are rebated upon the export of products, provided that certain conditions are met.

[144] Income or price supports often do not involve a financial transfer from government to producer, but rather, through government maintained prices, the transfer is from consumer, who must pay higher prices, to producer. Even though there may be no direct financial contribution from government under such schemes, income and price supports are still considered to fall within the Article 1 definition of subsidy.

commonly referred to as *de facto* specificity. Notwithstanding that there may be no express limitations on access to the subsidy, and objective criteria are used to determine eligibility, other factors may be considered in making a specificity determination. Although a subsidy may not appear to be specific, it may be in fact. The other factors that may also be reviewed in determining whether there is *de facto* specificity include the use of the subsidy by a limited number of certain enterprises, predominant use by certain enterprises, or the manner in which discretion, in practice, has been exercised under the particular subsidy programme. A consideration of these other factors may lead to a determination of *de facto* specificity.

Further elements of the specificity concept are then set out in the remaining paragraphs of Article 2. Paragraph 2 provides that, generally speaking, subsidies which are limited to geographical areas within the jurisdiction of the granting authority are considered to be specific.[145] Paragraph 3 states that any subsidy falling within the provisions of Article 3 (that is, a prohibited subsidy) is deemed to be specific. Finally, paragraph 4 requires that any determinations of specificity must be clearly substantiated on the basis of positive evidence.

(b) Part II: Prohibited Subsidies

Having defined the term "subsidy", the Agreement then proceeds to divide subsidies into three categories: prohibited (red light); permitted but actionable (yellow light); and permitted and non-actionable (green light). Part II of the Agreement (Articles 3 and 4) addresses those subsidies which are prohibited.

Paragraph 1 of Article 3 sets out the general prohibition on two types of subsidies. The first type of prohibited subsidies are all those, which in law or in fact, are made contingent on export performance—or, more commonly, export subsidies.[146] This prohibition is a significant expansion on the previously existing prohibition which, as discussed above, did not apply to export subsidies granted to primary products. No such distinction is made in the Agreement. The second type of prohibited subsidies are so-called import

---

[145] It is important to bear in mind that the specificity test here is based on the jurisdiction of the granting authority, which may not necessarily be the entire country. For example, if a state or provincial government is the granting authority, the jurisdiction is limited to that state or province. If the federal government is the granting authority, it is the entire country which is the relevant jurisdiction.

[146] Paragraph 1(a) of Article 3 notes that prohibited export subsidies include those listed in Annex I to the Agreement. Annex I (which is essentially the Illustrative List of Export Subsidies which was attached to the Tokyo Round Subsidies Code) then provides an illustrative list of 12 different types of subsidies that are to be considered to be contingent upon export performance. Among others, these subsidies include those that are directly linked to export performance, currency retention schemes and differential transportation charges.

replacement subsidies, or those which are made contingent on the use of domestic over imported goods. Members are prohibited from granting any new subsidies of this type and, subject to Articles 27 and 28, were required to eliminate any existing programmes as of January 1, 1995.[147]

It is important to note that both these prohibitions of Article 3 are made subject to the *Agreement on Agriculture*. The exception for rights contained in the *Agreement on Agriculture* was necessary because, as noted above, that Agreement does not completely prohibit the use of export subsidies on agricultural products, but rather only imposes certain restrictions on their use.[148]

Article 4 then provides a multilateral remedy specific to prohibited subsidies which is available to any Member where another Member is allegedly granting a prohibited subsidy. First, if a Member has reason to believe that prohibited subsidies are being granted it has the right to request consultations with the subsidizing Member. Once requested, the consultations are to commence as quickly as possible with the goals of clarifying the facts and arriving at a solution. If no solution is reached within 30 days of the request for consultations, any of the consulting Members may then refer the matter to the DSB for the immediate establishment of a dispute settlement panel. Once established, the dispute settlement panel may request the assistance of the Permanent Group of Experts ("PGE")[149] to determine whether the subsidy is one which falls within the prohibited category. If such a request is made, the PGE is to review immediately the evidence and report back to the panel. In doing so, the PGE is to provide an opportunity to the Member granting the subsidy to demonstrate that it is not a prohibited subsidy. Any conclusions of the PGE on the issue before it are then binding on the panel.

Once the panel has finished its review of the subsidy at issue, it must first distribute its report to the disputing Members. If the subsidy is found to fall within the prohibited category, the panel is to recommend that the subsidizing Member withdraw the subsidy within a time period to be specified in the panel's report. The panel's report is to be circulated to all Members within 90 days of establishment of the panel's composition and its terms of reference. The DSB must then adopt that panel's report within 30 days of its circulation to all Members, unless either one of the disputing parties notifies the DSB that it is appealing the report, or the DSB decides by consensus not to adopt the report.

---

[147] Articles 27 and 28 set out certain conditions under which prohibited subsidies may be continued after January 1, 1995. See the discussion below at pages 174-175.

[148] See pages 81-83 for the discussion of the export subsidy provisions of the *Agreement on Agriculture*.

[149] The PGE is established under Article 24 of the Agreement, discussed below at pages 172-173.

If the report is appealed, the Appellate Body[150] is normally required to issue a decision on the appeal within 30 days from the date the appeal was formally commenced. In special cases, the Appellate Body may take up to 30 additional days to decide the case. The decision of the Appellate Body must then be adopted by the DSB within 20 days of its issuance, unless the DSB decides by consensus that it should not be adopted.

If the panel has found the subsidy to be prohibited and the subsidizing Member does not eliminate the subsidy within the specified period of time, the DSB may then grant authorization to the complaining Member to take appropriate and proportionate countermeasures. Any dispute concerning the appropriateness of any countermeasures that are taken may be taken to arbitration in accordance with Article 22 of the Dispute Settlement Understanding.[151]

(c) Part III: Actionable Subsidies

Part III of the Agreement (Articles 5 through 7) addresses the category of permitted but actionable (or yellow light) subsidies. These are subsidies which are not prohibited under the Agreement, but action may still be taken against them if they have certain specified detrimental effects.

Article 5 provides that, subject to Article 13 of the *Agreement on Agriculture*,[152] no Member should cause, through the use of any specific subsidy, "adverse effects" to the interests of any other Member. The article then defines what is meant by the phrase "adverse effects" by providing three specific examples of such effects. These adverse effects are: (a) injury to a domestic industry of another Member; (b) nullification and impairment of benefits accruing to other Members; and (c) serious prejudice to the interests of another Member.

Article 6 then extensively elaborates upon the concept of "serious prejudice" for the purposes of Article 5(c).[153] Paragraph 1 establishes a presumption that in four specific circumstances serious prejudice will be deemed to exist. These circumstances are where:

(a) the total value of a subsidy exceeds 5 percent of a product's value;[154]

---

[150] The so-called "Appellate Body" is established under the DSU to consider appeals of certain types of decisions. See discussion of the Appellate Body in chapter 7, pages 321-323.

[151] For a discussion of Article 22 of the DSU, see pages 324-325.

[152] Article 13 of the *Agreement on Agriculture*, more commonly referred to as the "peace clause", exempts certain subsidies granted to agriculture from actions provided for under Parts III and V the *Agreement on Subsidies and Countervailing Measures*. See the discussion of the peace clause above at pages 83-84.

[153] As is the case with Article 5, paragraph 9 of Article 6 provides that Article 6 does not apply to subsidies maintained on agricultural products as provided for in Article 13 of the *Agreement on Agriculture*.

[154] The calculation of *ad valorem* subsidization is to be made in accordance with the provisions of Annex IV (Calculation of the Total Ad Valorem Subsidization (paragraph 1(a) of Article 6)).

(b) the subsidies are covering operating losses sustained by an industry;

(c) the subsidies are covering operating losses sustained by an enterprise (subject to an exemption for certain non-recurring benefits); and

(d) direct forgiveness of debt.

Paragraph 2 then provides that the presumption of serious prejudice in paragraph 1 may be rebutted if the subsidizing Member can demonstrate that the subsidy at issue, although it falls within the scope of paragraph 1, is not having any of the effects specified in paragraph 3.

Paragraph 3 sets out four circumstances, based on the effects that a subsidy is having, where serious prejudice can, in fact, exist. These are in addition to those where serious prejudice will be deemed to exist. Serious prejudice may arise in any case where the effect of the subsidy is to:

(a) displace or impede imports of a like product into the subsidizing Member;

(b) displace or impede exports of a like product of another Member in a third country;[155]

(c) result in significant price undercutting, suppression, depression, or lost sales;[156] or

(d) result in an increase in the world market share for the subsidized primary product or commodity.

In situations where the displacement or impediment may have occurred, paragraph 7 notes that serious prejudice will not arise where the other specified circumstances other than subsidization exist, such as a prohibition or restriction on imports or exports, *force majeure,* certain governmental arrangements, and non-conformity with standards or other regulatory requirements.

Article 7 then provides a multilateral remedy that a Member may invoke whenever it has reason to believe that another Member is granting any subsidy which is having adverse effects as defined. This remedy is similar in procedure to that set out in Article 4 for use in cases of prohibited subsidies.

The first step under Article 7 is to request consultations with the subsidizing Member. Once the consultations are requested, they are to commence as quickly as possible with the goals of clarifying the situation and arriving at a

---

[155] Paragraph 4 of Article 6 notes that the displacement of exports includes any case where it is demonstrated that there has been a change in relative market shares to the disadvantage of the non-subsidized like product.

[156] Paragraph 5 provides that price undercutting includes any case of undercutting that can be demonstrated by a comparison of prices of the subsidized product with those of a like non-subsidized product supplied to the same market.

mutually agreed solution. If the matter has not been resolved within 60 days, any consulting Member may refer the matter to the DSB for the establishment of a dispute settlement panel. The DSB is then required to establish a panel unless it agrees by consensus not to. The composition of the panel and its terms of reference must be provided within 15 days of the panel's establishment.

Once the panel is finished its review of the subsidy at issue, it is first to distribute its report to the disputing Members. The panel's report is to be circulated to all Members within 120 days of establishment of the panel's composition and its terms of reference. The DSB is then to adopt the panel's report within 30 days of its circulation to all Members, unless either one of the disputing Members notifies the DSB that it is appealing the report, or the DSB decides by consensus that the report will not be adopted.

If the report is appealed, the Appellate Body is normally required to issue a decision on the appeal within 60 days from the date the appeal was formally commenced. In special cases, the Appellate Body may take up to 30 additional days to decide the case. The decision of the Appellate Body must then be adopted by the DSB and unconditionally accepted by the Members to the dispute within 20 days of its issuance, unless the DSB decides by consensus that it should not be adopted.

Where a panel has found that the subsidy in question has resulted in adverse effects, the subsidizing Member is then required to remove the adverse effects or withdraw the subsidy.[157] If the subsidizing Member does not remove the adverse effects or withdraw the subsidy within six months from the adoption of the report by the DSB, and in the absence of an agreement between the disputing Members on compensation, the DSB may then authorize the complaining Member to take commensurate countermeasures. Any dispute concerning the appropriateness of any countermeasures that are taken may itself be taken to arbitration in accordance with Article 22 of the Dispute Settlement Understanding.

(d) Part IV: Non-actionable Subsidies

Part IV of the Agreement (Articles 8 and 9) sets out a special set of rules for a limited subset of subsidies or "green light" subsidies, which, although they may be "specific subsidies" within the meaning of Article 1, are still excluded from actionability under Parts III (Actionable Subsidies) and V (Countervailing Measures) of the Agreement.

Paragraph 1 of Article 8 identifies two types of subsidies which are to be considered non-actionable under the Agreement: those subsidies which are

---

[157] Note that, unlike Article 4, a Member is only required to remove the adverse effects, which may not necessarily require elimination of the subsidy in its entirety.

not specific within the meaning of Article 2, and those subsidies which, even though they may be specific, fall within the terms of paragraphs 2(a) to (c) of Article 8. Paragraph 2 then provides that, notwithstanding Parts III and V of the Agreement (and the right to take actions against subsidies provided in those parts), three specified and strictly limited types of subsidies are not actionable under the Agreement. These non-actionable subsidies are: (a) certain pre-competitive research and development assistance;[158] certain regional development assistance;[159] and (c) certain environmental adaptation assistance.[160]

If a Member intends to rely on the non-actionable exemption for a particular subsidy or programme, it must first notify the Committee on Subsidies and Countervailing Measures[161] in advance of the subsidy's implementation and in a manner sufficient to allow other Members to evaluate the consistency of the subsidy with the relevant non-actionable exemption being relied upon. Once a programme or subsidy is notified, the information provided must be updated on an annual basis.

At the request of any Member, the WTO Secretariat is required to review any non-actionable subsidy notification, and, if necessary, request that additional information be provided on the programme or subsidy. The Secretariat is to report its findings to the Committee. If requested, the Committee is required to review any findings of the Secretariat, or any notification, to determine whether the requirements of the applicable non-actionable exception have been met. A Member can then have the Committee's determination (as well as any violation found thereunder) submitted to binding arbitration. Generally speaking, the arbitrating body will then be subject to the DSU and must present its conclusions to the Members within 120 days.

Even though a programme may fall within the requirements for non-actionability under Article 8, there is the potential that it could still cause

---

[158] Among other requirements, in order for this type of assistance to be non-actionable it must be limited to certain specified amounts, and must be used exclusively for the costs of personnel, certain equipment and facilities costs, overhead and running costs.

[159] Among other requirements, in order to qualify for non-actionability status this type of assistance must be given to disadvantaged regions within a general framework of regional development and must be granted on a non-specific basis within that eligible region. There are also a number of requirements as to what constitutes a disadvantaged region for purposes of this exclusion.

[160] This assistance is limited to covering some of the costs of existing facilities adapting to new environmental requirements when those new requirements result in constraints or financial burden. Among other requirements, the assistance must be non-recurring, limited to 20 percent of the costs of adaptation, and available to all firms which can adopt the new equipment or processes.

[161] The Committee on Subsidies and Countervailing Measures (the "Committee") is established under Article 24 of the Agreement. See the discussion below at page 172.

adverse effects to the interests of other Members. Article 9 provides an additional procedure to address this possibility. If a Member believes that a non-actionable subsidy has resulted in serious adverse effects to one of its domestic industries, that Member may request consultations with the subsidizing Member. The requested consultations are to be commenced as quickly as possible, with the goals of clarifying the situation and arriving at a mutually acceptable solution. If no solution is reached within 60 days, the requesting Member may refer the matter to the Committee. The Committee is required to immediately review the situation and present its conclusions within 120 days. If it determines that the alleged effects do exist, it may recommend that the subsidizing Member modify the subsidy so as to eliminate those effects. If this recommendation is not then followed, the Committee is required to authorize the requesting Member to take commensurate countermeasures.

(e) Part V: Countervailing Measures

Part V of the Agreement, Articles 10 to 23, addresses the remedy that is most widely used against subsidies affecting international trade—the "countervailing duty". A countervailing duty is defined to be a special duty levied for the purpose of offsetting any subsidy bestowed directly or indirectly upon the manufacture, production or export of any merchandise. From its onset, GATT Article VI has allowed for the application of countervailing duties and set out certain basic requirements for their imposition. However, disputes often arose because of the vagueness of these GATT obligations. The uncertainty surrounding the application of countervailing duties was remedied somewhat with the entry into force of the Tokyo Round's Subsidies Code. Part V of the new Agreement builds upon the Subsidies Code and further clarifies the many procedural obligations that must be met by Members in applying countervailing duties against allegedly subsidized imports.

Article 10 sets out a general obligation concerning observance of the Agreement, requiring Members to take all necessary steps to ensure that any countervailing duty which is imposed only in a manner consistent with GATT Article VI and the Agreement. Countervailing duties may only be imposed pursuant to investigations that are initiated and conducted in a manner consistent with the Agreement and the *Agreement on Agriculture.*

A footnote to Article 10 then clarifies the relationship between Parts II, III and V of the Agreement and the various remedies provided under those parts. It is possible that the procedures provided for under Part II (prohibited subsidies) or III (actionable subsidies) may be invoked in parallel with a countervailing duty investigation. However, in the end, the Member may only apply one of the remedies to any particular subsidy—that is, the Member must choose between either authorized countermeasures under Part II or III, or a countervailing duty under Part V, but not both. This footnote also clarifies that a countervailing duty cannot be applied against a subsidy that is non-actionable under the terms of Part IV. However, in the context of a counter-vailing duty investigation, Members are still permitted to investigate a subsidy to determine whether or not it is specific. In addition, Members are also permitted to investigate other types of non-actionable subsidies if those subsidies have not been notified to the Committee as required under Article 8(3). However, they may not be countervailed if they are found to be the requirements for non-actionability as set out in Article 8.

(i) Initiation of an Investigation

The procedural requirements for the initiation and subsequent investiga-tion in a countervailing duty action are addressed in Article 11. Except in special circumstances, a countervailing duty investigation is only to be initi-ated after a written request has been received from or on behalf of the relevant "domestic industry".[162] The request for an investigation must provide suffi-cient evidence of the existence of a subsidy (and if possible, its amount), injury to the domestic industry, and a causal link between the subsidized imports and the injury being caused. Simple allegations without substituting evidence are insufficient. The request must also contain other information that is reasonably available to the petitioner, including: a complete description of the petitioner; all known domestic producers of the product at issue, along with volume and value of domestic production; a description of the allegedly subsidized product and its country or countries of origin, the foreign manufac-turers and domestic importers; evidence regarding the amount and nature of the subsidy; and evidence relating to injury, including volumes of imports and their effects on domestic prices.

Once the petition is filed, the relevant investigating authority is required to review the evidence to ensure that it is sufficient to justify the initiation of an investigation. The evidence of both the subsidy and injury are to be reviewed simultaneously. A petition is to be rejected and an investigation terminated as soon as it is determined that the evidence of subsidization or injury is insufficient to justify proceeding or where the subsidization is found to be de minimis[163] or the injury negligible.

---

[162] The term "domestic industry" is defined in detail for purposes of the Agreement by Article 16. Generally, the term is to be taken to mean the domestic producers as a whole of the like products or to those of them whose collective output of the like product constitutes a major proportion of the total domestic production of those products. However, in exceptional circum-stances, the territory of a Member may, for the production in question, be divided into two or more "regional markets" and the producers located in those regional markets may be regarded as separate industries. In order to be considered a regional market, the producers within the market must sell all or almost all of their production into that market, and demand in that market cannot be supplied to any substantial degree by producers located elsewhere in the territory of the Member.

[163] A subsidy is to be considered de minimus if it totals less than one percent of the product's value.

Moreover, an authority is not permitted to initiate an investigation without first examining the extent to which the petition is supported or opposed by the relevant domestic industry. The authority can consider a petition to have been filed on behalf of a domestic industry where it is supported by domestic producers whose collective production accounts for at least 50 percent of total domestic production of the relevant product. No investigation may be commenced where the domestic producers who expressly support the petition account for less than 25 percent of total domestic production.

The authority is not to publicize the fact that a petition has been filed until a decision has been made whether or not to initiate an investigation. Once an investigation has been initiated, it is normally to be completed within one year (or within 18 months in special circumstances), and while ongoing it is not to hinder normal customs clearance procedures.

(ii) Obligations Concerning Evidence to be Relied Upon

Article 12 addresses issues concerning the evidence that is provided or gathered during investigations. Once an investigation is initiated, a copy of the petition is to be provided to all known exporters and made available, upon request, to all interested parties.[164] Any interested Members and all interested parties must be given notice of the information which the investigating authority requires and must be provided with ample opportunity to present all relevant evidence. Exporters, foreign producers and interested Members which receive questionnaires must be given at least 30 days from the date of receipt to respond. Subject to confidentiality protections, evidence presented by one party must be made available to all other parties participating in the investigation. Other obligations under Article 12 concerning the evidence used in an investigation include:

- the authority must provide timely opportunities for all parties to review information that may be relevant to the presentation of their case and prepare presentations based on this information;
- interested Members and interested parties are to have the right, upon justification, to present their information orally, followed by written submissions;
- the investigating authority may only base its decision on information and arguments that are on the record;
- with respect to any confidential information provided to the investigating authority, the authority is not permitted to disclose that information without the permission of the party which provided it; if a party

---

[164] "Interested parties" is defined in Article 12(9) to include exporters, foreign producers, importers and domestic producers of the product which is the subject of the investigation.

provides confidential information, it must also provide a sufficient non-confidential summary of that information;

- generally speaking, the authority is required to satisfy itself that the information upon which its findings are based is accurate; however, if a party refuses or does not provide the necessary information within a reasonable time period, the authority is permitted to make its determinations on the basis of the facts that are available to it;

- before a final determination is made the authority must inform all parties of the essential facts under consideration; and

- industrial users of the relevant good and, where the good is normally sold at the retail level, consumer organizations, must also be provided with the an opportunity to provide relevant information.

The investigating authority is also permitted to undertake investigations in the territory of another Member as required, subject to that other Member's permission. In addition, the authority may also undertake investigations on the premises of a foreign firm and may examine the records of the firm if the firm so agrees. The procedures to be used in these so-called "on-the-spot" investigations are set out in detail in Annex VI to the Agreement. As the main purpose of these investigations is to verify information which that firm has already provided, generally speaking, such investigations should not be carried out until after the firm has already had the opportunity to respond to the authority's questionnaire.

(iii) Member-to-Member Consultations

Article 13 addresses Member-to-Member consultations. As soon as possible after a petition has been accepted and before an investigation is initiated, the investigating Member is required to invite those Members whose products may be the subject of an investigation to consult, with the aim of clarifying the situation and reaching a satisfactory solution. Members whose products are the subject of an investigation have the right to request consultations throughout the period of the investigation and must be granted access to all non-confidential information.

(iv) Calculating the Benefit of a Subsidy

The rules and procedures with respect to calculating the actual amount of any subsidy which is to be countervailed under the procedures of Part V are set out in Article 14. Recall that one of the basic requirements of Article 1(1) is that a benefit must be bestowed on the recipient of any subsidy. Article 14 then confirms that the amount of a subsidy for countervailing duty purposes is to be measured on the basis of its "benefit to the recipient", not its cost to the granting government. In all cases, the method of calculating this benefit must be set out in statute or regulation and, in any specific case, the method used must be transparent and adequately explained.

Article 14 sets out four additional guidelines which must also be met in calculating a subsidy:

- in the case of government equity infusions, these are not to be considered as conferring a benefit on the recipient unless the investment would not have been made on the same terms by private investors;
- with respect to loans, there will be no benefit to the recipient unless the rate of interest charged by the government is less than the comparable commercial rate;
- loan guarantees shall not be considered to confer a benefit on the recipient unless the firm obtains a lower interest rate on its loan because of the government guarantee; and
- where goods or services are being provided by the government to the recipient, there shall be no benefit conferred unless the good or service is being provided for less than adequate remuneration. Where the firm is providing goods to the government, there will be no benefit bestowed unless the good is being supplied for more than adequate remuneration. In both cases, the adequacy of the remuneration is to be determined in relation to the prevailing market conditions for the good or service in the country of provision or purchase.

(v) The Injury Determination

The factors that are to be considered and procedures to be followed in determining injury are set out in Article 15. "Injury" for the purposes of Article 15 is defined to mean material injury to a domestic industry, threat of material injury thereto, or the material retardation of the establishment of such an industry.[165] A determination of injury for purposes of a countervailing duty determination must be made on the basis of positive evidence and must involve an objective examination of the volume of subsidized imports and their effect on prices in the domestic market, and the impact of these imports on domestic producers.

With respect to the volumes of subsidized imports, it must be considered whether there has been a significant increase in such imports. With respect to

---

[165] Generally speaking, the injury determination must be made by reviewing the entire domestic industry as a whole. However, where two or more regional markets exist within the territory of a Member, injury can be determined to be occurring to producers located within one of the regional markets even where a major proportion of the entire domestic industry is not being injured, if there is a concentration of subsidized imports into the regional market and such imports are causing injury to producers of all or almost all production within that market.

price effects, it must be determined whether there has been price undercutting or other similar price effects, such as price erosion or suppression. It is noted that no one or several of these factors can necessarily give decisive guidance to the investigating authority. Other requirements with respect to injury determinations include:

- where imports from more than one country are being investigated simultaneously, the investigating authority will generally be permitted to assess injury on a cumulative basis, reviewing the effects of all imports as a group, provided that, among other factors, such an assessment is appropriate in light of the conditions of competition in the market;

- in assessing the effect of subsidized imports on the domestic industry, the investigating authority is to review and evaluate all relevant economic factors including actual and potential declines in output, profits, capacity utilization, wages, and employment; and

- there must be a causal nexus between the subsidized imports and the injury being caused—that is, it must be demonstrated that the imports, through the effects of the subsidy, are causing the injury alleged.

In some cases, injury may not be occurring at the time of the petition, but it may be threatened to occur in the future. With respect to such threats of future injury, any such determination must be based on facts and not mere allegations, conjecture or remote possibility. The change in circumstances in which a subsidy not currently causing injury would do so in the future must be clearly foreseen and imminent. Factors to be taken into account when making a determination of threat of material injury include: the nature of the subsidy at issue; the rate of increase in imports and the likelihood of increased imports in the future; the capacity utilizations of foreign producers and any pending additions; the current prices of subsidized imports and likely price effects; and inventories of the subject product. Considered together, in order for there to be a finding of threat of injury, these factors must lead to the conclusion that further exports are imminent and, unless protective action is taken, material injury will occur.

(vi) Provisional Measures

The issue of provisional measures or temporary duties which may be imposed while an investigation is ongoing is addressed in Article 17. Provisional measures in the form of temporary countervailing duties may only be applied in certain limited circumstances: a countervailing duty investigation must have been initiated; there must have been a preliminary determination that the relevant product is being subsidized and that injury is being caused to the domestic industry; and provisional measures are considered necessary to prevent any injury from being caused during the investigation. Any provisional countervailing duty is to be equal to the provisionally determined level of subsidization, cannot be applied sooner than 60 days after the investigation was initiated, and cannot remain in place longer than four months.

(vii) Undertakings

In some cases, Members that are the subject of a countervailing duty investigation, or the exporters themselves, may wish to eliminate the subsidy so that their products will not be subject to a countervailing duty. The possibility for such arrangements, or "undertakings", is provided for in Article 18. An investigation may be terminated without provisional or final countervailing duties being imposed whenever a satisfactory undertaking can be provided to the investigating authority. Such an undertaking may be given by either the exporting Member (whereby it agrees to eliminate or limit the subsidy), or by the exporter (whereby it agrees to raise its prices to eliminate the injurious effects of the subsidy).

Undertakings must be completely voluntary and cannot be sought or accepted until there has been a preliminary determination of both subsidization and injury. In any case, the investigating authority is not obliged to accept an undertaking if, in its view, the undertaking would be impractical (because, for example, too many exporters are involved). If an undertaking is accepted, the authority must complete the investigation if the exporting Member requests (or the importing Member decides). If the investigation is continued and a final determination of no subsidization or injury is made the undertaking must automatically lapse, unless it is determined that the negative determination was, in large part, due to the existence of the undertaking.

The investigating authority may require periodic information to determine that the undertaking is being complied with. If an undertaking is violated, the investigating authority is permitted to take immediate action, such as the imposition of a provisional countervailing duty, based on the best information available. In some cases, definitive duties may also then be applied retroactively to products which were already imported prior to the imposition of the provisional duty.

(viii) Imposition and Collection of Countervailing Duties

Once a Member has met its obligations under the Agreement relating to a countervailing duty investigation and has made final and positive determinations of both injury and subsidization, it may then apply a final countervailing duty in accordance with the provisions of Article 19.[166] Even though all the

---

[166] Note that Article 17.5 provides that the obligations of Article 19 also apply to provisional countervailing duties.

requirements for imposition have been met, the application of a final duty is still permissive. In addition, if a duty rate less than the total amount of subsidization will still be effective in eliminating the injury, the authority should have the ability to impose a lower duty. Members should also establish procedures whereby the authority is given the ability to take into consideration submissions made by interested parties, such as industrial users of the product and consumers whose interests might be adversely affected by the imposition of the duty. In any case, a countervailing duty cannot be imposed on any imported product in excess of the amount of the subsidy that has been determined to exist.

Where a countervailing duty is imposed, it must be applied on a non-discriminatory basis on all imports from all sources found to be subsidized and causing injury (except those sources that have eliminated the subsidy or entered into undertakings). Any exporter whose exports are subject to a definitive duty but who was not specifically investigated shall then be entitled to an expedited review so that the authority may establish an individual countervailing duty rate for that exporter.

(ix) Retroactivity

Article 20 addresses the issue of when a countervailing duty may be applied to any goods which were imported into the country and cleared customs formalities prior to the imposition of the duty. Generally speaking, provisional duties may be applied to imports while a countervailing duty investigation is ongoing provided there have already been preliminary determinations of both subsidization and injury. Once a final determination of injury is made, duties may be definitively assessed on all imports of the product which had been subject to the preliminary duties. If the final definitive duty is determined to be higher than the preliminary duty, the difference cannot be collected on any product imported during the preliminary period. If the definitive duty is less, then the difference must be refunded to the importer.

If a positive final determination of threat of material injury is made, then duties may only be applied to goods imported into the country as of the date of that final injury determination. Duties cannot be assessed retroactively on any products imported during the preliminary period (unless there is a finding that injury would have occurred during the preliminary period but for the imposition of the preliminary duty) and any duties so collected or security posted must be returned. Where the final determination of either subsidization or injury is negative, any duties paid or security posted during the preliminary period must be returned and no definitive duty may be imposed.

In certain critical circumstances, a retroactive countervailing duty may be imposed on products that were imported into the country as early as 90 days before the imposition of preliminary duties. The authority must first determine that the injury has been caused by massive imports of products benefiting from prohibited export subsidies and that these products have been imported over a relatively short period of time. If these circumstances are met, duties may be imposed retroactively if the authority considers them necessary to prevent the injury from recurring.

(x) Duration and Review of Countervailing Duties and Undertakings

Article 21 addresses the duration of definitive countervailing duties. The Article also applies equally to any undertaking that has been entered into in lieu of a definitive duty. Generally speaking, a duty can remain in place only so long as is necessary to counteract the subsidization that has caused injury. The investigating authority must review the continued imposition of a duty whenever an interested party submits evidence that substantiates the need for such a review (evidence that the subsidy has been eliminated, for example). If such a review determines that the duty is no longer necessary, it must be discontinued immediately.

Paragraph 3 of Article 21 provides an important new obligation, often referred to as the "sunset" provision. Generally speaking, a definitive countervailing duty can remain in place for no more than five years, unless it is specifically determined prior to the end of that five-year period that the elimination of the duty would lead to a continuation or re-occurrence of both the subsidization and the injury. The obligations of Article 12 relating to acceptable evidence will apply to any such reviews. The review must normally be concluded within one year, although the duty may remain in place until the review is completed.

(xi) Public Notice and Explanation of Determinations

Obligations concerning public notification of countervailing duty investigations and their results are provided in Article 22. Where the investigating authority is satisfied that there is sufficient evidence to justify the initiation of a countervailing duty investigation, it must then must notify all interested parties known to the authority, as well as any Members whose products are included within the scope of the investigation. The authority must also issue a public notice announcing the investigation.

This public notice (or a separately available public report) must include certain specified information, including: the countries covered by the investigation, the subsidies at issue, information concerning alleged injury, the date of initiation, the applicable investigatory time limits, and the address to which submissions may be made. Public notice must also be given of both the preliminary and final determinations, any decision to accept an undertaking, and the termination of any definitive duty or undertaking.

With respect to public notice of the imposition of preliminary duties, the notice (or a separately available report) must contain sufficient detail concerning the determinations of subsidization and injury, including: names of suppliers or countries involved; description of the product; the amount of the subsidy; and the primary reasons for the findings. Similar minimum disclosure requirements are imposed for any public notifications of conclusions or suspensions of investigations, the acceptance of any undertakings, and the initiation and completion of sunset reviews.

(xii) Judicial Review

The final Article of Part V of the Agreement (Article 23) establishes basic obligations concerning independent judicial review of certain types of decisions relating to countervailing duties. Any Member whose domestic law provides for countervailing duties must also maintain judicial, arbitral or administrative tribunals or procedures that allow for prompt and independent review of administrative actions relating to final determinations and reviews of final determinations. This review body or procedure must be independent of the original investigating authorities and must also be accessible to all interested parties who participated in the original administrative proceeding.

(f) Part VI: Institutions

Part VI of the Agreement (Article 24) establishes the Committee on Subsidies and Countervailing Duty Measures and provides the Committee's mandate. The Committee is composed of representatives from each of the Members. It selects its own Chair[167] and is to meet not less than twice a year, or upon the request of a Member. The Committee is to carry out its defined mandate and provide Members with the opportunity to consult on countervailing duty issues.

The Committee may establish any subsidiary bodies that it considers appropriate, but was specifically required to establish a PGE, comprised of five individuals highly qualified in the areas of subsidies and trade.[168] The

---

[167] Mr. Victor Luiz Do. Prado of Brazil was elected to be the first Chair of the Committee.

[168] On March 6, 1996, the Committee elected the first five members of the PGE, those being:

(i) Mr. Robert Martin, a former Secretary of the Canadian International Trade Tribunal and a Canadian GATT negotiator;

(ii) Mr. Gary Horlick, a U.S. trade attorney in the Washington, D.C., office of O'Melveny & Myers (Chairman);

(iii) Mr. Friedrich Klein, a former Director in the EC Commission's Directorate for

PGE is to assist the Committee on issues relating to export subsidies in particular, as well as other subsidy issues as may be requested by the Committee. In addition, any Member may consult with the PGE and may request a confidential advisory opinion from the Group concerning any proposed or existing subsidy programme of that Member.

(g) Part VII: Notification and Surveillance

In an effort to improve the overall transparency of Members' subsidy programmes and countervailing duty laws and practices, Part VII of the Agreement (Articles 25 and 26) establishes extensive notification and surveillance obligations. These transparency obligations are in addition to those that already exist under GATT Article XVI:1.[169] (Note that the notification obligations of Article XVI:1 have been carried forward into the GATT 1994 and therefore also continue to apply.)

By July of each year, Members are required to notify the WTO of the existence of any subsidy programme that both falls within the definition of "subsidy" as set out in Article 1(1) of the Agreement, and is specific within the meaning of Article 2. These notifications must meet certain content requirements (including the form of subsidy, amount, policy objective and duration). Where a Member does not properly notify a programme as required, any other Member may bring this failure to the attention of that Member. If the programme still remains unnotified, the matter may then be brought to the attention of the Committee.

In addition to these notification requirements, a Member may also request information from any other Member concerning the nature and extent of any subsidy programme maintained by that other Member. If so requested, the Member must provide any such information as soon as possible. The information provided is to be sufficient to allow the requesting Member to assess the programme and determine its compliance with the Agreement.

In addition to subsidy programmes, all countervailing duty actions must also be notified to the Committee immediately. A Member must also submit a

---

Commercial Relations;

(iv) Mr. Seung-Wha Chang, a lecturer in international trade law at the National University in Seoul, Korea; and

(v) Mr. Akira Kotera, a professor of international relations at the University of Tokyo.

These initial members were elected to serve staggered terms of office ranging from one to five years. All subsequent members of the PGE will be elected for five-year terms.

[169] GATT Article XVI:1 provides that if any Member "grants or maintains any subsidy, including any form of income or price support, which operates directly or indirectly to increase exports of any product from, or to reduce imports of any product into, its territory, it shall notify the Contracting Parties". The specific form and content of these required notifications are set out at BISD, 9S/193-194.

semi-annual report detailing all countervailing duty actions taken by that Member during the preceding six months. In addition, the Committee must be informed of all Members' investigating authorities and their domestic countervailing duty procedures.

The Committee is charged with examining all subsidy notifications filed by Members under Article 25 and GATT Article XVI:1 at special sessions to be held every three years. Any updated notifications are to be examined at regular Committee meetings, as are any countervailing duty action reports.

(h) Part VIII: Special and Differential Treatment for Developing Country Members

Limited special and differential treatment is extended to developing country Members under the terms of Part VII of the Agreement (Article 27). The first relates to the continued use of subsidies that would otherwise be prohibited under the terms of Article 3(1) of the Agreement. Subject to a number of conditions, the prohibition on export subsidies contained in Article 3(1)(a) does not apply to a specified group of least-developed country Members,[170] and, subject to a number of conditions, will only apply to all other developing country Members after January 1, 2003 (or eight years after the entry into force of the WTO Agreement).[171] In addition, the Article 3(1)(b) prohibition on subsidies linked to the use of domestic over imported goods will not apply to developing country Members until January 1, 2000, and will not apply to least-developed country Members until January 1, 2003.

The second aspect of special and differential treatment under Article 27 relates to the various remedies provided for under the Agreement that may be used against the subsidy practices of developing country Members. First, export subsidies used by developing country Members are not *per se* prohibited. Thus, provided the developing country Member is in compliance with its export subsidy obligations under Article 27, another Member cannot challenge the export subsidy unless it is actually having verifiable negative trade effects. In addition, the presumption of serious prejudice set out in Article 6(1) does not apply to developing country Members. This means that serious

---

[170] This specified group of countries is set out in Annex VII to the Agreement, and includes all least-developed country Members, as designated by the UN.

[171] This special export subsidy exemption is subject to a number of conditions. First, a developing country Member is not permitted to increase its level of export subsidies. Second, developing countries subject to the eight-year rule must phase-out their export subsidy programmes within that eight-year period, although this period may be extended under certain circumstances. Third, once a developing country Member has reached a stage of export competitiveness in a given product, it must eliminate any export subsidy granted to that product within two years. Least-developed country Members have a total of eight years to eliminate an export subsidy once the relevant product has become export competitive.

prejudice as defined in Article 6 must be proved to be occurring in every case whenever a subsidy of a developing country Member, export or domestic, is challenged under the provisions of Article 7.

With respect to countervailing duty actions taken against products originating in a developing country Member, developing country Members benefit from higher *de minimus* thresholds than those generally applicable to products from developed country Members. The investigation as it applies to exports from a developing country is to cease as soon as the investigating authority determines that either total subsidization does not exceed 2 percent of the product's value,[172] or the volume of imports from that developing country Member is less than 4 percent of all imports of the subject product.[173] Upon the request of a developing country Member, the Committee is to review any specific countervailing duty measure to determine whether that measure is consistent with these special *de minimus* rules.

The final aspect of special and differential treatment for developing country Members relates to privatization efforts. Certain types of subsidies, such as direct forgiveness of debt, that are granted by a developing country Member as part of a privatization plan are still countervailable by another Member, but they cannot be subject to multilateral challenge under Part III of the Agreement, provided that the subsidy is properly notified to the Committee, is granted for only a limited period, and eventually results in the privatization of the enterprise concerned.

(i) Part IX: Transitional Arrangements

Part IX of the Agreement (Articles 28 and 29) sets out certain special arrangements relating to the transition to the new legal regime established by the Agreement. Article 28 deals with certain pre-existing inconsistent subsidy programmes. Provided that the programme was properly notified to the Committee by April 1, 1995, Members have until January 1, 1998 to bring pre-existing inconsistent subsidy programmes into compliance with the Agreement. Until the expiry of this three-year transitional period, any such properly notified subsidy cannot be subject to multilateral challenge under Part II of the Agreement as a prohibited export subsidy, although it may be challenged under Part III of the Agreement, and it may still be countervailed.

---

[172] Least-developed country Members are subject to an even higher three percent *de minimus* threshold. In addition, any other developing country Member can gain the benefit of this three percent threshold by eliminating all of its export subsidies prior to January 1, 2003.

[173] The four percent *de minimus* rule concerning import volumes will not apply where there are imports from more than one developing country Member and individually they each account for less than four percent of total imports, but collectively they account for more than nine percent. In such a case, the investigating authority will be permitted to cumulate all imports from all the developing country Members.

Article 29 sets out special obligations applicable to Members that are in transition from centrally planned to market-based economies. Generally speaking, these Members-in-transition are permitted to apply programmes and measures necessary to effect the transition. In addition, such Members have an additional four years, or until January 1, 2002, to eliminate the use of any prohibited subsidies. Special limits also apply concerning the actionability of other types of permitted subsidies.

(j) Part X: Dispute Settlement

Part X of the Agreement (Article 30) provides that disputes that arise under the Agreement are to be settled in accordance with GATT Articles XXII and XXIII, as elaborated and applied by the DSU.

(k) Part XI: Final Provisions

Part XI (Articles 31 and 32) provides the Agreement's final obligations. Article 31 notes that certain of the Agreement's provisions concerning non-actionable subsidies and deemed serious prejudice will only apply for a temporary period of five years—until January 1, 2000. The Committee is to review these obligations prior to their expiry to determine whether they should be amended and/or extended.

Article 32 sets out a number of miscellaneous obligations. Paragraph 1 confirms that no action may be taken against the subsidy of another Member except in accordance with GATT 1994 as interpreted by the Agreement. Each Member was required to take all necessary steps to bring themselves into compliance with all obligations of the Agreement as of January 1, 1995. The Agreement is to apply to all investigations and reviews of existing measures that are initiated after January 1, 1995. With respect to the five-year sunset provision of Article 21(3), all pre-existing countervailing duty orders are deemed to have entered into force January 1, 1995, meaning that all such orders must be reviewed prior to January 1, 2000 to determine whether they are still warranted. Members are required to notify the Committee of any changes to their relevant laws or regulations. Finally, the Committee is to review the implementation and operation of the Agreement annually and is also to report annually to the Council for Trade in Goods.

Part G:

Safeguards

1. INTRODUCTION

While the GATT 1947 attempted to encourage contracting parties to reduce their customs duties through negotiation, it was viewed as equally important that they were expected to "bind" any such reductions, meaning that contracting parties generally agreed that they would not increase any reduced tariffs in the future. However, it was accepted early in the GATT negotiations that unconditional tariff bindings were not likely to be acceptable to most countries. There was general agreement that contracting parties should be permitted to subsequently increase a bound tariff in a number of special circumstances. One of these accepted special circumstances was where imports of a particular product were increasing or "surging" at such a rate as to cause significant disruption to the relevant domestic industry. In such circumstances, contracting parties would be permitted to temporarily "escape" the relevant tariff binding and "safeguard" their domestic industry through the imposition of an import restraint. This exemption, entitled "emergency action" and included as Article XIX of the GATT 1947, has since become known as the "safeguard" or "escape" clause.

2. PRE-WTO OBLIGATIONS AND THE NEGOTIATIONS CONCERNING SAFEGUARDS

As originally drafted, Article XIX allowed contracting parties to take emergency action, in the form of increased tariffs or quantitative restrictions, when, as the result of an unforeseen development, a product was being imported in such increased quantities as to cause or threaten serious injury to the domestic producers of a like or directly competitive product. In such circumstances, a contracting party was, subject to certain additional obligations, free to suspend an obligation in whole or in part, or withdraw or modify a concession, to the extent and for such time as may be necessary to prevent or remedy the injury. Use of this emergency remedy was subject to two important limitations. First, it had to be applied on an MFN basis, meaning that imports of the product from all sources had to be treated equally, and the action could not be targeted on a selective basis, against imports from only one or more specific countries. Second, the contracting party taking the emergency action was generally expected to provide compensation, in the form of increased market access for other products, to those other contracting parties whose exports were affected by the emergency action. If the parties were not able to reach agreement on such adequate compensation, the affected exporting parties could then be authorized to take substantially equivalent retaliatory action.

During the 1970s, a number of problems with Article XIX became increasingly evident. Three problems in particular were seen as significantly impairing the utility of the safeguard remedy. First, the requirement of "serious" injury to the relevant domestic industry was considered by some to be too high a threshold. Second, the requirement of compensation was considered to be onerous in some cases, such as where significant levels of trade might be affected by the action. Finally, the MFN requirement meant that the remedy could not be targeted at imports from the one or more problem countries. These elements tended to significantly increase the "cost" of invoking the remedy, meaning that it was infrequently used. Instead, many contracting parties either increasingly resorted to anti-dumping or countervailing duty remedies or, even more problematic, began to employ remedies that operated largely outside of the GATT rules. This second type of measure, often initiated at the request of a domestic industry, usually involved a bilateral agreement between the importing and exporting country whereby the exporting country would "voluntarily" agree to limit its exports. While it was generally considered that such voluntary export restraints were inconsistent with the then existing GATT obligations, they were not clearly and specifically prohibited (such measures subsequently became known as "grey-area measures", "voluntary export restraints" or "VERs"). In a trading system designed to rely on comparative advantage, such VERs smacked of interventionalism, cartelization and market sharing. However, faced with difficulties of using the safeguard remedy, domestic political considerations often required some contracting parties to continue to employ such measures in order to protect their domestic producers regardless of their secondary trade effects or the existing GATT rules. The use of grey-area measures subsequently exploded during the 1970s and they began to constitute a serious threat to the entire GATT system.

The contracting parties, realizing the potential consequences of such a trend, placed the safeguard remedy on the negotiating agenda for the Tokyo Round of GATT negotiations, and during the Round an attempt was made at developing a "Safeguard Code" which would address the defects with the existing Article XIX remedy. Unfortunately, agreement on even a modest Code was not possible during the Round, with the MFN/selectivity issue being the primary point of division. Realizing the importance of the issue, the contracting parties agreed to continue negotiations on Article XIX after the Round had formally concluded. In November 1979, the GATT Council formed the Committee on Safeguards in order to continue with the negotiations. While negotiations did continue, no substantial progress could be made. Thus, by 1985 the "Leutwiler Report" was still able to comment that:

> We are in no doubt that the safeguard rules of GATT must outlaw discrimination. Time and again the negotiation of voluntary export restraints with one supplier . . . has been followed by a proliferation of bilateral deals with all efficient suppliers who are not in a position to refuse, leading to a virtual cartelization of world markets. The most obvious case in point is the Multifibre Arrangement, but cartelization of the steel sector is also far advanced. It is therefore untrue that "selective" action helps to limit the extent of disruptive trade. Moreover, the process of discrimination against the most efficient suppliers contravenes the principle of comparative advantage and maximizes the cost to the world economy of the protection granted to the inefficient.[174]

---

[174] *Trade Policies for a Better Future*, at 43.

As a result, the Leutwiler Report recommended not only that safeguard action be taken only in strict accordance with improved Article XIX rules, but that all then existing VERs and similar arrangements be eliminated or brought into conformity with these improved rules.

As in many other areas, the Leutwiler Report was very influential in developing the Uruguay Round's negotiating agenda as it applied to safeguards. The Ministerial Declaration setting out the negotiating agenda for the Round then mirrored much of the Leutwiler Report's safeguard recommendations, providing that:

(i) A comprehensive agreement on safeguards is of particular importance to the strengthening of the GATT system and to progress in the Multilateral Trade Negotiations.

(ii) The agreement on safeguards:

— shall be based on the basic principles of the General Agreement;

— shall contain, *inter alia*, the following elements: transparency, coverage, objective criteria for action including the concept of serious injury or threat thereof, temporary nature, degressivity and structural adjustment, compensation and retaliation, notification, consultation, multilateral surveillance and dispute settlement; and

— shall clarify and reinforce the disciplines of the General Agreement and should apply to all contracting parties.[175]

As of the Montreal Mid-term Meeting in 1988, some basic negotiating principles had still not been agreed to amongst the parties, with MFN/selectivity still remaining as the largest obstacle. However, over the next two years substantial progress was made in the negotiations to the point that a bracketed draft text could be produced for the Brussels Ministerial Meeting in late 1990. While this text was not complete, with a number of political decisions yet to be made, it is probable that a consensus could have been reached on these remaining issues during the Meeting had it not collapsed due to issues relating to agriculture. In any event, these remaining issues were resolved over the course of the next few years, and the *Agreement on Safeguards* was included in Annex IA to the WTO Agreement.

3. THE *AGREEMENT ON SAFEGUARDS*

The *Agreement on Safeguards* is a brief agreement, comprised of only 14 Articles. Its preamble notes that there is a need to clarify and reinforce the provisions of GATT 1994, particularly those of Article XIX, in order to re-establish multilateral control over safeguards, and eliminate measures which escape such control. The purpose of the Agreement is then re-confirmed in

---

[175] "Ministerial Declaration on the Uruguay Round", BISD, 33S/19, at 24-25.

Article 1, which provides that the Agreement establishes the rules for measures taken under GATT Article XIX.

Article 2 sets out the basic conditions under which the Article XIX safeguard remedy may be invoked. A Member[176] is only permitted to apply a safeguard if it has determined, in accordance with the Agreement, that the following two conditions exist:

- that the product is being imported into its territory in increased quantities, either absolute or relative[177] to domestic production; and

- such increased imports are causing or threatening to cause serious injury to the domestic industry producing a like or directly competitive product.

Paragraph 2 of Article 2 then re-confirms the basic MFN requirement that a safeguard measure is to be applied against an imported product, regardless of its source. Thus, selectivity in application of the safeguard remedy has generally been rejected, with an exception, discussed below, for the selective application of quantitative restrictions in certain limited circumstances. These primary elements of the safeguard remedy are then further developed in the remaining provisions of the Agreement.

(a) The Investigation

The provisions of Article 3 address issues relating to safeguard investigations. A safeguard can only be applied following an investigation that has been undertaken pursuant to published transparent procedures. The investigative process must include certain due process requirements, such as reasonable notice to all interested parties, and a public hearing or other process which provides for the presentation of evidence (with sufficient protections for confidential information) and the exchange of argument. A detailed analysis of the case under investigation, any findings and reasoned conclusions are then to be published by the investigating authority.

(b) The Injury Determination

Article 4 clarifies certain requirements that must be met in undertaking the required determination of serious injury or threat thereof. In making an

---

[176] A footnote to Article 2 provides that a customs union, such as the EU, may apply a safeguard either as a single unit, on behalf of all countries to the union, or on behalf of only one Member to the union. If applying the measure on behalf of the entire union, injury must be assessed on a union-wide basis. If the measure is being applied on behalf of only one Member, injury is to be assessed only within that one Member.

[177] Article 2 has now clarified that safeguard action may be taken for both absolute and relative increases in imports. This position was not entirely clear under Article XIX.

injury determination, "serious injury" is to be interpreted to mean a significant overall impairment in the position of a domestic industry. "Domestic industry" in turn means the producers, as a whole (or those producers representing a major proportion of domestic production), of a like or directly competitive product operating within the territory of the Member.

In determining injury, the investigating authority must evaluate all the relevant factors bearing on the domestic industry's situation, including, in particular: the rate of increase in imports; their share of the domestic market; and changes in the levels of sales, production, productivity, capacity utilization, profitability, and employment. Importantly, a finding of serious injury is not to be made unless the investigation determines, on the basis of objective evidence, that there is a causal link between the imports of the product and injury being suffered by the domestic industry.

(c) Application of Safeguard Measures

Article XIX provides that a safeguard measure may take the form of either a tariff or a quantitative restriction. This choice has not been altered under the Agreement. Article 5 provides that in either case, Members are only to apply a safeguard to the extent necessary to prevent or remedy the serious injury and facilitate adjustment. If a quantitative restriction is used, except in exceptional circumstances, the safeguard must not reduce imports to below the prevailing average level of imports over the last three representative years. In a slight deviation from the MFN obligation of Article 2, in certain circumstances a Member may further restrict imports below this level on a selective basis and for a limited period of time if the Member can demonstrate to the Committee on Safeguards[178] that imports from certain Members have increased disproportionately, and that such a selective reduction is equitable and can be justified.

In a specific application of GATT Article XIII, paragraph 2 notes that if a quota is to be allocated among the various exporting countries, the Member taking the action may seek agreement from those countries as to their respective shares. If such agreement is not practical, the Member taking the action may allocate quotas amongst the exporting countries based on representative levels of previous exports.

(d) Provisional Measures

Under Article 6, Members may impose a provisional or temporary measure pursuant to a preliminary injury determination in cases where there is clear

---

[178]The Committee on Safeguards (the "Committee") is established under Article 12 of the Agreement.

evidence that increased imports have or will cause serious injury, and where delay in the imposition of a definitive safeguard would cause damage that would be difficult to repair subsequently. Any such provisional measure must be in the form of an increased tariff and cannot be in place for any longer than 200 days, during which time a full investigation must be conducted. If it is then determined that the serious injury requirement has not been proved, all duties collected during the provisional period must be refunded.

(e) Duration and Review of Safeguard Measures

A safeguard measure has always been considered to be a temporary measure to be imposed only to allow the domestic industry time to adjust to import competition. It was not to be imposed indefinitely. However, no specific time limits on imposition were set out in Article XIX. Article 7 of the Agreement now specifies that a safeguard is only permitted to be in place for as long as is necessary to remedy the serious injury and facilitate the adjustment. Generally speaking, this period is to be no longer than four years. This can be extended, but only if a new investigation confirms that the safeguard remains necessary to prevent or remedy the injury and there is evidence that the domestic industry is adjusting. In any case, a safeguard can only be renewed for a further four years (for maximum of eight years in total).

In addition to specific time limits, Article 7 also introduces a "degressivity" requirement. Where a safeguard is expected to be in place for longer than one year, it must be progressively liberalized at regular intervals during its period of application. Measures in place for more than three years must be reviewed at their mid-term to determine whether the pace of liberalization can be increased or if the measure can be withdrawn completely. Any measure which is extended beyond its initial four years cannot be made any more restrictive on extension than it was at the end of its initial four-year term and its regular liberalization must continue.

In order to prevent Members from avoiding these time limits set out above, a safeguard measure cannot be applied against the same product more than once under the Agreement, unless a period of time has elapsed where there has been no safeguard in place against the product. This period must be a minimum of two years, but in any case must be at least equal to the length of time that the original safeguard was in place. However, if the original safeguard was in place 180 days or less, it may be applied again after only one year from the date the measure was originally imposed. In any such cases the safeguard may only be applied twice during a five-year period.

(f) Level of Compensatory Concessions

Generally speaking, under Article XIX, a Member imposing a safeguard is expected to maintain a substantially equivalent level of concessions with other Members affected by the safeguard. In some cases, this imposed a significant cost on the country wishing to invoke the remedy. Compensation remains voluntary under the Agreement, and all Members concerned may agree as to how an equivalent level of concessions might be maintained in particular circumstances. If no agreement can be reached, the Member remains free to impose the safeguard, but an exporting Member may then be authorized to suspend substantially equivalent concessions in retaliation. However, in an important limitation of the compensation/retaliation obligation, if the safeguard is otherwise consistent with the Agreement and has been taken as a result of an absolute increase in imports, no retaliation can be exercised by any Member for the first three years that the safeguard is in place. Thus, in effect, no compensation will be payable if a safeguard remains in place for three years or less. Not only is this likely to increase the overall attractiveness of the remedy, but it also provides a significant incentive to limit actions to under three years.

(g) Special and Differential Treatment for Developing Country Members

Article 9 provides for two types of special treatment applicable to developing country Members. First, a safeguard action cannot be applied against a product from a developing country Member if that Member's share of total imports is less than three percent, and that any such Members do not cumulatively account for more than nine percent of all imports of the product. Second, developing country Members are permitted to impose safeguards for up to a maximum of 10 years (rather than the eight years applicable to developed country Members) and they are permitted to re-impose safeguards on the same product sooner than are developed country Members.

(h) Safeguard Measures Which Pre-existed the WTO

Many measures previously taken under Article XIX of GATT 1947 were still in force at the time the WTO Agreement entered into force. As noted, such measures were not previously subject to any specific time limits for elimination. However, under Article 10 of the Agreement Members are now required to terminate all such pre-existing safeguards eight years after they first came into effect, or by January 1, 2000, whichever date is later.

(i) Prohibition and Elimination of VERs

Article 11 now specifically prohibits the use of VERs and other similar grey-area measures, and provides for the elimination of all such pre-existing measures. Paragraph 1 confirms that Members are only permitted to take safeguard actions in accordance with Article XIX and the Agreement (although it is noted that the Agreement only applies to actions taken under

Article XIX, and not pursuant to any other provisions of GATT 1994). In addition, Members are prohibited from seeking, taking or maintaining any voluntary export agreements or similar arrangements. Members are also prohibited from encouraging or supporting any similar non-governmental measures adopted or maintained by private or public enterprises.

Any non-conforming arrangements that were in existence on January 1, 1995 must be brought into conformity with the Agreement by January 1, 1999, according to time tables that were submitted to the Committee on Safeguards. Subject to notification and mutual agreement amongst the involved Members, each importing Member is, however, entitled to extend one such measure for one additional year, until December 31, 1999.[179]

(j) Notification, Consultation, Surveillance and Dispute Settlement

The Committee on Safeguards is established under Article 13. The Committee operates under the authority of the WTO's Council on Trade in Goods and is open to any Member wishing to participate. Among others, the following functions have been assigned to the Committee: monitor and report on the Agreement; investigate certain procedural complaints; assist in consultations; monitor the elimination of VERs as required under the Agreement; and review certain compensation-related issues.

Related notification and consultative obligations are set out in Article 12. Subject to certain protections for confidential information, Members are required to fully notify the Committee of a number of safeguard-related items, including: all safeguard-related laws and any changes thereto; the initiation of any safeguard investigations; the imposition of any provisional measures; any injury determinations and any decision to apply or extend a safeguard; and any VERs to be eliminated. Any Member proposing to apply a safeguard must consult, on request, with other substantially interested Members. The results of these, and any other consultations undertaken in accordance with the Agreement, are to be reported to the Council for Trade in Goods through the Committee on Safeguards.

With respect to dispute settlement, the provisions of Articles XXII and XXIII of GATT 1994, as elaborated and applied by the DSU, apply to consultation and dispute settlement under the Agreement.

---

[179]The Agreement specifies that Members have specifically accepted that the EU's VER on certain Japanese automobiles falls within this exception and is therefore to be eliminated on December 31, 1999.

Part H:

Technical Barriers to Trade

1. INTRODUCTION

As its title suggests, the WTO's *Agreement on Technical Barriers to Trade* ("TBT Agreement") attempts to regulate the development and application of technical standards and related measures which can sometimes act as unnecessary barriers to trade in goods. Technical standards and related measures are generally considered to include a significant number of mandatory and voluntary measures which attempt to regulate the characteristics of products and their methods of manufacture.

As is discussed below, the TBT Agreement is substantially based on the pre-existing GATT Standards Code, one of six non-tariff codes that were originally negotiated as part of the Tokyo Round of GATT negotiations.[180] In essence, the TBT Agreement expands upon and clarifies many of the previously existing obligations of the Standards Code. It is important to note at the outset that the TBT Agreement does not establish any specific technical standards itself. Rather, it imposes disciplines on the development and application of those standards, particularly as they apply to imported products. The over-arching goal of the Agreement is to ensure that such measures do not unnecessarily hinder trade.

2. PRE-WTO DISCIPLINES ON TECHNICAL STANDARDS AND THE URUGUAY ROUND NEGOTIATIONS

There is no GATT obligation which specifically addresses technical standards. Such measures are, instead, subject to a number of the GATT's general obligations, including, most importantly, the non-discrimination obligations of Articles I and III (MFN and national treatment) and the prohibition on quantitative restrictions (Article XI). In addition, the GATT's general exception, Article XX, also has application to these measures in a number of circumstances.

During the late 1960s and early 1970s, it had become apparent to many GATT contracting parties that tariffs were no longer the primary obstacles to international trade. Non-tariff barriers had assumed that role. Such non-tariff barriers can take many forms, one of which is discriminatory or otherwise unfair technical standards which act to isolate domestic producers from import competition. The contracting parties determined that the next round of GATT

---

[180] The Tokyo Round Standards Code is more formally known as the *Agreement on Technical Barriers to Trade* (GATT, BISD, 26S/8).

negotiations, the Tokyo Round, would attempt to develop new disciplines on many specific types of non-tariff barriers, including technical standards. One of the results of these negotiations was the Tokyo Round Standards Code, which entered into force on January 1, 1987. As was the case with all Tokyo Round Codes, accession to the Standards Code was voluntary. By the commencement of the Uruguay Round negotiations, only 34 GATT contracting parties had become signatories to the Standards Code, while a further 23 had been granted "observer" status.

Based primarily on the national treatment obligation of GATT Article III, the Standards Code provided a number of new disciplines on the development and application of technical standards. However, as was the case with most of the results of the Round, it was soon considered that the Code contained a number of deficiencies. By the time of the 1982 GATT Ministerial Meeting, less than two years after it had come into force, Ministers could already agree that the Standards Code, along with many of the other Tokyo Round Codes, should be reviewed to determine how it might be improved.

The Committee on Technical Barriers to Trade, which had been established under the Standards Code, undertook the task of identifying areas of the Code which could be improved. Immediately prior to the initiation of the Uruguay Round, the Committee decided to develop a non-exhaustive list of items that should be discussed as part of the negotiations. The issues identified were then divided into three broad categories: improvements that should be made to existing inadequate rules; clarifications to existing provisions which were considered unclear; and additional rules in new areas not then covered by the Code.[181] In early 1987, the Committee provided its list to the Uruguay Round's Negotiating Group on MTN Agreements and Arrangements, which had by then been established to negotiate improvements to a number of the Tokyo Round Codes.[182]

While resolution was not possible on a number of the issues the Committee identified, the fact that the issues had already been catalogued and discussed by the Committee assisted the Negotiating Group in refining the issues and identifying potential solutions. This assisted the negotiations as a whole, and, as a result, the Negotiating Group was able to table a substantially complete draft Agreement by the time of the Brussels Ministerial Meeting in late 1990. Only certain decisions relating to integration of the text into the final

---

[181] See the 1986 and 1987 Reports of the Committee on Technical Barriers to Trade, GATT, BISD, 33S/188 and 34S/174, respectively.

[182] The Negotiating Group on MTN Agreements and Arrangements was given a broad mandate as part of the final Uruguay Round agenda. Negotiations within this Group were to: "aim to improve, clarify, or expand, as appropriate, Agreements and Arrangements negotiated in the Tokyo Round of Multilateral Negotiations". See Ministerial Declaration on the Uruguay Round, GATT, BISD, 33S/19, at 25.

outcome of the Round and certain political issues remained. An agreement likely could have been finalized during the Brussels Meeting had the Meeting not collapsed due to the imbroglio over agriculture. Those few issues that did remain outstanding were then substantially addressed by Director-General Dunkel in his *Draft Final Act* presented to all participants in late 1991. The draft "Agreement on Technical Barriers to Trade" which appeared in the Dunkel Draft was then carried forward, substantially unchanged, into Annex IA of the WTO Agreement.

3. THE *AGREEMENT ON TECHNICAL BARRIERS TO TRADE*

The TBT Agreement is comprised of four major parts: (i) obligations concerning the development and implementation of technical measures (Articles 2 to 4); (ii) obligations relating to conformity assessment procedures (Articles 5 to 9); (iii) transparency enhancing obligations (Articles 10 to 12); and (iv) institutional and dispute settlement provisions (Articles 13 to 14). By way of introduction, it is important to note that one of the major failings of the Tokyo Round Standards Code was its limited membership. This shortcoming has now been addressed by inclusion of the TBT Agreement in Annex 1A to the WTO Agreement, meaning that all Members are now subject to the Agreement's obligations.

(a) Definitions, Scope and Coverage

Article 1 contains certain general provisions establishing the scope and coverage of the Agreement and provides certain important definitions. Generally speaking, in the area of technical standards, so-called "terms of art" used in the Agreement are normally to have the meanings given to them by other bodies within the United Nations system and other international standardizing bodies.[183] However, certain important terms used in the Agreement are specifically defined in Annex I. In particular, Annex I defines "technical regulation", "technical standard" and "conformity assessment procedure". Generally speaking, these definitions divide technical measures into two broad categories: mandatory and voluntary. A "technical regulation" is defined as a document which establishes a product's characteristics or its related process or production method, with which compliance is mandatory. The alternative, a "standard", is defined to be a document which provides rules, guidelines or characteristics for a product or a related process or production method, with which compliance is voluntary. The distinction between regulations and standards is important as the Agreement imposes different obligations concerning

---

[183] In particular, Annex I provides that the definitions found in the sixth edition of the ISO/IEC Guide 2:1991, "General Terms and Their Definitions Concerning Standardization and Related Activities", apply to those terms as used in the Agreement.

each type of measure. A "conformity assessment procedure" is then defined to be any procedure used, directly or indirectly, to determine whether the relevant requirements of a technical regulation or standard have been fulfilled. Such procedures include sampling, testing and inspection, evaluation, verification, and assurance of conformity with the relevant measure.

Paragraph 3 of Article 1 then establishes the scope and coverage of the Agreement. Generally speaking, all products, including industrial and agricultural products, are subject to the Agreement.[184] Paragraphs 4 and 5 set out certain exclusions from this coverage. First, purchasing specifications for government procurement purposes are not covered by the TBT Agreement but instead by the *Agreement on Government Procurement*.[185] Second, the TBT Agreement does not apply to sanitary and phytosanitary measures, which are instead covered by the WTO's *Agreement on Sanitary and Phytosanitary Measures*.[186]

(b) Technical Regulations and Standards

The Agreement's obligations relating to the establishment and application of technical regulations and standards are found in Articles 2 to 5. Obligations applicable to technical regulations are divided between those applicable only to central governments of Members (Article 2), and those applicable to local governments and non-governmental bodies (Article 3).

With respect to the application of technical regulations of central governments, Article 2 provides that Members must:

- promptly publish all adopted regulations or otherwise make them available to any interested party;
- ensure that, with respect to technical regulations, all imported products receive both MFN and national treatment;
- give positive consideration to accepting as equivalent the regulations of other Members, even if different from their own, if the Member is

---

[184] It is important to note that the Agreement is limited to "products". Technical regulations and standards applicable to services are therefore not covered.

[185] The *Agreement on Government Procurement* is discussed below in chapter 6, at pages 300-303.

[186] The *Agreement on Sanitary and Phytosanitary Measures* ("SPSM Agreement") is discussed above at pages 86-95. While the obligations of the TBT Agreement and the SPSM Agreement are similar in many respects, there is at least one important difference between the two agreements. In determining whether a particular measure is acting as an inconsistent barrier to trade, the TBT Agreement relies primarily on the non-discrimination obligations of MFN and national treatment. The SPSM Agreement, on the other hand, relies on the potentially more onerous requirements of scientific principles and risk assessments. The classification of a measure within one or the other of the two Agreements can therefore have significant implications.

satisfied that the other Member's regulations fulfill the required objectives of their own; and

- ensure that regulations are not prepared, adopted or applied so as to create unnecessary obstacles to trade.

This last important obligation was not found in the Tokyo Round Standards Code. In order to meet the obligation, technical regulations must not be more trade-restrictive than is necessary to meet a "legitimate objective", taking into account the risks non-fulfilment would create. "Legitimate objectives" are defined non-exhaustively to include: national security requirements; the prevention of deceptive practices; protection of human health or safety; animal or plant life or health; or the environment. In addition, technical regulations are not to be maintained if the circumstances that originally justified their enactment no longer exist or have changed so that a less trade-restrictive alternative is now available.

With respect to the development of new regulations, Members are required to:

- allow a reasonable period of time between the publication of a new technical regulation and its entry into force in order to allow other Members' exporters to adapt their products or methods of production to the new measure (except in urgent circumstances);
- generally speaking, specify technical regulations based on a product's performance requirements, rather than on design or descriptive characteristics; and
- base regulations on international standards, where such standards already exist or are imminent, unless these standards are inappropriate because of climatic, geographic or certain other factors.

In order to better develop the appropriate international standards, Members are expected to play a full part, within the limits of their resources, in the preparation of such international standards by the relevant international standardizing bodies. These international standards are important under the Agreement as whenever a technical regulation is in accordance with the relevant international standard and is being applied or adopted to meet a legitimate objective, the Agreement provides a rebuttable presumption that the regulation does not constitute an unnecessary obstacle to trade. There is, however, no reverse presumption which applies if a technical regulation is not based on an international standard.

Members have additional obligations in circumstances where a relevant international standard does not exist, or is otherwise not technically appropriate, and the technical regulation may have a significant effect on trade. In such cases, Members are required to: pre-publish the proposed regulation; notify other Members of the coverage of the proposed regulation through the WTO

Secretariat; provide particulars on request; allow a reasonable time for comments on the proposed regulation; discuss any comments on request; and take such comments and discussions into account. In urgent cases relating to safety, health, environmental protection, or national security, a Member is not required to take such steps in advance, provided that once the technical regulation is adopted the Member then properly notifies other Members of the regulation through the WTO Secretariat and allows for comment and discussion on the regulation.

Article 3 provides similar obligations applicable to the preparation, adoption and application of technical regulations by local government bodies and all non-governmental bodies. These obligations expand upon those found in the Tokyo Round Standards Code. Members are required to take all such reasonable measures as may be available to them to ensure that all local government bodies and non-governmental bodies comply with the obligations of Article 2, with the exception of certain notification provisions.[187] Members are required to ensure that the regulations of all local governments directly below the level of the central government (states and provinces, for example) are notified in accordance with provisions of Article 2, except when those regulations are substantially similar to previously notified central government measures. While in some cases they may not be subject to all the obligations of Article 2, Members are not permitted to take measures which require or encourage local government bodies or non-governmental bodies to act in a manner inconsistent with Article 2. Finally, an obligation not found in the Tokyo Round Standards Code provides that Members remain fully responsible under the Agreement for compliance with Article 2 and they are required to take positive steps to ensure such compliance by local government and non-governmental bodies.

Article 4 addresses certain general issues concerning the preparation, adoption, and application of the non-mandatory standards of central and local government bodies and non-governmental bodies. First, Members are required to ensure that central government standardizing bodies accept and comply with the Agreement's "Code of Good Practice" (discussed below). Thus, central government standardizing bodies are bound by the Code. Members must also take such reasonable measures as may be available to them to ensure local government and non-governmental standardizing bodies, as well as certain regional standardizing bodies within their territories, comply with the Code. These obligations apply to Members regardless of whether or not a relevant body has specifically accepted the Code.

The Code itself is found in Annex III to the Agreement. The Code is open to any standardizing body for acceptance. With respect to its substantive

---

[187]The obligation to take such reasonable measures as may be available to Members to ensure compliance substantially tracks the language of GATT Article XXIV:12 and the "Understanding on the Interpretation of Article XXIV:12", both discussed above at pages 65-66.

obligations, generally speaking they mirror those that apply to bodies that develop and apply technical regulations under Article 2. For example, among other obligations, standardizing bodies are required to:

- accord non-discriminatory treatment to imported products;
- ensure that standards do not create unnecessary obstacles to international trade;
- participate in international standards development;
- avoid duplication and make every effort to develop national consensus on standards they develop;
- specify standards based on product requirements in terms of performance rather than design or descriptive elements;
- publish a detailed work programme on a regular basis;
- except in urgent situations, allow for a 60-day comment period between publication of a draft standard and its adoption, and take any comments received into account; and
- promptly publish any adopted standard.

Any standardizing bodies that accept and are complying with the Code must be acknowledged by Members to be complying with the principles of the TBT Agreement.

(c) Conformity with Technical Regulations and Standards

The second major part of the Agreement (Articles 5 to 9) sets out certain obligations relating to determining the conformity of products with any relevant technical regulation or standard that has been established. These provisions expand upon similar obligations found in the Tokyo Round Standards Code. Article 5 first provides the obligations applicable to central government bodies. In cases where a positive assurance of compliance with a technical regulation or standard is required, Members must ensure that their central government bodies meet a number of specific obligations in assessing the compliance of products of other Members. Generally speaking, the conformity assessment procedures must meet the following requirements:

- they must accord non-discriminatory (MFN and national) treatment;
- they must not be prepared, adopted or applied so as to create an unnecessary obstacle to trade;
- they must be undertaken and completed as quickly as possible;
- the standard processing time must be published or provided on request;
- information requirements must be limited to what is necessary;
- confidentiality must be respected;

- any fees that are charged for assessing foreign products must be equitable in relation to those charged for assessing products of national origin, bearing in mind that certain additional costs may be incurred;

- the location of assessment facilities and the selection of samples must not cause unnecessary inconvenience; and

- procedures must be in place to review complaints and take corrective action if a complaint is justified.

Similar to the Agreement's obligations relating to the development of regulations and standards, Members are also required to ensure that their central government bodies employ, when available, the guides or recommendations of international standardizing bodies as the basis of their conformity assessment procedures. Members are also required to participate in the development of such guides or recommendations within the relevant international bodies. Except in urgent situations, in those cases where a relevant international guide or recommendation does not exist, or is inapplicable, and an assessment may have a significant effect on trade, Members are required to:

- pre-publish the proposed conformity assessment procedure;

- notify other Members of the proposed procedure through the WTO Secretariat; and

- allow a reasonable period for comment, discuss any comments upon request, and take these comments and discussions into account.

Members are permitted to avoid these transparency-enhancing obligations where urgent problems of safety, health, environmental protection or national security arise. In such cases, once the assessment procedure has been adopted the Member must then notify other Members, provide copies of the procedure to other Members on request, allow for comments and discussion, and then take any such comments and discussions into account.

Similar to the process involved in the implementation of regulations and standards, Members are required to publish or otherwise make available all conformity assessment procedures and, except in a case of urgency, allow a reasonable period of time between publication of a new procedure and its entry into force, thereby permitting producers in exporting Members time to adjust to the new procedure.

Article 6 then addresses issues related to the recognition of conformity assessments conducted by the central government bodies of other Members. Subject to certain qualifications, Members are required to ensure that their central government bodies extend recognition to the results of conformity assessment procedures of other Members, provided those procedures afford an equivalent assurance of conformity with the relevant technical regulation or standard. Members are also encouraged to negotiate mutual recognition agreements concerning conformity assessment procedures and to allow for the non-discriminatory participation of conformity assessment bodies from other Members in their conformity assessment procedures.

While Articles 5 and 6 address conformity assessment issues concerning central government bodies, Article 7 addresses those issues as they apply to local government bodies. With respect to such local government bodies, again, Members are required to take such reasonable measures as may be available to them to ensure that they comply with substantially all of the obligations of Articles 5 and 6 as described above. Members may not take measures which require or encourage their local governments to act in a manner inconsistent with those obligations, and, perhaps more importantly, Members remain fully responsible under the Agreement for the observance of all of the provisions of Articles 5 and 6 by local government bodies and they must take positive measures to ensure such compliance.

With respect to notification, Members are only obliged to ensure that the conformity assessment procedures of local governments on a level directly below the central government (state and provincial governments, for example) are properly notified, and Members are permitted to require that any communication concerning local government measures be conducted through the central government.

Certain issues concerning the conformity assessment procedures of non-governmental bodies are then addressed in Article 8. Members may have little control over the activities of such non-governmental bodies and therefore Members' obligations concerning them are correspondingly less. Members must take such reasonable measures as may be available to them to ensure that their non-governmental bodies conducting conformity assessments meet the obligations of Articles 5 and 6 (with the exception of certain of the notification obligations). Central government bodies are not permitted to rely on assessments conducted by non-governmental bodies unless those bodies meet the obligations of Articles 5 and 6. In addition, Members are prohibited from taking positive actions which may have the effect of requiring or encouraging such bodies to act in a manner inconsistent with Articles 5 and 6.

Article 9 concerns international and regional systems of conformity assessment. In situations where a positive assurance of compliance with the relevant technical regulation or standard is required, Members are required, if practical, to develop an international system of conformity assessment. Similar to the case with non-governmental bodies under Article 8, Members must take such reasonable measures as may be available to them to ensure that any such international or regional conformity assessment systems meet the obligations of Articles 5 and 6. Central government bodies are not to rely on such systems unless they meet the obligations of those Articles. In addition, Members are prohibited from taking any positive action which may have the effect of requiring or encouraging such systems to act in a manner inconsistent with Articles 5 and 6.

(d) Information and Assistance

Issues relating to information and assistance are addressed in the next Part of the Agreement, Articles 10, 11 and 12. For the most part, these provisions essentially repeat obligations found in the Tokyo Round Standards Code. Article 10 provides for greater transparency in the area of technical regulations, standards and conformity assessment procedures. First, Members must ensure that an "enquiry point" exists which can answer questions and provide information on a number of specified matters including technical regulations, standards and conformity assessment procedures. Members must also take reasonable measures to ensure that an enquiry point exists to answer enquiries relating to certain additional measures of non-governmental bodies.

With respect to notifications required under the Agreement, generally speaking Members must designate a single central government authority that has responsibility for meeting those notification obligations. All such notifications must be provided in one of the WTO's languages—that is, English, French or Spanish. If requested by another Member, developed country Members are required to provide English, French or Spanish translations of any notified document. Other than these obligations, nothing in the Agreement is to be construed as requiring a Member to provide any texts or information in other than its own langauge. In addition to the other notification obligations of the Agreement, Members are required to notify the WTO Secretariat of any international Agreement concerning technical regulations, standards or conformity assessment procedures which may have a significant effect on trade. (Members are then encouraged to consult on such Agreements on request.) The Secretariat is to circulate all notifications that it receives under the Agreement to all Members and interested international standardizing and conformity assessment bodies.

Issues relating to technical assistance to Members are addressed in Article 11. Generally speaking, if requested, Members are required to advise other Members on the preparation of technical regulations. Among the other types of required support, advice and technical assistance must be provided on request regarding the establishment of national standardizing bodies, the participation in international standardizing bodies, conformity assessment bodies, institutions and legal framework issues. In giving any such assistance, priority is to be given to the needs of least-developed country Members.

The special and differential treatment which is to be extended to developing country Members under the Agreement is provided for under Article 12. Members are to take into account the special development, financial and trade needs of developing country Members in a number of aspects, including in the preparation and application of technical regulations, standards and conformity assessment procedures, and in the implementation and operation of the Agreement generally. With respect to international standards and bodies, developing country Members should not be expected to use international standards as a basis for their domestic measures when such standards are not appropriate to their development, financial and trade needs. Members are to take such reasonable measures as may be available to ensure that international bodies are organized and operate so as to facilitate the participation of developing country Members.

The most important aspect of special and differential treatment is provided for under paragraph 8 of Article 12, where it is generally recognized that developing country Members may face special problems in meeting their obligations under the Agreement. Members are required to take this fact fully into account. Moreover, upon request, the Committee on Technical Barriers to Trade (established under Article 13) is permitted to grant certain time-limited exceptions from the Agreement's obligations for developing country Members.

(e) Institutions, Consultation and Dispute Settlement

The next Part of the Agreement deals with issues relating to institutions and dispute settlement. First, the Committee on Technical Barriers to Trade (the "Committee") is established under Article 13. The Committee is composed of representatives from each Member and is to meet as necessary, but no less than once a year, to allow for consultations on any matter affecting the operation of the Agreement. The Committee may establish any working parties or other bodies that it considers appropriate.

Article 14 addresses consultations and dispute settlement. In an important improvement on the Tokyo Round Standards Code, consultations and dispute settlement relating to the Agreement are to take place under the auspices of the DSB, in accordance with GATT Articles XXII and XXIII, as elaborated upon and applied by the DSU. Article 14 also confirms that Members may initiate the dispute settlement process if the measures or actions at issue relate to a local government or non-government body.

Because of the highly technical nature of disputes arising in the area, a dispute settlement panel established under the Agreement is permitted, either upon request of a party to the dispute, or on its own accord, to establish a technical experts group to assist the panel with technical issues. Any such technical experts group is to be governed by the special procedures set out in Annex II to the Agreement. The Annex provides that such groups are under the panel's control, which will establish the group's terms of reference. The rules concerning participation in such groups are very similar to those concerning WTO panelists generally. For example, participation in a group is limited to properly qualified individuals. Experts are to serve in their individual capacity and not as government representatives. Nationals of a Member that is involved in the dispute cannot serve in the group except under certain circumstances.

The group may seek information and advice from any source that it considers appropriate. Parties to the dispute are to have access to all non-confidential information provided to the group, in addition to all confidential information upon consent, or a non-confidential summary thereof. The group must first submit a draft report to the Members concerned for their review and comments, and must take any comments into account, as may be appropriate, in the drafting of the group's final report. The final report is then to be circulated to the concerned Members at the same time it is provided to the requesting panel.

(f) Final Provisions

The Agreement's final provisions are found in Article 15. Most importantly, paragraph 3 provides that the Committee shall annually review the implementation and operation of the Agreement. In addition, every three years the Committee is to review the Agreement with an eye towards recommending to the Council for Trade in Goods what changes should be made to the Agreement.

Part I:

The Agreement on Trade-Related Investment Measures

1. INTRODUCTION

This part of chapter 3 discusses the WTO's *Agreement on Trade-Related Investment Measures*. Trade-related investment measures ("TRIMs") are generally considered to be governmental measures relating to investment which have direct or indirect trade effects, intended or otherwise. In the past, many governments have imposed numerous types of requirements on investments in goods-producing enterprises, which then directly or indirectly affect the quantity of exports or imports. Such measures include requirements to use in local production a certain amount of domestically produced inputs (often referred to as "local-content requirements"), or requirements which link the amount of imports that may be used in local production to the amount of that production which is then exported (also known as "trade-balancing requirements"). Such TRIMs have long been argued to be justified for economic development or balance-of-payments purposes. And, as such measures are often tied to the regulation and control of foreign direct investment and multinational enterprises, any discussion of such measures raises sensitive questions relating to national sovereignty, particularly in the eyes of many developing countries.

2. PRE-WTO OBLIGATIONS AND THE NEGOTIATIONS CONCERNING TRIMs

At the time of the negotiation of GATT 1947, global flows of foreign investment were generally quite limited. International commerce was primarily confined to the cross-border movement of raw resources and finished products. As a result, there was considered to be little need for specific GATT rules regulating governmental behaviour in the area of foreign investment, other than those relating to balance of payments generally. However, since 1947 global investment flows have increased significantly, and, consequently, so have discussions concerning the need for increased governmental disciplines in the area.

In the GATT context, although no specific rules were developed, discussions indirectly related to foreign investment had been ongoing for over 20 years prior to the commencement of the Uruguay Round. An important difference of opinion which had been identified in the course of these discussions concerned the extent to which the then existing GATT rules already disciplined certain types of TRIMs. The prevailing view among developed countries was that GATT Articles III and XI, in particular, already prohibited those TRIMs which violated the national treatment obligation or acted to restrict imports or exports. This view was disputed by many developing countries which held the view that investment issues were entirely beyond the GATT's purview.

This issue remained a major point of contention within the GATT until 1982 when, in a dispute involving certain foreign investment measures of Canada's Foreign Investment Review Agency ("FIRA"), a GATT panel concluded that certain GATT obligations did apply to TRIMs in some circumstances, and that the Canadian measures at issue did, in fact, violate the national treatment obligation of GATT Article III.[188] While the panel's findings were not comprehensive in scope, the case did appear to settle the

---

[188] See *Canada—Administration of the Foreign Investment Review Act*, GATT, BISD, 30S/140. This dispute, between Canada and the United States, concerned certain measures that FIRA imposed on, or accepted from, foreign investors as a condition of approving certain types of foreign direct investment. Among others, these measures included a requirement to purchase domestically-produced inputs in preference to the like imported inputs (a clear local-content requirement). The GATT panel considered that such requirements to purchase domestically produced goods treated such goods more favourably than the like imported goods, thereby violating GATT Article III:4.

question as to whether the GATT had any competence to discipline TRIMs in some cases.

In spite of this outcome, many developing countries continued to dispute GATT's competence in the area of investment. After 1982, this debate continued on into the Preparatory Committee that had been charged with preparing the draft negotiating agenda for the Uruguay Round. Discussion within this Committee first centred on whether TRIMs should be the subject of any specific negotiations during the Round, and, if so, should the existing GATT disciplines be expanded or should their application merely be clarified. Any expansion of the existing GATT disciplines would take the GATT into a new uncharted area, much like the proposed negotiations on services and intellectual property. A compromise was eventually reached on this issue and, in the end, while TRIMs were placed on the agenda, a group of mostly developing countries was successful in having the agenda significantly restricted. The Ministerial Declaration on the Uruguay Round subsequently provided that:

> Following an examination of the operation of GATT Articles related to the trade restrictive and distorting effects of investment measures, negotiations should elaborate, as appropriate, further provisions that may be necessary to avoid such adverse effects on trade.[189]

As any subsequent negotiations would be required to follow the agenda set out in the Ministerial Declaration, the agreed agenda effectively limited the negotiations to only clarifying existing GATT obligations. Discussions would not venture beyond those measures which had trade-distorting effects. This agenda then effectively pre-determined much of the outcome of the TRIMs negotiations. Thus, while the TRIMs negotiations were considered by some to be a "new" area for the GATT, similar to the areas of services and intellectual property, in fact the TRIMs negotiations were much more conservative in scope, being restricted to discussing only those investment measures which had "trade restrictive and distorting effects". The negotiations would not be permitted to address the many other investment issues and measures which do not directly or indirectly affect trade.

While apparent agreement had been reached on a limited agenda and a negotiating plan, in a reflection of the overall sensitivity of the area, important differences continued to remain throughout the TRIMs negotiations. These differences proved to be so significant that even after four years of negotiations an agreed negotiating text could still not be produced for the Brussels Ministerial Meeting in December 1990.[190] In order to move the negotiations

---

[189] Ministerial Declaration on the Uruguay Round, GATT, BISD, 33S/19, at 26.

[190] It is interesting to note, however, that by this time the TRIMs negotiating group had identified 18 separate GATT Articles which could be applicable to TRIMs in various circumstances (including Articles I, II, III, VI, VIII, X, XI, XII, XIV, XV, XVII, XVIII and XIX).

along, three basic issues of divergence were identified for discussion by Ministers in Brussels. First, there continued to be disagreement concerning the potential coverage of any agreement. Should an agreement address measures imposed on existing enterprises or should it be limited to those measures imposed only at the time of making a new investment? Also related to coverage, should an agreement cover only mandatory obligations or should it also extend to measures related to the bestowing of all governmental advantages, such as subsidies? A second issue related to the level of discipline. Should an agreement impose *per se* prohibitions on trade-distorting TRIMs, or should measures only be subject to discipline if they have actual distorting effects in application? Finally, what special and differential treatment should be extended to developing countries in light of any agreement that might be reached on the first two issues? Unfortunately, the Brussels Ministerial Meeting collapsed over agricultural issues before substantive progress could be made on any of these TRIMs issues. Negotiations subsequently recommenced in early 1991.

These post-Brussels TRIMs negotiations proved to be equally as unsuccessful, and it was not until Mr. Dunkel produced his Draft Final Act in December 1991 that any consensus could be developed within the negotiating group. In light of the internal trade-offs that all participants were being asked to make within the Dunkel Draft's TRIMs Agreement, it generally found wide-spread, although begrudging, acceptance among the participants. This draft Agreement was then subsequently carried forward into the WTO Agreement largely unchanged. While few participants were pleased with the outcome of the TRIMs negotiations, most agreed that it was likely to be the best possible result in the circumstances. Any improvement to disciplines in the investment area would have to await future negotiations.

3. THE *AGREEMENT ON TRADE-RELATED INVESTMENT MEASURES*

Perhaps reflecting the minimalist outcome of the negotiations, the *Agreement on Trade-Related Investment Measures* (the "TRIMs Agreement") is the briefest Agreement within the WTO framework, comprised of only nine Articles. Its preamble repeats the applicable provision of the Ministerial Declaration concerning TRIMs, thereby indicating that the Agreement is largely limited to clarifying existing GATT obligations. This is further confirmed by Article 1, which provides that the Agreement applies only to investment measures related to trade in goods or "TRIMs". Thus, investment measures relating to services or intellectual property fall outside the scope of the Agreement.[191]

---

[191] This is not to say that investment measures relating to services or intellectual property fall outside of the WTO Agreement entirely. Rather, investment measures relating to services and intellectual property are addressed in certain respects within the *General Agreement on Trade in Services* and the *Agreement on Trade-Related Aspects of Intellectual Property Rights*. See the discussion of these agreements in chapters 4 and 5, respectively.

Article 2 then sets out the Agreement's substantive disciplines. Paragraph 1 first provides that, without prejudice to other rights and obligations under GATT 1994, Members are prohibited from applying any TRIM that is inconsistent with Articles III or XI of GATT 1994. The Agreement thereby incorporates a *per se* prohibition rather than an effects test. And, while in many respects this obligation can be seen as simply repeating existing GATT obligations, it is the first time that many developing countries have explicitly acknowledged that the GATT applies to investment measures.

An illustrative list of measures which are considered to offend GATT Articles III:4 and XI is then provided in an Annex (which is incorporated into the Agreement through paragraph 2 of Article 2). Importantly, measures listed in the Annex are not limited to mandatory or enforceable measures, but also include those non-mandatory measures which must be complied with by an enterprise in order to obtain the benefit of an advantage. With respect to violations of the national treatment obligation of Article III:4, the Annex lists the following prohibited requirements:

- requirements to purchase domestic products or from domestic sources, whether such requirements are specified in terms of volume, value, or a proportion of volume or value of local production; or

- requirements that link the purchase or use of imported products to the amount of locally produced products that are exported.

(Both these types of measures are generally considered to constitute "local-content requirements".)

With respect to violations of the prohibition on quantitative restrictions found in GATT Article XI, the Annex lists the following prohibited requirements:

- requirements which link an enterprise's imports to its local production or its exports ("trade-balancing requirements");

- requirements which limit an enterprise's imports by linking access to foreign exchange to the amount of foreign exchange inflow attributable to that enterprise (also known as "foreign-exchange-balancing requirements"); or

- requirements which limit the amount of local production that an enterprise may export.

It is important to note three other features of Article 2. First, the list of measures found in the Annex is illustrative, not comprehensive. Thus, other types of measures may still fall within the Article 2 prohibition if they violate GATT Article III or XI. Second, while the Article 2 prohibition does extend to all "advantages", including subsidies, the *Agreement on Subsidies and Countervailing Measures* also contains certain related disciplines on some types of subsidies. For example, Article 3(1) of that Agreement prohibits any subsidy which is linked to the use of domestic over imported goods.[192] Third, generally speaking, there are a number of investment-related measures which fall outside of the prohibition as they do not violate GATT Article III or XI. For example, minimum export requirements, technology transfer requirements, employment obligations and minimum equity requirements will, in most cases, not be disciplined by the Agreement.

Article 3 of the Agreement then clarifies that the prohibitions of Article 2 are not absolute. All the exceptions under GATT 1994 that are otherwise available to Members continue to apply to the obligations of the Agreement. This, of course, includes the important exceptions of GATT Articles XX and XXI. This provision is further elaborated upon by Article 4, which provides that developing country Members remain free to deviate from the prohibitions of Article 2 for balance-of-payments purposes, subject to certain continuing balance-of-payments obligations under GATT 1994.

Article 5 of the Agreement then provides certain notification and transitional obligations. Under paragraph 1, by the beginning of April 1995, all Members were to have notified the WTO's Council for Trade in Goods of all TRIMs that they were then applying which were inconsistent with the Agreement. Under paragraph 2, developed country Members were then to eliminate all such notified inconsistent measures by January 1, 1997. Developing country Members have an additional three years, until January 1, 2000, to eliminate such measures, and least-developed country Members have until January 1, 2002. These longer transition periods applicable to developing country Members can also be further extended by the Council in certain justifiable circumstances. While not specifically addressed in Article 5, it appears that a failure to notify a pre-existing inconsistent TRIM as required means that the measure cannot be protected during the applicable transition period and should have been eliminated as of January 1, 1995.

Paragraph 4 of Article 5 provides that during the applicable transition period a Member is not permitted to amend a notified inconsistent measure so as to increase its inconsistency with the prohibitions of Article 2. In addition, any inconsistent TRIM introduced by a Member less than 180 days prior to January 1, 1995 cannot benefit from the transition periods of paragraph 2.

Paragraph 5 provides an additional exception to Article 2, designed to ensure that certain new investments will not be placed at a competitive disadvantage during the transition period. Notwithstanding Article 2, and during the applicable transition period only, a Member is permitted to apply a TRIM to a new investment if the products of the new investment are like

---

[192] Article 3(1) of the *Agreement on Subsidies and Countervailing Measures* is discussed above at pages 157-158.

products to those being produced by an existing enterprise that is already subject to an existing and notified TRIM, and where the new TRIM is necessary to avoid distorting the competition between the existing enterprise and the new investment. Among other obligations, any such new TRIM must be eliminated at the same time as the existing TRIM.

The issue of increased transparency is addressed in Article 6. In particular, Members have re-affirmed certain existing notification obligations that are already considered to be applicable to TRIMs. In addition, Members must notify the WTO Secretariat of publications where their TRIMs can be found, accord sympathetic consideration to requests for information, and afford adequate opportunity for consultation on any matter arising from the Agreement. Should any such consultations prove unsuccessful, Article 8 provides that GATT Articles XXII and XXIII, as elaborated upon by the DSU, apply to consultation and dispute settlement under the Agreement.

The Committee on Trade-Related Investment Measures is established under Article 7. The Committee is open to all Members and is to meet not less than once a year, or otherwise as requested by any Member. It is to monitor the operation and implementation of the Agreement, reporting annually to the WTO's Council for Trade in Goods. It is also to carry out any other tasks that might be assigned to it by the Council.

Perhaps most importantly, under Article 9 the Council is to review the operation of the Agreement by January 1, 2000, and is to then propose any amendments to the Agreement which might be appropriate. In the course of this review, the Council is to consider whether the Agreement should be complemented with additional provisions dealing more broadly with investment and competition policies. In other words, the Council is to determine whether a more comprehensive investment Agreement can and should be negotiated within the WTO in the future.[193]

Part J:

Conclusions

Trade in goods has been the principal focus of international trade law for much of the past 50 years. In many ways, the WTO Agreement reflects this historical focus. For example, in quantitative terms the Agreements and related documents that make up the Multilateral Agreements on Trade in Goods comprise over 70 percent of the WTO Agreement. However, in spite of

---

[193]The potential for future WTO negotiations in the area of investment is discussed below in chapter 8.

the fact that the historical focus of trade law has been trade in goods, there were still a growing number of areas of continuing and seemingly intractable difficulty relating to trade in goods. Over the course of its life, the GATT had struggled to address many of these issues, often unsuccessfully. For example, trade in agricultural products was one of the first areas to develop problems. Yet, hampered by vague rules and weak disciplines, the GATT made little progress in addressing the problems being experienced in this sector. Problems in agriculture were followed by problems in textiles and clothing. Rather than addressing the underlying problems in this sector, it was dealt with by adopting a policy of denial—by simply excluding clothing and textile trade from the otherwise applicable GATT rules. More recently, the trade remedies of safeguards and anti-dumping and countervailing duties became increasingly controversial. The GATT's failure to address concerns in these areas meant that the rules were being increasingly side-stepped through the use of so-called "grey-area" measures, producing a cartelization of some major product and geographic markets. Attempts made during the Tokyo Round to address many of these problems in some ways merely increased systemic deficiencies, and thereby generated further problems and disputes.

In contrast to past attempts, the WTO, through its Multilateral Agreements on Trade in Goods, has made a comprehensive attempt at addressing all outstanding trade-in-goods issues. Considering the length of time many of these problems have dogged the international trading system, the results of this attempt, at least initially, should be considered impressive. For example, the *Agreement on Agriculture*, while it has not produced many immediate improvements in market access, has commenced the elimination of the special rules that had previously dominated agricultural trade, leaving it for future negotiations to produce greater market access under the framework of these improved disciplines. The *Agreement on Textiles and Clothing* should result in the full integration of textiles and clothing into the global trading system for the first time in two decades. The *Agreement on Safeguards* has also addressed longstanding perceived deficiencies in the rules. Further, the "single undertaking" approach of the WTO now means that all WTO Members are signatories to all the Multilateral Agreements, thereby eliminating the problem of differing rights and obligations created by the Tokyo Round and bringing developing countries more fully into the global trading system. Finally, all these improvements are now overseen by an official multilateral organization and enforced with the assistance of a much-improved and effective dispute settlement system.

While the results of the Uruguay Round as it applies to trade in goods should be considered impressive, there remains much work to be done. And, it must be noted, a fair degree of uncertainty continues to exist. While agriculture and textiles and clothing are being integrated into the system, this process will take years, and perhaps decades to accomplish fully. Disputes in these areas are likely to arise as market access, and resulting competition in domestic markets, increases. Further, concern has been expressed that in some areas (such as anti-dumping in particular) the rules have been permitted to regress, making it easier to take protective action against imports. This is of major concern. Demands for protective action increase with the level of competition in the domestic market. Such increased competition, or what is now being referred to as "increased contestibility" of domestic markets, is one of the underlying goals of trade liberalization. What may be gained on the one hand through improved WTO rules may be taken away with the other through increasing recourse to trade remedies.

And yet, even while areas of uncertainty and concern do exist, the creation of the WTO has fundamentally changed the dynamics of these remaining problems. The mandate of the WTO is, in part, to ensure that such problems are not allowed to fester until the political consequences of possible solutions make resolution domestically unacceptable. Work is already underway in some areas, such as agriculture, to prepare for the next round of negotiations. While the WTO has not resolved all trade-in-goods issues and produced free access in all sectors, it has produced real and substantive improvement in many areas.

4

The General Agreement on Trade in Services

1. INTRODUCTION

It has been estimated that the production and supply of services now accounts for about 70 percent of all employment and 65 percent of gross domestic product in Canada.[1] The total North American services market has recently been estimated to be as large as US$4.2 trillion.[2] Yet, in spite of this significant and growing economic importance, there existed few disciplines regulating the international trade in services prior to the completion of the Uruguay Round. Because of the relative economic importance of trade in goods at the time the GATT was first negotiated, that Agreement only addressed issues arising out of such trade in goods. In fact, one of the continuing criticisms of the pre-Uruguay Round GATT system was that it was becoming increasingly irrelevant as services gained in importance in the global economy. Unless steps were taken to begin addressing issues arising out of the international trade in services, the GATT would likely become increasingly marginalized as services continued to represent an increasing proportion of global economic activity and world trade.

While the Uruguay Round was the first multilateral international negotiation to address trade in services in any comprehensive manner, the issue of trade in services first appeared on the international agenda in the late 1970s, largely as a result of increasing United States interest in the issue. The GATT itself first began reviewing issues related to trade in services in the early 1980s. During its meetings in 1981, the Consultative Group of Eighteen[3] reviewed a preliminary analysis of certain trade-in-services issues prepared by the GATT Secretariat.[4] While views apparently varied widely among the Group's members as to the advisability of extending the GATT's work into the area of services, no member of the Group opposed further exploratory work being undertaken by the Secretariat. Subsequently, the Ministerial Declaration issued following the 1982 Meeting of the Contracting Parties included three carefully worded paragraphs relating to services. The Contracting Parties had decided:

---

[1] See, for example, M. Walker, "Behind the North American Free Trade Agreement," in *Fraser Forum* (January 1993), at 5-12.

[2] H. Broadman, "International Trade and Investment in Services" (1991) 27 *Int'l Lawyer* 623 at 625.

[3] The Consultative Group of Eighteen ("CG-18") was established by the GATT Council in July 1975 to assist the GATT Contracting Parties in carrying out their responsibilities under the General Agreement (see Decision of the GATT Council, BISD 22S/15). The Group's original membership, which was "balanced and broadly representative", included Canada, the U.S., the EC (as it then was) and a number of developing countries. The Group was initially established as a temporary body but, after two extensions, was made permanent in 1979.

[4] See *Report of the Consultative Group of Eighteen to the Council of Representatives*, GATT, BISD 28S/71, at 74.

1. To recommend to each contracting party with an interest in services of different types to undertake, as fast as it is able, national examination of the issues in this sector.

2. To invite contracting parties to exchange information on such matters among themselves, *inter alia*, through international organizations such as the GATT. The compilation and distribution of such information should be based on as uniform a format as possible.

3. To review the results of these examinations, along with the information and comments provided by relevant international organizations, at their 1984 Session and to consider whether any multilateral action in these matters is appropriate and desirable.[5]

In late 1983, the GATT's Director-General then asked "seven eminent persons" if they would serve as an independent group to study and report on the problems facing the international trading system. Chaired by Mr. Fritz Leutwiler of Switzerland, the Group issued its report, *Trade Policies For a Better Future*, in February 1985.[6] Among other things, the Group recommended that "[g]overnments should be ready to examine ways and means of expanding trade in services, and to explore whether multilateral rules can appropriately be devised for this sector."[7]

While support was clearly building among the developed countries for the view that the GATT should begin addressing issues arising out of services trade, this view was not shared by most developing countries. Many resisted strongly any U.S.-led attempt to press for further GATT work in the trade-in-services area. The debate between the United States and the developing countries continued on through 1985 and into early 1986.

It was not until the September 1986 GATT Ministerial Meeting, called to launch the Uruguay Round, that many developing countries finally relented and allowed trade in services to be placed on the Round's negotiating agenda. While this was viewed by some as being an important early breakthrough, there is probably little question that the United States would not have agreed to commence the Uruguay Round without the inclusion of services on the agenda. The Ministerial Declaration launching the Round provided that:

Negotiations in this area shall aim to establish a multilateral framework of principles and rules for trade in services, including elaboration of possible disciplines for individual sectors, with a view to expansion of such trade under

---

[5] *Ministerial Declaration of the Thirty-eighth Session*, GATT, BISD 29S/9, at 21-22.

[6] Consequently, the Group's report subsequently became known as the "Leutwiler Report". The Group's recommendations formed the basis of many proposals for reform which were ultimately adopted as part of the Uruguay Round.

[7] *Trade Policies For A Better Future: Proposals For Action* (Geneva: GATT, 1985), at 45-46.

conditions of transparency and progressive liberalization and as a means of promoting economic growth of all trading partners and the development of developing countries. Such framework shall respect the policy objectives of national laws and regulations applying to services and shall take into account the work of relevant international organizations.[8]

In an attempt to address some of the concerns relating to the negotiation of services-related rules, two functionally separate negotiating groups were established: the Group Negotiations on Goods ("GNG"), which had responsibility for goods-related issues, and the separate and distinct Group of Negotiations on Services ("GNS"), which had responsibility for the services negotiations. Both groups were to report to the Trade Negotiations Committee ("TNC"), the ministerial level group established to oversee the complete negotiations.

2. THE NEGOTIATIONS

There are two distinct features of services and their international trade which initially made rule development conceptually difficult. First, there are significant qualitative differences between the many types of services that are already being traded internationally.[9] For example, there is relatively little in common between financial services and engineering, or between telecommunications and maritime shipping. Developing general rules that are to be comprehensively applicable to all the various types of services is a demanding task when the potential issues that might face suppliers, consumers and regulators can be so vastly different across service sub-sectors.

Second, in contrast to goods, where there is only one possible mode of trade (that is the physical export and import of a good), it was generally recognized that, with respect to the trade of services, there are four methods or modes whereby a service can be traded or supplied internationally. First, the service can be provided to a user in one country from a supplier located in its home jurisdiction (accounting advice given over the telephone or by facsimile transmission, for example). Second, the service-supplier could establish an office or commercial presence in the territory of the user and the service can then be supplied on a face-to-face basis (a U.S. engineering firm opening an office in Canada, for example). Third, rather than establish a commercial presence, the service-provider could enter the jurisdiction of the user, on a temporary basis only, to provide the service as and when needed (for example, a Canadian lawyer meeting a client at the client's business office in the U.S.).

---

[8] *Ministerial Declaration on the Uruguay Round*, GATT, BISD 33S/19, at 28.

[9] For example, the Reference List of Sectors that was employed during the Uruguay Round negotiations (which itself relies on the Central Product Classification system) lists over 600 different types of services. See GATT Doc. MTN.GNS/W/50, 13 April 1989.

Finally, rather than the supplier of the service travelling to the consumer, the consumer of the service could travel to the supplier's jurisdiction or place of business and purchase and consume the service at that locale (many travel or tourism services would be examples of this mode of supply). These four modes of supply each present significantly different issues, meaning that generally applicable rules will tend to be much more complex in application. Moreover, rules would also be required to address a number of issues that had previously been unknown in the trade-in-goods area, such as "right of establishment", "commercial presence" and "labour mobility".

3. SOME IMPORTANT NEGOTIATING ISSUES

Through previous GATT negotiations, many nations had developed significant institutional expertise in negotiating trade-in-goods issues. A multilateral agreement that comprehensively addressed trade in services was something new. Many of the issues that would confront negotiators were unconventional. There would be little or no previous negotiating experience or underlying analytical work to draw upon. Even leaving aside these entirely new issues solely related to services, the fundamental differences between the nature of trade in goods and trade in services meant that even the tried and true solutions had to be re-assessed and re-tested to ensure that they remained equally applicable to trade in services. The novelty and complexity of the area and the lack of negotiating experience and analytical background work significantly complicated and lengthened the negotiations. Before the content of the final Agreement is discussed in detail, it is useful to review briefly some of the more important issues that confronted the negotiators.

(a) Scope and Coverage of the Agreement

One of the first issues that must be addressed in any trade negotiation is the "scope and coverage" of the potential Agreement. In other words, what services are going to be covered by the Agreement? However, because of the novelty of the area, even before negotiations on scope and coverage could commence in substance one had to determine what was actually being talked about. What is a "service"? Therefore, as a first step, definitions would have to be developed for basic terms, such as "services" and "trade in services". Once these definitional problems are resolved, the issue of what services will be covered by the Agreement can be addressed. Was the Agreement to be comprehensive, meaning that all types of services would be covered? Or, alternatively, would the Agreement only cover certain specified service sectors, and if so, which ones, and how would this be determined? An issue related to scope and coverage was whether certain service sectors were so different from other sectors or so difficult to regulate that they required their own special sets of rules. Early in the negotiations, sectors such as financial services, transportation and telecommunications were identified as possibly requiring different or additional rules. A final issue related to scope and coverage concerned pre-existing agreements that addressed trade in certain services, such as bilateral air transportation agreements. Would these agreements be integrated into the services agreement or would those services sectors be excluded from the new agreement?

(b) Structure of the Agreement

Beyond coverage, consensus also had to be reached on the form and structure of the agreement. Perhaps the most important structural issue concerned membership. Would membership be universal, similar to the GATT, for example, or would the agreement's structure be more analogous to the Tokyo Round Codes, where membership was optional?

Beyond the membership issue, a determination had to be made as to the agreement's primary obligations. Would it be similar to the GATT and include, for example, the basic national treatment and MFN obligations? While these non-discriminatory rules are the cornerstones of the GATT, as the negotiations commenced there was not unanimous agreement that they should be included in a services Agreement. For example, with respect to national treatment, many nations wished to retain the ability to discriminate against foreign service-providers in some circumstances. With respect to MFN treatment, the United States, in particular, was concerned about the inclusion of an unconditional MFN obligation. Most developed countries already had substantially open service markets. The inclusion of an unconditional MFN obligation could mean that developed countries would be required to provide access to suppliers from developing countries, but would likely obtain little or no access to developing-country services markets in return.

Another important area which had to be addressed was temporary entry of individual service-providers. In the case of some services, if an individual is not able to enter the home jurisdiction of the consumer it is not practically possible to supply the service on a cross-border basis. Thus, negotiators first had to determine whether rules in this area were necessary, and, if so, what would those rules be, bearing in mind that almost every country has immigration, employment and national security-related concerns about foreign persons entering their territory.

Related structural issues concerned the manner in which the obligations would apply to any covered service. Would the agreement apply to all services immediately, would there be a phase-in period, or would there be some form of offering up and scheduling of concessions, as has been done traditionally with tariff concessions in the GATT context?

(c) Institutional Issues

With respect to institutional issues, the negotiators had to determine what institutional structures would be necessary. Was there a need for a secretariat similar in form and function to the GATT Secretariat? What provisions concerning dispute settlement would have to be included? Would there be any formal linkage between the services agreement and the GATT, so as to allow for cross-sectoral retaliation, for example?

(d) Developing Countries

The participation of developing countries had to be carefully considered. It was only with great reluctance that many developing countries finally agreed to begin negotiations in the services area. Many developing countries were concerned that any services agreement would lead to their newly developing service sectors being overwhelmed by large multinational service-providers from developed countries. Thus, the negotiators had to consider to what extent developing countries might benefit from some special and differential treatment, while at the same time providing foreign service-providers with meaningful access to their service markets.

4. THE GENERAL AGREEMENT ON TRADE IN SERVICES

The *General Agreement on Trade in Services*[10] ("GATS") is comprised of three essential elements: (i) the basic framework agreement which includes its general obligations and disciplines; (ii) a number of Annexes to the Agreement which establish special or different rules for specific types of services; and (iii) the Member-specific GATS Schedules that set out each Member's specific market access concessions. In some cases, the general obligations or special Annexes have also been further supplemented by separate Decisions or Declarations that make up part of the Uruguay Round's final package.

(a) The Basic Framework Agreement

In discussing the basic framework of the GATS, it is important to bear in mind that the framework Agreement itself does not provide for market access to any particular service sector. Specific market access commitments are instead only found in each Member's GATS Schedule. This structure is important to note in advance as the Agreement's essential obligations are divided between its Parts II and III. Disciplines found in Part II (entitled "General Obligations and Disciplines") for the most part apply generally to all services covered by the GATS, regardless of whether a Member has listed any particular service sector concession in its Schedule. In contrast, the disciplines of Part III (entitled "Specific Commitments") apply only to those sectors specifically listed in a Member's Schedule.

---

[10] The *General Agreement on Trade in Services* is attached as Annex 1B to the WTO Agreement.

(i) Part I: Scope and Definitions

Part I of the Agreement (Article 1) addresses the scope and coverage of the Agreement and sets out certain important definitions. The Agreement is stated to apply to "measures of Members affecting trade in services". All the terms used in this provision are then defined and, through these definitions, the scope and coverage of the Agreement is established. The first important definition is that of "services". This term is defined expansively to include any service except those services supplied in the exercise of government authority.[11] This means that, generally speaking, the scope of the Agreement is comprehensive, intending to cover all types of services.

"Trade in services" is then defined as meaning the supply of a service by any one of the four methods or modes of service delivery discussed above. These are:

(a) from the territory of one Member into the territory of another Member (accounting advice given over the telephone or by facsimile transmission are examples of this mode of supply);

(b) in the territory of one Member to the consumer of another Member (aviation or travel/tourism services, for example);

(c) by service-supplier of a Member, to the consumer of the service located in the territory of another Member, by way of a commercial presence in the territory of the other Member (a U.S. engineering firm opening an office in Canada, for example); and

(d) by the service-supplier of a Member, through presence of a natural person, in the territory of another Member (for example, a Canadian lawyer meeting a client at the client's business office in the U.S.).

Consequently, all four of the generally recognized modes of service delivery are covered by the Agreement.

Finally, Article 1:3(a) defines what is meant by the phrase "measures by Members". This definition is important in that it is "loaded"—it not only defines a term, but it also imposes an obligation. First, measures are stated to include not only those measures taken at the national level, but also those measures taken at the regional and local level, meaning that the Agreement applies to the measures of state, provincial and municipal governments, in addition to those of national governments. Second, measures are also stated to include those measures taken by non-governmental bodies in the exercise of

---

[11] The exclusion for "services supplied in the exercise of governmental authority" is then further clarified by Article 1:3(c), which defines this phrase to mean any service which is supplied neither on a commercial basis nor in competition with one or more service-suppliers. Thus, the extent to which a service is supplied in the exercise of governmental authority can only be determined on a case-by-case basis and will vary from Member to Member.

powers delegated to them by any of the three levels of government. Such non-governmental bodies are normally delegated regulatory authority through legislation or regulation and could include, for example, securities commissions, stock exchanges, and the self-governing regulatory organizations that oversee and regulate most professions.

The final paragraph of Article 1:3(a) provides an "extent of obligations" provision very similar in wording and intent to that found in GATT Article XXIV:12.[12] Under GATS Article 1:3(a), Members are required to take such reasonable measures as may be available to them to ensure that regional and local governments and non-governmental bodies observe the obligations and commitments of the Agreement. Because of the similarity of language between this provision and GATT Article XXIV:12, it is reasonable to assume that existing jurisprudence concerning the interpretation of Article XXIV:12 will be persuasive in the interpretation of Article 1:3(a).[13] Thus, while the provision does not appear to impose an absolute obligation on federal governments to ensure such compliance, the similarity in language between this provision and the GATT obligation likely means that federal governments such as Canada and the United States have accepted a "best efforts" type of obligation, and will still be required to undertake "serious, persistent and convincing efforts" to ensure compliance with the GATS by sub-federal bodies.[14]

---

[12] Generally speaking, under international law a country is not able to invoke provisions of its internal law as a justification for its failure to meet its treaty obligations. However, the separation of constitutional jurisdiction in many federal states means that the federal government often does not have the constitutional jurisdiction to force a sub-national government to adopt or amend measures in particular subject areas. Thus, many international Agreements will include a provision which addresses this domestic constitutional issue.

[13] For a further discussion of GATT Article XXIV:12 see pages 65-66.

[14] It should also be noted that there is a significant difference between the application of the Agreement on the one hand, and the obligation to ensure compliance on the other. As noted above, the Agreement is specifically stated to apply to sub-national governments, and therefore all such governments are required to observe the obligations of the Agreement. However, there may be some cases where a sub-federal government refuses to observe the applicable GATS obligation. At this point the provisions of Article 1:3(c) are applicable, and to the extent to which the federal government is able to force the sub-national government to comply will depend upon the constitutional authority granted to the federal government under that country's constitution. If the federal government is constitutionally unable to ensure compliance, it will not be, strictly speaking, in violation of its GATS obligations. However, the government will remain responsible to other Members for the resulting loss of market access created by the actions of the sub-national government and this may mean that it could be required to offer up compensation in other areas in return, or face the possibility of authorized retaliation. In this respect, see the discussion of GATS Article XXIII:2 and Article 22(9) of the *Understanding on Rules and Procedures Governing the Settlement of Disputes* (DSU), below at pages 228-231.

(ii) Part II: General Obligations and Disciplines

As noted above, the primary obligations of the GATS are divided between its Parts II and III. Generally speaking, Part II contains those obligations that apply to all service measures covered by the Agreement, regardless of whether a Member has listed a particular service in its GATS Schedule or not. Part II of the Agreement is comprised of Articles II to XV.

Article II—Most-favoured-nation Treatment. The potential inclusion of an MFN obligation was one of the more controversial aspects of the GATS negotiations. Some developed countries were concerned that the inclusion of an MFN obligation would lead to "free-riding", in that all Members would automatically gain the benefit of another Member's concessions without having to offer up any equivalent market access in return. This concern led to a compromise whereby the MFN obligation is stated to apply generally to all services, but Members are able to avoid the MFN obligation under certain specified circumstances.

Article II:1 sets out the basic MFN obligation. Generally speaking, unconditional MFN treatment must be accorded and Members are not able to discriminate among the services and services-suppliers of other Members. With respect to any measure covered by the Agreement, Members are required immediately and unconditionally to accord to services and service-suppliers of any other Member treatment no less favourable than the treatment that Member accords to the services or service-providers of any other country.

Paragraphs 2 and 3 of Article II then provide two exceptions to the basic MFN obligation.[15] First, similar to GATT Article XXIV:3(a), paragraph 3 provides a limited exception for certain advantages granted in relation to contiguous frontier zones. A more important exception is found in paragraph 2, as further supplemented by the Annex on Article II Exceptions. Paragraph 2 provides that a Member is able to maintain a measure which is inconsistent with the MFN obligation (that is, a Member is able to discriminate between services and service-suppliers of other Members based on their country of origin) if the Member has reserved the relevant discriminatory measure by listing it in the Annex on Article II Exceptions, and the measure otherwise meets the conditions of the Annex. In effect, this exception allows for "conditional MFN treatment" in certain circumstances.[16] It should be noted that, subject to certain sector-specific exceptions, the Annex on Article II

---

[15] There are a number of additional exceptions to the unconditional MFN obligation of Article II provided throughout the Agreement, including one for free trade areas under Article V, and for government procurement under Article XIII.

[16] Conditional MFN treatment generally means that MFN treatment will not be extended to services or service-providers unless the country of export meets the appropriate conditions. Such conditions are often linked to reciprocity, meaning that a country must extend reciprocal market access or it will be denied MFN treatment.

Exceptions only sets out the conditions under which a Member may be exempt from its MFN obligations under the GATS as of the date of entry into force of the Agreement. It does not address any new MFN exemptions that may be requested by a Member after January 1, 1995.[17] Most Article II reservations that have been taken by Members under the Annex can be divided into two general groups.[18] The first group of reserved measures are of a horizontal type which applies across many or all service sectors. Often this type of reservation concerns preferential treatment extended on a bilateral basis under pre-existing bilateral agreements. For example, Canada has taken a reservation for the dispute settlement provisions of its bilateral foreign investment protection agreements that Canada currently has in place with a number of countries. Among other measures, the United States has taken a reservation for certain temporary entry and taxation measures. The second type of Article II reservation taken by many Members is for sector-specific or vertical measures, relating to specific service sub-sectors, such as maritime services, air transport, financial services or basic telecommunications. In some cases, these sub-sectors are subject to further negotiations or are addressed under the provisions of their own sector-specific GATS Annex, as discussed below.[19]

Paragraph 3 of the Annex provides that the Council for Trade in Services[20] is to review all MFN exceptions that have been taken for longer than five years. The first such review is to be undertaken no later than January 1, 2000. In this review, the Council is to examine whether the conditions which created the need for those MFN exceptions still exist. The Council is also to set the date for any further review.

While any Article II exemption that has been taken is to terminate on the date specified in the exception itself, in fact most of the Article II exceptions that have been listed do not set out any express expiry date, and, thus, without

---

[17] Any new exemptions from Article II requested by a Member after January 1, 1995 (the date the WTO Agreement entered into force) must be dealt with under Article IX:3 of the WTO Agreement. As is discussed above at pages 40-41, Article IX:3 of the WTO Agreement is that Agreement's primary waiver provision. Under that Article, the WTO's Ministerial Conference may decide, in exceptional circumstances and on three-fourths majority vote, to waive any obligation imposed on a Member under any of the Multilateral Trade Agreements.

[18] While the complete list of measures reserved under the Annex is appended to the treaty copy of the WTO Agreement, most published versions of the Agreement do not reproduce that lengthy list. Recourse must therefore be had to each Member's GATS Schedule, which, if applicable, usually includes a "Final List of Article II (MFN) Exceptions" for that Member.

[19] For example, specific exclusions from the MFN obligations of Article II and the Annex on Article II Exceptions are set out in the Second Annex on Financial Services, the Annex on Maritime Transport Services and the Annex on Telecommunications.

[20] The Council for Trade in Services (the "Council") is established under GATS Article XXIV.

any further obligation to eliminate them such exceptions could be maintained indefinitely. Paragraph 6 of the Annex, in part, addresses this concern by providing that, in principle, exemptions should not exceed 10 years, and, in any event they must be subject to negotiation in subsequent negotiating rounds. As provided in GATS Article XIX:1, the next such negotiating round for services is to commence no later than January 1, 2000.

Article III—Transparency. GATS Article III and Article III *bis* provide the Agreement's basic transparency obligations. Members are required to promptly publish all measures of general application that are covered by or that might affect the operation of the Agreement. Other relevant international Agreements are also to be published. Members are also required to promptly notify the Council of the introduction of any new measures or any amendments to existing measures.[21] By January 1, 1997, each Member is to have established an "enquiry point" which can be contacted by other Members and which can provide information on the Member's services-related measures. Members are required to respond promptly to any information requests from other Members, including those requests made by a Member to an enquiry point. In many situations, a Member is permitted to afford special protection to confidential information under Article III *bis* and therefore disclosure of that type of information may not be required. Finally, Members may notify the Council of any measure of another Member which it considers to be affecting the operation of the Agreement.

Article IV—Increasing Participation of Developing Countries. One of the major issues that had to be addressed during the negotiations was the participation of developing countries. It was only with great reluctance that many developing countries agreed to begin negotiations in the services area. Many such countries were concerned that any Agreement would lead to their newly developing service sectors being overwhelmed by large multinational service-providers. While developing country concerns were taken into account during the negotiations, generally speaking this did not translate into special and differential treatment under the Agreement. This means that developing country Members have accepted the same GATS obligations applicable to developed country Members. There are, however, a number of provisions such as Article IV which have been designed to address developing country concerns and assist those Members in attaining maximum benefit under the Agreement.[22]

---

[21] Note that there is no obligation under the GATS to provide advance notice of a measure prior to its adoption, nor to consult with other interested Members prior to adoption.

[22] Other examples include paragraphs 2 and 3 of Article XIX (which concern the expectations placed upon developing country Members in any future liberalization negotiations under the Agreement) and paragraph 2 of Article XXV (which provides that the WTO Secretariat is to provide technical assistance to developing countries).

Rather than extending special and differential treatment, paragraph 1 of Article IV notes that the increasing participation of developing country Members in world services trade is to be achieved through the negotiation of specific commitments under the Agreement, including improved access to technology, distribution channels and information networks, and through improved market access in service sectors and modes of supply of interest to developing country Members. In addition, by January 1, 1997 developed country Members were required to have established "contact points" that will be able to assist the service-providers of developing country Members in obtaining information relating to, for example, market access requirements such as the registration and licensing requirements for professionals. Other Members are also required to establish such contact points to the extent possible.[23]

Article V and Article V bis—Economic and Labour Market Integration. Article V provides a further exception to the MFN obligation of Article II for bilateral or plurilateral Agreements to liberalize services trade. Such Agreements would include, for example, the NAFTA and the EU. This Article is similar in structure and intent to GATT Article XXIV, which is the equivalent MFN exception for free trade areas and customs unions in trade-in-goods area.[24] Paragraph 1 of Article V provides that the GATS does not prevent Members from entering into such preferential Agreements liberalizing services trade, provided certain conditions are met, and subject to review by the Council.

Any such Agreement need not be comprehensive in its sectoral coverage, but, at a minimum, its coverage must be "substantial". As further clarified by a footnote, this requirement is to be measured by the number of sectors and modes of supply covered, and the volume of trade affected by the Agreement. In order to meet this requirement, it is specifically noted that the Agreement should not provide for the *a priori* exclusion of any of the four modes of service supply. Second, the Agreement must essentially require that national treatment be extended to all covered services, either on the Agreement's entry into force or on the basis of a reasonable implementation time-frame. Under paragraph 3, the requirements of paragraph 1, particularly the national treatment requirement, are relaxed to a limited degree where developing countries are parties to such Agreements.

In order to ensure that such preferential Agreements do not act so as to restrict trade with non-signatories, in addition to the requirements of paragraph 1, the Agreement must also be designed to facilitate trade between its

---

[23] Article XXV:1 also provides that service-suppliers of other Members that are in need of such assistance shall also have access to these contact points.

[24] With respect to GATT Article XXIV, see discussion above at pages 65-66.

signatories and must not raise the overall level of barriers to trade in services that may be imposed on non-signatories. This provision is further reinforced by a requirement that service-providers of non-signatories that are juridical persons incorporated under the laws of a signatory to such an Agreement must receive the same preferential treatment provided for under the regional Agreement, provided that the juridical person engages in substantial business operations within the territory of the signatories.[25]

The review of such preferential services Agreements by the Council is provided for under paragraph 7. Member signatories are required to notify the Council of any such Agreement or any enlargement[26] or significant modification of a previously notified Agreement. Any relevant information requested by the Council is to be provided by the signatories. The Council may also establish a working group to review the Agreement and report back to the Council on its consistency with the requirements of Article V. Based on the report of any such working group, the Council may make appropriate recommendations to the signatories.

Article V *bis* provides an additional exclusion for labour market integration Agreements. This special exclusion, of which there is no comparable GATT obligation, was apparently included at the request of the Nordic countries whose labour markets are highly integrated. As described in a footnote to the Article, such labour market integration Agreements provide citizens of the signatory countries with a right of free entry to the employment markets of all signatory countries. A strict application of the Agreement's MFN and national treatment obligations would mean that signatories to such labour Agreements would be required to extend equivalent labour market access to all individual service-providers who are citizens of any Member country. However, by virtue of Article V *bis*, such Agreements will not be subject to the GATS, provided the Agreement exempts citizens of signatory countries from residency and work permit requirements and the Agreement is notified to the Council.

Article VI—Domestic Regulation. So as to ensure that apparent market access on paper cannot be undermined by a Member through unfair or prejudicial application of its domestic laws, Article VI sets out certain transparency and due process requirements relating to the domestic regulation of services and service-providers. Paragraph 1 provides that, only with respect to those sectors where specific commitments have been undertaken, each Member is required to ensure that all measures of general application are being

---

[25] This requirement is relaxed in cases where the Agreement is only among developing country Members. See Article V:3(b).

[26] Although not specified, presumably the Council would have to be notified of any enlargement of the Agreement on either a sectoral or a geographic basis.

administered in a reasonable, objective and impartial manner. Under paragraph 2, subject to certain constitutional or legal restraints, each Member is also required to maintain judicial, arbitral or administrative tribunals or procedures which can be invoked by service-suppliers to obtain prompt, objective and impartial reviews of any administrative decision that has been taken affecting trade in services.[27]

Most Members require that many types of service-suppliers be registered, licensed or obtain similar approval before the supplier is permitted to commence providing the relevant service within a Member's territory (the mandatory licensing of professional service-providers, for example). Article VI provides four important obligations relating to licensing and similar qualification-related requirements.

First, in those sectors where specific commitments have been undertaken, if an authorization is required before a service can be provided, the Member's competent authorities are required to provide a decision on a completed application within a reasonable period of time after the application has been made. These authorities are also required to provide information concerning the status of any application upon request and without undue delay. Second, with a view to ensuring that measures relating to qualifications and licensing requirements do not themselves act as unnecessary barriers to trade, the Council has been directed to develop what it considers to be any necessary additional disciplines on such requirements. These additional disciplines are expected to ensure, for example, that any such requirements are based on objective and transparent criteria and are no more burdensome than is necessary.[28] Third, until the Council is able to develop these additional disciplines, Members may not apply licensing or qualification requirements so as to undermine their specific commitments. This could occur, for example, by the imposition of requirements that are unreasonable, non-transparent or more burdensome than is necessary to ensure the quality of the service. Finally,

---

[27] Paragraphs 1 and 2 of Article VI are based on GATT Articles X:3(a) and (b), as discussed above at page 59.

[28] This "further negotiations" provision was supplemented by a Ministerial Decision included as part of the Uruguay Round final package. The "Decision on Professional Services" recommended that the Council, at its first meeting, adopt a specified decision relating to professional services. Among other things, the specified Decision establishes a Working Group on Professional Services. This Working Group is to recommend to the Council what further disciplines on professional licensing and qualification requirements may be required. The Working Group is to give priority to the accountancy sector. The Council adopted the specified Decision and established the Working Party at the Council's first meeting in early 1995. The Working Group began its work in earnest in late October 1995. In May of 1997, the Council adopted a set of non-binding guidelines for mutual recognition agreements in the accountancy sector which had been developed by the Working Group on Professional Services. The purpose of these guidelines is to facilitate the mutual recognition of accountancy qualifications.

where Members have undertaken specific commitments related to professional services, they are also required to provide adequate procedures for verifying the competency of the relevant professionals of other Members.

Article VII—Recognition. Related to issues of licensing and qualification requirements are issues concerning mutual recognition. Using medical doctors as an example, the education, training and licensing requirements for doctors in Canada may be very similar to the education, training and licensing requirements of doctors in the United States. If these types of requirements are substantially similar between the two countries, should the United States still require Canadian doctors to re-qualify in the United States (by again completing their education or training in the United States) before they can be licensed to practice medicine in the United States, and *vise versa* with respect to American doctors wishing to practice in Canada? In situations where education, training and other requirements are substantially similar between countries, the responsible licensing authorities have often entered into mutual recognition Agreements under which both authorities agree to accept the education, training or other formal requirements of the two jurisdictions as being equivalent. While these Agreements usually do not eliminate the requirement that the service-provider be licensed in both jurisdictions, in many cases they will simplify the licensing procedure by relieving an applicant from having to re-complete some or all of their formal education or training. In some cases, the relevant licensing authorities will also act unilaterally, recognizing the education or training gained in another jurisdiction without expecting reciprocal recognition in return. Article VII is intended to address a number of issues that arise out of these types of recognition situations.

First, paragraph 1 notes that a Member remains free, subject to certain disciplines, to recognize the education, experience, requirements, licences or certifications gained or met in other countries. Such recognition may be accorded unilaterally, or pursuant to an Agreement between two or more countries.

Such recognition raises issues relating to MFN treatment. For example, recognizing the certification of a service-provider gained in one country but not a similar certification gained by a second service-provider gained in a second country can be argued to be a denial of unconditional MFN treatment, in that service-providers from one country are being treated more favourably than those from other countries. While paragraphs 2 and 3 of Article VII do not explicitly exempt recognition from the Agreement's MFN obligation, they do so by implication, provided that certain other disciplines are still observed. In the case of mutual recognition Agreements, Members who are parties to any such Agreement are not required to automatically extend the Agreement to all Members, but instead must afford an adequate opportunity to any interested Member that may wish to either accede to the Agreement or to negotiate a similar Agreement. Where recognition is extended unilaterally, again Members are not required to extend such treatment automatically to all other Members, but the Member must afford an adequate opportunity to any Member to show that its education or comparable requirements should also be recognized on a similar basis. Finally, paragraph 3 provides an over-arching obligation that in any case Members cannot apply recognition in a discriminatory fashion nor use it as a disguised restriction on trade in services.

Paragraph 4 acts to improve the transparency of any existing or future recognition measures. First, by January 1, 1996, Members were required to notify the Council of all existing recognition measures. Second, Members are required to notify the Council promptly of the commencement of any negotiations aimed at concluding any new mutual recognition Agreement. This will allow other Members the opportunity to express their interest in participating in the negotiations. Members are also required to notify the Council of the adoption of any new recognition measures or the modification of any existing measures.

Finally, paragraph 5 notes that whenever appropriate, recognition should be based on widely accepted criteria. Members should also work with intergovernmental bodies and non-governmental organizations in an effort to develop common recognition criteria and international standards for the professions and other service trades.

Article VIII—Monopolies and Exclusive Service-Suppliers. Article VIII sets out special rules applicable to monopolies and exclusive service-suppliers so as to ensure that such entities cannot be used to undermine a Member's obligations under the Agreement. Monopoly service-providers are quite common in a number of service sectors, such as telecommunications and electrical generation and distribution. Paragraph 5 of Article VIII notes that the obligations of the Article apply not only to monopolies, but also to oligopoly situations, where a Member, either formally or in effect, permits only a small number of service-providers to operate in the sector and prevents competition among those providers.

Generally speaking, the establishment of new monopolies and maintenance of existing monopolies is not prohibited under the Agreement. However, a Member is still required to ensure that any such entity does not, in the supply of the relevant service within the Member's territory, violate the Member's MFN obligations under Article II, or any of the Member's specific commitments. Where the entity also provides other non-monopolized services, and those other services are the subject of a specific commitment, the Member is also required to ensure that the entity does not abuse its monopoly position (by cross-subsidizing, for example) nor act contrary to the Member's commitments. Members were required to provide the Council with information concerning the operation of any monopoly service-provider or exclusive supplier when such information is requested.

Finally, a Member must notify the Council of any new monopoly or exclusive supplier that it permits, if the entity will be supplying a service that is already subject to a specific commitment. The designation of a new monopoly may be, in effect, a unilateral modification of a Member's commitments. Unilateral modifications to a Member's concessions are generally not permitted. And, as a result, certain provisions of Article XXI (Modification of Schedules) will then become applicable. Any Member that may be affected by the establishment of the new monopoly has the right to negotiate a compensatory adjustment in concessions under the provisions of Article XXI.[29]

Article IX—Business Practices. Members have recognized that there are certain types of unfair business practices, in addition to those that can be undertaken by monopolies, that might be undertaken by other service-suppliers, that can have the effect of restraining competition and thereby restricting the international trade in services. While Article IX sets out certain obligations applicable to such practices, it does not specify what those "certain business practices" might be. It is likely, however, that such business practices could include acts such as predating pricing and other generally accepted anti-competitive behaviour. The Article contains no binding obligation to eliminate such practices. Instead, Members are only required to provide information to other Members and enter into consultations on request with a view to eliminating any such offending practices.

Article X—Emergency Safeguard Measures. Some Members were concerned that the liberalization of their service sectors under the Agreement would result in a surge of foreign services and service-providers into their markets, thereby having a destabilizing effect on their domestic service-providers and labour markets. The potential for such import surges have long been recognized and addressed in the trade-in-goods area (under GATT Article XIX, for example). While the concern over import surges in the services area was generally accepted as being legitimate in some circumstances, Members were unable to reach agreement on the structure of any such safeguard mechanism prior to the conclusion of the Round. As a result, Article X provides for both further negotiations on the issue and an interim safeguard mechanism. First, with respect to future negotiations, Members are to negotiate an agreement on an emergency safeguard based on the principle of non-discrimination; this agreement is to become effective no later than January 1, 1998.[30] Being based on non-discrimination, Members will likely be obliged to impose any such safeguard on an MFN basis, meaning that Members will not be able to restrict the services or service-providers of only one or a few Members.

---

[29] Article XXI is discussed in depth below at pages 227-228.

[30] These negotiations are being conducted within the Working Party on GATS Rules, established in March of 1995 by the GATS Council.

Paragraph 2 then provides a type of interim safeguard that is to be in effect only while negotiations on a permanent mechanism are continuing. Members are permitted to modify or withdraw any of their specific commitments after a period of one year from the date a given commitment becomes effective. While the requirements of paragraph 2 are not entirely clear, it appears that a Member will be required to demonstrate to the Council that there is an import surge of the relevant service which justifies the immediate modification or withdrawal of the commitment. And, again, while not entirely clear, paragraph 2 does appear to be linked to certain of the requirements of Article XXI, meaning that if safeguard action is taken, the Member will be required to negotiate acceptable compensation with other Members.

Articles XI and XII—Restrictions on Payments and Transfers. Restrictions on currency transactions and payments has long been recognized as a way by which countries are able to indirectly restrict import or export trade. However, it is also recognized that there are legitimate reasons as to why a government may wish to restrict currency transactions (to safeguard its balance of payments, for example). In the trade-in-goods area, GATT Article XII recognizes this reality and permits currency restrictions in certain specified situations. GATS Articles XI and XII, in essence, apply this GATT balance-of-payments exception to services trade. Article XI provides that, in those sectors where a Member has granted specific commitment, the Member is only permitted to apply restrictions on international transfers and payments for current transactions for balance-of-payments reasons, and in accordance with the requirements of Article XII. Article XII:2 then sets out the basic requirements for any restrictions that may be employed. These requirements include non-discrimination, consistency with IMF obligations and temporary nature. The remaining paragraphs of Article XII then set out additional obligations that must also be met, such as required notification to the Council and prompt consultations with the Committee on Balance-of-Payments Restrictions.[31]

Article XIII—Government Procurement. Government procurement is the purchase of goods and services by governments, government departments or government corporations for their own use. Governments often favour their own national suppliers when making such purchases. It can be argued, however, that by favouring its own national suppliers a Member would be in violation of its non-discrimination obligations under the Agreement. Thus, Article XIII:1 provides an exception from the relevant non-discriminatory obligations in Articles II (MFN Treatment), XVI (Market Access) and XVII (National Treatment) for government procurement.[32] Thus, Members are still

---

[31] The Committee on Balance-of-Payment Restrictions is established under the *Understanding on Balance-of-Payments Provisions of the General Agreement on Tariffs and Trade.* See the discussion of that Understanding above at page 60.

[32] In the trade-in-goods area, a similar exclusion for government procurement is provide in GATT Article III:8.

able to favour their own service-providers when procuring services for their own use.[33] In addition, Members commenced negotiations on government procurement of services in January 1997.[34]

Articles XIV and XIV bis—*General and Security Exceptions.* At the time the GATT was originally negotiated, it was widely recognized that there were certain situations where countries would be justified in taking action that could be inconsistent with their GATT obligations. For the most part, these exceptions were set out in GATT Articles XX and XXI.[35] In a slightly modified form, these same GATT exceptions have been incorporated into the GATS through Articles XIV and XIV *bis.* Under Article XIV, subject to a number of requirements, Members are permitted to take certain necessary measures, such as those to protect public morals, maintain public order and protect human, animal or plant life or health.[36] Additional exceptions have been provided for certain taxation measures in paragraphs (d) and (e) of Article XIV.

Article XIV *bis*, similar to GATT Article XXI, provides the Agreement's security exemption. For example, nothing in the Agreement is to be construed so as to prevent a Member from taking any action in order to meet its obligations under the *United Nations Charter*. As a result, there will be no violation of the GATS if a United Nations Security Council Resolution

---

[33] It should be noted, however, that some Members, including Canada, the United States and the EU, have accepted certain additional disciplines on their services procurements under the *Agreement on Government Procurement*, the scope and coverage of which has now been extended to cover certain services for the first time. See pages 300-303 for a discussion of this Agreement.

[34] These negotiations are being conducted within the Working Party on GATS Rules, discussed above at page 222, and are in addition to the obligations accepted by some Members under the *Agreement on Government Procurement*. These negotiations have not yet progressed beyond the issue-definition stage.

[35] See pages 63-64 for the discussion of GATT Articles XX and XXI.

[36] An issue arises as to whether measures necessary to protect the environment would be covered under the Article XIV(b) exception. A similar issue arises with respect to the relationship between GATT Article XX(b) and environmental measures. As discussed below at pages 338-340, Ministers have established a Committee on Trade and the Environment to investigate issues relating to trade and the environment. The Council, at its first meeting held on March 1, 1994, adopted an additional Ministerial Declaration specifically relating to services. The Council's *Decision on Trade in Services and the Environment* states that measures necessary to protect the environment may sometimes conflict with the GATS, but, at the same time, such measures typically have as their objective the "protection of human, animal or plant life or health". It is therefore not clear whether there is any need to modify Article XIV(b) to specifically except potentially inconsistent environmental measures. The Council requested the Committee on Trade and the Environment to examine and report on the relationship between services trade and the environment, including the issue of inter-governmental environmental Agreements and their relationship to the GATS. The Committee provided its report on this and a number of other environmental issues at the WTO's first Ministerial Conference, held in Singapore in December 1996. See the discussion at pages 338-340.

imposes economic sanctions against a Member and requires all other Members to terminate their economic relationships with that Member, including all services trade.

Article XV—Subsidies. While subsidies have long been recognized as being a problem in international trade, the development of adequate disciplines has proved illusive. In the trade-in-goods area, attempts to develop subsidy disciplines have been ongoing for almost 50 years. It is therefore not surprising that Members were unable to develop a comprehensive set of rules governing the granting of subsidies to services and service-providers during the Uruguay Round negotiations. All that Members were able to reach consensus on were future negotiations on the issue and a right to consultations on request in the interim. Article XV:1 provides that Members will enter into negotiations to develop disciplines on trade-distorting subsidies. In the trade-in-goods area, in certain circumstances such trade-distorting subsidies can be offset by a special or "countervailing" duty applied at the border by the importing country to the subsidized goods. The GATS subsidy negotiations will determine whether similar countervailing measures might also be appropriate in the services area. There is little doubt that any investigation in these areas will raise a multitude of conceptual questions much more complex than those that arise in the trade-in-goods area. This likely means that these negotiations will take many years to complete, even if consensus can be reached on any of the myriad of issues that are likely to arise.[37]

(iii) Part III: Specific Commitments

Part II of the Agreement, entitled "General Obligations and Disciplines", for the most part provides a series of obligations that apply generally to Members regardless of any specific commitments of a given Member. The title of Part III of the Agreement, "Specific Commitments", is a clear indication of the nature of the obligations contained in this Part. It bears repeating that Part III, comprised of Articles XVI (Market Access), XVII (National Treatment) and XVIII (Additional Commitments), sets out a series of obligations that are only applicable to those specific commitments made by each individual Member and listed in their own individual Schedules to the Agreement. Thus, Members are not required to automatically extend market access and national treatment to all services and service-providers of other Members. Those market access and national treatment obligations that have been accepted are specified in each Member's Schedule. According to the obligations of Article II, these specified concessions must then be extended to all Members on an MFN basis.

---

[37] These negotiations are currently being conducted within the Working Party on GATS Rules, discussed above at page 222. To date, the Working Party has largely focused its efforts on emergency safeguards and government procurement and has not addressed subsidies to any significant degree.

Article XVI—Market Access. The first obligation under Article XVI is that Members must accord the treatment that they have agreed to accord to specific services and service-providers under their respective Schedules. Paragraph 2 of Article XVI then lists six specific types of market-restricting measures that Members are not permitted to adopt or maintain in those sectors where a Member has undertaken market-access commitments, unless the Member has specifically reserved such offending measures in its Schedule. For example, Members are not permitted to establish quotas on service-providers, either in the form of absolute numbers or value. They cannot restrict or require any specific type of legal entity through which the provider must supply the service. And, perhaps most importantly, a Member is not permitted to impose limits on foreign ownership or investment.

Article XVII—National Treatment. Article XVII:1 sets out the Agreement's basic national treatment obligation. In summary, in those sectors included in a Member's Schedule (and subject to any terms and conditions specified in that Schedule) a Member cannot discriminate between its own services and service-providers and those of other Members. It is important to note two additional aspects to this national treatment obligation. First, it extends broadly, not just to measures directly relating to the relevant service, but to all measures affecting the supply of that service.[38] Second, as is further elaborated upon in paragraphs 2 and 3, the national treatment obligation of paragraph 1 is *de facto* as opposed to *de jure* national treatment. This has two implications. First, a Member need not extend formally identical treatment to both domestic and foreign services and service-providers in order to meet the national treatment obligation. It is sufficient if the conditions of competition between the two are equal. Second, and perhaps more importantly, formally identical treatment may not meet this national treatment obligation. If a measure accords to foreign services or service-providers treatment that is formally identical to that accorded to domestic services or service-providers, but still modifies the conditions of competition in favour of domestic services or service-providers, the measure will likely run afoul of Article XVII.

Article XVIII—Additional Commitments. Article XVIII provides that, if they wish, Members are able to negotiate and list in their Schedules commitments in addition to those relating strictly to market access and national treatment. For example, Members have negotiated specific commitments relating to licensing and qualification matters governed by Article VI. Members might also wish to negotiate issues relating to mutual recognition or even specific subsidy limitations or other disciplines.

---

[38] "Measures by Members affecting trade in services" is then defined broadly in Article XXVIII to include among other things, measures respecting the purchase, payment and use of a service, and the presence of persons in the territory of a Member.

(iv) Part IV: Progressive Liberalization

Part IV of the Agreement, comprised of Articles XIX, XX and XXI, provides for progressive liberalization through further negotiations and for the modification of Members' Schedules under certain other circumstances.

Article XIX—Negotiation of Specific Commitments. The initial liberalization and commitments that have been achieved under the Agreement are only the first step. Under Article XIX, Members have already agreed to continue to progressively liberalize service trade through additional and successive rounds of negotiations. The first such round is to be commenced no later than January 1, 2000, with continuing rounds thereafter. These periodic negotiations are generally expected to be comprehensive in their sectoral scope, and are in addition to, and should not be confused with, the ongoing GATS issue and sector-oriented negotiations. While these further negotiations have not been stated to be formally linked to a next round of comprehensive WTO negotiations, this appears to likely be the case in practice.

Article XX—Schedules of Specific Commitments. Article XX sets out how Members are to structure their respective Schedules. First, Members are to set out those specific commitments they accepted in their respective Schedules. If applicable, with respect to each sectoral commitment, Members must specify any limitations or qualifications that may be applicable to the commitment, including limitations and conditions on market-access and national treatment, along with any applicable dates for entry into force or implementation of the obligations. Any measures which are considered to be inconsistent with the market access obligation under Article XVI or the national treatment obligation under Article XVII, must also be specifically inscribed in the relevant column in the Schedule. It should be noted that a failure to specifically list qualifications, limitations or other non-complying measures in a Member's Schedule would likely mean that the Member is required to eliminate such measures. These Schedules are annexed to and form an integral part of the Agreement.

Article XXI—Modification of Schedules. Once a Member has listed a specific commitment in its Schedule it is expected to live up to the terms of that commitment. At the same time, Schedule commitments are not cast in stone. In addition to the ability to take emergency action under Article X, a Member is permitted to modify or withdraw a commitment at any time after three years have elapsed from the time the commitment became effective, subject to the requirements of Article XXI.[39]

---

[39] The ability to modify or withdraw a commitment and the procedures set out in Article XXI for this process are substantially similar to those provided under GATT Article XXVIII in the trade-in-goods area. See pages 67-68 for a discussion of GATT Article XXVIII.

The Member must first notify the Council of its intent to modify or withdraw a commitment. Second, the Member must enter into negotiations with any other Member that considers that it may be adversely affected by the modification or withdrawal with a view to reaching an agreement on compensation for the modification or withdrawal. If these Members are unable to reach an agreement on appropriate compensation, the adversely affected Member may then request arbitration on the issue of compensation. In such a case, the Member may not modify or withdraw its commitment until it has provided compensation in accordance with the findings of the arbitrator. A Member could be subject to substantially equivalent retaliation if it does not comply with the arbitrator's findings but proceeds to modify or withdraw its commitment without providing adequate compensation. A Member is free to modify or withdraw a commitment if no other Member has requested arbitration on the proposed action.

(v) Part V: Institutional Provisions

Some of the more important issues that had to be addressed during the negotiations concerned the Agreement's institutional structures and provisions. Was there a need for a secretariat similar in form and function to the GATT Secretariat? What provisions concerning dispute settlement would have to be included? Would there be any formal linkage between the services agreement and the GATT, so as to allow for cross-sectoral retaliation, for example? In the end, many of these issues were settled when the decision was made to establish the new WTO and provide for consolidated dispute settlement under the new *Understanding on Rules and Procedures Governing the Settlement of Disputes.*[40] The need for independent institutional provisions within the GATS was correspondingly reduced as a result. Among other things, the institutional provisions of Part V of the Agreement (Articles XXII to XXVI) link dispute settlement under the Agreement with the DSU and establish the Council for Trade in Services.

Articles XXII and XXIII—Consultation and Dispute Settlement. Articles XXII and XXIII provide for the settlement of disputes arising under the Agreement. As a first step in the process, under Article XXII:1 a Member is required to consult with another Member, on request, concerning any matter affecting the operation of the Agreement. The relevant provisions of the DSU will apply to any such consultations. If the consulting Members are unable to find a satisfactory solution through consultation, any of them may request the

---

[40] See pages 308-327 for discussion of the *Understanding on Rules and Procedures Governing the Settlement of Disputes* ("DSU").

assistance of the Council or the Dispute Settlement Body ("DSB"). A special dispute settlement rule applies in the case of taxation measures falling within the scope of so-called double taxation agreements.[41]

The next phase of dispute settlement under the Agreement is the initiation of the panel process. In cases where one Member is of the view that another Member is in violation of its obligations under the Agreement, Article XXIII:1 establishes the link between the GATS and the DSU.[42] This Article provides that if a Member considers that another Member is failing to carry out its obligations or specific commitments under the Agreement, the complaining Member may have recourse to the DSU. It should be noted that while consultations under Article XXII may be requested regarding "any matter affecting the operation" of the Agreement, under Article XXIII:1, the provisions of the DSU may only be invoked for a more limited subset of matters, those concerning a Member's failure "to carry out its obligations or specific commitments" under the Agreement.

If the complaining Member is successful in its complaint under Article XXIII:1, elimination or amendment of the offending measure would normally be the result. In addition, Article XXIII:2 provides that if the defending

---

[41] A Member is not permitted to allege that another Member's measure violates the national treatment obligations of Article XVII if that measure falls within the scope of a double taxation Agreement to which they are both party. Issues concerning taxation measures that fall within the scope of such double taxation Agreements must be resolved within the scope of those Agreements. However, in some cases there may be a question as to whether or not the measure at issue does fall within the scope of the relevant double taxation agreement. If the relevant agreement has come into force after January 1, 1995, either Member may bring the issue before the Council, and the Council must then refer the matter to binding arbitration for final resolution. If the double taxation agreement was in force prior to January 1, 1995, the issue of coverage can only be placed before the Council with the consent of both parties.

[42] The linkage between the GATS and the DSU has been supplemented by a Ministerial Decision adopted by the Council at its first meeting held on March 1, 1995. The *Decision on Certain Dispute Settlement Procedures for the General Agreement on Trade in Services* provides for the establishment of a specialized roster of potential dispute settlement panelists that can be used to assist in the selection of a panel to hear any complaint initiated under GATS Article XXIII. Members may suggest individuals for inclusion on this roster. The roster is to be maintained and administered by the WTO Secretariat in consultation with the Chair of the Council. In any case, a panel established to hear a GATS Article XXIII complaint is to be composed of well-qualified governmental and/or non-governmental individuals who have experience in GATS or trade-in-services issues, and who will serve in their personal capacities. Where a dispute concerns a specific service sector, the panel is also required to have the necessary sectoral expertise. Paragraph 4 of the first Financial Services Annex then specifically applies this expertise requirement to financial services disputes by stating that panels for disputes on prudential issues or financial matters are required to have the necessary expertise relevant to the specific financial service under dispute.

Member fails to bring its measure into compliance with its obligations under the Agreement, the DSB is authorized to permit retaliation against the Member in accordance with the provisions of Article 22 of the DSU.[43]

One additional basis of complaint, that of "non-violation nullification and impairment", is provided for under Article XXIII. In some cases, a Member could adopt a services-related measure which, although technically consistent with its obligations under the Agreement, might nonetheless act to restrict the market access that other Members previously enjoyed or expected to enjoy in that Member's service markets. In such a case, because the Member adopting the new measure is technically in compliance with its obligations under the agreement, there is no inconsistent measure, and therefore there is no basis for a complaint under Article XXIII:1. However, paragraph 3 of Article XXIII provides a separate but limited basis of complaint for such "non-violation" nullification and impairment. There are three requirements for such non-violation complaints under paragraph 3. First, the measure at issue must be related to a specific market access commitment that the responding Member has accepted under Part III of the Agreement and listed in its GATS Schedule. Second, that specific commitment must have given rise to a reasonable expectation of the complaining Member that some benefit would accrue to it as a result of the commitment (for example, it would now have market access in a previously restricted service sector). Finally, the reasonable expectation of that benefit is being nullified or impaired by the measure of the responding Member. In addition, although not specifically required, it appears likely that in order to be successful in a non-violation case the measure at issue will have to be a new measure, adopted or amended after the specific commitment has

---

[43]Note that the provisions of Article XXIII:2 and the reference to Article 22 of the DSU have three additional effects. First, Article 22(4) of the DSU notes that the DSB is not permitted to authorize retaliation (technically referred to as "suspension of concessions") if the relevant covered Agreement prohibits such action. Thus, one of the effects of GATS Article XXIII:2 is to ensure that the DSB has specific authority, if necessary, to authorize retaliation. Secondly, Article 22(3) of the DSU also allows for cross-retaliation in some circumstances—that is, a Member may be authorized to suspend a concession under the GATS for another Member's failure to remove an offending measure covered under the GATT or the TRIPS Agreement. GATS Article XXIII:2 therefore allows the DSB to order the suspension of a concession under the GATS in such cross-retaliation cases. Finally, Article 22(9) of the DSU further clarifies the status of measures of sub-federal governments under the GATS by noting that the dispute settlement provisions of the GATS may be invoked in respect of sub-federal measures. When the DSB has ruled that the relevant sub-federal measure is not in compliance with the GATS, the defendant federal government is then required to take all reasonable measures as may be available to it to ensure compliance. Where the federal government still has not been able to secure the required compliance, the compensation and retaliation provisions of Article 22 of the DSB will apply, meaning that the federal government will be required to offer up equivalent compensation to adversely affected Members or face the possibility of retaliation.

come into force.[44] If the DSB determines that there has been nullification or impairment, the defending Member is not required to eliminate or modify the measure. Rather, Article XXI:2 will apply, meaning that the defending Member is obliged to enter into negotiations with the complaining Member in order to reach satisfactory agreement on compensation. If the defending Member agrees, this negotiated compensation may, but is not required to, include elimination or modification of the measure at issue. If the Members are not able to reach agreement on acceptable compensation, then Article 22 of the DSU will apply and the complaining Member will be able to apply to the DSB for authority to impose retaliation. The matter may then be referred to arbitration to determine the quantity of any such authorized retaliation.

Article XXIV—Council for Trade in Services. The Council for Trade in Services has been established under Article XXIV. It is required to carry out those functions as may be assigned to it, presumably by the WTO's General Council. The Services Council may establish such subsidiary bodies as it considers appropriate. Pursuant to two Ministerial Decisions adopted by the Services Council at its first meeting held on March 1, 1994, a Working Group on Professional Services and a Committee on Financial Services have been established.[45] Membership in the Council and any of its subsidiary bodies is open to all Members. The Chair of the Council is to be elected by all the Members, and not by the Council. The first Chair of the Services Council, Ambassador Christer Manhusen of Sweden, was elected during the General Council's first meeting on January 31, 1995.

(vi) Part VI: Final Provisions

The Agreement's final provisions, which address denial of benefits, the Agreement's annexes, and provide certain additional definitions, are found in Part VI, Articles XXVIII to XXIX.

---

[44] The fact that a measure was already in force at the time the specific commitment was given and the Member did not agree to eliminate the measure as part of its commitment would go some way to defeating a claim of another Member that it had a reasonable expectation of benefit accruing to it under the specific commitment.

[45] The two Ministerial Decisions, the *Decision on Institutional Arrangements for the General Agreement on Trade in Services*, and the *Decision on Professional Services*, were part of the final package adopted by Ministers at Marrakesh on April 15, 1994. The *Decision on Professional Services* is briefly discussed above at page 219. The *Decision on Institutional Arrangements*, in addition to establishing the Committee on Trade in Financial Services, sets out certain responsibilities for subsidiary bodies and sectoral committees established by the Council. For example, any sectoral committee (such as the Committee on Trade in Financial Services) is to, among other things, continuously monitor the application of the Agreement to the sector concerned, provide a forum for technical discussions, and provide technical assistance to developing country Members. Subsidiary bodies are permitted to settle their own rules of procedure, establish any of their own subsidiary bodies that they consider appropriate, and are required to report at least annually to the Council.

Article XXVII—Denial of Benefits. Article XXVII allows Members to deny the benefits of the GATS to the services and service-suppliers of other Members under certain circumstances. For example, a Member may deny benefits to the supplier of a service if the Member establishes that the service is supplied from or in the territory of a non-Member. In the case of a service-supplier that is a juridical person, a Member may deny the benefits of the Agreement if the Member establishes that the person is not a service-supplier of a Member.[46] Certain additional rules are provided in the case of maritime transport services.

Article XXVIII—Definitions. Definitions for a number of important terms used in the Agreement are provided in Article XXVIII. These are in addition to a number of other important definitions set out in Article I. Recall that Article I provides that the Agreement applies to "measures" of Members. "Measure" is defined broadly here to include not only laws and regulations, but also procedures, decisions and administrative actions. "Supply of service" has also been defined broadly to capture not just the actual provision of service, but also its production, distribution, marketing and sale. A number of definitions provided under Article XXVIII relate to the denial of benefits under Article XXVII. These include "service of another Member", "person", "natural person of another Member", "juridical person of another Member", and "owned", "controlled" and "affiliated". It should be observed that the definitions in Article XXVIII have not been arranged in alphabetical order.

(b) The Annexes to the Agreement[47]

The second set of obligations under the GATS is found in a number of Annexes to the Agreement. These Annexes serve two purposes. The first is to provide for additional rights and obligations that apply to certain complex types of services—financial services, for example. The second purpose is to provide for further negotiations in a number of specific sectors (maritime services, telecommunications, *etc.*) and to allow for incorporation of the results into the Agreement once the negotiations have been completed. In most cases, these Annexes are then further supported by Ministerial Decisions that were issued as part of the final Uruguay Round package.

(i) The Annex on Movement of Natural Persons Supplying Services Under the Agreement

Recall that one of the modes of supplying a service that is covered under the Agreement is by a service-supplier of one Member, through the presence

---

[46] Among other things, such a determination would be based on the definition of "service of another Member" and "juridical person of another Member" provided in Article XXVIII. These and other definitions in Article XXVIII ensure that service-suppliers from non-Members will not be able to obtain the benefits of the Agreement by establishing shell corporations in Member countries.

[47] The Annex on Article II Exceptions, is discussed above, at pages 214-216.

of natural persons of a Member in the territory of any other Member. The example of this mode of supply that was used above was that of a Canadian lawyer meeting a client at the client's office in the United States. Thus, one of the ancillary issues that had to be negotiated was that of temporary access or entry to the territory of Members for individual service-providers of other Members. The Annex on Movement of Natural Persons Supplying Services Under the Agreement, among other provisions, addresses this issue.

The Annex makes it clear that the Agreement does not apply to measures that affect persons seeking employment in the territory of a Member, nor to those measures relating to citizenship, residence or employment on a permanent basis. The obligations of the Agreement are restricted to that temporary entry necessary in order to supply a service. Members may negotiate specific commitments, in accordance with Parts II and IV of the Agreement, applying to the movement of persons supplying services under the Agreement. Thus, the issue of temporary entry is one that is to be negotiated on a case-by-case basis and any commitment in this regard will be included in a Member's GATS Schedule. A Member is not automatically required to grant temporary entry to all types of service-suppliers from all other Members. However, once a Member has committed to allowing the temporary entry of a certain type of supplier, the Member must allow natural persons covered by that specific commitment to supply the service in accordance with that commitment.

Finally, paragraph 4 of the Annex notes that the Agreement does not prevent a Member from regulating temporary entry generally, provided that those measures are not applied so as to nullify or impair any benefits. Thus, Members are still permitted to impose application and visa requirements, reasonable time limits on temporary entry, and basic entry criteria, such as good character and health requirements.

The original negotiations on the movement of natural persons were not entirely successful. While many Members did schedule some commitments in the area, in a reverse of the normal situation that prevailed during the negotiations, some developing country Members were of the view that developed country Members had not offered up sufficient commitments in this regard. It was therefore decided to continue the negotiations on the movement of natural persons beyond the formal conclusion of the Uruguay Round.[48] A Negotiating Group on Movement of Natural Persons was established. Further negotiations commenced in late 1994 and were concluded on July 28, 1995.[49]

---

[48] See *Decision on Negotiations on Movement of Natural Persons*, a decision of Ministers issued on April 15, 1994 in Marrakesh as part of the final Uruguay Round package.

[49] These negotiations were originally scheduled to be completed by June 30, 1995. However, on June 30 the Services Council extended the deadline until July 28, 1995, to coincide with an extension agreed to for the financial services negotiations. This was largely the result of certain developing country Members attempting to link the results of these two functionally separate negotiations. Certain developing country Members were only prepared to offer significant commitments in the financial services sector if developed country Members were prepared to make significant commitments on temporary entry.

These further negotiations were moderately successful in obtaining additional commitments from some Members relating to temporary entry.

(ii) The Annex on Air Transport Services

Air transportation services presented unique problems during the negotiations because of the number of pre-existing bilateral air agreements between Members governing landing and traffic rights negotiated under the auspices of the *Chicago Convention*.[50] The provisions of the Annex on Air Transport Services effectively exclude these bilateral agreements from coverage under the Agreement. Paragraph 3 of the Annex specifically states that the Agreement only applies to measures affecting "aircraft repair and maintenance services", "the selling and marketing of air transport services" and "computer reservation services", all as further defined in the Annex. The Agreement and its dispute settlement procedures are specifically stated not to apply to measures affecting traffic rights, however granted, or to services directly related to the exercise of traffic rights.

The Council is required to periodically review developments in the air transportation sector and it is possible that such reviews may lead to an extension of the Agreement and to full coverage of this sector under the Agreement in the future.

(iii) Annexes Relating to Financial Services

It was determined relatively early in the negotiations that because the regulatory structures governing the area were relatively unique and complex, financial services would require its own set of additional and special rules. The Annex on Financial Services and the Understanding on Commitments in Financial Services were included for this purpose. It also soon became clear that negotiations on specific commitments (as opposed to the general obligations) in the financial services sector would also be difficult. The difficulty lay in a prevailing United States concern over "MFN free-riding". Many of the developed countries already had relatively open markets with respect to financial services. The United States, in particular, was concerned that developing country Members would not agree to open their financial services markets to a similar degree, yet the GATS' MFN clause would still guarantee that their financial-service-providers would have access to the markets of most developed country Members. As the Uruguay Round concluded, the United

---

[50]These bilateral landing rights Agreements govern issues such as the airlines of one country that will be permitted to land in the other country, the cities at which the flights will be permitted to land, the routes to be followed, and total number and capacity of flights that will be allowed.

States remained dissatisfied with the financial service commitments being offered by many developing country Members, and it took an MFN reservation for many of its financial services commitments. Some viewed this move as indicating a significant failure in the negotiations. However, rather than concede defeat in this most important of service sectors, Members agreed instead to continue the financial services negotiations after the Round had been concluded.[51] These continuing negotiations therefore necessitated an additional Ministerial Decision on further negotiations in the sector and a Second Annex on Financial Services.

(1) The Annex on Financial Services. The Annex on Financial Services provides certain general rights and obligations related to the financial services sector. The Annex is stated to apply to measures affecting the supply of "financial services" by any of the four modes set out in Article I:2 of the GATS.[52] The exclusion from coverage under the Agreement provided in Article I:3(b) for "services supplied in the exercise of governmental authority" has been specifically defined for the purposes of financial services in paragraph 1(b) of the Annex to exclude monetary and exchange rate policies. In addition, provided that such services are not provided within the territory of a Member on a competitive basis, statutory social assistance, public retirement plans, and activities conducted by a public entity for the account of or with the guarantee of or using the financial resources of the government, will also be excluded from coverage under the Agreement.

Paragraph 2 of the Annex addresses certain issues arising from the domestic regulation of the financial services sector. Generally speaking, the sector is intensively regulated to ensure consumer protection and institutional solvency. First, notwithstanding any other provisions of the GATS, a Member is free to take measures for prudential reasons—that is, measures to protect investors, depositors and policy-holders, and to ensure the safety and security of the Member's financial system. Second, nothing in the Agreement is to be read as requiring a Member to disclose any confidential or proprietary information, or information relating to individual financial services customers.

---

[51] In terms of the importance of the financial services, the WTO Secretariat has estimated that the financial services is the largest single services sector covered by the GATS, and that OECD exports of banking services alone totalled over US$40 billion in 1992. See *WTO Focus* Newsletter, May-June 1995, at 12.

[52] "Financial service" is expansively defined in paragraph 6 of the Annex to mean "any service of a financial nature offered by a financial service supplier of a Member". The Annex then sets out an extensive list of specific examples of what constitutes a financial service, including insurance and insurance-related services, all forms of banking, lending and financial leasing, securities, settlement and clearing services, and financial advice.

Similar to GATS Article VII, paragraph 3 of the Annex addresses issues arising out of recognition; in the case of financial services it is the recognition of the prudential measures of another country. First, a Member is permitted to recognize the prudential measures of others in determining how the Member will apply its own measures. For example, a Member may permit the financial-service-providers of another Member to enter its territory because it considers the prudential measures of the other Member to be equivalent to its own. Such recognition can be accorded either unilaterally or by agreement. The Member according recognition is not required to extend such recognition on an unconditional MFN basis, but must provide an adequate opportunity to other interested Members to obtain a similar agreement or unilateral recognition.

(2) *The Understanding on Commitments in Financial Services.* With respect to those obligations relating to market access, the Understanding on Commitments in Financial Services (the "Understanding") provides additional disciplines in many areas. While the Understanding is not formally part of the GATS, almost all developed country Members have made their specific financial services commitments on the basis of the Understanding.[53] The Understanding is essentially an alternative approach to that provided under Part III of the GATS for making commitments in the financial services sector.[54]

First, with respect to monopolies in the financial services area, in addition to GATS Article VIII (Monopolies and Exclusive Service Providers), each

---

[53] For example, the GATS Schedules of Canada, the United States and the EU all specifically provide that financial services commitments contained in their Schedules have been undertaken in accordance with the Understanding. Some Schedules incorporate the Understanding by reference. Thus, each Member's specific Schedule must be reviewed in order to determine whether its financial services commitments have been made on the basis of the additional disciplines contained in the Understanding.

[54] Part III of the GATS includes Articles XVI (Market Access) and XVII (National Treatment). Thus, those Members that have agreed to make commitments on the basis of the Understanding have agreed to a more specific and rigorous set of obligations than those found in Articles XVI and XVII. This approach can be seen as being similar to the voluntary "Code" approach adopted during the Tokyo Round. This approach raises several issues, many of which are addressed in the Understanding's preamble. First, the Understanding merely provides disciplines which are in addition to, but not in conflict with, those of the Agreement. Second, application of the Understanding is completely voluntary. Members remain free to make financial services commitments under Part III of the Agreement, rather than applying the Understanding to those commitments. Third, those Members that do employ the Understanding to their financial services commitments must still apply their commitments and the additional obligations on an MFN basis, to all Members. Finally, the Understanding does not itself give rise to specific market access commitments. It only sets out additional disciplines that will apply to those market access commitments that a Member has made based on the Understanding.

Member was required to list in its Schedule any existing monopoly rights in the financial services sector and make attempts to reduce or eliminate the scope of those monopolies. This includes activities conducted by a public entity for the account of or with the guarantee of or using the financial resources of the government, which are otherwise excluded from the Agreement by virtue of paragraph 1(b)(iii) of the first Annex on Financial Services.

With respect to the government procurement of financial services, notwithstanding Article XIII (which basically excludes government procurement of services from coverage under the GATS), a Member's public entities must accord non-discriminatory treatment to financial-service-suppliers of any Member established in the Member's territory when procuring financial services.

With respect to the cross-border trade in financial services (that is providing a financial service from the territory of one Member into the territory of another), each Member is required to permit non-resident suppliers to supply certain types of insurance and financial information and data processing services. In addition, each Member must allow its residents to purchase most covered financial services from the territory of another Member. This includes certain insurance services, banking, lending, securities, data processing and financial advice. This obligation means that although a Member may not have undertaken a specific commitment allowing the financial-service-providers of other Members to establish a presence within its territory, the Member must not restrict the ability of its residents to purchase services from providers located within the territory of another Member. In other words, consumers must be free to choose where and from whom they purchase their financial services.

With respect to the commercial presence of a financial-service-provider of one Member in the territory of another, Members are required to grant such a service-provider of other Members the right to establish a commercial presence within its territory, or expand that presence, including through the acquisition of existing enterprises. Members are still permitted to impose terms, conditions and procedures for obtaining authorizations relating to commercial presence, provided that they do not undermine the basic commercial presence obligation. In addition, the exception for prudential measures will also continue to apply. Once a service-supplier has established a presence in a Member's territory, the Member must allow the supplier to offer any "new financial service" within its territory.[55]

---

[55] A "new financial service" is defined as "a service of a financial nature, including services related to existing and new products or the manner in which the product is delivered, that is not supplied by any financial service supplier in the territory of a particular Member but which is supplied in the territory of another Member".

Many large financial-service-suppliers have centralized their data processing on a global basis, in one or more locations around the world. Paragraph 8 of the Understanding ensures that such rationalization will be permitted by prohibiting Members from taking any measures to prevent transfers of information or the processing of financial information where such operations are necessary for the conduct of the ordinary business of the supplier.

With respect to temporary entry of personnel of financial-service-suppliers, the Understanding goes beyond the Annex on Movement of Natural Persons Supplying Services Under the Agreement. Where a supplier has or is establishing a commercial presence in the territory of a Member, the Member must permit the temporary entry into its territory of certain specialists and senior management personnel. A lesser obligation, subject to labour availability within the territory of the Member, applies with respect to the temporary entry of certain other types of specialists, such as computer, actuarial and legal specialists.

Paragraphs 10 and 11 of the Understanding address non-discriminatory measures which, although they may be consistent with the obligations of the Agreement, may still act to restrict financial services trade. Members have accepted that they will endeavour to remove or limit any significant adverse effects on financial-service-suppliers of other Members that may result from the application of such non-discriminatory measures. These measures can include those which limit the types of services that can be provided by a supplier (a measure which prevents all banks from selling insurance services, for example) and those that limit the expansion of service-suppliers.

With respect to national treatment, the provisions of the Understanding are in addition to those of Article XVII. Members must provide access to payment and clearing systems operated by public entities and official funding and re-financing facilities on national treatment terms to financial-service-providers of any other Member located in the Member's territory. This obligation does not apply to access to the Member's lender of last resort. Where membership in any self-regulating body or similar organization is required in order to provide a given financial service (stock exchanges, for example) Members must also ensure that these entities accord national treatment to financial-service-suppliers of other Members.

(3) *The Decision on Financial Services.* As a result of the decision to extend the financial services negotiations beyond the formal conclusion of the Uruguay Round, on April 15, 1994, the Ministers issued the Decision on Financial Services as part of the Round's final package. This Decision provided that Members' financial services commitments that had already been accepted would enter into force on an MFN basis on January 1, 1995. No later than June 30, 1995, Members were to finalize their positions with respect to

their MFN exemptions relating to financial services. During this six-month period, any MFN exceptions that had been made conditional on the level of commitments undertaken by other Members would be suspended. This meant that the application of the MFN reservation that the United States had taken at the end of the financial services negotiations would be temporarily delayed. The Decision also provided that the Committee on Trade in Financial Services was to monitor the continuing negotiations and report to the Services Council.[56]

(4) The Second Annex on Financial Services. The Second Annex on Financial Services was then required to put this Ministerial Decision into practical effect. Paragraph 1 of the Annex provides that, notwithstanding the MFN obligation of Article II and the Annex on Article II Exemptions, for a 60-day period starting May 1, 1995, Members would still be permitted to list in the Article II Annex those financial services measures that were inconsistent with the MFN obligation. In addition, notwithstanding Article XXI, for a 60-day period starting May 1, 1995, Members would be free to improve, modify or withdraw all or part of their financial services commitments without having to offer up compensation in return. The additional provisions of this Second Annex therefore gave Members the necessary flexibility to adjust their financial services commitments in light of the results of the continuing negotiations.

(5) The Post-Marrakesh Negotiations. The financial services negotiations were re-commenced almost immediately following the Marrakesh meeting of April 15, 1994. From the perspective of the United States, the goal was to attempt to improve the concessions offered up by most developing country Members. One continuing concern of the United States was that many developing country Members still refused to commit to maintaining even their existing measures. This would mean, for example, that there would be no recourse to dispute settlement under the GATS if these Members subsequently acted to further restrict foreign ownership or force a divestiture of financial services assets. From the perspective of other developed country Members, the goal was to try to persuade the developing country Members to improve their offers sufficiently so as to prevent the United States from taking an unpleasant and precedent-setting MFN exception.

While many developing country Members did improve their offers, on June 29, 1995, the United States again announced that it was still not sufficiently satisfied with the results of the negotiations and it notified the participants that it would be withdrawing most of its offer and would be taking an

---

[56]The Committee on Trade in Financial Services was not actually established until the first meeting of the Services Council on March 1, 1995. During that period the negotiations were overseen by the Interim Group on Financial Services. Both the Group and the Committee were chaired by Mr. Frank Swedlove, an official with Canada's Department of Finance.

MFN exemption for all future measures across the entire financial services sector (banking, securities, insurance and diversified financial services). The United States did note that it would continue non-discriminatory treatment for all then existing investments in its financial services sector. This exception would allow the United States to adopt a policy of reciprocity in financial services and thereby discriminate against those Members who continued to refuse to allow reciprocal access to their markets to United States financial-service-providers.

It initially appeared as though the United States' announcement would scuttle the negotiations. Many of the participants were of the view that there was no point in concluding any agreement in financial services if the United States was not a party. However, the EC, in particular, was of the view that good progress had been made in the negotiations and that this progress should be "harvested" to the greatest extent possible. Additional progress might then be made in future negotiations. In an emergency session of the Services Council it was agreed that the original June 30, deadline would be extended a further 28 days during which time the EC could attempt to build support among the other participants for its position.

There were three main elements to the EC's proposal. First, an agreement would be accepted by all participants, with the exception of the United States, based on the existing market access offers on the table as of June 30, 1995. Second, the agreement would not come into force until August 1, 1996. In the interim, a "standstill" would be in effect, meaning that until the agreement entered into force, Members would not take measures inconsistent with their agreed-to commitments. The agreement would an interim one, to remain in force only until December 31, 1997. For a 60-day period beginning November 1, 1997, Members would again be free to maintain, improve or withdraw any or all of their commitments under the agreement, notwithstanding GATS Article XXI. Finally, a new and more comprehensive round of financial services negotiations would be completed before the December 31, 1997 expiry of the interim agreement.

In the end, the EC was able to gain sufficient support for this proposal. All Members who participated in the negotiations, with the exception of the United States, accepted the interim agreement. The protocol was open for signature until June 30, 1996 to allow signing Members sufficient time for their domestic ratification procedures. The United States refused to relent. While it agreed to maintain its existing regime for foreign financial-service-suppliers already operating in the U.S., it withdrew its financial services offer and retained its MFN exemption. Twenty-nine participants (counting the EC as one) signed the protocol. As planned, further negotiations aimed at improving the level of market access commitments in the financial sector and in broadening the level of participation were re-commenced in April of 1997 and are expected to conclude by the end of the year.

(iv) The Annex on Negotiations on Maritime Transport Services

Much like air transport and financial services, maritime transport services are characterized by a number of bilateral and plurilateral Agreements in addition to complex regulatory regimes. A number of countries require that their ocean-going imports or exports be carried by nationally flagged and/or owned vessels. Additional problems relate to liner conferences, coasting or cabotage trade (that is, pick-ups and deliveries within the territory of the same country), and access to and use of port facilities. Some Members, most particularly the United States, were reluctant to negotiate on maritime services within the context of the GATS. While much progress was made during the Uruguay Round itself, at the last minute the United States withdrew its maritime services offer. The EC then followed suit. It was then decided that commitments in the maritime services area would also be put on hold and negotiations on maritime services would be re-commenced after the formal completion of the Uruguay Round. The Annex on Negotiations on Maritime Transport Services and the Ministerial Decision on Negotiations on Marine Transport Services were then adopted to give effect to this decision.

The Ministerial Decision on Negotiations on Marine Transport Services provided that further negotiations in the maritime sector (including shipping, auxiliary services, and access to and use of port facilities, but excluding cabotage) were to be re-commenced no later than May 16, 1994. The Negotiating Group on Maritime Transport Services ("NGMTS") was established to carry out this mandate, with participation in the Group open to all interested Members on a voluntary basis. A number of Members agreed to participate in the Group, including Canada, the United States and the EC. The negotiations were to conclude no later than the end of June 1996, and the results were to be implemented at a later date to be determined by the NGMTS.

Until the negotiations were concluded, the MFN obligation of Article II (and the relevant provisions of the Annex on Article II Exemptions) was not to apply to the maritime services sector. At the end of the negotiations, Members were to be permitted to finalize their commitments in the area, and could claim an MFN exemption if they chose to. Any resulting commitments were to then be included in each Member's Schedule and thereby would become subject to all the provisions of the Agreement. If negotiations could not be successfully concluded by June 1996, the Services Council was then to determine whether the negotiations would be extended or terminated.

The participants also agreed to a "standstill" while the negotiations were ongoing. Commencing on April 15, 1994, and continuing until the results of the negotiations were implemented, no participant was to apply any new restrictive measure that would affect trade in maritime transport services or improve their negotiating leverage. The standstill was to be monitored by the NGMTS and participants could notify the NGMTS of any violations.[57]

Because of these continuing negotiations and the Decision's provisions concerning the suspension of the MFN obligation, the Annex on Negotiations on Maritime Transport Services was also required. The Annex provided that, with the exception of any specific commitments that may already be in effect,[58] the MFN obligations of Article II and the Annex on Article II Exemptions would not enter into force for the maritime transport sector until either the implementation date of the negotiated results, or, if the negotiations were unsuccessful, the date of the Negotiating Group's final report. Between the conclusion of the negotiations and their implementation, Article XXI would not apply and Members would be free to modify, improve or withdraw any or all of their specific commitments in the maritime services sector without being required to offer up compensation in return.

As the negotiations approached the June 28 deadline, the United States remained substantially dissatisfied with the offers of the other Members that were then on the table. It announced to the other participants that it would not be tabling an offer. The negotiations subsequently collapsed. But, unlike the financial service negotiations, there was no appetite in the maritime negotiations for any form of temporary agreement. The NGMTS was faced with a decision of either terminating the negotiations or merely "suspending" them. On June 28, 1996, the Council for Trade in Services issued its Decision on Maritime Transport Services, thereby announcing that the maritime services negotiations were being suspended. The negotiations are to resume in the year 2000 as part of the next round of comprehensive service negotiations which are mandated under GATS Article XIX. All participating Members then had

---

[57] In July 1995, the EU along with several other Members notified the NGMTS of what it considered to be a United States violation of the maritime standstill. Since the Arab oil embargo of 1973, the United States had prohibited all exports of Alaskan oil. In July 1995, a bill made its way through Congress which eliminated this export prohibition. However, the bill also included a cargo reservation provision that restricted the carriage of all Alaskan oil exports to U.S.-flagged carriers. The cargo reservation was apparently included in order to gain support for the legislation from U.S. seafarers' unions. Measures such as this type of cargo reservation would likely be prohibited if maritime services were brought fully into the GATS.

The United States' position with respect to the alleged violation of the standstill was that Alaskan oil had not been carried by foreign carriers for over 22 years and this would not change under the legislation. Moreover, the United States took the position that the standstill was not a binding obligation. The EU view was that this was a new measure which acted to increase U.S. leverage in the negotiations and thus violated the standstill. (See "Japan, EU Assail Alaska Oil Plan", *Journal of Commerce*, 3 November 1995, at page A1.) The bill which eventually entered into force included the disputed provision.

[58] Almost all Members retracted their maritime services offers when the negotiations collapsed just prior to the completion of the Round and therefore few Members currently have any scheduled maritime services commitments in effect.

30 days during which time they could modify or withdraw any maritime services commitments that had been made during the Uruguay Round or the subsequent negotiations.

The Council's Decision provides a "standstill" whereby it is understood that Members will not adopt any new measures in the maritime services sector that would have the effect of improving their negotiating leverage, except in response to the measures of others. The Decision also extends the suspension of the unconditional MFN obligation of GATS Article II until the end of the resumed negotiations, at which time Members will be permitted to take an MFN exemption for maritime services if they so choose.

While the WTO negotiations are suspended, the countries of the Organization for Economic Co-operation and Development ("OECD") are simultaneously pursuing international rule development in maritime services along other avenues outside the scope of the WTO. It has been reported that the Maritime Transport Committee of the OECD is attempting to reach a nonbinding agreement on fair competition in the maritime transport sector with willing countries in Asia and Latin America.[59] While this appears to be a positive development, there are three aspects of this extra-WTO initiative that should be noted. First, unlike WTO obligations, the obligations of these MOUs are not binding on the parties. Second, even if these MOUs were binding, because they are not part of the WTO, the dispute settlement provisions of the WTO cannot be invoked to enforce any of their obligations. Finally, the MOUs are more limited in subject-matter than the ongoing maritime negotiations. Moreover, the United States has apparently reserved the right to carry government and military cargoes on U.S.-flagged ships. Thus, these MOUs should be seen to be a second-best alternative to the negotiation of a more comprehensive agreement on maritime services within the WTO/GATS framework.

(v) Telecommunications

Like many of the other service sectors that required their own sector-specific Annex, the telecommunications sector is noted for its complex domestic legal structures and its highly regulated business environment. The capital-intensive nature and national security aspects of domestic telecommunications infrastructures have generally produced nationally owned and highly regulated monopolies in many segments of the telecommunications

---

[59]This agreement would apparently be similar to a Memorandum of Understanding ("MOU") on the same issue that the OECD countries signed with certain Eastern European countries in 1993. See, for example, "OECD May Set Global Maritime Deal", in *Journal of Commerce*, 21 November 1995, at B10, and OECD Press Release SG/Press (93)37 of 10 June 1993.

sector. Unlike many other service sectors, however, there are two separate and distinct aspects to the provision of telecommunications services. First, basic telecommunications, such as telephone service, is considered to be the provision of a service or distinct economic activity in and of itself. As a result, the usual issues of national treatment, MFN treatment, ownership restrictions and market access issues arise with respect to the supply of these services. Second, there are many service-suppliers operating within other sectors unrelated to telecommunications, such as financial-service-suppliers, for example, that rely on access to a telecommunications infrastructure in order to support and adequately supply their unrelated service to consumers. This aspect of telecommunications raises an additional set of independent issues, such as non-discriminatory access to and use of the telecommunications infrastructure.

Related to this distinction is another often made between basic telecommunications, such as the provision of basic telephone, television and radio services, and enhanced or secondary telecommunications services, such as voicemail services, e-mail, and online data processing and research services. Basic telecommunications services are usually supplied by large highly regulated monopolies, while the supply of secondary telecommunications services is usually marked by a greater number of suppliers and a correspondingly higher degree of competition among those suppliers. The current treatment of telecommunications under the applicable GATS Annexes essentially tracks this distinction between the basic and secondary telecommunications services.

(1) The Annex on Telecommunications. With respect to secondary services, the Annex on Telecommunications essentially elaborates and supplements the applicable GATS provisions so as to require transparent and non-discriminatory access to and use of "public telecommunications transport networks and services".[60]

More specifically, paragraph 4 of the Annex addresses transparency issues, requiring Members to ensure that all relevant information concerning access to and use of networks and services is publicly available. This includes information relating to matters such as tariffs, terms of service, technical specifications and licensing or registration requirements.

Paragraph 5 sets out the Annex's obligations relating to access to and use of networks and services. Sub-paragraph (a) sets out the basic obligation.

---

[60] In order to determine the precise scope of the Annex it is necessary to review the definitions provided by para. 3 of the Annex. "Telecommunications" is defined to mean the transmission and reception of signals by any electromagnetic means. This would include, for example, radio, television, telephone and satellite transmission. "Public telecommunications transport service" is defined to mean any non-enhancing telecommunications transport service required by a Member to be offered to the public generally, including telephone, telex and telegraph. Public networks are those telecommunications infrastructures which permit telecommunications between and among network termination points. However, there are a number of specific exclusions from the scope of the Annex, such as one for measures which affect the cable or broadcast distribution of radio or television programming.

Where a Member has included a particular service sector in its GATS Schedule (financial services, for example), that Member must ensure that all applicable service-suppliers are accorded access to and use of public networks and services on reasonable and non-discriminatory terms and conditions so as to permit them to supply that scheduled service.[61] Sub-paragraphs (b) to (f) then provide further elaboration on this basic obligation.

The remaining provisions of the Annex address issues related to technical cooperation and the relationship between the Annex and other international Agreements and organizations that address the same or related issues such as the International Telecommunications Union.[62]

(2) The Decision on Negotiations on Basic Telecommunications. As noted above, measures relating to basic telecommunications are not addressed in the Annex on Telecommunications. Like a number of other difficult service sectors that were under negotiation during the Uruguay Round, Members were unable to arrive at an agreement on basic telecommunications services prior to the end of the Round. Again, one of the major stumbling blocks was the United States' position that many Members were not prepared to offer up serious commitments in the area and it was threatening to take an MFN exemption for the basic telecommunications sector. Rather than have this occur, Members agreed to continue negotiations on basic telecommunications after the formal conclusion of the Round. This was confirmed by the Ministers' Decision on Negotiations on Basic Telecommunications, included as part of the Uruguay Round final package.

The Decision provided that negotiations were to be commenced on a voluntary basis with a view to progressive liberalization in basic telecommunications. The Negotiating Group on Basic Telecommunications ("NGBT") was established to carry out this mandate. Canada, the United States, the EC and a number of other Members agreed to participate in the

---

[61] Note that Members themselves often, but not always, own or operate public networks or services operating within their territories. For example, many public telephone networks are owned and operated by highly regulated but privately-owned companies. In such cases, there is an issue as to what a Member's obligation might be to ensure compliance with the obligations of the Annex by these companies. Footnote 14 of the Annex, an "extent-of-obligations" provision, provides the answer. There is an absolute obligation on Members to take whatever measures may be necessary to ensure that the obligations of the Annex are being met by those entities actually supplying the public networks and services.

[62] The International Telecommunications Union ("ITU") is a specialized agency of the UN with responsibility for telecommunications. It was originally established in 1865 as the International Telegraph Union, but its name was changed to the ITU in 1934. It became a specialized agency of the UN in 1947. The purposes of the ITU, as set out in the 1982 *International Telecommunications Convention* (also known as the "Nairobi Convention") include allocating and registering the radio frequency spectrum, and promoting developments relating to technical telecommunications facilities.

NGBT. Negotiations commenced shortly after the Marrakesh meeting, and were to be concluded no later than April 30, 1996. Once the negotiations were complete, the results were to be incorporated in each participating Member's GATS Schedule. Paragraph 7 of the Decision provided a "standstill" for the sector while negotiations were continuing. Until the negotiations were completed and the results implemented, no participant was to apply any measure so as to improve its negotiating position or leverage. The NGBT was charged with overseeing the standstill, and any participant was able to notify the Group of any act of another Member that it believed to be contrary to the standstill obligation.

(3) The Annex on Negotiations on Basic Telecommunications. The Decision on Negotiations on Basic Telecommunications was further supported by the Annex on Negotiations on Basic Telecommunications. Similar to other GATS Annexes concerning ongoing negotiations, this Annex provided that, subject to any specific commitment that may already be in effect, the MFN obligation of Article II was suspended for basic telecommunications until either the results of the negotiations were implemented or, if negotiations failed, the date of the NGBT's final report. This meant that, subject to the basic telecommunications standstill, Members remained free to discriminate among suppliers of basic telecommunications until the negotiations were concluded. And, as was the case with respect to financial services, Members then would be permitted to take an exemption under the Annex on Article II Exemptions for their basic telecommunications measures, if they so chose.

(4) The Negotiations on Basic Telecommunications. Negotiations within the NGBT commenced shortly after the Marrakesh meetings of April 1994. By December 1995, 45 Members were participating in the negotiations with another 27 observing. The United States was very much the driving force in the negotiations and was one of the first Members to table a comprehensive offer in late July 1995. Underlying the United States' offer was the strong belief that improved market access or the elimination of foreign ownership restrictions, by themselves, would be insufficient in a regulatory environment dominated by national monopolies. Any market access offers had to be supported by certain additional regulatory commitments that would guarantee a pro-competitive business climate. The United States' offer was comprised of five inter-related commitments designed to achieve this goal. First, with the exception of certain limits on foreign ownership of radio stations and measures at the state level, the U.S. was prepared to offer unlimited foreign access to the U.S. telecommunications market. However, this access was stated to be reciprocal, meaning that it would only be extended to companies based in Members that eliminated their own foreign ownership restrictions applicable to U.S. companies. Second, a fair and economical interconnection system would be assured. Third, telecommunications regulators would be independent of the service-providers they regulate. Fourth, the rate-making and other

aspects of the regulatory process would be fair and transparent. Finally, there would be competitive safeguards to prevent dominant players from acting unfairly to restrict competition (through cross-subsidization, for example). The net effect of this package of commitments would be to not only improve market access on paper, but also to require dominant suppliers to provide access to their systems to other competing suppliers at public, non-discriminatory, cost-based rates.

The United States' offer met with mixed reviews. Many other developed country Members, such as Japan and Canada, supported the U.S. approach. In contrast, the EC, which did not table an offer until the beginning of October, was more sceptical. The EC offer stressed market access and national treatment, and, while it accepted that the U.S. approach had merit, the EC was of the view that such an approach may be too ambitious to be negotiated by the April 1996 deadline.

Despite some initial hesitation, subsequent to the tabling of the U.S. offer, negotiations did proceed on a set of pro-competitive "Regulatory Commitments", as proposed by the U.S., which could be used to support Members' market access concessions made as part of the negotiations. A final version of the Regulatory Commitments was approved by the NGBT on April 24, 1996, and was subsequently incorporated into what became known as the "Reference Paper". The Reference Paper set out a series of additional obligations related to certain pro-competitive safeguards, interconnection, transparency, universal service, licensing criteria, independence of regulators and the allocation and use of scarce resources (such as frequencies, numbers and rights of way). Similar to the Understanding on Commitments in Financial Services, the intention was that the Regulatory Commitments would act as additional disciplines on Members in the area of basic telecommunications. This would be accomplished by participating Members making their telecommunications concessions subject to the Reference Paper, either by specifically repeating the Regulatory Commitments in their respective GATS Schedules, or by incorporating the Reference Paper by reference.

The agreement on the Regulatory Commitments was considered to be a significant advancement in the negotiations and while it seemed that a successful conclusion to the negotiations was then within reach, the U.S. still remained dissatisfied with the majority of offers that had been tabled by the participants up to that time. The U.S. again threatened to withdraw from the negotiations. Rather than allow these negotiations to collapse when success was so close, and in order to save what progress had been made to date, Members quickly reached an agreement on extending the April 30, 1996 deadline and re-commencing the negotiations after a short recess.

The agreement to re-commence the negotiations was modelled after previous such agreements in the financial and maritime services negotiations, and was comprised of four elements. First, all offers on the table as of April 30, 1996 would remain "frozen" until January 15, 1997. (Most such offers had already incorporated some or all of the Regulatory Commitments discussed above.) Second, negotiations aimed at improving these existing offers were to re-commence in late July 1996 and were to conclude prior to a new deadline of January 15, 1997. Third, as of January 15, 1997, Members would have a 30-day period, until February 15, 1997, during which time they would be able to modify, improve or withdraw those offers based on the results of the further negotiations. Finally, participants agreed to an interim standstill which provided that they would not take any measures that would be inconsistent with their undertakings resulting from the negotiations until their new telecommunications obligations entered into force.

These further negotiations commenced as planned in late July 1996 and continued right up until a revised deadline of February 15, 1997. In the end, the further negotiations were substantially successful in increasing the scope of both pre-existing and new offers. By February 15, 55 schedules of commitments, representing 69 Members, had been agreed to. These new schedules will be annexed to the Fourth Protocol to the GATS, which will remain open for signature until November 30, 1997. The new commitments are scheduled to enter into force on January 1, 1998 (although many Members did provide for a post-implementation phase-in of their commitments). Generally speaking, almost all commitments are to be implemented on an MFN basis. However, nine Members did take certain limited MFN exemptions. Of the 69 Members making concessions, 63 included commitments on regulatory disciplines in their respective Schedules, while 57 Members adopted the disciplines of the Reference Paper either substantially or in their entirety. The WTO estimated that the 69 Members covered by the new telecommunications commitments represented over 90 percent of global telecommunications revenues in 1995.

5. CONCLUSIONS

There is no doubt that the GATS with its associated Annexes, Decisions, Schedules and further negotiations can be a bewildering maze of documentation. It should always be borne in mind, however, that it is based on certain "tried and true" principles that are fundamental to trade law generally. The first such principle is MFN treatment. A Member must not discriminate among service-providers from others Members. The second is *de facto* national treatment. In those sectors where a Member has scheduled concessions, it cannot discriminate between its own services and service-providers and those of other Members. The final principle is one of transparency. Members are required to regulate services within their territories in a fair and transparent manner. When problems arise under the Agreement it is always useful to return to these first principles for an initial assessment of the issues involved.

It must be acknowledged that the GATS has been subject to some criticism. Some have suggested that the Agreement does little more than codify existing protectionism. Others argue that some provisions, such as those relating to MFN exclusions, "gut" the Agreement of any real substance. Still others have commented that market access has not been substantially improved. The GATS is not a perfect agreement, nor did any of the negotiators ever believe that it could be. Like any international agreement of substance, the GATS is a product of compromise. Give and take was required by all Members in order to reach a consensus. At a minimum, the Agreement has foreclosed increasing protectionism in a number of service sectors. This development, in and of itself, is a substantial improvement on the situation that existed previously. But it is unfair to compare the results of the GATS negotiations with the degree of openness that now exists in the area of trade in goods. It has taken almost 50 years to achieve the degree of market access that currently exists for goods. And it should not be forgotten that two important areas, agriculture and textiles and apparel, have only now been brought within the international rules. Viewed in this light, the GATS as it now stands should be compared with the GATT as it was in 1947, as only the very first step of a long journey of liberalization in the area of trade in services. More steps will be taken when the ongoing negotiations are complete. Still more will be taken when the succeeding rounds of comprehensive service negotiations are commenced and then completed. In other words, we may be a long way from free trade in services, but an impressive first step has been made.

One final cautionary comment should be made with respect to sectoral negotiations. These negotiations have demonstrated again the difficulty of negotiating on single issues in isolation. While most Members have some interest in the sectors under negotiation, there is often no ground-swell of support for any one of them. Even among the developed country Members, there are varying degrees of enthusiasm for the negotiations depending upon the sector at issue. This has led to attempts to link the sectoral negotiations so that a concession in one sector might be traded-off for a potential gain in another. For example, many developing country Members tried to link the results of the financial services negotiations with those on temporary entry. The EC attempted to link the telecommunications negotiations with those on maritime transport. To some degree this is probably unavoidable when presented with two or more simultaneous sectoral negotiations. It also demonstrates, however, that the best results for service negotiations likely will not be attainable within the context of individual sectoral negotiations, but within comprehensive services negotiations, or, potentially even better, within the context of an entirely new round of WTO negotiations, where concessions can be exchanged across goods, services, investment and intellectual property and where the results can be easier sold to domestic constituents as a total package. While at the time of writing there apparently is little appetite among

WTO Members for a new and punishing round of comprehensive trade negotiations similar to the Uruguay Round, it appears that a desire to achieve genuine improvements in international service liberalization may drive Members to initiate such a new comprehensive round in the future.

5

The Agreement on Trade-Related Aspects of Intellectual Property Rights

1. INTRODUCTION

The 1970s and 1980s saw an escalating conflict between two competing trends in intellectual property. The first was the increasing importance of technology and knowledge-based enterprises to economic growth and development. The "high-tech" industries, such as computers, computer software, chemicals, pharmaceuticals and related scientific research and development, began to account for an increasing proportion of economic activity in most of the world's developed countries. At the same time, however, a competing trend of intellectual property piracy and trade in counterfeit goods was expanding at an alarming rate, thereby significantly reducing the potential economic benefits being generated by the first trend. It has been estimated that in one year, 1986, U.S. businesses alone lost between US$43 and $61 billion due to inadequate intellectual property protection around the world.[1]

There had been a number of previous attempts at addressing these two competing trends. Most such attempts proceeded along two tracks. First, attempts were made to improve the minimum levels of intellectual property protection already provided for under certain existing international Agreements, usually by attempting to negotiate improvements to those existing international Agreements. Second, efforts had been made to improve compliance with, and enforcement of, the existing standards of protection by, for example, explicitly linking these recognized levels of protection to trade laws. The result of such a linkage would have been that a violation of the former could then lead to trade sanctions being imposed under the latter.

In essence, the *Agreement on Trade-Related Aspects of Intellectual Property Rights* (or the "TRIPS Agreement") proceeds down both tracks simultaneously.[2] In summary, the TRIPS Agreement:

  (i) applies certain basic GATT principles, such as national treatment and MFN treatment, to intellectual property;

  (ii) establishes certain minimum levels of protection that must be extended by all Members to a number of specific types of intellectual property;

  (iii) requires Members to implement certain enforcement obligations to ensure that those levels of protection are in fact observed within their respective territories; and

  (iv) links the obligations of the TRIPS Agreement with those of the WTO Agreement, thereby ensuring that, in certain circumstances, a violation of the TRIPS Agreement can be disciplined through the use of trade-related sanctions, such as increased duties.

---

[1] See *Foreign Protection of Intellectual Property Rights and the Effects on U.S. Industry and Trade*, USITC Pub. No. 2065, Inv. No. 332-245 (February 1988), at H-3.

[2] The TRIPS Agreement is attached as Annex 1C to the WTO Agreement.

(a) What are Intellectual Property Rights?

Before discussing what improvements the Uruguay Round might have brought to the international legal regime governing the protection of intellectual property, it must first be determined what its Members were attempting to protect. What is meant by the phrase "intellectual property"? Generally speaking, intellectual property is a property right that is held in ideas. The expression is now generally considered to encompass three major intangible property rights—patents, trademarks and copyright—and several other lesser-known rights, including trade secrets, plant breeders' rights, industrial designs, geographical indications of origin, and the rights in layout designs of computer chips.[3]

(i) Patents

Patents are creatures of statutory law. Most governments will normally grant a patent for new "inventions"—that is, a method, process, apparatus, or any combination thereof, that is inventive. Patents are usually only granted for inventive advancements that would not be obvious to someone skilled in the relevant art. Patents are, in effect, similar to temporary government-sanctioned monopolies. For a specified period of time, the government grants the patent-holder the exclusive right to work, licence and sell the patented item or process in exchange for disclosing the secrets of the patentee's success to the public. While a patent is similar to a monopoly, and monopolies are generally frowned upon, the theory behind the granting of a patent is that overall public welfare will be increased by the temporary monopoly because desirable inventive activity and investment will be encouraged by the prospect of temporary exclusivity and its resulting profits.

(ii) Trademarks

A trademark is a mark or distinguishing guise that is used by a trader to distinguish its goods or services from those of its competitors. A trademark can be a word or words, including a slogan, or a design. Unlike patents, trademarks are not pure creatures of statute. For some time the common law of many countries has recognized and protected unregistered trademarks at a local level under the law of unfair competition or "passing-off". While common law trademarks are still recognized and enforced in many countries, registration of a trademark under the applicable statute generally provides the registrant with significantly improved statutory rights relating to enforcement.

---

[3] Historically, the term "intellectual property" was used only to describe copyright. Patents, trademarks and other rights were described by the term "industrial property". The subtle distinction between these two terms is rarely observed today and the term "intellectual property" is now generally used as being all-encompassing.

The theory behind trademark protection is based primarily on the notions of unfair competition and consumer protection. Passing-off goods or services as being produced by or somehow associated with those of another trader when there is no such connection is commercially unfair to the other trader and deceptive or misleading to the consumers of these goods or services.

(iii) Copyright

As with patents, copyright is also a creature of statutory law. Copyright is the exclusive right granted under statute to an author, artist or musician to prevent others from copying his or her work for a specified period of time. Copyright is generally considered to also include the right to control and prohibit the translation, performance, recording, filming, or transmission of a work. The theory behind the exclusive nature of copyright is similar to that of patents. Creativity will be encouraged by the prospect of exclusive protection and the resulting potential profits, and society as a whole will thereby be better off. Copyright in a work is generally considered to legally subsist from the moment of its creation, without any need to formally register that creation. However, registration usually provides the registrant with the benefits of certain additional rights and presumptions.

(iv) Other Intellectual Property Rights

Some of the lesser-known, but still important intellectual property rights include geographical indications of origin, industrial designs and lay-out designs (or mask works). Geographical indications of origin, more commonly referred to as appellations of origin, are indications that identify a good as originating within a particular geographical region. While most commonly used in association with wine (Burgundy, Bordeaux and Champagne, for example), such indications are also often used in association with a wider variety of food and other products (such as Roquefort cheese or Parma ham).

An industrial design is the shape or ornamentation of a product employed for its aesthetic rather than its functional value. For example, the exterior shapes of many small kitchen appliances have been registered as industrial designs. These designs can be protected independently from any patent or trademark that may also be related to the product.

Finally, lay-out designs, computer mask works or topographies are the plans or configurations for integrated circuits or "computer chips". Generally, such configurations are essential to a chip's attributes and are unique to each particular type of chip.

(b) Pre-WTO History of Intellectual Property Protection

The Uruguay Round was certainly not the first attempt to build international consensus on the appropriate levels of intellectual property protection.

In fact, the history of multilateral cooperation in improving intellectual property protection can be traced back over 100 years. In 1883, 11 countries met in Paris and signed the *International Convention for Protection of Industrial Property*.[4] This has since been followed by a number of additional international agreements that have attempted to improve international intellectual property protection in some areas, including: the 1886 Berne Convention[5]; the 1961 Rome Convention[6]; and the 1989 Washington Treaty.[7] Since 1967, the Paris, Berne and Rome Conventions have all been administered by the World Intellectual Property Organization ("WIPO"), a specialized agency of the United Nations, headquartered in Geneva.[8]

In spite of this long history of international cooperation in intellectual property matters, for numerous reasons these Agreements had become subject to an increasing number of criticisms. First, their membership was not universal. For example, while over 100 countries signed the Paris Convention, only 88 signed the Berne Convention, and only 32 countries signed the Rome

---

[4] *Convention for the Protection of Industrial Property*, 828 U.N.T.S. 305 (the "Paris Convention"). This Convention, last revised in 1967, is still in force today. It is intended to protect a number of intellectual property rights of the industrial variety, including patents, trademarks, trade names, industrial designs, and appellations of origin. It requires signatories to extend national treatment to foreign works and, in some cases, sets out certain minimum levels of protection. Over 100 countries are now signatories to this Convention.

[5] *Convention for the Protection of Literary and Artistic Works*, 1161 U.N.T.S. 198 (the "Berne Convention"). This Convention is now the primary international Agreement protecting copyright. As with the Paris Convention, its primary obligations are national treatment and certain minimum standards of protection. It also includes special rules for developing countries. Almost 90 countries are now signatories to this Convention.

[6] *International Convention for the Protection of Performers, Producers of Phonograms and Broadcasting Organizations*, 496 U.N.T.S. 44 (the "Rome Convention"). As the full name of this Convention implies, it provides for the protection of works of performers, producers of phonograms and broadcasting organizations, works that are not normally subject to copyright protection under the Berne Convention. Again, the basic obligations of the Rome Convention are national treatment with certain minimum levels of protection. Only 32, mostly developed, countries have signed the Rome Convention.

[7] *Treaty on Intellectual Property in Respect of Integrated Circuits*, adopted at Washington 26 May 1989, 28 I.L.M. 1477 (1989) (the "IPIC Treaty" or the "Washington Treaty"). While this Treaty was intended to protect lay-out designs, or mask works, because of what are seen to be certain major flaws, very few countries have become signatories to it and it has not yet entered into force.

[8] The WIPO was created by the 1967 *Convention Establishing the World Intellectual Property Organization*, 828 U.N.T.S. 3. The Convention entered into force in 1970 and the WIPO became a specialized agency of the UN in 1974. The primary objectives of the WIPO, as stated in the Convention, are to improve intellectual property protection around the world and administer certain intellectual property agreements (or "unions" as they are often called). Currently the WIPO administers 17 such intellectual property unions, including the Paris, Berne and Rome Conventions.

Convention. The United States did not sign the Berne Convention until 1988. The result is differing levels of protection for all forms of intellectual property around the world.

Second, the obligations or the standards of protection required by most of these Agreements are considered by some to be insufficient. Most of these Agreements only impose a national treatment obligation and generally do not specify any minimum levels of protection that signatories must provide to a particular intellectual property right. For example, while one of the Paris Convention's basic obligations is national treatment, the Convention's provisions applicable to patents do not specify what types of products or processes must be eligible for patent protection, nor do they establish any minimum patent term.

Third, many of the Agreements are viewed as being void of adequate provisions relating to dispute settlement and enforcement of obligations. Not only do they usually not oblige signatories to enforce the relevant intellectual property laws within their respective jurisdictions, they also do not provide for adequate international dispute settlement should signatories fail to live-up to those minimum obligations that they have agreed to accept.[9] This lack of effective dispute settlement is then matched by a corresponding lack of effective sanctions for violations.

The final problem relates to the difficulty of affecting any real improvement to those existing Agreements within the confines of the WIPO. In some cases, this problem relates to the divergent views of developed and developing countries on intellectual property issues.[10] For example, when a group of developed countries proposed amendments to the Paris Convention so as to establish certain minimum standards of protection and increase its enforcement obligations relating to patents, a group of developing countries responded by proposing instead a weakening of the Convention's obligations in some areas. While preparatory meetings and negotiations continued on these proposed amendments for over nine years, in the end neither view prevailed

---

[9] While, in theory, most of these Agreements would allow a signatory to bring a complaint before the International Court of Justice, this has never occurred in practice.

[10] Generally speaking, the prevailing view in developed countries is that intellectual property is a private right that should be protected just like any other object of private property. In contrast, the prevailing view in many developing countries is that intellectual property is more of a public good than private property, and therefore any benefits that might be derived from that property should be made available to all, so as to promote overall welfare and economic development within the country. Thus, again generally speaking, developed countries will tend to seek improved protection, while developing countries will tend to seek rules that reduce protection and promote technology transfers at little or no cost. As is discussed below, these generalizations do not always hold true in practice. There are some areas, such as in the areas of pharmaceuticals and "culture", for example, where even developed countries cannot agree on what should be the minimum levels of protection.

and consequently the Convention remained unaltered and its basic problems remained unresolved.[11]

As multilateral efforts within the WIPO and elsewhere were failing to bear fruit, the United States, in particular, began searching for alternative methods of improving global intellectual property protection. Pressed by domestic interests that were suffering direct economic harm by poor protection in other countries, the option of bilateral action became an increasingly attractive alternative. To encourage such bilateral action the United States Congress, among other things, made intellectual property protection explicitly actionable under section 301 of the *Trade Act of 1974*. This was followed by the introduction of "Special 301" as part of the *Omnibus Trade and Competitiveness Act of 1988* (an Act that came into force after the Uruguay Round had already commenced).[12] While U.S. bilateral actions under these and other legislative provisions met with varying degrees of success, the clear message being sent by the U.S. was that the status quo with respect to global intellectual property protection was unacceptable and that it was determined to have these problems addressed—one way or the other.[13]

There were also some previous attempts within the GATT to address intellectual property issues.[14] Until the Uruguay Round, these efforts had generally met with no better success than the efforts within the WIPO. For

---

[11] Divisions within the WIPO have not always been along developed/developing country lines. In the past, Eastern European countries often expressed divergent views, and on some issues the United States and the Western European countries have also been known to be at odds with one another.

[12] What is commonly referred to as "Special 301" is, in fact, a process established under Sections 301 to 310 of the *Trade Act of 1974*, which generally provides the U.S. President with a domestic process to enforce U.S. rights under international trade Agreements. "Special 301" is section 182 of the *Trade Act of 1974*, added to that Act by Section 1303 of the *Omnibus Trade and Competitiveness Act of 1988*. Among other features, Special 301 requires the U.S. Trade Representative to identify annually those countries that are denying adequate and effective protection to intellectual property rights or fair and equitable market access to U.S. persons that rely on intellectual property protection. In certain situations, such countries may then become subject to an investigation under Section 301.

[13] One problem the United States had to confront when resorting to such bilateral actions was its existing GATT obligations. In most cases, the U.S. was unable to impose any form of trade sanctions against other GATT contracting parties as to do so would conflict with that other party's rights and U.S. obligations under the GATT. As a result, this bilateral strategy was most successfully employed against those countries that were not GATT contracting parties (such as Taiwan and China) or against developing countries to which the U.S. had extended unilateral trade benefits that were not protected by U.S. GATT obligations.

[14] It should be noted that the GATT 1947 already contained some provisions which indirectly addressed certain intellectual property issues. For example, GATT Article III:4 required contracting parties to extend national treatment to imported goods. Article XX(d) allowed contracting parties to take measures necessary to secure compliance with laws relating to the protection of patents, trademarks and copyright. These provisions have been carried over into GATT 1994.

example, the issue of counterfeit goods was subject to some discussion during the Tokyo Round, but no Agreement could be reached on the issue prior to the completion of the Round. After the Tokyo Round had been completed, the United States, with the support of the EC, Japan and Canada, persisted with the counterfeit goods issue and during the 1982 GATT Ministerial meeting attempted to have the GATT's developing work plan expanded to include issues relating to counterfeit goods. In spite of strong opposition voiced by some developing countries (who expressed the view that the issue was beyond the purview of the GATT) the 1982 Ministerial Declaration did provide for some work to be done in the area of counterfeit goods only.[15] This was soon followed by a U.S. proposal that the next round of trade negotiations should not be limited to issues solely related to counterfeit goods but should be expanded to include discussion of all trade-related intellectual property rights. This proposal again met with strong objections from a number of developing countries, who continued to express the view that the WIPO, not the GATT, was the proper forum for negotiating intellectual property issues.

While support continued to build during this period for the broad inclusion of intellectual property issues on the Uruguay Round negotiating agenda, there was still no consensus that this should be the case. It was not known if a consensus could be achieved even up to the time of the September 1986 Ministerial Meeting called to finalize the agenda and initiate the Round. In the end, Ministers were able to reach Agreement on a negotiating mandate for "trade-related intellectual property issues". The Ministerial Declaration provided:

Trade-related aspects of intellectual property rights, including trade in counterfeit goods

In order to reduce the distortions and impediments to international trade, and taking into account the need to promote effective and adequate protection of intellectual property rights, and to ensure that measures and procedures to enforce intellectual property rights do not themselves become barriers to legitimate trade, the negotiations shall aim to clarify GATT provisions and elaborate as appropriate new rules and disciplines.

Negotiations shall aim to develop a multilateral framework of principles, rules and disciplines dealing with international trade in counterfeit goods, taking into account work already undertaken in the GATT.

---

[15] See Ministerial Declaration (of the Thirty-Eighth Session at the Ministerial Level), GATT, BISD 29S/9, at 19. The relevant portion of the Declaration provides:

The Contracting Parties instruct the Council to examine the question of counterfeit goods with a view to determining the appropriateness of joint action in the GATT framework on the trade aspects of commercial counterfeiting and, if such joint action is found to be appropriate, the modalities for such action, having full regard to the competence of other international organizations. For the purposes of such examination, the Contracting Parties request the Director-General to hold consultations with the Director-General of WIPO in order to clarify the legal and institutional aspects involved.

These negotiations shall be without prejudice to other complementary initiatives that may be taken in the World Intellectual Property Organization and elsewhere dealing with these matters.[16]

When negotiations first commenced in earnest, countries were divided along developed/developing country lines (often referred to during the negotiations as the "North-South debate") on most of the contentious issues. Developed countries were pushing developing countries to improve the scope and effectiveness of their intellectual property regimes and to strictly limit compulsory licensing practices. Generally speaking, the developing countries were not enthusiastic participants in the TRIPS negotiations. They opposed most developed country proposals and continued to dispute the jurisdiction of the GATT over intellectual property issues. However, textiles and agriculture were the important areas to most developing countries. Many were prepared to acknowledge that they could accept a comprehensive TRIPS Agreement if there was sufficient progress in the textiles and agricultural areas. In addition, many developing countries were becoming concerned with the increasing unilateralism of some developed countries with respect to intellectual property issues. A multilateral negotiation which addressed these issues could increase the negotiating leverage of individual developing countries, and could result in treaty-based disciplines on the use of unilateral remedies. It is also interesting to note that as the negotiations continued the developing-versus-developed country dichotomy did break down on occasion, and in a number of cases the developed countries faced-off against one another.[17]

By the time of the Brussels Ministerial Meeting in late November 1990, two draft Agreements had largely been completed. These two Agreements were reflective of the two basic approaches to the question of GATT's mandate to address intellectual property issues and the relationship of any resulting agreement with the GATT. The developed country approach, represented in a comprehensive draft TRIPS Agreement, contemplated that the draft agreement would be implemented as an integral part of the GATT. The developing country approach contemplated two separate agreements. The first, a draft agreement dealing only with issues relating to trade in counterfeit goods, would be implemented within the GATT. A second agreement, which would provide certain standards and principles generally applicable to intellectual property, would then be negotiated and implemented within the appropriate international organization, likely the WIPO. It had previously been agreed at the Montreal Mid-term Review in 1988 that a final decision on the institutional implementation of the TRIPS negotiations would be made by Ministers once the final and complete outcome of the Round had become

---

[16] Ministerial Declaration on the Uruguay Round, GATT, BISD 33S/19, at 25-26.

[17] For example, the developed countries were at odds over moral rights, certain patent-related issues, and use of border measures, among others.

known. In the end, the approach advocated by the developed countries, that of one agreement, implemented as an integral part of the GATT (or the new WTO), was finally accepted by all Members.

2. SOME IMPORTANT NEGOTIATING ISSUES

In some respects, the overall negotiating agenda on intellectual property that was advanced by the developed countries can be easily summarized: establish minimum standards of protection and provide for effective enforcement of those standards. Of course, such a summary hides a host of difficult issues on which a consensus had to be reached in order to achieve an effective Agreement. The major issues that arose during the negotiations can be divided into two categories: horizontal issues (that is, those general issues that affect all types of intellectual property) and vertical issues (those issues that relate to only a specific type of intellectual property).

(a) Horizontal Issues

(i) Structure of the Agreement and Institutional Provisions

As already noted, a consensus had to be reached on the basic form and structure of any agreement. The fact that developing countries continued to dispute the GATT's jurisdiction over intellectual property made this issue that much more difficult. As a result, two different approaches concerning the relationship between any agreement and the GATT outlined above were advocated. Related to this basic structural issue were the agreement's institutional provisions. Would there be a need for a separate secretariat such as the GATT Secretariat? What provisions concerning government-to-government dispute settlement would be necessary? Would there be any formal linkage between the agreement and the GATT so as to allow enforcement through the introduction of trade sanctions, if necessary?

(ii) Relevancy of International Standards

A second major horizontal issue related to the applicability of those numerous international standards of protection that already existed under other agreements such as the Paris, Berne and Rome Conventions and the Washington Treaty. Were these existing standards sufficient or were they in need of specific improvements? If they were sufficient, should those standards be incorporated into the agreement or should they simply be referred to? What should be done in those areas where no minimum standards yet existed?

(iii) Applicability of Basic GATT Obligations

To what extent should basic GATT obligations, such as national treatment, MFN treatment and transparency, be incorporated into the agreement?

While most existing agreements already provided for national treatment, in many cases there was no minimum standard of protection required. The introduction of different or higher levels of minimum standards could potentially introduce new concerns over the application of any national treatment obligation. With respect to MFN treatment, such a provision was largely unknown in previous intellectual property agreements. If these obligations were included, would any exceptions be permitted? For example, would those preferential trading arrangements which included intellectual property provisions be exempt from any MFN obligation? Finally, to what extent would general exceptions similar to GATT Articles XX and XXI be applicable to an intellectual property agreement?

(iv) Provisions Relating to Effective Enforcement

What provisions would be necessary concerning enforcement? Would it be limited to border measures, or would enforcement obligations be stricter, requiring signatories to enforce the minimum standards within their territories? Would the agreement include any obligations with respect to civil remedies, which would allow a right-holder to enforce its rights and seek damages for infringement?

(v) Participation of Developing Countries

Due to the prevailing view amongst developing countries concerning GATT's jurisdiction, their participation in any agreement had to be carefully considered. As was the case with respect to services, intellectual property was an area where many developing countries only very reluctantly agreed to negotiations. At the same time, however, some viewed developing countries as part of the problem. Extending any special or differential treatment to those countries would have the potential to significantly undermine the effectiveness of any agreement.

(b) Important Vertical Issues

(i) Patents:

- **Patentable Subject-matter:** Some countries would not grant patents to many products or processes normally patentable in other countries, particularly with respect to new agricultural chemicals and pharmaceuticals.
- **Length of Patent Protection:** Considerable debate focused on what was the appropriate length or "term" for patent protection. The prevailing developed country view was 20 years, measured back to the date of

filing the patent application, although this view was not universal. Developing countries usually provided shorter periods of protection, often combined with liberal compulsory licensing schemes.

- **Compulsory Licences:** Most developing countries (and some developed countries) employed liberal compulsory licence systems for patents. If a patent was not being "worked", the government could award a compulsory licence to a local company to work the patent, with little or no royalties payable to the right-holder. Often the definition of "work" required the product or process to be manufactured or used within the country. Simply importing a patented product would therefore not meet the "work" requirement. In some cases, a patent could even be revoked for a failure to meet the work requirement.

(ii) Trademarks

- **Use Requirement to Obtain Registration:** There was no consensus as to the requirements concerning use of a trademark. Some countries required that a trademark be in use before an application to register could be filed. Others, such as Canada and the U.S., permitted applications to be filed based on intended use, but required that a trademark be in use before a registration would be granted. Others would permit a trademark to be registered before use had commenced, but would then cancel the registration if the mark was not used within a specified period of time.

- **Use Requirement to Maintain Registration:** Most countries required that trademarks must be continued to be used or the registration was liable to be "expunged" or removed from the register. While this use requirement was generally accepted, in some cases new duties, import restrictions or government requirements made sales of the trademarked product difficult or impossible, technically resulting in non-use of the trademark and potential loss of the registration.

- **Unauthorized Registrations:** In many developing countries it was possible for unauthorized persons to apply and register internationally well-known trademarks. This made legitimate use of the trademark within the country by its true owner difficult, if not impossible.

- **Service Marks:** Many countries only protected trademarks used in association with goods, not services.

(iii) Copyright

- **Complete Lack of Protection:** Many countries completely lacked any type of copyright law.

- *Protection for Computer Software and Databases:* Most developed countries protected computer software and databases as literary works under copyright laws, but this means of protection was not universally recognized.

- *Neighbouring Rights:* Under the provisions of the Rome Convention, some countries recognized that performers, broadcasters and producers of sound recordings had the right, related to copyright, to protect their own transmission, fixation or rendition of a performance, independent of any copyright which may subsist in the underlying material being performed. Because of the limited number of countries that have signed the Rome Convention recognition of these "neighbouring rights" was by no means universal.

- *Moral Rights:* A copyright is generally considered to be comprised of two separate rights: an economic right (to copy the work, for example) and a non-economic or "moral" right. Article 6bis of the Berne Convention provides that:

   > Independent of the author's economic rights, and even after the transfer of those rights, the author shall have the right to claim authorship of the work and to object to any distortion, mutilation, or other modification of, or other derogatory action in relation to that work that would be prejudicial to his honour or reputation.

   Some countries, including the U.S., did not explicitly recognize and protect these moral rights.

- *Discrimination Against Foreign Works:* Some countries provided adequate protection for domestically-created works, but did not protect foreign-created works.

- *Collective Licensing:* Some countries imposed special copyright levies designed to compensate copyright owners for losses incurred through unauthorized copying of their works. For example, in France a tax was charged on all sales of video and audio recorders, and on blank video and audio cassettes, with the resulting revenue being divided among authors, performers, French distributors, and French arts groups. Foreign copyright owners were discriminated against in that they were only able to claim a share of the authors' portion. Germany had a similar collective licensing system in place.

- *Rental Rights:* Some countries did not recognize an independent rental right in all copyright material. This means that some right-holders had no ability to prevent the rental of their works, such as compact disks, videos, or computer programmes. With existing technology, inexpensive rentals often leads to widespread unauthorized copying of the material, particularly compact disks and computer programmes.

3. AGREEMENT ON TRADE-RELATED INTELLECTUAL PROPERTY

The TRIPS Agreement is divided into seven parts. Part I (Articles 1 to 8) sets out certain general provisions and basic principles. Part II (Articles 9 to 40) then provides specific standards concerning the availability, scope and use for each specific type of intellectual property covered by the Agreement. Part III (Articles 41 to 61) sets out certain obligations relating to the enforcement of intellectual property rights. The procedural processes of acquisition and maintenance of intellectual property rights are addressed in Part IV (Article 62). Part V (Articles 63 and 64) sets out the Agreement's Member-to-Member dispute settlement procedures. Part VI (Articles 65 to 67) deals with transitional issues and Part VII (Articles 68 to 73) sets out certain institutional and final provisions.

(a) Part I: General Provisions and Basic Principles

Part I of the Agreement (Articles 1 to 8) sets out certain basic obligations including national treatment and MFN treatment.

(i) Article 1—Nature and Scope of Obligations

The scope and coverage of the Agreement is established, in part, by paragraph 2 of Article 1. For the purposes of the Agreement, "intellectual property" is defined to include all the categories of intellectual property specifically addressed in Part II. Seven categories of intellectual property are specified in Part I: copyright and related rights; trademarks; geographical indications; industrial designs; patents; lay-out designs of integrated circuits; and confidential information.[18]

The scope of Members' obligations under the Agreement is further clarified by paragraph 3 of Article 1, which provides that Members are required to extend the treatment provided for under the Agreement to "nationals" of other Members.[19]

---

[18]This appears to be an exhaustive list. Other intellectual property rights that are not specifically mentioned in Part II are not covered by any of the Agreement's substantive obligations.

[19]The term "national" is further defined by incorporating by reference certain provisions of the Paris, Berne, and Rome Conventions and the Washington Treaty. Depending upon the intellectual property right at issue, whether a legal or natural person falls within the definition of "national" under the TRIPS Agreement will be determined by reference to the other applicable international Agreement. In certain cases, signatories are able to limit their obligations in this respect under the Rome Convention. This ability is continued under the TRIPS Agreement, but a Member doing so must provide notification to the Council for Trade-Related Aspects of Intellectual Property Rights.

Paragraph 1 of Article 1 provides that Members are required to give effect to the provisions of the Agreement.[20] In light of the diverse nature of Members' legal systems, the Agreement does not specify how Members are to implement the Agreement domestically and therefore Members generally remain free to determine the manner in which the Agreement is to be implemented within their own legal systems. Paragraph 1 also notes that the Agreement only establishes the minimum levels of protection that must be accorded to intellectual property. Members remain free to accord higher levels of protection provided such protection is otherwise consistent with the Agreement.

(ii) Article 2—Intellectual Property Conventions

Because of the number of pre-existing intellectual property Agreements such as the Paris, Berne and Rome Conventions, Members had to address the inter-relationship between these other international Agreements and the TRIPS Agreement. In part, this is done in Article 2, although there are a number of other provisions throughout the Agreement that address additional specific inter-relationships. Generally speaking, the TRIPS Agreement does not require Members to become signatories to these other Agreements; Members must simply comply with certain specifically identified obligations.

With respect to the Paris Convention, paragraph 1 of Article 2 provides that Members are required to comply with Articles 1 to 12, and 19 of that Convention.[21] Paragraph 2 notes that nothing in Parts I to IV of the TRIPS Agreement is intended to derogate from any existing obligations that a Member might have under the Paris, Berne, and Rome Conventions, and the Washington Treaty.

(iii) Articles 3, 4 and 5—National Treatment, MFN Treatment and Exceptions

Article 3 sets out the Agreement's basic national treatment obligation.[22] Members are required to accord to the nationals of other Members no less

---

[20]This obligation, combined with the lack of a federal-state clause, appears to impose an absolute obligation on the central governments of federal states, such as Canada and the U.S., to ensure compliance with the Agreement by their sub-national governments.

[21]The Paris Convention is comprised of 30 Articles in total. Its substantive obligations are found in Articles 1 to 12. Article 19 is entitled "Special Agreements" and allows signatories to enter into additional Agreements for the protection of intellectual property and thus permits the TRIPS Agreement. The remaining Articles of the Convention generally address institutional issues and therefore were not considered relevant in the context of the TRIPS Agreement.

[22]Recall that one of the criticisms of most existing intellectual property agreements was that they only required national treatment and did not specify any minimum levels of protection. In the TRIPS Agreement, this problem has been addressed by requiring national treatment, but also by supplementing this obligation with specified minimum levels of protection in Part II.

favourable treatment than they accord to their own nationals in the protection of intellectual property.[23] This basic national treatment obligation is then subject to a number of exceptions. Subject to certain limitations set out in paragraph 2 of Article 3, Members are still able to rely on any applicable exceptions to national treatment specified in the Paris, Berne and Rome Conventions or the Washington Treaty.[24] With respect to performers, producers of phonograms and broadcasting organizations, the national treatment obligation is strictly limited to only those rights provided by the TRIPS Agreement itself. In certain cases, if a Member intends to rely on some of the national treatment exceptions set out in these other Agreements, it must notify the Council for Trade-related Aspects of Intellectual Property Rights (the "TRIPS Council")[25] to that effect.

Paragraph 2 of Article 3 specifies that with respect to judicial or administrative procedures, Members are permitted to rely on the exceptions outlined in paragraph 1 of Article 3 only to the extent necessary to ensure compliance with laws and regulations which are themselves not inconsistent with the Agreement and where such practices are not applied in a manner that would constitute a disguised restriction on trade.

Article 4 provides the Agreement's MFN obligation and sets out certain exceptions to that obligation. With regard to the protection of intellectual property, any advantage, favour, privilege or immunity granted by a Member to the nationals of another Member must be immediately and unconditionally extended to the nationals of all other Members. As MFN treatment was generally considered to be somewhat foreign to intellectual property, a number of exceptions were provided. The Article itself specifies four exceptions to the basic obligation. The first is for international agreements concerning law

---

[23] Footnote 3 to the Agreement notes that the use of the term "protection" in both Articles 3 and 4 is intended to be broadly interpreted to mean that the national treatment and MFN obligations apply to all matters affecting availability, acquisition, scope, maintenance, and enforcement of intellectual property rights in addition to those matters affecting use. The effect of this footnote is to provide that Articles 3 and 4 apply generally to all aspects of intellectual property covered by the Agreement, even though the Agreement may not specify any minimum obligations with respect to all such aspects of covered property.

[24] For example, Article 6 of the Berne Convention provides an exception to national treatment concerning certain works of authors who are nationals of non-Union countries. Perhaps the most important exception is found in Article 16(a) of the Rome Convention, which sets out the national treatment exemption applicable to collective licensing schemes. This appears to exclude from the national treatment obligations the collective licensing schemes currently in effect in some Members, such as France and Germany, and contemplated by Canada. One common feature of these schemes is that they often discriminate against foreign copyright holders.

[25] The TRIPS Council is established under Article 68 to oversee the operation of the TRIPS Agreement.

enforcement, judicial assistance, or similar agreements of a general nature.[26] The second exception is for those advantages, favours, privileges or immunities that are granted on a non-MFN basis in accordance with certain provisions of the Berne or Rome conventions. The third exception, mirroring one of the national treatment exceptions, limits the MFN obligation to only those rights provided to performers, producers of phonograms and broadcasting organizations under the Agreement. Under certain conditions, a fourth exception is provided for those international agreements related to the protection of intellectual property that entered into force prior to January 1, 1995. This may exclude from the MFN obligation more favourable treatment extended among signatories to pre-existing preferential trading arrangements.[27]

Article 5 sets out a further general exception which applies to both the national treatment and the MFN treatment obligations. These obligations do not apply to procedures provided for under certain other WIPO Agreements relating to the acquisition and maintenance of intellectual property rights.[28]

(iv) Articles 6, 7 and 8—Miscellaneous Provisions

Article 6 essentially excludes the issue of exhaustion of intellectual property rights from coverage under the Agreement.[29] The Article provides

---

[26] This would presumably exclude, for example, Canada's Mutual Legal Assistance Treaties ("MLATs"). Canada has negotiated a series of 15 bilateral MLATS and is currently in the process of negotiating a further 20. These MLATS provide for bilateral cooperation in the investigation of mainly criminal or quasi-criminal offences. In some cases, the provisions of an MLAT might be invoked in the investigation of an offence related to the misuse or abuse of an intellectual property right. The U.S. has a similar system of bilateral legal assistance treaties.

[27] It should be noted that the TRIPS Agreement does not include a general MFN exclusion for preferential trading arrangements as is the case under GATT Article XXIV. Thus, while TRIPS Article 4(d) may exclude some existing agreements under certain specified circumstances, it will not serve to exclude any future agreements from the MFN obligation. It should also be noted that in many cases the TRIPS Agreement's basic national treatment obligation will continue to apply to the Member, which will act to diminish the effect of this MFN exception.

[28] This exception will serve to exclude, for example, the provisions of the *Patent Cooperation Treaty*, CTS 1990/22, 28 UST 7645 ("PCT"). The PCT is a procedural Agreement, administered by the WIPO, that provides a simplified system for multi-country patent applications. In effect, patent applications can be filed simultaneously in any or all of the signatory countries by the filing of one application with the applicant's home-country authority. The PCT does not, however, govern the subsequent review of the applications, nor the granting of any patents. Over 70 countries are now signatories to the PCT.

[29] Exhaustion in the intellectual property context is based on the notion that once a rightholder allows a product to be released into the chain of commerce, any subsequent sales or transfers of the product cannot then be controlled by them as the relevant intellectual property right has been exhausted by that first sale. For example, a manufacturer of patented widgets which sells some widgets for export to country X may not be able to prevent the purchaser from

that, subject to the national and MFN treatment obligations, nothing in the Agreement is to be used to address the issue of exhaustion of intellectual property rights.

Article 7 sets out certain objectives for the protection and enforcement of intellectual property and clearly displays the tension between developed and developing country Members over these issues. Such protection should contribute to promoting innovation and technology transfer, to the mutual benefit of both producers and users of knowledge, and in a manner conducive to social and economic welfare. While not a binding obligation in and of itself, it could be used as a guide to interpret other of the Agreement's rights and obligations.

Article 8 further clarifies the application, scope and coverage of the Agreement. First, Members remain free to adopt measures relating to public health and nutrition or to promote the public interest in vital sectors provided that any such measures are consistent with the Agreement. Second, again provided that such measures are consistent with the Agreement, Members remain free to adopt measures needed to prevent the anti-competitive abuse of intellectual property rights by right-holders.

(b) Part II: Standards Concerning the Availability, Scope and Use of Intellectual Property Rights

Part II of the Agreement (Articles 9 to 40), sets out the required standards of protection for each specific type of intellectual property covered under the Agreement. Part II is divided into seven separate sub-parts, with each sub-part addressing a specific type of intellectual property.

(i) Section 1: Copyright and Related Rights

Section 1 of Part II (Articles 9 to 14) addresses copyright and certain other related rights. Article 9 establishes the relationship between the TRIPS Agreement and the Berne Convention. While the Article does not require Members to become signatories to the Berne Convention, it does incorporate by refer-

---

subsequently selling those widgets to a further purchaser in country Y. Exhaustion in the context of international trade is often related to exclusive marketing arrangements or "grey marketing" where a right-holder attempts to segment the global market and extend exclusive rights to market a product to different people in different countries. Unauthorized sellers obtain the product through a legitimate market purchase in one country but then export and sell the product into another country, much to the annoyance of the exclusive distributor for that market. An international consensus on the issue of exhaustion has not yet developed. According to the intellectual property laws of many countries there is no illegality involved in such transactions. However, the laws of some countries will allow grey-marketed goods to be detained at the border in some circumstances.

ence Articles 1 to 21 of the Convention and its Appendix. This means that Members are required to comply with these obligations even though they may not be signatories to the Convention. Articles 1 to 21 and the Appendix are the Berne Convention's substantive provisions, which include, for example, the basic obligation of protecting copyright works, national treatment, the term of protection, and certain special treatment for developing countries.[30] Also included is Article 18 of the Convention, which addresses the extension of protection to formerly unprotected works.

The obligation to adhere to the substantive obligations of the Berne Convention is subject to one important exception—Article 6bis. Article 6bis establishes the Convention's obligations concerning so-called "moral rights". Because of the widely differing views on the issue of protection of moral rights, this exclusion means that the protection of moral rights by a Member cannot be subject to dispute settlement under the TRIPS Agreement.

Paragraph 2 of Article 9 serves to clarify that copyright protection cannot be extended to ideas, procedures, methods of operation or mathematical methods in and of themselves. Protection is only to be extended to the expression of those concepts. Thus, an idea cannot be protected by copyright unless it has been expressed in some protectable form, such as in writing.

Article 10 addresses issues related to computer programmes and compilations of data. While the Berne Convention does not specifically address the protection of computer programmes and data compilations, most developed countries have extended copyright protection to them as literary works, although in some cases not specifically. Article 10 requires Members to protect computer programmes (whether in source or object code) as literary works under the Berne Convention. Paragraph 2 requires the same protection to be extended to compilations of data or other material provided that the selection or arrangement of such data or material constitutes an intellectual creation.

The issue of rental rights, which is not addressed in the Berne Convention, is, in part, dealt with in Article 11. The concern with the rental of copyright material is that it can lead to widespread unauthorized re-production of the copyright material. Article 11 establishes certain obligations concerning rental rights in computer programmes and cinematographic works (movie videos and laser disks, for example), while Article 14(4), discussed below, addresses rental rights in phonograms (records, compact disks and audio tapes). With respect to computer programmes, Members are required to provide to authors and their successors in title the right to control the commercial rental of their copyrighted works. This obligation will not apply

---

[30] Articles 22 to 38 of the Convention, which have not been incorporated into the TRIPS Agreement, primarily address procedural and institutional issues such as establishment of the Berne Union and its operation.

where the programme is not the essential object of the rental (for example, where a computer is being rented and operating software is included as part of that rental).

This rental right obligation will not apply to cinematographic works unless such rentals are leading to widespread unauthorized copying of the material. It is generally considered that the general availability of movie video rentals has not resulted in substantial unauthorized copying. Article 11 will therefore allow such rentals to continue.

The minimum term of copyright protection specified in Article 7 of the Berne Convention is the life of the author plus 50 years. Article 12 provides further clarification as to the minimum term of protection whenever that term is calculated on a basis other than the life of a natural person (when the "author" is a corporation, for example). In such cases the minimum term of protection must be no less than 50 years. This minimum period does not apply to works of applied art or photographic works.

Article 9(1) of the Berne Convention establishes that authors have the basic right to control the reproduction of their work in any manner or form. However, Article 9(2) provides that signatories are able to permit unauthorized reproductions in special cases, provided that such reproductions do not conflict with the normal exploitation of the work and does not unreasonably prejudice the legitimate interests of the author. This exception allows copying for the purposes of study, for example. Article 13 of the TRIPS Agreement expands the coverage of this limited exemption. Under the Article, Members must confine their limitations and exceptions to all the exclusive rights (not just the reproduction right) attached to copyright and related rights to special cases which will not conflict with the normal exploitation of the work and will not unreasonably prejudice the legitimate interests of the rightholder. While not specifically addressed, this obligation appears to preclude the use of compulsory licences on copyright material except in unusual and special circumstances.

Article 14 addresses the issue of protection of performers, producers of sound recordings and broadcasting organizations—or so-called neighbouring rights. Recall that the issue of neighbouring rights is not addressed in the Berne Convention, but in the Rome Convention, which has only been signed by 32 countries. It is interesting to note that unlike Article 9 of the TRIPS Agreement, which requires adherence to certain provisions of the Berne Convention, Article 14 does not specifically require adherence to any of the obligations of the Rome Convention.

Paragraph 1 sets out certain obligations with respect to performers. Members are required to provide performers with the right to prevent the unauthorized broadcast or communication to the public of a live performance, and the unauthorized recording (or fixation) of a live performance and any reproduction of such a recording.[31] Under paragraph 5, the term of protection for this right must be a minimum of 50 years from the end of the year in which the performance took place.[32]

Under paragraph 2, producers of sound recordings are to be provided the right to control the reproduction of their recordings. As with performers, paragraph 5 provides that the term of protection for this right must be a minimum of 50 years from the end of the year in which the recording took place.[33] The issue of rental rights in sound recordings is then separately addressed in paragraph 4. Under this provision, producers of sound recordings are to be given the right to control the rental of their works to the public. This rental right is subject to special exclusion which grandfathers certain rental systems that were already in operation in some Members prior to April 15, 1994, and then only under certain limited circumstances. Apparently Japan and Switzerland are the only Members which have systems in place which will qualify for this rental right exclusion.

With respect to broadcasting organizations, paragraph 3 provides that Members, at their option, must either grant broadcasting organizations the right to prohibit the unauthorized recording, reproduction of recordings, and re-broadcast of their television broadcasts, or provide similar rights to owners of the copyright in the subject-matter of the broadcast. Under paragraph 5, the term of protection for these rights must be a minimum of 20 years from the end of the year in which the broadcast took place.

Paragraph 6 incorporates into the Agreement the conditions, limitations, exceptions and reservations of the Rome Convention. With respect to the rights conferred under paragraphs 1, 2 and 3 of Article 14, Members are still permitted to rely on these provisions. For example, Article 15 of the Rome Convention provides that a signatory may establish its own exclusions from protection for, among other things, teaching or scientific research. However, Paragraph 6 also provides that Article 18 of the Berne Convention, which addresses the extension of new protections to formerly unprotected pre-existing works, will now also apply to the rights of performers and producers' sound recordings, but not to broadcasting organizations.[34]

---

[31] The unauthorized recording of live performances is often referred to as "bootlegging".

[32] This is an extension of the minimum 20-year term of protection required under Article 14 of the Rome Convention.

[33] As is the case with performers, this is an extension of the minimum 20-year term of protection required under Article 14 of the Rome Convention.

[34] Paragraphs 1 and 2 of Article 18 of the Berne Convention provide:

(1) The Convention shall apply to all works which, at the moment of its coming into force, have not yet fallen into the public domain in the country of origin through the expiry of the term of protection.

(ii) Section 2: Trademarks

Section 2 of Part II of the Agreement (Articles 15 to 21) establishes the Agreement's obligations specific to trademarks.

Article 15 establishes what subject-matter must be protectable under a Member's trademark laws and the conditions for obtaining and maintaining a trademark registration. Any "sign" (such as words, names, designs and colours) or combination of signs capable of distinguishing the goods and services of one trader from those of another shall be capable of constituting a trademark. Where a sign is not inherently distinctive (for example, a person's name) Members may condition registrability of such a sign on an acquired distinctiveness, meaning that the sign has been used in association with a trader's goods or services so as to have become associated with those goods or services.

Paragraph 2 clarifies the relationship between the obligations of paragraph 1 and the Paris Convention by providing that Members remain able to deny a trademark registration on other grounds, provided those grounds are consistent with the obligations of the Paris Convention. For example, Article 6ter of the Paris Convention sets out certain limitations on the registrability of state emblems, official marks, and emblems of inter-governmental organizations.

Paragraph 3 addresses the issue of "use". Members are entitled to make use of a trademark as a requirement for its registrability, meaning that the trademark must be in use before it will be registered. But Members are not permitted to make use of a condition for the filing of an application for a registration. Nor, under paragraph 4, are Members permitted to condition registrability on the type of goods or services to which the trademark is being applied.

Finally, paragraph 5 provides that Members must publish each trademark either prior to registration or promptly after registration and they must provide a reasonable opportunity for an application or petition to cancel the registration because, for example, the registration may be in conflict with the pre-existing rights of another trader. Members may also extend to others an opportunity to oppose the registration of a trademark.

Article 16 establishes the specific rights that Members must confer on the owner of a trademark registration. Under paragraph 1, owners of registered

---

(2) If, however, through the expiry of the term of protection which was perviously granted, a work has fallen into the public domain of the country where protection is claimed, that work shall not be protected anew.

For a discussion of the issues raised by the extension of new protections to formerly unprotected works, see the U.S. *Statement of Administrative Action*, at pages 992-999. While this discussion is specifically concerned with the situation in the United States, it highlights the complexities resulting from the application of Article 18.

marks must be provided with the exclusive right to prevent third parties from unauthorized use of confusingly similar marks. Members may make these rights contingent on actual use of the registered trademark.

Paragraphs 2 and 3 of Article 16 address certain aspects of so-called "well-known" marks, expanding and clarifying the obligations of Article 6bis of the Paris Convention. Article 6bis provides that, at the request of an interested party, signatories are required to refuse or cancel a trademark registration, and prohibit the use of well-known trademarks owned by someone other than the applicant. However, under the Convention this right is limited to trademarks applied to goods, not services, and Article 6bis provides little guidance as to what constitutes a "well-known" trademark. Paragraph 2 addresses both these deficiencies. First, Article 6bis will now apply equally to trademarks applied to both goods and services. Second, in determining whether a trademark is well-known, Members are required to take into account the knowledge of the trademark in the relevant sector of the public. Paragraph 3 then provides that under certain conditions, the rights conferred by Article 6bis must also be extended to goods and services beyond those covered by a well-known registered trademark to include similar or related goods and services.

Under Article 17, concerning exceptions, Members may provide limited exceptions to the rights conferred by registration, such as fair use of descriptive terms, for example, provided that any such exceptions take into account the interests of the owner and third parties.

The term of protection conferred by registration is addressed in Article 18. The initial registration must be for a term of not less than seven years. This initial registration must then be renewable indefinitely for successive terms of seven years.

Articles 19 and 20 set out further provisions related to use and other requirements. Recall that Article 15(3) provides that Members may make registrability of a trademark dependent on actual use. Article 19 then provides that if use is required to maintain such a registration, the registration can only be cancelled for non-use after an uninterrupted period of at least three years, and subject to any special circumstances beyond the owner's control which may have justified such non-use. Authorized use by a person other than the owner (under licence, for example) must be recognized as valid use of the mark necessary to maintain the registration. Article 20 then provides that Members cannot make use of a trademark subject to unjustifiable special requirements, such as tying use of one trademark to use of another trademark, or use in some special form or format.

Obligations concerning the licensing and assignment (or transference of ownership) of trademarks are found in Article 21. Generally speaking, subject to the other obligations of Article 21 and the Agreement's general obligations,

Members are free to determine their own conditions for licensing and assignment of trademarks. Compulsory licensing of trademarks is not permitted. In addition, the owner of a registered mark must have the right to assign the mark with or without the business to which the mark belongs.

(iii) Section 3: Geographical Indications

The protection of geographical indications of origin (more commonly known as "appellations of origin") is addressed in Section 3 of Part II, Articles 22, 23 and 24.

Paragraph 1 of Article 22 defines a "geographical indication" as an indication which identifies a good as originating in the territory of a Member, or a region or locality thereof, where the good's quality, reputation or other characteristic is essentially attributable to its geographical origin.

Members are required to provide the legal means for interested parties to prevent the use of misleading or false geographical indications. Members must also provide legal procedures to refuse or invalidate trademark registrations which contain or consist of misleading geographical indications. These protections also extend to the use of those geographical indications which, though literally correct, are still misleading.

Article 23 sets out certain additional protections for geographical indications of wines and spirits. Paragraph 1 expands on the obligations of Article 22(2). Not only must Members provide protection against the false or misleading use of geographical indications relating to wine and spirits, but these protections must apply even where the true origin of the goods is also indicated (California Burgundy or Japanese Scotch, for example) or where the indication is used in translation or accompanied by expressions such as "type" or "style" ("Champagne-style", for example). Members must also provide legal procedures to refuse or invalidate trademark registrations which contain or consist of misleading geographical indications identifying wines or spirits.

The protection obligations of Articles 22 and 23 are subject to the exceptions set out in paragraphs 4 to 9 of Article 24. First, nonconforming geographical indications that have been in continuous use for more than 10 years are "grandfathered" under paragraph 4. Paragraph 5 extends, under certain conditions, a similar exception to trademarks which have been applied for or registered in good faith prior to the Agreement's entering into force. Paragraph 6 provides an exclusion from protection for common or customary terms and grape varieties. Under paragraph 7, Members are permitted to impose a five-year limitation period on requests to invalidate trademark registrations containing misleading geographical indications. The ability of an individual to use, in the course of trade, his or her name is not to be effected by the obligations of Section 3, except where the name is used in such a way as to mislead. Finally, there is no obligation to protect indications that are not protected in their country of origin or have fallen into disuse in that country.

Future negotiations concerning additional protections of geographical indications for wines and spirits are provided for under paragraph 4 of Article 23 and paragraphs 1, 2 and 3 of Article 24. First, paragraph 4 of Article 23 provides that in order to facilitate the protection of geographical indications for wine, negotiations concerning the establishment of a multilateral notification and registration system for such indications are to be undertaken within the TRIPS Council.[35] Paragraph 1 of Article 24 provides that Members are not to use the exceptions outlined below as a basis for refusing additional negotiations aimed at increasing protection for individual geographic indications. It is likely that these future negotiations will centre on those indications that have slipped into common usage in some Members, but which are still subject to protection in others. For example, the EC now has strict controls on the use of the term Champagne, limiting its use to true Champagne, while the term Champagne is widely used in other countries to refer to sparkling wine of any origin or production method.

Under paragraph 2 of Article 24, the TRIPS Council is to review the application of provisions relating to the protection of geographical indications. The first such review took place in the fall of 1996. Members are able to bring any matter affecting the operation of the relevant provisions of the Agreement to the attention of the Council. The Council may then take such action as may be agreed upon to facilitate the operation of these provisions.

Finally, paragraph 3 of Article 24 provides that in implementing their obligations concerning the protection of geographical indications, Members are not permitted to diminish the protections that were already in existence immediately prior to January 1, 1995.

(iv) Section 4: Industrial Designs

The protection of industrial designs is addressed in Section 4 of Part II, Articles 25 and 26.

Article 25 establishes the basic obligations relating to protection of industrial designs. Subject to certain limitations, paragraph 1 states that Members are required to provide for the protection of new or original industrial designs. (Industrial designs have traditionally been protected through a registration system similar to that used for trademarks.) Members need not protect designs which are similar to pre-existing designs or designs which are dictated by technical or functional considerations.

---

[35] Preparations for those negotiations commenced in February 1997.

Paragraph 2 deals with one specific type of designs, that of textile designs. Members are required to protect textile designs either under industrial design or copyright law. Members are also to ensure that requirements for obtaining such protection do not unreasonably undermine the opportunity to seek that protection.

Article 26 then specifies the type of protection that Members must extend to industrial designs. Subject to limited exceptions, owners of protected designs must have the right to prevent unauthorized commercial copying, selling or importing of goods bearing or embodying those protected designs. The term of protection is to be no less than 10 years.

(v) Section 5: Patents

The protection of patents is addressed in Section 5 of Part II, Articles 27 to 34. The obligations of the Paris Convention applicable to patents essentially only require national treatment and, beyond some basic requirements for patentability, the Convention is generally void of substantive obligations in the patent area. As a result, many of the TRIPS negotiating issues concerned patents. In light of both the narrow scope of the Paris Convention and the number of problems associated with patent protection, it is not surprising that Section 5 goes into more elaborate detail than many of the other Sections of Part II.

Article 27 addresses issues relating to what inventions or processes may actually be patented, an issue commonly referred to as "patentable subject-matter". Many countries significantly limit the types of things that may be patented and thereby reduce the scope of protection that may be available. For example, pharmaceutical chemicals cannot be patented in many countries. Subject to the exceptions set out in paragraphs 2 and 3, paragraph 1 requires that provided that the invention is new, inventive (or "non-obvious") and capable of industrial application (or "useful"), patents must be available for any type of product or process invention, in all fields of technology. Again, subject to certain limited exceptions, patents must be available and patent rights enjoyable on a non-discriminatory basis, regardless of the place of invention, the field of technology or whether the products are imported or manufactured locally.[36]

Exceptions to these basic obligations concerning patentable subject-matter are found in all three paragraphs of Article 27. First, paragraph 1 specifies that the basic patentability obligation is subject to paragraph 4 of Article 65 and paragraph 8 of Article 70. Because the obligations of Article 27

---

[36] This obligation combined with the obligations of Article 31 concerning compulsory licensing appear to preclude the use of a "lack of local working" as a basis for a compulsory patent licence, although this is apparently disputed by some developing countries.

will require some Members to extend protection to products and processes that were previously not protectable under their laws, a number of transitional issues had to be addressed. Paragraph 4 of Article 65 permits developing country Members an additional transition period for compliance with the relevant obligations of the TRIPS Agreement when such Members are required by the Agreement to extend product patent protection to areas of technology that had not previously been subject to protection within their territories. Similarly, paragraph 8 of Article 70 sets out special provisions applicable where a Member did not provide patent protection for pharmaceutical or agricultural chemical products on January 1, 1995. In such a case, the Member must, as of January 1, 1995, establish a provisional system whereby patent applications for these products can be filed during the applicable transition period.[37] Once the Member's transition period has ended, it must then review all such applications and extend patent protection for the remainder of the patent's term, measured back to the date of the original filing.[38]

Paragraphs 2 and 3 of Article 27 set out special exclusions from the broad scope of patentable subject-matter specified in paragraph 1. Paragraph 2 sets out a general public protection exception, providing that Members may exclude from patentability those inventions which, if commercially exploited, would have a detrimental effect on public order, morality, human, animal or plant life or health, or seriously prejudice the environment. Paragraph 3 sets out two specific exclusions from patentability: one for diagnostic, therapeutic and surgical methods, and another for plants, animals (other than microorganisms) and biological processes for the production of plants and animals. While Members are not required to provide protection for plants, they are still required to protect plant varieties through either their patent laws or a similar system. As many developed country Members were dissatisfied with the broad scope of the exclusion permitted for plants and animals, this exclusion is to be re-visited after January 1, 1999, and it is likely that some Members will attempt to have it eliminated at that time.

Article 28 sets out what rights a patent must confer on the right-holder. Where the subject-matter of the patent is a product, the owner must have the exclusive right to prevent unauthorized parties from making, using, selling,

---

[37] Transitional periods under the Agreement are discussed in depth below as pages 289-291.

[38] Under paragraph 9 of Article 70, where a product is the subject of an application under paragraph 8, a Member is required to grant exclusive marketing rights for a five-year period after the product receives marketing approval, or until the patent is granted or rejected, whichever period is shorter. In order to qualify for this period of exclusivity, a patent application has to have been filed and a patent granted for that product in another Member and marketing approval obtained in such other Member. These special provisions will provide protection similar to patent protection until the applicable transition periods have ended and patent protection then becomes available.

offering for sale, or importing[39] the product. Similarly, where the subject-matter of a patent is a process, the owner must have the exclusive right to prevent unauthorized parties from using the process or from using, selling, offering for sale, or importing a product obtained from that process. Patent owners must also have the right to assign the patent or transfer it by succession and to enter into patent licensing agreements.

Article 29, which concerns conditions applicable to patent applications, provides that Members must require applicants to disclose the nature of the inventions in a sufficient manner when applying for a patent. Members may require applicants to disclose information concerning the applicants' other foreign applications and grants for their invention.

The exclusivity rights that must be conferred on a patent owner by virtue of Article 28 are subject to the exceptions set out in Articles 30 and 31. Article 30 provides a general exception, stating that Members may provide limited exceptions to the exclusive rights conferred by a patent, provided that any such exception will not conflict with the normal exploitation of the patent and will not unreasonably prejudice the interests of the owner.[40]

Article 31 sets out obligations applicable to the specific exception concerning other uses of a patent without the authority of the owner, more commonly referred to as "compulsory licensing". Unlike most other types of intellectual property covered by the Agreement, Article 31 does permit the compulsory licensing of patents, but only under tightly circumscribed circumstances.

Where a Member does allow for use of a patent without the authorization of the owner, the obligations of paragraphs (a) to (l) of Article 31 must be observed. Among other requirements, such use can only be permitted after the proposed user has made efforts to obtain authorization from the owner on reasonable commercial terms. Any such use must be on a non-exclusive basis. The owner must be adequately remunerated. And the authorization for use must be subject to termination when the circumstances giving rise to it cease

---

[39] Footnote 6 to the Agreement notes that patent rights with respect to importing are, like all other rights conferred under the Agreement in respect to the use, sale, importation or other distribution of goods, subject to the provisions of Article 6. This Article essentially excludes the issue of exhaustion of intellectual property rights from the Agreement.

[40] A similar exception applicable to copyright is found in Article 9(2) of the Berne Convention and, in essence, is repeated in Article 13 of the TRIPS Agreement. The Article 30 exception might be relied upon to exclude price controls on patented products. For example, many countries impose some form of price controls on patented pharmaceuticals. Such controls could meet the terms of Article 30, provided the prices were not so low as to "unreasonably prejudice the legitimate interests of the patent owner".

to exist.[41] It is thought that these stringent conditions, linked with the other obligations of Section 5 of Part II, generally preclude the granting of compulsory licences where the patented product is being imported rather than being worked locally.

The term of protection that must be provided for patents is specified in Article 33 to be a minimum of 20 years counting from the date on which the patent application was originally filed. Members are permitted to use a different starting date in determining patent term (such as the date of the granting of the patent) provided that the term of protection still effectively meets the 20-year requirement. Twenty years is only a minimum period. Members remain free to establish a longer period of protection if they so choose.

Article 34, the final obligation of Section 5, provides a form of reverse onus or burden of proof that is applicable to civil infringement actions concerning process patents. It is sometimes very difficult for the owner of a process patent to prove that an infringer actually employed the patented process to produce an identical product. Members are therefore required to grant their judicial authorities power to the order that the defendant prove that the process which it used to produce an identical product was not the patented process. In certain circumstances, failing such proof, the defendant will be deemed to have employed the patented process.

(vi) Section 6: Lay-out Designs (Topographies) of Integrated Circuits

Section 6 of Part II (Articles 35 to 38) address the protection of lay-out designs or topographies of integrated circuits. It had become widely recognized that this type of intellectual property was not protectable through copyright or patent law under either of the Paris or Berne Conventions. The lack of international consensus on the issue had sparked a proliferation of differing national legislation, some of which did not accord unconditional national treatment to the lay-out designs originating in other countries.[42] This situation was to have been remedied by the 1989 negotiation and implementation of an international agreement in the area, the Washington Treaty (the "IPIC Treaty"), negotiated under the auspices of the WIPO. This was not to be the case. The developed/developing country dichotomy pervaded the negotiations, and in the end many of the participating developed countries considered the result to be fatally flawed, particularly in the areas of term of

---

[41] Paragraph (k) notes that many of these requirements are not applicable when the compulsory licence is authorized in order to remedy an anti-competitive practice related to the patent.

[42] For example, the United States' *Semiconductor Chip Protection Act of 1984* provides for national treatment only to foreign nationals who are from a country which is party to a treaty protecting mask works to which the U.S. is also a party.

protection and compulsory licensing. As a result, only four countries ever signed the IPIC Treaty and it has never entered into force.[43]

Article 35 addresses the relationship between the TRIPS Agreement and the Washington Treaty. Members are required to provide protection to lay-out designs in accordance with certain specified Articles of the Washington Treaty, in addition to the remaining provisions of Part 6 of the TRIPS Agreement. The incorporation of only certain select provisions of the Washington Treaty means that its problematic obligations have not been incorporated.[44]

Article 36 addresses the required scope of protection. Subject to certain limited exceptions in paragraph 1 of Article 36, the unauthorized commercial importation, selling, or other distribution of a protected lay-out design, an integrated circuit incorporating a protected lay-out design, or a product incorporating such an integrated circuit, is to be considered unlawful under Members' laws.

Article 37 addresses the issue of "acts not requiring the authorization of the right-holder", the most important being compulsory licensing. While compulsory licensing of a lay-out design is permitted in certain circumstances, paragraph 2 of Article 37 provides that the conditions imposed on the compulsory licensing of patents under subparagraphs (a) to (k) of Article 31 are

---

[43] Over 70 states were represented at the Diplomatic Conference that negotiated and drafted the Treaty. The final Treaty was approved with the support of only 49 of those states. The U.S. and Japan, which represent the majority of global computer chip production, voted against approving the Treaty, while five other states (Canada, the Holy See, Liechtenstein, Sweden and Switzerland) abstained from the vote. To date, only Ghana, Liberia, Yugoslavia and Zambia have signed the Treaty.

[44] Article 35 of the TRIPS Agreement incorporates by reference Articles 2 to 7 (other than paragraph 3 of Article 6), Article 12 and paragraph 3 of Article 16 of the Washington Treaty. Article 2 provides the relevant definitions, including those of "integrated circuit" and "lay-out design (topography)". Article 3 sets out the basic obligation to protect lay-out designs. Article 5 provides the Treaty's basic national treatment obligation. Article 6 specifies the scope of protection that must be provided, including a prohibition against unauthorized reproduction. Article 7 deals with issues concerning exploitation, registration and disclosure. Article 12 clarifies that the Treaty is not to affect any obligations under either the Paris or Berne Conventions. Paragraph 3 of Article 16 addresses the protection of lay-out designs that are in existence at the time the Treaty enters into force.

Perhaps more importantly are those provisions that have not been incorporated into the TRIPS Agreement. These are Article 1, paragraph 3 of Article 6, Articles 8 to 11, and 13 to 15, paragraphs 2 and 3 of Article 16, and Articles 17 to 20. Many of these provisions relate to procedure and administration of the Treaty and therefore need not be incorporated in the context of the TRIPS Agreement. However, two of the most controversial provisions of the Treaty have not been incorporated by reference. These are paragraph 3 of Article 6, which provides broad scope for compulsory licensing, and Article 8, which established a term of protection of a minimum of only eight years. These obligations have been modified by other obligations in Section 6 of the TRIPS Agreement.

also applicable to any compulsory licensing of lay-out designs.[45] Most importantly, subparagraph (c) of Article 31 significantly limits the purposes for which the compulsory licensing of semi-conductor technology is permitted, to include only public non-commercial use or use to remedy a practice determined after judicial or administrative process to be anti-competitive. These conditions appear to be significantly more onerous than the controversial provisions concerning compulsory licences found in paragraph 3 of Article 6 of the Washington Treaty.

Paragraph 1 of Article 37 deals with another type of non-authorized user—that of an innocent, but still unauthorized, importer, seller or distributor. Members are not to consider unauthorized importation, sales or distribution to be unlawful if the person performing or ordering the acts did not know and had no reasonable grounds to know that the good being imported, sold or distributed incorporated an unlawfully reproduced lay-out design. However, once such a person has been notified of the unauthorized use, they are to be permitted to liquidate their remaining stock on hand or already on order, but must then pay the right-holder a reasonable commercial royalty with respect to any sales of these items. Presumably, any future importations or sales beyond this liquidation made by that person after receiving notice would no longer be innocent and therefore would be considered unlawful under Article 36.

Article 38 deals with the term of protection and improves upon what was seen to be the inadequate term provided under Article 8 of the Washington Treaty. Where a Member requires registration of a lay-out design in order to obtain protection, the minimum term of protection must be at least 10 years from the date of filing for registration, or from the first commercial exploitation of the design, wherever in the world that exploitation occurs. Where a Member does not require registration in order to obtain protection, the minimum term must be at least 10 years from the first commercial exploitation of the design. Alternatively, Members may simply provide for a term of protection of 15 years from the date of creation of the lay-out design.

(vii) Section 7: Protection of Undisclosed Information

Section 7 of Part II (Article 38) addresses the protection of the last type of intellectual property covered by the Agreement, that of undisclosed information, more commonly referred to as "confidential information" or "trade secrets". Paragraph 2 provides that natural and legal persons must have the

---

[45] As discussed above, these subparagraphs impose significant conditions on the use of compulsory licences, including the requirement that such licences can only be issued after the proposed user has made attempts to obtain a licence on normal commercial terms from the right-holder and the right-holder must be paid adequate remuneration.

ability under a Member's laws to prevent the unauthorized use or disclosure of undisclosed information, provided that the information is secret and is maintained as secret, and has value because it is secret. Paragraphs 1 and 3 address confidential information and data that may be submitted to governments or governmental agencies. Paragraph 1 applies the provisions of paragraph 2 to governments and government agencies, requiring them to protect any undisclosed information or data that may be provided to them. Paragraph 3 addresses undisclosed data supplied to governments as a condition of obtaining marketing approval for pharmaceutical or agricultural chemicals. In some countries, it is common practice to release such data publicly or to the applicant's commercial competitors. Generally, Members must protect such data from disclosure and unfair commercial use.

(viii) Section 8: Control of Anti-competitive Practices in Contractual Licences

Section 8 of the Agreement (Article 40) addresses issues relating to the control of anti-competitive practices in contractual licences of intellectual property rights. Members have agreed that some licensing practices or conditions that restrain competition may have adverse effects on trade and hamper the transfer of technology. Paragraph 2 therefore provides that nothing in the Agreement is to prevent Members from specifying under their laws those licensing practices or conditions that may restrain competition.[46] Members are permitted to adopt appropriate measures to control such practices, provided such measures are otherwise consistent with the other obligations of the Agreement. Paragraphs 3 and 4 provide for Member-to-Member consultations in certain situations where such anti-competitive licensing practices or conditions are at issue.

(c) Part III: Enforcement of Intellectual Property Rights

With Part III, the Agreement shifts focus from establishing what basic levels of protection must be provided for intellectual property to establishing specific obligations respecting the enforcement of those protections. Recall that one of the main criticisms of the pre-existing global intellectual property regime was that even in those areas where minimum standards of protection existed, some countries still failed to enforce the standards of protection provided for under their domestic laws. Part III of the Agreement attempts to address this concern by establishing a number of specific rights and remedies that Members must extend to right-holders under their domestic laws.

---

[46]"Exclusive grantback conditions", "conditions preventing challenges to validity" and "coercive package licensing" have been specifically identified as being the types of conditions that may have an adverse effect on competition.

(i) Section 1: General Obligations

The first section of Part III (Article 41) sets out a number of general obligations relating to the enforcement of intellectual property rights. First, Members are required to ensure that all the enforcement procedures that are otherwise specified under Part III are available under domestic law so as to allow for effective action to be taken against intellectual property infringement. These procedures must be fair and equitable, and must not be unnecessarily complicated, costly or lengthy. With respect to any decisions on the merits required under such procedures, such decisions can only be based on evidence which the participating parties have had an opportunity to meet. Written reasons are preferred but not mandatory, and they must be made available, at least to the parties to the proceeding, on a timely basis. With the exception of acquittals in criminal cases, parties to a proceeding must have the right to a further judicial review of most final administrative or judicial decisions that may be made in a proceeding.

Finally, paragraph 5 notes that nothing in Article 41 creates any obligation with respect to the distribution of law enforcement resources as between intellectual property and law enforcement generally, meaning that Members remain free to establish their own law enforcement priorities and allocate resources accordingly.

(ii) Section 2: Civil and Administrative Procedures and Remedies

Section 2 of Part III (Articles 42 to 49) addresses required civil and administrative procedures (as distinct from criminal procedures, which are addressed in Section 5).

Procedures that must be made available are set out in Articles 42 and 43. Article 42 requires that Members must make available to intellectual property right-holders civil judicial procedures that will allow those right-holders to enforce the rights covered under the Agreement. Such judicial procedures must be fair and equitable in that they must require that defendants receive timely written notice of the claim, parties must be allowed to be represented by independent legal counsel, present all relevant evidence, and any requirements concerning mandatory personal appearances must not be overly burdensome. Article 43 sets out certain obligations concerning evidence in such judicial procedures. Judicial authorities must have the ability to order the production of evidence under the control of a party in certain circumstances. Where a party to a proceeding does not provide or refuses access to necessary information, judicial authorities may be permitted to make preliminary or final findings or decisions on the basis of evidence before them.

Remedies that must be made available are specified in Articles 44 to 46. Injunctions in civil or administrative actions are addressed in Article 44.

Judicial authorities must have the authority to issue injunctive relief in intellectual property proceedings. Under Article 45, judicial authorities must be able to order the infringer to pay adequate compensatory damages to the right-holder and to also pay the right-holder's expenses relating to the action, including appropriate attorney's fees. Finally, Article 46 provides that in order to create an effective deterrent to intellectual property infringement, judicial authorities must also have the power to order that all infringing goods be disposed of or destroyed without compensation to the infringer. With respect to counterfeit trademarked goods, simply removing the trademark cannot be considered sufficient to permit release of the goods.

Certain miscellaneous issues are addressed in Articles 47 to 49. The right-holder's ability to obtain certain further information is provided for under Article 47. Although not required, judicial authorities may be granted the power to order that infringers provide the right-holder with the identity of any third parties that may be involved in the production and distribution of infringing goods or services, and their channels of distribution.

Article 48 addresses the indemnification of defendants in certain circumstances. Judicial authorities must be able to award that a right-holder pay adequate compensation and expenses to a defendant when the right-holder has abused any enforcement procedure and that abuse has injured the defendant. With respect to public officials administering the enforcement of intellectual property law, Members are only permitted to exempt such officials from potential liability where the relevant action has been taken or intended in a good faith administration of the law. Finally, Article 49 provides that where a civil remedy can be ordered as a result of administrative, as opposed to judicial, procedures such procedures must also conform with all of the obligations set out in Articles 42 to 48, discussed above.

(iii) Section 3: Provisional Measures

Section 3 of Part III (Article 50) addresses certain temporary or preliminary measures that may arise in the context of enforcement actions. First, paragraph 1 provides a general obligation that judicial authorities must be able to order prompt and effective provisional measures, such as injunctive relief, in order to prevent an infringement from occurring or to preserve relevant evidence relating to an infringement. In appropriate circumstances, these measures must be available *ex parte*, particularly where delay is likely to cause irreparable harm or there is a risk that evidence will be destroyed. Where a measure has been ordered on an *ex parte* basis, the defendant must then be provided with notice upon execution of the measure at the latest, and the defendant must then have the right, on request, to be heard on the issue as to whether the measures should be modified, revoked or confirmed.

Prior to ordering the imposition of such provisional measures, judicial authorities may require the applicant to prove that it is the right-holder, that its rights are being infringed, or that such infringement is imminent. The applicant may be ordered to provide security sufficient to protect the defendant and prevent abuse of process. The applicant may also be required to provide other information necessary to identify the goods.

Where provisional measures have been ordered, the defendant may apply to have the measures revoked if the right-holder does not initiate a proceeding leading to a decision on the merits in the case within a reasonable period of time. Where the measures are then revoked, or in a subsequent decision on the merits it is determined that there was no infringement, judicial authorities must have the ability to order the right-holder, upon request of the defendant, to pay adequate compensation to the defendant for any injury caused by wrongly imposed provisional measures.

Finally, to the extent that a provisional measure can be ordered as a result of administrative, as opposed to judicial proceedings, those procedures must also conform with all of the other obligations of Article 50.

(iv) Section 4: Special Requirements Related to Border Measures

Section 4 of Part III (Articles 51 to 60) addresses special requirements that arise with respect to intellectual property enforcement at the border. Of course, such border enforcement is not practical within customs unions where internal border controls on the movement of goods have generally been eliminated. As a result, footnote 12 specifies that the provisions of Section 4 do not apply to a Member that has dismantled substantially all controls over the movement of goods across its borders with another Member with which it forms customs unions.[47] Another exception is provided under Article 60. Members may, but are not required to, exclude from the scope of Section 4 small amounts of non-commercial imports contained in travellers' luggage or otherwise sent in small consignments.

Article 51 establishes a general obligation requiring Members to provide certain border measures. Members are required to provide procedures that allow a right-holder who has grounds to suspect the importation of counterfeit trademarked or pirate copyrighted goods to apply to have the suspect imported goods detained by customs authorities. Members may extend this procedure to other types of intellectual property infringement and to infringing exports, if they so choose. The obligations of Article 51 are further clarified by footnotes 13 and 14. Footnote 14 defines "counterfeit trademarked goods" and "pirated copyrighted goods" for the purposes of the Agreement. Footnote 13 again addresses the issue of exhaustion by noting that there is no obligation under Article 50 to apply these border procedures to imports put on the market in another country by or with the consent of the right-holder.

---

[47] Note that only Members of customs unions, not free trade areas, are exempted from Section 4.

The basic obligations of Article 51 are then elaborated upon by the remaining articles of Section 4. Article 52 requires that any person applying to invoke a border measure must be required to provide adequate *prima facie* evidence of infringement and a sufficient description of the infringing goods. The competent authorities are then required to advise the applicant within a reasonable period of time as to whether the application has been accepted and, if applicable, the period of time for which the measures will apply. The issue of security is addressed in Article 53. An applicant may be required to provide security or equivalent assurances sufficient to protect the defendant, the competent authorities and prevent abuses of the process. Where goods have been detained which may concern the infringement of industrial designs, patents, lay-out designs or undisclosed information, and 10 (or in some cases 20) working days have expired without the granting of other provisional relief, the owner, importer or consignee of the goods must then be entitled to have the goods released. The owner, importer or consignee must post security sufficient to protect the right-holder from any infringement that may occur as a result, but that security is to be subsequently released if the right-holder does not then pursue an action on the merits of the case within a reasonable period of time.

Under Article 54, the importer and the applicant must be promptly notified in any case where border measures have been invoked and goods detained. Once the applicant has received notice of a detention, the time periods specified in Article 55 become effective. If within 10 working days of receipt of the notice of detention the applicant has not commenced a proceeding on the merits of the case or obtained other provisional measures (such as an injunction), the detained goods must be released. In appropriate cases, this deadline can be extended for an additional 10 working days. In those cases where a proceeding leading to a decision on the merits has been initiated, the defendant must be able to request a review of the detention to determine whether its continuation is justified. Where goods have been wrongly detained or where they have been released under Article 55 when no proceedings have been initiated by the applicant, the relevant authorities must have the ability to order the applicant to compensate the importer, consignee and owner for any damages caused by the detention.

Article 57 provides that a right-holder must be permitted sufficient opportunity to have detained goods inspected in order to substantiate the right-holder's claim. Importers must be given the equivalent opportunity of inspection. Where a decision on the merits has upheld the right-holder's claim, the competent authorities may be permitted to provide the right-holder with certain details of the importations, such as the names and addresses of the importer, the consignor and the consignee.

In some situations, the relevant authority may take action on its own accord without being prompted by a complaint or application from a right-holder. Members are free to confer such powers on their competent authorities provided they meet the requirements of Article 58. The authorities must have *prima facie* evidence that an intellectual property right is being infringed, the importer and right-holder must be promptly notified of any suspension and, where the defendant then appeals the suspension, the requirements of Article 55 (with respect to subsequent release of the goods within 10 or 20 working days) will apply.

Article 59 deals with the ability of authorities to destroy or otherwise deal with detained goods. Without prejudice to either of the other remedies, a right-holder may have or, to a defendant's review rights, competent authorities must have the ability to order the destruction or disposal of infringing goods without payment of any compensation. With respect to counterfeit trade-marked goods, re-exportation of the infringing goods in an unaltered state must not be permitted.

(v) Section 5: Criminal Procedures

The final remedy that must be specified under a Member's domestic law is that of criminal sanctions. As a minimum, Article 61 provides that criminal sanctions must be available at least in cases of wilful commercial trademark counterfeiting and copyright piracy. Members may extend criminal sanctions to other types of intellectual property infringement if they so choose, but this is not required. The precise extent of criminal sanctions, be it imprisonment and/or fines, is not specified, but in any case such sanctions must be sufficient to act as a deterrent. In appropriate cases, available remedies must also include seizure, forfeiture and destruction of offending goods, materials and implements.

(d) Part IV: Acquisition and Maintenance of Intellectual Property Rights and Related *Inter Partes* Procedures

Part IV of the TRIPS Agreement (Article 62) addresses certain procedural issues relating to the acquisition and maintenance of intellectual property rights. Generally speaking, Members may require right-holders to comply with reasonable procedures and formalities in order to acquire and maintain intellectual property rights, provided that they are consistent with the other obligations of the Agreement. Where acquisition of a right is subject to the right being granted or registered (such as the grant of a patent or the registration of a trademark) such procedures must result in a granting or registration of the right within a reasonable period of time. Paragraph 3 specifies that Article 4 of the Paris Convention, which is concerned with applications in more than one country and priority rights that may arise as a result, shall also apply to applications for services marks. Procedures concerning the acquisition and maintenance of rights (including procedures such as trademark oppositions and expungements) must be fair and equitable, and must not be unnecessarily complicated, costly or lengthy. With respect to any decisions on the merits required under such procedures, such decisions can only be based on evidence which the participating parties have had an opportunity to meet. Written reasons are preferred but not mandatory, and they must be made available, at least to the parties to the proceeding, on a timely basis. With some limited exceptions, all final administrative decisions made under such acquisition and maintenance procedures must be subject to further review before a judicial or quasi-judicial authority.

(e) Part V: Dispute Prevention and Settlement

With Part V (Articles 63 and 64), the Agreement shifts to Member-to-Member dispute settlement. One criticism of the pre-existing intellectual property regime was that of ineffective dispute settlement. Even those international agreements which did contain dispute settlement provisions were generally considered to be ineffective. A country was therefore free to flaunt even its existing international obligations with impunity. While improved dispute settlement was often an issue for discussion at the WIPO, these discussions generally led to no substantive improvement. Improving substantive obligations under the TRIPS Agreement was considered by many to be only addressing one-half of the problem. These new standards of protection had to then be supported by effective Member-to-Member dispute settlement provisions in order for the Agreement to prove effective over the longer term. Part V of the Agreement is the result of these concerns.

One of the tried and true methods of improving adherence to international obligations is improved transparency. Article 63 therefore applies this concept to the intellectual property area. First, all laws, regulations, and final judicial and administrative decisions of a Member pertaining to matters covered under the Agreement must be published or made publicly available. Certain intergovernmental agreements must also be published. Second, Members must notify the TRIPS Council (established under Article 68) of all such laws and regulations. This notification obligation may eventually be waived in the future if the Council is able to negotiate the establishment of a common legal and regulatory registry with the WIPO. Finally, all Members must be prepared to supply to any requesting Member information on all their relevant laws, regulations, and final judicial and administrative decisions. Nothing under Article 63 is to be interpreted as requiring Members to disclose certain types of confidential information.

The settlement of disputes that may arise between or among Members is addressed in Article 64. Generally speaking, paragraph 1 of Article 64 applies the dispute settlement provisions of GATT 1994 (Articles XXII and XXIII), as further elaborated upon and applied by the Dispute Settlement Understanding, to the TRIPS Agreement.[48] One of the key results of this application of the Understanding to the TRIPS Agreement is the availability of cross-sectoral sanctions if a Member fails or refuses to implement a panel decision in a timely manner. Thus, in some situations a Member may be able to impose tariffs on imports of another Member when that other Member is in violation of its obligations under the TRIPS Agreement.[49]

Generally speaking, GATT Article XXIII provides three bases for complaint: (a) there is an alleged violation of an obligation; (b) the measure at issue is not in violation of any obligation, but it is still nullifying or impairing a Member's anticipated benefit; (c) and any other situation. During the negotiations of the TRIPS Agreement there was significant support for the view that the bases of complaint under subparagraphs (b) and (c) had little or no role to play in the intellectual property context. The debate could not be concluded prior to the completion of the negotiations and it was therefore decided that the issue would be subject to further review. Thus, paragraph 2 of Article 64 provides that only the first basis of complaint, a direct violation of an obligation, will be available to Members until January 1, 2000. During this five-year period, the TRIPS Council will examine whether the type of complaints provided for under GATT Articles XXIII (b) and (c) are appropriate in the intellectual property context and, if so, how should such complaints be brought before the DSB. The Council is to submit any recommendations it may have in this regard to the Ministerial Conference. Any decision made by the Conference with respect to the Council's recommendations must then be made by consensus.

(f) Part VI: Transitional Arrangements

Because of the substantial change represented by the TRIPS Agreement, the transition from the existing system of intellectual property protection to

---

[48] See pages 308-327 for a complete discussion of the Dispute Settlement Understanding.

[49] The provisions of Article 64(1) also appear to preclude the use of unilateral remedies whenever the subject of a dispute falls within the scope of the TRIPS Agreement. However, a specific statement to this effect which at one time appeared in the negotiating text was eventually deleted. For example, Article 67 of the *Agreement on Trade Related Aspects of Intellectual Property Rights, including Trade in Counterfeit Goods*, tabled at the 1990 Brussels meeting (MTN.TNC/W/35, pages 196-231) would have provided very broad protection against unilateralism. That provision stated:

PARTIES shall not have recourse in relation to other PARTIES to unilaterally decided economic measures of any kind. Furthermore, they undertake to modify and administer their domestic legislation and related procedures in a manner ensuring the conformity of all measures taken thereunder with the above commitment.

This issue is comprehensively addressed in Article 23 of the DSU. See discussion of Article 23 at page 325.

the new system had to be clearly and carefully addressed. Part VI of the Agreement (Articles 65 to 67) sets out the special transitional arrangements. Generally speaking, these provisions allow developing country Members additional time in which to bring their domestic legal regimes governing intellectual property into compliance with the obligations of the TRIPS Agreement.

Paragraph 1 of Article 65 establishes the general date on which the TRIPS Agreement entered into force. The Agreement generally entered into force on January 1, 1996, one year after the WTO Agreement generally entered into force. This generally effective date is then modified for many Members by paragraphs 2, 3 and 4 of Article 65. Under paragraphs 2 and 3, developing country Members and "Members in transition"[50] may delay implementation of most of the Agreement's substantive obligations until January 1, 2000. This delay does not apply to obligations under Articles 3 (National Treatment), 4 (Most-Favoured-Nation Treatment) and 5 (Multilateral Agreements on Acquisition or Maintenance of Protection), which become applicable to all Members without exception as of January 1, 1996.

Paragraph 4 of Article 65, applicable only to developing country Members, provides for a further transition period of an additional five years for product patents, in certain limited cases. To the extent that a developing country Member is required by the Agreement to extend product patents to areas that were not previously patentable under its laws, the Member may further delay the application of the Agreement's product patent provisions (found in Section 5 of Part II) to these areas until January 1, 2005. However, this exception is subject to the obligations of paragraph 8 of Article 70, discussed below, which specifically addresses pharmaceutical and agricultural chemicals.

Paragraph 5 of Article 65 provides for a standstill during the transition periods provided for in paragraphs 1, 2, 3 and 4. Any Member making changes to its intellectual property measures during an applicable transition period is not permitted to increase the degree of inconsistency of these measures with the obligations of the Agreement.

Least-developed country Members are extended special treatment under Article 66. Such Members are not required to implement the Agreement (other than Articles 3, 4 and 5) until January 1, 2006, or 10 years from the date the Agreement becomes generally effective. The TRIPS Council is able to grant

---

[50] Article 65 describes a Member in transition as being a Member "which is in the process of transformation from a centrally-planned into a market, free enterprise economy and which is undertaking structural reform of its intellectual property system . . ." It is generally recognized that these former communist countries, such as those of the former Soviet Union and Eastern Europe, may face special problems in implementing an intellectual property regime, and therefore require an additional period of time.

further extensions of this period if appropriate. Developed country Members are to provide incentives to business and institutions in order to encourage technology transfers to least-developed country Members. In addition, Article 67 provides for technical cooperation between developed countries and other Members. In order to facilitate the Agreement's implementation, developed country Members are to provide certain forms of technical and financial assistance to developing and least-developed country Members.

(g) Part VII: Institutional Arrangements: Final Provisions

Institutional arrangements and certain final issues, such as issues relating to existing subject-matter and general exceptions, are addressed in Part VII of the Agreement (Articles 68 to 73).

Article 68 provides for the establishment of the Council for Trade-Related Aspects of Intellectual Property Rights (the "TRIPS Council" or the "Council for TRIPS"). The Council is to monitor the operation of the Agreement, provide a forum for consultation on trade-related intellectual property matters and assist in dispute settlement. The Council may consult with and seek information from any source that it considers appropriate. In particular, the Council was directed to establish a formal relationship with the WIPO and its subsidiary bodies.[51]

Beyond the formal consultative relationship established under the Council, pursuant to Article 69 Members have agreed to cooperate with each other with a view to eliminating international trade in goods that infringe on intellectual property rights. This would include, but is not limited to, counterfeit trademark goods and pirate copyright goods. In order to further this goal, Members are required to establish contact points that will be able to exchange information on trade in such goods.

The implementation of the Agreement will require the substantial revision of the intellectual property laws of many Members. Among many other complex transitional issues, in many Members the implementation of the Agreement will extend protection to previously unprotectable intellectual property. Thus, one of the most important transitional issues concerns existing subject-matter. What was to be done with that intellectual property which existed prior to the implementation of the Agreement and all actions relating thereto, which immediately became subject to protection as a result of the implementation of the Agreement? Article 70 addresses this difficult and complex issue.

---

[51] Pursuant to this direction, a formal cooperation agreement was negotiated with WIPO. The agreement entered into force on January 1, 1996. It provides for formal cooperation between the WTO and WIPO in three main areas: (i) notification and access to national laws; (ii) implementing procedures for Article 6ter of the Paris Convention (relating to national emblems) for purposes of the TRIPS Agreements; and (iii) technical cooperation.

First, paragraph 1 provides that nothing in the Agreement gives rise to any obligations with respect to any acts that occurred prior to the date of application of the Agreement to that Member.[52]

Second, generally speaking, the Agreement applies to all protectable subject-matter that is in existence as of the date the Agreement applies to the Member. This general rule of application is then subject to a number of exceptions. First, copyright obligations applicable to existing works are to be determined solely under the provisions of Article 18 of the Berne Convention.[53] Generally speaking, this means that copyrighted works which have fallen into the public domain may not be protected anew. This rule of application also applies to the rights of producers of phonograms and performers in existing phonograms. The third rule of application, somewhat related to these first two, is that there is no obligation to restore protection to any subject-matter that has fallen into the public domain of the Member.

Third, with respect to ongoing acts which had previously been legal or acceptable, but which became infringing once a Member's implementing legislation became effective, Members are permitted to limit a right-holder's available remedies in such cases, so that the right-holder may not be able to legally terminate the continuing infringements, provided that the act in question had already commenced or a significant investment had already been made prior to the Member's acceptance of the WTO Agreement[54] but, at a minimum, the right-holder is to be paid equitable remuneration for these continuing acts.

The fourth exception found in paragraph 5 concerns rental rights in copyrighted works. The Agreement's obligations concerning such rental rights, found in Articles 11 and 14(4), will not apply to originals or copies of such works that were purchased prior to the date the Agreement applies to the Member.

---

[52] "The date of application" is the date on which the Agreement applied to the Member as determined under Articles 65 and 66. This obligation is itself subject to the standstill obligation of Article 65(5).

[53] The relevant provisions of Article 18 provide:

(1) This Convention shall apply to all works which, at the moment of its entry into force, have not yet fallen into the public domain in the country of origin through the expiry of the term of protection.

(2) If, however, through the expiry of the term of protection which was previously granted, a work has fallen into the public domain of the country where protection is claimed, that work shall not be protected anew.

[54] Note that the date of a Member's acceptance of the WTO Agreement, the date the WTO Agreement became effective and the TRIPS Agreement becomes effective are likely to all be different dates, the earliest of which is likely to be the date the Member accepted the WTO Agreement. This date may differ from Member to Member.

Fifth, with respect to existing compulsory patent licences, paragraph 6 provides that Members are not required to comply with the Agreement's obligations concerning such compulsory licences where such licences were granted by the government prior to the date the TRIPS Agreement became known.

In cases where an intellectual property right is conditional on registration, Members must permit that any applications for such registration which are pending with the Member on the date the Agreement becomes effective for that Member can be amended by the applicant if it so chooses, in order to claim the benefit of any enhanced protection that will occur as a result of the Agreement's implementation.

Paragraph 8 of Article 70 provides for special transitional protection for pharmaceutical and agricultural chemicals. Where, as of January 1, 1995, a Member does not already provide patent protection for pharmaceutical and agricultural chemicals (as required under Article 27), then, as of January 1, 1995, that Member must: (i) provide an interim system whereby patent applications for these chemicals can be filed (notwithstanding the transitional provisions of Part VI); (ii) when the applications are finally examined, novelty of the invention must be determined as of the date of filing; and (iii) where the application is accepted and a patent granted, the term of protection must still extend for 20 years, measured back to the filing date of the application (as is required under Article 33).[55]

Where a patent application is filed for a pharmaceutical or agricultural chemical under this interim system, and the product subsequently receives marketing approval prior to the granting of a patent, the Member must extend to the applicant the exclusive right to market the product for a period of five years, or until the patent is granted or rejected, whichever is shorter. While the transitional provisions of Part VI do not apply to this obligation, its potential benefit is limited in that in order to qualify for the exclusive marketing right the applicant must, after January 1, 1995, have filed a patent application, been granted a patent, and received marketing authority for the product in another Member. It will therefore not apply to any applications filed prior to January 1, 1995.

The review and potential amendment of the TRIPS Agreement is specifically provided for under Article 71. Under paragraph 1, the TRIPS Council is to undertake its first review of the Agreement's implementation after January

---

[55] For example, assume that a patent application is filed on January 1, 1995 under this provision, but the Member, subject to the Agreement's transitional provisions, does not provide for patentability of the subject product until January 1, 2005. If the applicant is then granted a patent on January 1, 2005, the Member must provide patent protection until January 1, 2015, or for a 20-year term, measured back to the date of filing. This provision is often referred to as the "mailbox" provision.

1, 2000, with subsequent reviews to take place every two years thereafter. Any potential changes to the Agreement that might result from such reviews would then be subject to the procedures established under Article X of the WTO Agreement.[56]

The effect on the TRIPS Agreement of potential amendments to other multilateral intellectual property Agreements is addressed in paragraph 2 of Article 71. Where an amendment to another multilateral Agreement has the effect of increasing the level of protection accorded to intellectual property rights, and that amendment has been accepted under the terms of the other Agreement by all WTO Members, the TRIPS Council may refer the matter to the Ministerial Conference on the basis of a consensus proposal, and the TRIPS Agreement will be amended thereby in accordance with the terms of Article X:6 of the WTO Agreement.[57]

Article 72 provides that no Member may take a reservation from any of the Agreement's obligations without the consent of the other Members. Article 73 sets out a final security exception, substantially similar to GATT Article XXI. Nothing in the Agreement is to be construed as requiring a Member to compromise its national security interests as they may be related to certain specified information, goods or events, nor is anything in the Agreement intended to prevent a Member from taking any action required of it under its United Nations obligations (such as the imposition of economic sanctions, for example).

4. CONCLUSIONS

In reviewing the TRIPS Agreement, one is immediately struck by both its broad scope and its complexity. Both these attributes are double-edged swords. Its broad scope and complexity mean that many of the goals that were established prior to commencement of the negotiations have been achieved in the text. But it also means that disputes are inevitable.

With respect to the Agreement's complexity, one interesting aspect is the underlying reason for much of this complexity. In many ways, the TRIPS Agreement marks a substantial departure from previous trade-related agreements. For example, for the most part, the GATT and the GATS only impose general disciplines on Members. They do not attempt to harmonize the laws of Members or establish specific domestic rules which Members must adopt. In contrast, the TRIPS Agreement imposes general disciplines, but then goes much further to, in essence, require the harmonization of many aspects of

---

[56] For the discussion of Article X of the WTO Agreement, see pages 40-41.

[57] Article X:6 of the WTO Agreement provides that any proposed amendment to the TRIPS Agreement meeting the requirements of Article 71(2) may be adopted by the Ministerial Council of the WTO without requiring a further formal acceptance process.

intellectual property laws among Members. This fundamental difference in approach to rule development is a notable example of the "deepening" of international trade law. To an ever-increasing degree, the domestic laws of most countries are being directly affected by international trade negotiations.

The Agreement does have its critics. Many in the developed countries argue that the Agreement did not go far enough in some areas and often target the long transition periods extended to developing countries. Critics in the developing world take the opposite view, arguing that the Agreement has gone too far and that it will hinder economic development and technology transfers. There appears to be little doubt that the developed countries achieved much of what they were pursuing. Developing country Members have agreed to accept very substantial increases in intellectual property protection, although it will be phased-in over time. Whether this will actually improve economic development and increase the rate of technology transfers as the developed countries have argued will only be determinable 15 to 20 years hence.

One final comment relates to the relationship of the TRIPS Agreement and the WTO to the WIPO. In many respects, the infant WTO does not yet have the experience, expertise, or even, perhaps, the desire, to oversee the global intellectual property regime. As a result, the success of the TRIPS Agreement will, to a great degree, depend on the working relationship that develops between the WTO and the WIPO.

6

The Plurilateral Trade Agreements

1. INTRODUCTION

Under the "single undertaking" approach to WTO membership, Members are generally required to accede to all WTO Agreements without reservation. However, there are four plurilateral exceptions to this requirement—the *Agreement on Trade in Civil Aircraft*, the *Agreement on Government Procurement*, the *International Dairy Agreement* and the *International Bovine Meat Agreement*—where accession is optional. These four Agreements are collectively defined in the WTO Agreement as the Plurilateral Trade Agreements.[1] As noted above in chapter 2,[2] Article II:3 of the WTO Agreement sets out the status of the Plurilateral Trade Agreements within the WTO framework. That Article provides:

> The Agreements and associated legal instruments included in Annex 4 (hereinafter referred to as "Plurilateral Trade Agreements") are also part of this Agreement for those Members that have accepted them, and are binding on those Members. *The Plurilateral Trade Agreements do not create either obligations or rights for Members that have not accepted them.* [Emphasis added]

This special status of the Plurilateral Trade Agreements is confirmed through a number of additional provisions of the WTO Agreement which state that the general obligations of the WTO Agreement are specifically subject to the rights and obligations of the Plurilateral Trade Agreements.[3]

All of the Plurilateral Trade Agreements were originally negotiated and concluded as part of the Tokyo Round negotiations. With the exception of the *Agreement on Trade in Civil Aircraft*, the Plurilateral Trade Agreements were amended in varying degrees during the course of the Uruguay Round. As discussed below, the most comprehensive amendments were made to the *Agreement on Government Procurement* (but the negotiations concerning this Agreement were, in fact, not formally part of the Uruguay Round). While the other three Plurilateral Agreements were discussed within the MTN Agreements and Arrangements Negotiating Group during the Round, no substantive changes were negotiated to these other Agreements, primarily due to an overall lack of enthusiasm for any such changes.

2. THE *AGREEMENT ON TRADE IN CIVIL AIRCRAFT*

The *Agreement on Trade in Civil Aircraft* first entered into force on January 1, 1980. At the time of writing, 22 Members plus the EC, are

---

[1] The four Plurilateral Trade Agreements are found in Annex 4 to the WTO Agreement.

[2] See above at pages 35-36.

[3] For example, the following provisions of the WTO Agreement provide that the obligations of the WTO Agreement, generally applicable to all the Multilateral Trade Agreements, are subject to the specific provisions of the Plurilateral Trade Agreements: Article IV:8 (structure); Article IX:5 (decision-making); X:10 (amendments); XII:3 (accessions); XIII:5 (non-application); XIV:4 (acceptance and entry into force); Article XVI:2 (withdrawals); and Article XVI:5 (reservations).

signatories to the Agreement.[4] The Agreement covers trade in all civil aircraft, and civil aircraft parts, components and sub-assemblies, civil aircraft engines, engine parts and components, and all ground flight simulators and their parts and components.[5]

The main goal of the Agreement was to establish free trade in civil aircraft and related parts and components. This was generally accomplished by requiring Signatories to eliminate all customs duties and other charges levied on imported civil aircraft, parts, components and repairs by January 1, 1980 (or upon accession). The Agreement also imposes certain other disciplines on government-directed purchasing of civil aircraft. These provisions encourage the free selection of aircraft suppliers on the basis of commercial and technological factors by prohibiting Signatories from requiring or pressuring purchasers into obtaining civil aircraft from a particular source. Article 5 of the Agreement also prohibits the use of quantitative restrictions, and import and export licensing systems in a manner inconsistent with the applicable GATT obligations.

Other important obligations of the Agreement attempt to discipline the use of government support and export credits often used in the aircraft industry to stimulate sales. Signatories have agreed to seek to avoid adverse effects on trade in civil aircraft that can result from such subsidization. They have also agreed generally to avoid unreasonably low pricing by noting that the pricing of civil aircraft should be based on a reasonable expectation of recoupment of all the costs of production.

Finally, the Agreement establishes a Committee on Trade in Civil Aircraft to oversee and conduct annual reviews of the operation of the Agreement. The Committee is also charged with issuing rulings and recommendations concerning disputes under the Agreement. Unfortunately, the Members were unable to conform the Agreement to the WTO during the Uruguay Round, and the Agreement therefore remains in its Tokyo Round form. The consultation and dispute settlement provisions of the WTO technically apply to disputes under the Agreement since the WTO is a successor Agreement to the GATT. However, the Signatories to the Agreement have complained that there is considerable legal uncertainty surrounding the Agreement in its current form.[6]

---

[4] Austria, Belgium, Canada, Denmark, Egypt, France, Germany, Ireland, Italy, Japan, Luxembourg, Macao, Netherlands, Netherlands Antilles, Norway, Portugal, Romania, Spain, Sweden, Switzerland, United Kingdom, the United States, and the European Communities.

[5] Article 1 of the Agreement. For purposes of the Agreement, "civil aircraft" refers to all aircraft other than military aircraft. "Civil aircraft" is used here to collectively refer to all products subject to the Agreement.

[6] For example, while Article 1(1) of the WTO's Dispute Settlement Understanding states that the Understanding applies to the *Agreement on Trade in Civil Aircraft*, this application has not been noted within the Agreement itself.

3. THE *AGREEMENT ON GOVERNMENT PROCUREMENT*

Governments, governmental agencies and government-owned companies are the largest purchasers of goods and services in many countries. Consequently, almost all governments find it irresistible to use this buying power to pursue their economic development objectives. This pursuit usually takes the form of discriminating in favour of local or national suppliers of goods or services to the detriment of those from other countries.

While original proposals for the Havana Charter would have prohibited such overt violations of national treatment, these proposals were soon abandoned under the belief that attempting to negotiate any substantive non-discriminatory rules for government procurement would have been virtually impossible at the time. Consequently, a specific exclusion for government procurement found its way into the GATT's national treatment obligation (in Article III:8(b)), meaning that, subject to certain basic requirements, government procurement was "carved out" of the GATT 1947 and contracting parties remained virtually free to discriminate as they saw fit in their procurement practices.

During the late 1960s and early 1970s, increasing concerns over the discriminatory and trade-distorting aspects of government procurement resulted in the issue being placed on the agenda for the Tokyo Round of GATT negotiations. These discussions then led to the conclusion of the first *Agreement on Government Procurement* (the "Government Procurement Code"), which entered into force for its Signatories on January 1, 1980. This Code formed the basis for the new *Agreement on Government Procurement*.

One important provision of the Tokyo Round Government Procurement Code was Article IX:(6)(b), which provided that the Signatories would undertake further negotiations on a regular basis so as to broaden and improve the Code. The Government Procurement Committee established under the Code then subsequently established the so-called "Informal Working Group on Negotiations" to oversee and implement this obligation. The first such negotiations resulted in a number of improvements being accepted and implemented into the Code in 1988. And prior to the issuance of the Ministerial Declaration that initiated the Uruguay Round, the Informal Working Group on Negotiations had already commenced a second set of negotiations aimed at further broadening and improving the Code. Thus, negotiations on a new government procurement agreement were already underway in a different forum at the time of the commencement of the Uruguay Round, making inclusion of government procurement within the Round somewhat duplicative and inappropriate.

In addition to the already commenced negotiations, there was a concern among some participants that these government procurement negotiations would be co-mingling discussions on goods and services. It was therefore decided that the issue of government procurement would remain within the Code's Informal Working Group on Negotiations and would not be formally brought within the Uruguay Round negotiations. Thus, the government procurement negotiations continued on contemporaneous with, but formally separate from, the Round. In the end, the Informal Working Group was able to negotiate a new *Agreement on Government Procurement*, which was also signed by participating countries at Marrakesh on April 15, 1994.

The new *Agreement on Government Procurement* entered into force on January 1, 1996. It has 14, mostly developed country, Signatories,[7] and now covers, for the first time, the procurement of both goods and services (including construction services), and some procurement at the sub-central government and public utilities levels. Government procurement has been substantially liberalized as a result of the new Agreement, with some estimating an increase in coverage of 10-fold over that of the Tokyo Round Code.

It is important to first note the limited scope and coverage of the Agreement. Not only does the Agreement only apply between and among its Signatories, but it also only applies to procurements over certain specified financial thresholds and undertaken by those entities specifically listed in the Annexes provided for each of the participating Signatories.

With respect to covered entities, the Annexes to the Agreement generally include three types of entities: national governments (and their ministries and other governmental bodies); sub-national governments (and their ministries and other governmental bodies); and an "all others" category (such as government-owned utilities).

With respect to financial thresholds, different thresholds apply depending upon what type of entity is undertaking the procurement and what is being procured. There are also some different country-specific thresholds. The generally applicable thresholds are as follows:

- *National Government Entities*
  - 130,000 Special Drawing Rights ("SDRs")[8] for goods or services, other than construction services;
  - 5 million SDRs for construction services;
- *Sub-national Government Entities*
  - 200,000 SDRs for goods or services, other than construction services;

---

[7] Canada, the European Communities, Finland, France, Israel, Japan, Luxembourg, Norway, the Republic of Korea, Spain, Sweden, Switzerland, the United States, and the Netherlands on behalf of Aruba.

[8] An SDR is a unit of account of the International Monetary Fund and its equivalent in national currency is determined by each Signatory. An SDR is equivalent to approximately US$1.40.

— 5 million SDRs for construction services;

• *Other Governmental Entities*

— 400,000 SDRs for goods or services, other than construction services; and

— 5 million SDRs for construction services.

A principal feature of the Agreement is the national treatment and non-discrimination obligations of Article III that apply to those procurements falling within the scope and coverage of the Agreement. Under these obligations, each Party must provide to products, services and suppliers of other Parties treatment that is no less favourable than the treatment accorded to domestic products, services and suppliers, as well as products, services and suppliers from any other Party. That is to say, generally speaking, Parties may not favour domestic products, services or suppliers in the procurement process. The Agreement also provides that Parties may not apply special rules of origin for government procurement purposes. This particular provision of the Agreement will be amended to incorporate the results of the harmonization of rules of origin once those rules have been negotiated and adopted as contemplated under the *Agreement on Rules of Origin.*[9]

A substantial portion of the Agreement establishes transparency-enhancing rules applicable to virtually all aspects and stages of the procurement process. These rules apply to: the valuation of contracts; technical specifications; tendering procedures; the qualification of suppliers; invitations to participate in intended procurement; selection procedures; time limits for tendering and delivery; tender documentation; the submission, receipt and opening of tenders; the awarding of contracts; negotiations; notice requirements; and challenge procedures.

As with many WTO Agreements, the *Agreement on Government Procurement* provides for special and differential treatment for developing countries. Under the Agreement, Parties are encouraged to facilitate increased imports from developing countries and to bear in mind the special economic circumstances of developing countries. Developed countries must, upon request, provide technical assistance to developing countries and must establish Information Centres to respond to requests by developing countries. Developing countries are authorized to negotiate mutually acceptable exclusions from the national treatment requirement and may modify their coverage lists.

The Agreement also establishes the Committee on Government Procurement to oversee the operation of the Agreement. The Committee, composed of representatives from each Party, is to meet at least once a year and is charged with reviewing the operation and implementation of the Agreement. Through

---

[9] See pages 121-124 for discussion on these negotiations.

the Committee, the Parties are required to consult concerning the use of technology in the government procurement process to ensure that the Agreement does not become an obstacle to technical progress.

Disputes arising under the Agreement may be resolved in one of two ways. First, Parties are required to establish challenge procedures under domestic law which may then be utilized by a supplier to challenge a particular procurement that the supplier believes constitutes a violation of the Agreement by the procuring entity. These procedures must generally accord due process to the aggrieved supplier, and must provide for a review of the supplier's challenge by an impartial and independent review body (with a subsequent right of appeal) or by a court. The second dispute settlement process, to be used in the case of disputes between Parties, provides for recourse to the WTO's Dispute Settlement Understanding, using the terms of reference set forth in the Agreement. Parties are encouraged to accelerate a dispute settlement proceeding whenever possible.

Finally, Article XXIV:7(b) of the Agreement provides for further negotiations to commence no later than January 1, 1999 with a view to improving the Agreement and expanding its scope and coverage to the greatest extent possible. This will include not only eliminating exceptions and lowering applicable thresholds, but also expanding the number of covered entities and Parties to the Agreement.

4. THE *INTERNATIONAL DAIRY AGREEMENT*

The *International Dairy Agreement* originally came into force on January 1, 1980 as part of the implementation of the results of Tokyo Round negotiations, effectively replacing both the *Arrangement Concerning Certain Dairy Products* (of 1970) and the *Protocol Relating to Milk Fat* (of 1973). This Agreement was slightly revised during the course of the Uruguay Round. Only 11 Members plus the EC are signatories to it.[10] The Agreement is intended to provide greater stability in dairy trade by avoiding surpluses, shortages and undue fluctuations in prices. The Agreement applies to the dairy products sector generally and provides for the establishment of minimum export prices for certain products.

Article VII:1 establishes the International Dairy Council to oversee the Agreement's operation. The Council is comprised of representatives of each participant in the Agreement, and decisions of the Council are taken by consensus. Parties are required to regularly submit marketing information to the Council so that it is able to monitor and assess the overall market for dairy products. If, after evaluating the world market for dairy products, the Council

---

[10] Argentina, Bulgaria, Chad, the European Communities, Finland, Japan, New Zealand, Norway, Romania, Sweden, Switzerland, and Uruguay.

finds serious market disequilibrium or the threat of serious disequilibrium, the Council is to make recommendations to participants to assist in resolving the situation.

The Agreement also encourages food aid and requires the participants to inform the Council in advance of their proposed contributions of food aid. The Agreement contemplates food donations through bilateral and multilateral arrangements, including the World Food Programme.

As noted, the Agreement also provides for the establishment of minimum export prices for the following products: skimmed milk powder, whole milk powder, buttermilk powder, anhydrous milk fat, butter and cheese. The Agreement provides a mechanism for making adjustments to these minimum export prices based upon milk-fat content, packaging, terms of sale, end use, special conditions of sale, and transactions other than normal commercial transactions. In October 1995, the International Dairy Council suspended the application of the Agreement's minimum-export-price provisions until December 1997 largely because a number of large dairy exporting countries were not signatories to the Agreement, making minimum prices unsupportable.

In late September 1997, the signatories to the Agreement agreed to terminate it at the end of 1997. It will then be deleted from the list of Plurilateral Agreements annexed to the WTO Agreement.

5. THE *INTERNATIONAL BOVINE MEAT AGREEMENT*

Like the Dairy Agreement, the *International Bovine Meat Agreement* was also originally concluded as part of the Tokyo Round, and has been brought under the WTO umbrella without substantive modification. At the time of writing there are 19 Signatories to the Agreement.[11] The Agreement specifically covers live cattle, meat and by-products, and is intended to liberalize and stabilize the international meat and livestock market.

The *International Bovine Meat Agreement* established an International Meat Council, comprised of representatives of each participant. Decisions of the Council are taking by consensus. The Council serves as a forum for the exchange of information concerning the international meat market and is charged with monitoring the conditions of that market. The Council meets twice annually to consult on matters affecting trade in bovine meat and to evaluate conditions in the market. If, after this evaluation, the Council finds a serious imbalance or the threat of an imbalance in the international meat market, it is to recommend solutions to the participants. The Council also

---

[11] Argentina, Australia, Brazil, Bulgaria, Canada, Chad, Colombia, the European Communities, Finland, Japan, New Zealand, Norway, Paraguay, Romania, South Africa, Sweden, Switzerland, the United States, and Uruguay.

maintains a database of information from participating countries and publishes an annual situation and outlook report. Participants are accordingly required to furnish the Council with information required for it to compile its annual report.

One noticeable difference between the Dairy and the Bovine Meat Agreements is that the Bovine Meet Agreement includes no provisions relating to minimum export pricing. The greater number of signatories to the Bovine Meat Agreement is largely attributable to this factor.

As with the International Dairy Agreement, in late September of 1997, the signatories to the *International Bovine Meat Agreement* agreed to terminate the Agreement at the end of 1997. The Agreement will then be deleted from the list of Plurilateral Agreements annexed to the WTO Agreement.

6. CONCLUSION

Compared to the WTO Agreement, the Plurilateral Trade Agreements have few signatories. However, all of the Plurilateral Trade Agreements contain provisions for accession by additional WTO Members. The significance of the post-Uruguay Round Plurilateral Trade Agreements is the fact that even though multilateral consensus could not be reached or was not appropriate for the issues covered by these Agreements, the signatories to them, and all other WTO Members, recognized the value of bringing these Agreements within the overall framework of the WTO. As part of the WTO, the Plurilateral Trade Agreements will now operate and develop under WTO principles, as well as be subject to the WTO's Dispute Settlement Understanding. At a minimum, this fulfills one of the important overall goals of the Uruguay Round, by improving and ensuring the overall consistency and integrity of the new global trading regime.

7

The Understanding on Rules and Procedures Governing the Settlement of Disputes

1. INTRODUCTION

Lawyers can be heard to remark that "there is no right without a remedy". In other words, rules, in and of themselves, will not provide effective disciplines unless there is some method whereby they can be enforced. The WTO Agreement is no different than any other set of rules in this respect. An effective enforcement and dispute settlement mechanism was therefore considered essential to the Agreement's overall success. Consequently, the dispute settlement and enforcement provisions of the WTO Agreement are often referred to as a cornerstone of the new WTO system. These provisions are found in the *Understanding on Rules and Procedures Governing the Settlement of Disputes*.[1] Reflecting its importance to the overall effectiveness of the WTO system, the Understanding itself provides that "[t]he dispute settlement system of the WTO is a central element in providing security and predictability to the multilateral system".[2] This chapter reviews these important provisions in detail. Part 2 below first provides a brief overview of the evolution of the GATT dispute settlement system and the Uruguay Round negotiations. Part 3 then reviews the provisions of the Understanding in depth.

2. PRE-WTO PROCEDURES AND THE URUGUAY ROUND NEGOTIATIONS

(a) The Pre-Uruguay Round GATT Dispute Settlement Process

It is important to appreciate that the Understanding is very much an Agreement borne of experience, based on over 40 years of dispute settlement under the GATT 1947. Much was learned through this experience. The original dispute settlement provisions of GATT 1947 were limited to two brief Articles—Articles XXII and XXIII. This lack of substantive dispute settlement procedures in the original GATT can be attributed primarily to the intended temporary nature of the GATT, which was to remain in force only until such time as the Havana Charter and the ITO came into effect. The Havana Charter had been equipped with more substantive procedures, including the ability to refer interpretive issues to the International Court of Justice. The drafters did not consider it necessary to repeat these procedures in the temporary GATT.

The ITO never came into being, leaving the Contracting Parties to address dispute settlement as best they could within the existing provisions of Articles XXII and XXIII of the GATT. This they had to do almost immediately after

---

[1] *Understanding on Rules and Procedures Governing the Settlement of Disputes* (the "Understanding" or the "DSU") is attached as Annex 2 to the WTO Agreement.

[2] Article 3.2 of the Understanding.

the Agreement came into effect, developing procedures that could be used to attempt to resolve disputes between contracting parties. The first process to be used was so-called "working parties". If one contracting party was concerned with the measure of another, a working party was formed to review and clarify the situation. These working parties were small groups of interested contracting parties, including the disputing countries themselves, which would review the situation and attempt to develop an appropriate negotiated solution. These working parties never had the ability to render binding decisions or enforce compliance, but rather were used to clarify the issues involved.

While the working party process initially met with some success, it was soon determined that a more effective mechanism had to be developed. By the early 1950s, a somewhat different "panel of experts" procedure was gradually and quietly replacing the working party process. Under this procedure, *ad hoc* panels of trade diplomats, stationed with contracting parties in Geneva, would review and report on individual disputes. This new process began to take on the appearance of arbitration, including, for example, the rather formal presentment of written and oral argument to the panel. The panel would then draft a report (often including a conclusion as to the legal consistency of the measure at issue) for presentation to the Contracting Parties. This change in procedure was accompanied by a subtle and evolving change in the stature of the GATT Secretariat, which began to play a more important role in the dispute settlement process. The development of this panel process was the first step in the "legalization" of the GATT's dispute settlement process—a trend which has now reached a new apex in the procedures of the DSU.

In response to concerns expressed by some developing countries that this process was not adequately protecting their interests, in 1966 the panel procedures were supplemented by the adoption of certain special procedures that could be employed when a developing country was one of the disputing parties.[3] While based on the then existing panel process, these special procedures improved upon it by providing for the participation of the GATT's Director-General in an *ex officio* capacity, providing an automatic right to a panel and setting specific time periods for each stage.

By the time of the commencement of the Tokyo Round negotiations in 1973, many flaws in this panel process had been exposed. Perhaps most problematic was the fact that the entire process was based on consensus. The process could not move forward unless there was a consensus among all contracting parties to do so. If one of the disputing parties was intent on delaying the establishment of a panel or the adoption of a panel report, it could do so by blocking any consensus. Consequently, losing parties often temporarily, or in some cases permanently, blocked the formation of panels, or the

---

[3] "Procedures Under Article XXIII", Decision of 5 April 1966, GATT, BISD 14S/18.

implementation of panel reports, or both. This ability to delay or stymie the panel process rendered it ineffective in some cases.

By the time the Tokyo Round had commenced, the flaws in the system were generally well-known and the negotiations did produce some improvements to the existing dispute settlement procedures. In particular, the *Understanding Regarding Notification, Consultation, Dispute Settlement and Surveillance* was agreed to, along with its accompanying Annex, the "Agreed Description of Customary Practice".[4] In addition to this Understanding, many of the Tokyo Round Codes incorporated their own separate dispute settlement processes based, but improving upon, the then-existing panel process.

While the Tokyo Round Understanding did serve to clarify many procedural aspects of the panel process (including setting some general guidelines on the timing for each step), some contracting parties refused to accept any changes to the consensus requirement which continued to dominate the process. Consequently, the Tokyo Round Understanding left considerable scope for individual contracting parties to delay or disrupt the process in any given case. It was not long before further changes were considered necessary.

Additional procedural improvements were subsequently made in late 1982[5] and again in late 1984. In particular, in 1984 the Contracting Parties adopted a proposal which: (i) provided for the inclusion of non-governmental experts as panelists (so as to increase the depth of expertise available and thereby increase the overall quality and objectivity of panel decisions); (ii) permitted the Director-General to select and appoint panelists in the event that the disputing parties were unable to agree on the composition of a panel (refusing to accept nominated panelists had by then become a popular method of delay); and (iii) where written submissions were involved, panels were directed to set precise deadlines and disputing parties were expected to respect those deadlines (failing to file written argument on time had become another popular method of delay).[6] While the adoption of these procedural changes had introduced further incremental improvement to the system, they had done nothing to address the consensus rule.[7]

In 1985 the Leutwiler Report recommended that still more changes should be made to the system. While noting that often the underlying rules themselves were more to blame for dispute settlement failure than the procedures, the Report recommended a number of improvements to increase speed and effectiveness. The Report noted that:

---

[4] See GATT, BISD 26S/210.

[5] The changes introduced in 1982 were part of the 1982 Work Programme. See GATT, BISD 29S/13.

[6] See "Dispute Settlement Procedures", GATT, BISD 31S/9.

[7] The consensus rule was, in fact, re-affirmed in the 1982 decision, although it was also stated that obstruction of the process was to be "avoided".

Panels should be set up, and should complete their work, more speedily than in some past instances. Panels should always clearly indicate the rationale for their findings so as to give the GATT Council a firm basis for decision. The panels should be composed of experts fully familiar with the increasingly complex GATT legal system.

. . .

We further suggest that greater and more flexible systemic attention be given to the implementation of panel reports. Fixing dates for carrying out their recommendations, and regular Council reviews of how this is being carried out, would be steps in the right direction.[8]

(b) The Uruguay Round Negotiations

By the time the agenda was being developed for the Uruguay Round there had developed a widely held view that the dispute settlement provisions remained in need of substantive improvement, and, consequently, wide-spread support for the inclusion of dispute settlement on the Round's agenda. With little debate over the issue, the Ministerial Declaration subsequently provided that:

> In order to ensure prompt and effective resolution of disputes to the benefit of all contracting parties, negotiations shall aim to improve and strengthen the rules and procedures of the dispute settlement process, while recognizing the contribution that would be made by more effective and enforceable GATT rules and disciplines. Negotiations shall include the development of adequate arrangements for overseeing and monitoring of the procedures that would facilitate compliance with adopted recommendations.[9]

A separate Negotiating Group on Dispute Settlement was established to carry out the mandate. Once negotiations commenced, there immediately was a great deal of common ground on a number of procedural issues and the Group was able to reach agreement on many procedural improvements by late 1987. There remained, however, a significant divergence of views on the role that dispute settlement should play in the GATT system generally. Two views were expressed which diverged on the role that disputing parties themselves should play in the process. On the one hand, the United States, generally supported by Canada, was of the view that the existing system should be further "legalized" by the adoption of fully automatic procedures. GATT dispute settlement should be very similar to domestic court, and the consensus requirement should therefore be dispensed with as the primary barrier to greater effectiveness.

On the other hand, the EC, supported by Japan, resisted any further legalization of the GATT process. The system should remain true to the

---

[8] *Trade Policies for a Better Future: Proposals For Action* (GATT, Geneva: 1985), at 46-47.

[9] "Ministerial Declaration on the Uruguay Round", GATT, BISD 33S/19, at 25.

"diplomatic" nature of the original GATT Articles XXII and XXIII. This diplomatic nature necessitated a mutually agreeable negotiated resolution to all disputes. Under this view of the process, the consensus rule was an essential feature, ensuring that the resolution in any given case would be mutually acceptable and protecting the diplomatic nature of the process from further legal incursions.

By early 1988, the Negotiating Group was able to divide all issues before it into two groups: (i) a series of procedural improvements, for which there was broad support; and (ii) substantive changes, for which no consensus had yet developed and where further negotiations were still required. Because of the degree of support for the procedural improvements the Negotiating Group was able to produce a draft interim agreement for the Montreal Mid-term Meeting in late 1988 that would introduce a number of procedural improvements to the dispute settlement system, and which could be adopted immediately. These improvements included the adoption of standard terms of reference and, most importantly, the establishment of specific time periods for each phase of the panel process. These improvements were accepted by the Ministers as part of the Decisions taken following the Montreal Mid-term Meeting, and were adopted on a trial basis commencing May 1, 1989.[10]

With these procedural improvements temporarily adopted, the Negotiating Group could then turn to the negotiation of the more substantive issues. In addition to issues surrounding the consensus requirement, the Montreal Mid-term Meeting also added a number of new issues to the Group's agenda. For example, by this time many of the other negotiating groups were independently considering dispute settlement issues and some had begun to develop their own procedures. The Dispute Settlement Group was therefore asked to consider issues relating to the integration of all such separate dispute settlement provisions. The Group was also asked to review certain issues relating to so-called non-violation nullification and impairment complaints.

By June 1990, broad Agreement had been reached on many substantive improvements to the system. Most importantly, a proposal for the introduction of a formal appeal process into the system had paved the way for agreement on substantially automatic processes, including panel establishment and adoption of panel reports. By the time of the Brussels Ministerial Meeting in December 1990, the Chair of the Dispute Settlement Group could produce a broadly acceptable draft Agreement. Only three major issues remained unresolved, these being certain aspects of non-violation complaints, integration of all dispute settlement provisions, and a pledge against unilateral action. Only one of these issues was even discussed in Brussels prior to that Meeting's collapse over agricultural issues.

---

[10] See "Improvements to the GATT Dispute Settlement Rules and Procedures", Decision of 12 April 1989, GATT, BISD 36S/61.

Between the negotiations re-commencement in February 1991 and December of that year, agreement was reached on these three remaining issues and a draft "Understanding on Rules and Procedures on Dispute Settlement" was finalized. A second related Agreement had also been drafted, proposing an integrated dispute settlement system which would apply to all the Agreements then being developed as part of the Uruguay Round. This draft "Elements of an Integrated Dispute System" proposed the establishment of a centralized Dispute Settlement Body to settle all disputes that might arise under any of the new Agreements and, in order to provide for better enforcement, also proposed that cross-sectoral retaliation would be available in certain circumstances. Both these draft Agreements were included as part of the Draft Final Act circulated by Mr. Dunkel in late December 1991. While many other aspects of the Draft Final Act proved contentious, there was broad acceptance of the dispute settlement provisions. While further work was done to integrate the two draft Agreements into one comprehensive Understanding, few substantive changes were made and these two Agreements were essentially carried forward into the WTO Agreement as one integrated text.

3. THE *UNDERSTANDING ON RULES AND PROCEDURES GOVERNING THE SETTLEMENT OF DISPUTES*

(a) Coverage and Application

The Understanding provides the primary rules for dispute settlement under the WTO Agreement. This is confirmed in Article 1, which provides that the rules and procedures of the DSU apply to all disputes brought pursuant to the consultative provisions of those WTO Agreements listed in Appendix 1 to the Understanding, as well as disputes concerning rights and obligations under the WTO Agreement itself. [11]Some of the Agreements listed in Appendix 1 contain certain additional dispute settlement rules. In such cases, the general rules of the Understanding are made subject to those more specific rules. Article 1 also provides certain "conflict" rules in the event that two or more rules of dispute settlement conflict with one another.

(b) The Dispute Settlement Process

(i) The Dispute Settlement Body

Article 2 of the Understanding creates the WTO's Dispute Settlement Body ("DSB"), the WTO committee charged with administering the Under-

---

[11]Appendix 1 to the DSU lists the WTO Agreement, the Multilateral Agreements on Trade in Goods (including the GATT 1994 and the 12 other Annex 1A Agreements), the *General Agreement on Trade in Services* (Annex 1B), the *Agreement on Trade Related Aspects of Intellectual Property Rights* (Annex 1C), and the Understanding itself. The DSU refers to these Agreements as the "covered Agreements". Appendix 1 also includes the Plurilateral Trade Agreements, but the application of the DSU to these Agreements is subject to the adoption of a decision by the parties to each of those Agreements establishing, in each individual case, the terms of application of the DSU to that Agreement.

standing's rules and procedures. Among its functions, the DSB is authorized to establish dispute settlement panels, adopt reports, oversee the implementation of rulings and recommendations, and authorize suspension of concessions and other obligations under the covered Agreements. The DSB is comprised of all Members of the WTO Council,[12] and is to meet as often as may be necessary to carry out its functions under the DSU. Under paragraph 4 of Article 2, where the rules and procedures of the Understanding require the DSU to take a decision, it must do so by consensus.[13]

(ii) General Provisions

Article 3 of the Understanding (drawing heavily on the Tokyo Round Understanding and its attached "Agreed Description") sets out a number of general provisions which constitute important contextual guides to the entire WTO dispute settlement process. Among its features, Article 3 requires that Members:

- affirm their adherence to prior dispute settlement practice as occurred under GATT 1947, Articles XXII and XXIII;

- recognize that dispute settlement is necessary to preserve and clarify WTO rights and obligations (importantly, however, the dispute settlement process cannot add to or diminish those rights and obligations);

- emphasize that the overall purpose of dispute settlement under the DSU remains to achieve a mutually satisfactory solution of all matters; however, any solutions that may be achieved must still be consistent with the WTO;

- in an attempt to avoid unnecessary cases, Members are to exercise their judgment before initiating the dispute settlement process; however, use of the process is not to be considered a contentious act, and Members should still attempt to resolve all disputes in good faith;

- in the absence of a mutually acceptable resolution, the first objective is the removal of the relevant offending measure; compensation (in the form of improved market access in another area or sector) should only be resorted to if removal of the offending measure is impractical, or pending the removal of that measure; a suspension of concessions (so-called "retaliation") should only be used as a last resort, and then only with the prior authorization of the DSB;

---

[12] While the DSB is comprised of all Members of the WTO Council, when a dispute arises under one of the covered Plurilateral Trade Agreements, only those Members that are parties to that Plurilateral Agreement may participate in DSB decisions or actions pertaining to that dispute.

[13] Consensus is deemed to exist if no Member, present at the relevant meeting, formally objects to the proposed decision.

- an inconsistent measure is *prima facie* considered to have resulted in "nullification and impairment" and, as a result, the measure is deemed to have had an adverse impact on Members;
- complaints and counter-complaints concerning separate matters should not be linked; in such cases, separate and distinct proceedings should be initiated;
- the DSU only applies to disputes initiated after January 1, 1995; disputes initiated prior to that date are to be settled according to the applicable rules and procedures in effect at the time the dispute was originally commenced;[14] and
- developing country Members retain the option of using the procedures of the DSU or those special dispute settlement procedures for developing countries set out in the 1966 Decision.[15]

(iii) Consultations

The dispute settlement procedure under the DSU actually consists of several separate, but inter-related procedures: consultations, good offices, conciliation, mediation, arbitration, panel review, and appellate review of panel determinations. The first layer of dispute settlement under the Understanding is a consultative process whereby the disputing Members first attempt to negotiate a mutually acceptable settlement of the problem at hand. Article 4.2 of the Understanding provides that each Member is required to accord sympathetic consideration to and afford adequate opportunity for consultation regarding any representations made by another Member concerning measures affecting the operation of any covered Agreement.

Upon receipt of a written request for consultations, the Member to which the request is made must reply within 10 days of receipt of the request and enter into good faith consultations within 30 days of its receipt. A failure to respond to such a request within the required time means that the requesting Member may immediately request the establishment of a panel. Any Member making a request for consultations must notify the DSB and any Council or Committee responsible for the relevant agreement. The request must include the reasons for the request, the measure at issue and the legal basis for the complaint.

Consultations are without prejudice and are confidential. Through the consultation process, the disputing Members are to attempt to reach a mutu-

---

[14] This issue is also addressed in a decision adopted by the Preparatory Committee for the WTO ("Co-existence of the GATT 1947 and the WTO Agreement, adopted 8 December 1994) which provides for the priority of WTO dispute settlement.

[15] Procedures under Article XXIII, Decision of 5 April 1966, GATT, BISD 14S/18. See above at page 309.

ally satisfactory resolution of the matter. If consultations fail to resolve the dispute within 60 days of receipt of the request, the complaining Member may then request the establishment of a panel.[16] The complaining Member may request a panel review prior to the expiration of the 60-day period if the disputing Members agree that the consultations have failed.

In cases where a third Member considers that it has a substantial trade interest in the consultations, it may notify the consulting Members of its desire to join the consultations. If the responding Member does not consider that this third Member has a substantial interest in the matter it may refuse that request to participate. If its request is refused the third Member remains free to initiate its own consultations on the matter.

(iv) Good Offices, Conciliation and Mediation

Under Article 5 of the DSU, Members may, on a voluntary basis, use good offices, conciliation or mediation as alternate means of resolving disputes.[17] The WTO's Director-General is free, acting in an *ex officio* capacity, to offer such good offices, conciliation and mediation to assist Members in settling disputes. These procedures may be initiated or terminated at any time during the dispute settlement process without prejudice to the rights of any Member to pursue further proceedings. If good offices, conciliation or mediation is pursued within 60 days of receipt of a request for consultations, the complaining Member must then wait 60 days from the date of receipt of the request for consultations before requesting the establishment of a panel. The complaining Member may request a panel prior to the expiration of the 60-day period if the disputing Members agree that the good offices, conciliation or mediation has failed. Good offices, conciliation or mediation may continue while the panel process is ongoing if the disputing Members agree.

(v) Establishment of a Panel

Assuming that consultations or the other alternatives have failed to settle the dispute, the next phase is the initiation of the panel process under Articles 6 to 16 of the Understanding. These panels are charged with assisting the DSB

---

[16] Paragraph 8 of Article 4 provides an accelerated time-frame applicable to urgent cases, including those concerning perishable goods. In such cases, Members must enter into consultations within a period of no more than 10 days after the date of receipt of the request. If the consultations fail to settle the dispute within a period of 20 days after the date of receipt of the request, the complaining Member may then request the establishment of a panel.

[17] In addition to these alternatives, arbitration is also made generally available under the provisions of Article 25 (in addition to a number of specific instances elsewhere in the Understanding). Arbitration may be undertaken upon the mutual Agreement of the disputing Members and may prove particularly useful in cases where the issues have already been clearly defined.

in making recommendations and issuing rulings. Under Article 6, if a complaining Member so requests, a dispute settlement panel is to be established by the DSB, at the latest, at the first DSB meeting following the meeting at which the request for a panel first appeared as an item on the DSB's agenda. The DSB must establish a panel unless it decides, by consensus, not to establish the panel.[18] Any such request for a panel must include certain specified information, including the measure at issue and the legal basis for the complaint.

Article 7 then sets out the panel's standard terms of reference which are to guide the panel in considering the dispute. The standard terms are to examine, in light of the relevant WTO provisions, the matter referred to the DSB and make relevant findings and recommendations to the DSB. Panels are to employ these standard terms of reference unless the disputing Members agree otherwise. Panels are also required to address the relevant provisions of any agreement cited by the disputing Members.

The composition of panels is addressed in Article 8. In order to facilitate the panel selection process, the WTO Secretariat is directed to maintain an "indicative list" of qualified individuals who are available to serve as dispute settlement panelists.[19] This list includes the pre-existing roster of qualified individuals that was compiled for use under the GATT procedures, as well as the names of other individuals that may periodically be provided by Members.[20] The composition of individual panels is to be determined with a view to ensuring a sufficiently diverse background and a wide spectrum of experience. In order to protect the independence of the panels, panelists may not be citizens of Members whose governments are parties to the dispute, unless the disputing Members otherwise agree. If selected to serve on a panel, panelists serve in their individual capacity, not as representatives of their governments, and Members are not permitted to instruct or influence their citizens while acting as panelists.

---

[18] The employment of the "reverse consensus" requirement at this stage of the process is the first example of the method that has been adopted to overcome the problems of blocking that the consensus rule had caused under the dispute settlement rules of the GATT 1947.

[19] Paragraph 1 of Article 8 sets out certain necessary panelist qualifications. Generally speaking, panels are to be composed of well-qualified governmental and/or non-governmental individuals, including persons who have: (i) served on or presented a case to a panel; (ii) served as a representative of a Member or a contracting party to GATT 1947, or as representative to the Council or Committee of any covered Agreement or its predecessor Agreement; (iii) served in the Secretariat; (iv) taught or published on international trade law or policy; or (v) served as a senior trade policy official of a Member.

[20] In addition, a decision of Ministers accepted as part of the Uruguay Round final package provides that, with respect to disputes arising under the GATS, a special GATS roster is to be developed, comprised of experts in trade in services. Where the dispute concerns the GATS, panels should be comprised of these experts.

Under paragraph 5 of Article 8, panels are ordinarily to be comprised of three individuals, unless the disputing Members agree to a panel of five within 10 days of the establishment of the panel. Upon the establishment of a panel by the DSB, the WTO Secretariat proposes panelist nominations to the disputing Members. Members may only object to proposed panelists "for compelling reasons". If the disputing Members cannot agree on the composition of the panel within 20 days of its establishment, the WTO's Director-General is to appoint the panel, after consultations with the disputing Members, the Chair of the DSB and the Chair of any relevant Council or Committee.

Article 9 provides the procedures to be followed in cases involving more than one complaining Member. In the event that more than one Member requests the establishment of a panel concerning the same matter, the Understanding encourages the establishment of a single panel whenever feasible. When a single panel is convened, the panel is directed to ensure that its examination of the matter and its presentation of its findings do not impair the rights that the various Members would have enjoyed if separate panels had been established. If more than one panel is established, the panels' composition should remain the same to the greatest extent possible and the timetables for the panels should be harmonized.

In many instances, Members who are not parties to the dispute may still have a direct or indirect interest in the outcome of the dispute. For example, the dispute may involve the interpretation of an important obligation that could affect future disputes. Article 10 of the Understanding requires that panels take into account not only the interests of the disputing Members, but also the interests of other Members. If a Member has a substantial interest in a matter before a panel and that Member notifies the DSB of that interest, the Member will be allowed to participate in the panel process as a third party. Third parties to panel reviews have the right to be heard by the panel, to make written submissions and to receive the submissions of the other Members. While those third-party Members do not participate in a number of preliminary matters, such as consultations and panel selection, they remain able to initiate their own complaint concerning the matter if they wish.

With respect to the function panels play under the DSU, Article 11 provides that they are to assist the DSB in discharging its responsibilities under the Understanding. As a result, panels are to make objective assessments of the matter before them, and make such findings as will assist the DSB in making its rules and recommendations.[21]

---

[21] One unsettled issue is the standard of review panels are to apply in their review of disputes. While the Understanding does not contain an explicit standard of review, it is considered by many that an implicit standard of review may be gleaned from the Understanding's general

Another significant achievement of the Understanding is the establishment of fixed time periods for the completion of panel reviews. While tentative improvements adopted following the 1988 Montreal Mid-term Meeting formed the basis for certain procedural provisions of the Understanding, these improvements only set out a general timetable for the completion of panel reviews. Article 12 of the Understanding has gone one step further and establishes specific time limits of no more than six months and a maximum time limit of no more than nine months for the completion of panel reviews. In urgent cases, the panel should issue its final ruling within three months of its establishment. If a panel believes that it cannot issue its report within the specified time limit, it must inform the DSB in writing of the reasons for the

provisions. All provisions of the Understanding are governed by the general principle that WTO dispute settlement "serves to preserve the rights and obligations of Members under the covered agreements, and to clarify the existing provisions of those agreements in accordance with customary rules of interpretation of public international law". In addition, a panel is charged with "mak[ing] an objective assessment of the matter before it, including an objective assessment of the facts of the case and the applicability of and conformity with the relevant covered agreements". These broad standards are tempered only by the caveat that "[r]ecommendations and rulings of the DSB cannot add to or diminish the rights and obligations provided in the covered Agreements". These standards appear to give mediators, arbitrators or panelists, as the case may be, a wide degree of discretion in resolving matters before them. The settlement of disputes is subject only to the constraints of the customary rules of interpretation of public international law and objectivity. This suggests that a "correctness" standard is the proper standard of review to be applied by panels.

These broad standards became quite controversial in the closing days of the Uruguay Round. The United States delegation became concerned that WTO panels would not pay appropriate deference to domestic agencies rendering decisions that could be subject to WTO review. In particular, the United States was concerned that WTO panels would not afford the same degree of deference to agency determinations in anti-dumping and countervailing duty matters as is afforded by U.S. courts reviewing the determinations. In 1993, the U.S. proposed a more deferential standard of review be applicable in all disputes involving administrative determinations. This proposal was apparently abandoned when U.S. intellectual property interests opposed granting this type of deference to foreign patent and copyright office decisions. Later that year, less than one month before the conclusion of the Uruguay Round in December 1993, the United States submitted a revised proposal to amend only the *Anti-dumping Agreement* to provide a more deferential standard applicable to panel review of anti-dumping determinations. After much negotiation, a more deferential standard of review, similar to the U.S. proposal was added to the *Anti-dumping Agreement*. Although the United States sought parallel changes to the *Agreement on Subsidies and Countervailing Measures*, no such standard appears in that Agreement. The United States did succeed in obtaining two Ministerial Decisions as part of the final package relating to standard of review. One calls for the consistent resolution of disputes arising from anti-dumping and countervailing measures, suggesting that the standard of review should be the same in each type of dispute (see "Declaration on Dispute Settlement Pursuant to the *Agreement on Implementation of Article VI of the General Agreement on Tariffs and Trade* or Part V of the *Agreement on Subsidies and Countervailing Measures*"). The other Decision provides that Article 17.6 of the *Anti-dumping Agreement* will be reviewed in three years to consider whether it is capable of general application (see "Decision on Review of Article 17.6 of the *Agreement on Implementation of Article VI of the General Agreement on Tariffs and Trade 1994*").

delay and provide an estimate of the additional time that will be required to complete its report.

Article 12 and Appendix 3 of the Understanding set forth panel working procedures. Whenever practicable, within one week after the composition of the panel and the terms of reference have been agreed upon, the panel should fix a timetable for the completion of the process.[22] The panel is expected to set precise deadlines for written submissions and the Members are expected to meet those deadlines. The general working procedures for panels provide for both initial and rebuttal written submissions by the disputing Members and any third parties, as well as two substantive meetings with the disputing Members and a meeting with any third parties. Panels may hold additional meetings as necessary, and may, at any time, put questions to the disputing Members and ask them for explanations either during any meeting or in writing. *Ex parte* meetings between the panel and any party are prohibited.

All meetings of the panel are to be held in closed session, with the disputing Members and any third parties being present only upon invitation of the panel. In addition, deliberations of the panel and documents submitted to it are to be kept confidential, except that Members are permitted to disclose their own submissions to the panel if they so choose.[23]

Article 13 of the Understanding authorizes panels to seek information from any relevant outside source, although if a panel wishes to seek information or advice from any individual or body within the jurisdiction of any Member, it must inform the authorities of the Member before doing so. Confidential information submitted to the panel may not be publicly disclosed without the formal authorization of the individual, body or authority that submitted that information. Paragraph 2 of Article 13 also permits panels to seek advisory reports from expert review groups. The rules and procedures for establishing an expert review group, which operates under a panel's authority, are found in Appendix 4 to the Understanding.

The panel prepares an interim report following the submission of written arguments and the presentation of oral arguments. The deliberations of the panel are confidential and panel reports are drafted outside of the presence of the disputing Members. Panel opinions are anonymous. The process then moves to an interim review stage under Article 15. The interim review stage is

---

[22] Appendix 3 includes a proposed timetable for the panel process.

[23] While the confidential nature of panel review has historically been employed to encourage the negotiated settlement of disputes, the resulting lack of transparency has recently raised some concerns about the legitimacy of the system. The United States, in particular, has pressed the WTO to make its dispute resolution process more open and transparent, to include, for example, public hearings and the opportunity for non-governmental groups to make submissions to the panel. To date there has been little support for moves in this direction, although the WTO has made some effort to provide greater public access to its documents.

a two-step process. The panel first drafts the factual and argument portions of its report and circulates these portions to the disputing Members for their review. The Members are then provided with the opportunity to review and comment on these portions of the panel's report. This review ensures that the panel properly understands the facts of the case and the arguments put before it. After this review has been completed, the panel then completes the drafting of the interim report and circulates the entire document, including the panel's findings, to the disputing Members for review and comment. The disputing Members are then permitted to request that the panel revisit precise aspects of its report prior to the circulation of the report to all Members.

This interim review is an interesting aspect of the WTO dispute settlement process. WTO dispute settlement aims for a mutually agreed resolution of the dispute at every level of the process. The interim review discloses the panel's decision to the disputing Members on a confidential basis and thereby provides one last opportunity to settle the dispute before a final report is circulated among the WTO Members. The interim review also acts as an informal appeal process by ensuring that the panel has not made basic errors based on a misunderstanding of the facts or the arguments before it.

If the disputing Members fail to reach a mutual settlement following this interim stage, the panel will issue its final report to the DSB. If no comments have been received from the disputing Members, the interim report will be considered to be the final report of the panel. Otherwise, the panel will prepare a final report that addresses the arguments raised by the disputing Members at the interim review stage. Under Article 16, the final panel decision is then circulated among all WTO Members and will be adopted by the DSB within 60 days of its circulation unless a Member to the dispute formally notifies the DSB of its decision to appeal the decision under Article 17, or if the DSB decides, by consensus, that the report will not be adopted.

(vi) Appellate Review

In exchange for the adoption of an automatic process and in order to improve the overall quality of panel reports, the Understanding provides a formal appeal process that can be used by any of the disputing Members when they consider that the panel has made a legal error. All panel decisions rendered under Articles 6 to 16 may be appealed to the WTO's Appellate Body established under Article 17. The Appellate Body consists of seven people, each of whom serves a four-year term.[24] Three members of the Appellate Body serve on each case on a rotating basis. Appellate Body

---

[24] Each member may be re-appointed once. The terms of three of the seven individuals appointed immediately after the entry into force of the Agreement will expire after two years. These three individuals were chosen by lot.

members must be of recognized authority, with demonstrated expertise in law, international trade and the general subject-matter of the WTO Agreement.[25] Persons serving on the Appellate Body may not be affiliated with any government and must be available at all times and on short notice. In order to ensure the independence of the Appellate Body, it has been provided with its own Appellate Secretariat, which is associated with, but which operates formally outside the WTO Secretariat.

Paragraph 4 of Article 17 limits the right of appeal to parties to the dispute; third parties may not appeal a panel decision but may participate in an appeal initiated by a disputing party. Under paragraph 6, appeals of panel determinations are limited to issues of law covered in the panel report and legal interpretations developed by the panel.

In order to overcome concerns that a formal appeal process might be used to delay the dispute settlement process, paragraph 5 of Article 17 establishes an accelerated timetable for any appellate review. Appellate Body proceedings generally should not exceed 60 days, but in any case, may not exceed 90 days from the date a party notifies the DSB of its intent to appeal.

The Appellate Body was charged with developing its own working procedures, which were issued by the Body in February 1996.[26] These procedures require that notices of appeal be filed simultaneously with the DSB and the WTO Secretariat. Among other information, appeal notices must contain the title of the panel report under appeal, the name of the Member to the dispute filing the appeal (the appellant), and a brief statement of the nature of the appeal, including the specific allegation of legal error.

Within 10 days of filing the Notice of Appeal, the appellant must then file a written submission detailing the allegation of legal error and the nature of the relief sought. The respondent or any other party to the dispute that wishes to respond to the appellant's allegations must file a written submission within 25 days of the filing of the appeal notice. All submissions to the Appellate Body must be served on all parties to the dispute. The Appellate Body will generally hold a hearing 30 days after the filing of the appeal notice.

Similar to the panel review process, the Appellate Body review is conducted in private, submissions to the Body are confidential, and the reports of

---

[25] On November 29, 1995, the DSB, after much lobbying by the Members, announced the appointment of the first seven Members of the Appellate Body: the Honorable James Bacchus of the United States, Ambassador Christopher Beeby of New Zealand, Professor Claus-Dieter Ehlermann of Germany, Doctor Said El-Naggar of Egypt, Justice Florentino Feliciano of the Philippines, Ambassador Julio Lacarte of Uruguay and Professor Mitsuo Matsushita of Japan. The members of the Appellate Body were chosen from a list of 32 candidates nominated by 23 countries.

[26] See *Working Procedures for Appellate Review*, WT/AB/WP/1, 15 February 1996.

the Appellate Body are drafted outside of the presence of the parties to the dispute. In addition, no *ex parte* communications may take place between the original panel and the Appellate Body. Appellate Body reports are anonymous, and the Appellate Body is authorized under Article 17.14 to uphold, modify or reverse the legal findings and conclusions of the panel. Most significantly, the Appellate Body report will be adopted by the DSB and must be unconditionally accepted by the disputing Members, unless the DSB decides by consensus not to adopt the Appellate Body's report within 30 days of its circulation.

(c) Enforcing Panel Determinations—The Remedies

The ability of the WTO to enforce panel determinations is largely based upon the cooperation of the Members and the possibility of the imposition of certain remedies known as compensation and the suspension of concessions (or more commonly referred to as "retaliation"). Under Article 19, when a panel or the Appellate Body has determined that a measure is inconsistent with a covered Agreement, it may only recommend that the Member concerned bring the measure into conformity with the relevant obligations. While a panel or the Appellate Body can recommend changes to a WTO Member's law or practice, the DSB cannot directly enforce such recommendations. In addition, panel and Appellate Body decisions are interpretive only; they cannot add to or diminish the rights and obligations provided for under the covered Agreements.

Article 21 of the Understanding expresses the view that prompt compliance with recommendations or rulings of the DSB is essential in order to ensure effective resolution of disputes to the benefit of all Members. To further this goal of prompt compliance, Article 21 directs a Member to which a panel or Appellate Body determination is directed to inform the DSB of its intentions with respect to implementation of the recommendations and rulings of the DSB at a meeting held within 30 days after the adoption of the panel or Appellate Body report.

If the Member is not able to comply with the DSB's recommendations immediately (because, for example, the recommendation may require the amendment of a domestic law) the Member concerned may have a reasonable time in which to bring itself into compliance. This reasonable time period may be a period proposed by the Member concerned so long as that period is approved by the DSB. In the absence of DSB approval, the reasonable period of time may be a time mutually agreed upon between the disputing Members or a period determined through binding arbitration.[27]

---

[27] Article 21.3(c) sets a guideline for arbitrators of 15 months from the adoption of the panel or Appellate Body report by the DSB for the implementation of that report.

The DSB is also charged with monitoring the implementation of any recommendations or rulings. To this end, the implementation of a recommendation or ruling will be placed on the agenda of the DSB meeting six months after the establishment of the reasonable time period for implementation, and will remain on the DSB agenda until the matter has been finally resolved.

Article 22 addresses compensation and retaliation. Compensation and retaliation are to be considered temporary measures, to be used only in the event that recommendations or rulings cannot be implemented within a reasonable period of time. Neither are preferred to full implementation of the relevant recommendation or ruling. Where a Member fails to bring itself into compliance with the relevant obligations within the prescribed reasonable period of time, the Member concerned must, on request of the complaining party, enter into negotiations to determine mutually acceptable compensation for the nullification or impairment of benefits. Compensation is completely voluntary and, if granted, must still be consistent with all WTO obligations.

Under paragraph 3 of Article 22, if compensation negotiations do not result in an Agreement on mutually acceptable compensation within 20 days, or if the Member concerned is not willing to negotiate compensation, the injured Member may then request authorization from the DSB to suspend the application of concessions (or retaliate) against the non-complying Member.[28] Like compensation, the suspension of concessions is considered a temporary measure that is not preferred to the implementation of the recommendations or rulings of the panel or Appellate Body.

Perhaps more importantly, the provisions of Article 22 provide the potential for so-called "cross-sectoral retaliation" in certain circumstances. In determining which concessions may be suspended, the Understanding provides that the complaining Member must first look to suspend concessions in the same sector as that which was the subject of the dispute.[29] For example, if the complaint involved automobiles, the complaining party could suspend concessions on automobiles, chickens, steel or any other type of good. If it would be impracticable or ineffective for the complaining Member to suspend concessions in the same sector, the complaining Member may seek authoriza-

---

[28] The suspension of concessions refers to a complaining Member's ability to withdraw, on a discriminatory or non-MFN basis, from certain obligations that it agreed to with the other Member concerned. For example, if the complaining Member has agreed to bind its tariff on automobiles at two percent, the complaining Member could suspend that concession with respect to imports of automobiles from the other Member concerned by raising the tariff on automobiles.

[29] With respect to complaints involving goods, the Understanding defines sector to mean all goods. For services, "sector" is defined by reference to the Services Sectoral Classification List referred to in the GATS. For intellectual property rights, "sector" is defined by reference to the categories of intellectual property rights found in the TRIPS Agreement.

tion to suspend concessions in other sectors under the same Agreement.[30] Finally, if it would be impracticable or ineffective to suspend concessions in other sectors under the same agreement and the circumstances are serious enough, the complaining party may seek to suspend concessions under another agreement. This potential to retaliate across sectors is likely to greatly increase the deterrent effect of the retaliation option, thus improving overall compliance with recommendations and rulings.

It is important to note that the complaining Member must first receive authorization from the DSB before suspending concessions and, in all cases, the level of concessions to be suspended must be equivalent to the level of nullification or impairment that has occurred. The suspension of concessions will be authorized by the DSB within 30 days of the expiration of the reasonable period for implementation of the relevant ruling, unless the DSB decides by consensus to reject the request. Thus, like the adoption of panel and Appellate Body rulings, the Member concerned cannot block the authorization of the suspension of concessions. However, if the Member concerned objects to the level of concessions that have actually been suspended, that issue can be settled through arbitration under paragraphs 6 and 7 of Article 22.

(d) Strengthening the Multilateral System

Article 23, entitled "Strengthening the Multilateral System", is aimed at improving the functioning of the multilateral trading system and dispute settlement under that system, by preventing Members from taking unilateral actions without prior recourse to the WTO dispute settlement system. Where Members seek redress for alleged violations of WTO obligations, they are specifically required to have recourse to and abide by the rules and procedures of the Understanding. Paragraph 2 of Article 23 specifies a number of obligations in this respect. In particular, Members:

- are not to make unilateral determinations of violations of WTO rights and obligations;
- must follow the procedures of Article 21 concerning reasonable periods of time for the implementation of panel reports; and
- must also follow the procedures of Article 22 concerning compensation and prior authorization for retaliation.

(e) Special Procedures for Least-developed Countries

As with many other of the WTO Agreements, the Understanding contains special provisions for disputes involving least-developed country Members.

---

[30] For goods, the term "Agreement" means all of the Agreements listed in Annex 1A of the WTO Agreement and all Plurilateral Agreements to which both the complaining Member and the other Member concerned are signatories. With respect to services, the term "Agreement" means the GATS, and for intellectual property, the term "Agreement" means the TRIPS Agreement.

Article 24, in particular, along with many other provisions of the Understanding, directs Members to give due consideration to the special situation of least-developed country Members. To this end, Members are encouraged to exercise restraint in bringing proceedings against least-developed countries and in asking for compensation or seeking authorization to suspend concessions when a nullification or impairment is found. In addition, Article 24 requires the WTO's Director-General and the Chair of the DSB to offer their good offices, conciliation or mediation at the request of a least-developed country involved in a dispute.

(f) Non-violation Nullification and Impairment Complaints

Article 26 of the Understanding concerns "non-violation" nullification and impairment complaints. Nullification and impairment can occur in two types of situations. First, under Article 2.8, nullification and impairment is, in effect, presumed to exist where a violation of a WTO obligation is found. The second type of nullification and impairment is often referred to as "non-violation" because there is no specific violation of a WTO obligation. In such cases, a Member has adopted a measure which, although technically consistent with its WTO obligations, is having the effect of nullifying benefits that other Members had reasonably expected would accrue to them under the WTO Agreement. Some, but not all of the WTO Agreements permit Members to initiate complaints under the DSU on the basis of non-violation nullification and impairment. Paragraph 1 of Article 26 sets out certain obligations respecting such complaints. The complaining Member must present a detailed justification in support of the complaint. Unlike the situation of violation complaints, nullification and impairment is not presumed to exist. It must be proved to exist in the case of non-violation complaints. Again, unlike a violation complaint, if nullification and impairment is determined to exist, there is no obligation on the responding party to withdraw the measure at issue. In such cases, the panel or the Appellate Body is instead to recommend mutually satisfactory compensation.

(g) Responsibilities of the WTO Secretariat

Under Article 27 responsibility for certain aspects of the dispute settlement process are placed on the WTO Secretariat. The Secretariat has the responsibility of assisting panels. This assistance takes the form of not just secretarial and technical support; more importantly, the Secretariat is to provide assistance on legal, historical and procedural aspects of the dispute settlement process. Secretariat staff therefore play an important advisory role in the dispute settlement process. In addition, the Secretariat is to provide legal assistance to developing country Members, on request, and is to conduct special training courses for all Members on the dispute settlement procedures.

4. CONCLUSIONS

At the time of writing, the WTO Agreement has been in force for almost three years, yet during this brief period there have been over 100 requests for consultations under the DSU. In less than three years, the WTO has now seen one-third as many requests for consultations than the GATT saw in 50 years. A number of panel reports have proceeded through the appellate process, numerous panels are ongoing and requests for the establishment of over 30 panels are possible based on existing consultations. Several cases have been settled at the consultation stage. While it may be too early to draw definitive conclusions concerning the functioning and effectiveness of the new procedures, there does appear to be at least initial confidence in the system.[31]

And, although there has been a limited amount of experience to date, some general observations can still be made. First, the scope of the WTO Agreement is much broader than that of the GATT 1947. Consequently, there are likely to be many more disputes under the WTO than under the GATT 1947. This conclusion already appears to be borne out by the number of cases to date.

Second, the new Appellate Body appears to be functioning as planned. Recourse to the Body may, unfortunately, become standard practice, although the Body appears to be up to the task and its reports to date have been of a high quality, helping to further clarify rights and obligations.

Third, there is little doubt that the automatic processes introduced through the Understanding are at least partly responsible for the smoother functioning of the dispute settlement system. An additional factor in this regard may also be the improved clarity of the underlying rules which, in some cases, has made panel review a somewhat easier task.

Finally, if there is a concern on the horizon it is that the procedures may, in fact, prove too popular for their own long-term benefit. The WTO has been provided with limited resources. If these resources become stretched too thinly, the quality of dispute settlement results will begin to decline, as will Members' confidence in the process.

---

[31] As part of the Uruguay Round final package, Ministers decided that by January 1, 1999, the WTO's Ministerial Conference will review the dispute settlement system. Once this review is completed the Ministerial Conference will then decide whether to continue, modify or terminate the rules and procedures (see "Decision on the Application and Review of the Understanding on Rules and Procedures Governing the Settlement of Disputes"). Thus, there is a formal review process already in place should this initial confidence begin to wane.

8

The Road Ahead for the WTO

1. INTRODUCTION

As significant an achievement as negotiating and implementing the WTO Agreement is, this will not mark the end of multilateral trade negotiations. Rather, the Uruguay Round has culminated in the creation of a multilateral institution intended, in part, to serve as the forum for continuing trade negotiations and consultations on new or developing trade-related issues. Thus, far from being the conclusion of international trade negotiations, the WTO and the new rules of global trade will now continue to develop on an ongoing basis, with specific areas of development being dependent on a constantly evolving agenda. In this regard, after less than three years in existence, the agenda of issues to be addressed which now faces the WTO and its Members—that is, the road ahead—is already somewhat daunting.

Issues already on, or anticipated to be placed on, the WTO's work agenda derive primarily from two sources. The first source is the WTO Agreement itself. The Agreement has an extensive "built-in agenda". Many of the WTO Agreements have already specifically identified a number of subject areas for continued or new negotiations under, in some cases, specified negotiating timetables. In addition to this built-in agenda, a number of other issues also flow out of the WTO Agreement, including implementation and transparency issues, issues related to regionalism, the extensive list of ongoing accession negotiations and provision for biennial Ministerial level meetings (the first of which was held in Singapore in December 1996).

These issues flowing out of the WTO Agreement alone represent an enormous amount of work yet to be done. However, there is a second source of additional, and perhaps even more challenging issues. This second source is the so-called "trade and" issues. These issues relate to a host of regulatory subject areas which can have indirect effects on trade (and *vice-versa*). International rules addressing these inter-relationships remain vague or non-existent. These areas include the environment, labour, investment and competition policy. Using these two expansive and complex sets of issues as a map, this chapter previews the road ahead for the WTO.

2. ISSUES RELATED TO THE WTO AGREEMENT

(a) The WTO's Built-in Agenda

As noted, the WTO Agreement has an extensive agenda of negotiating issues already built into the document. The entry into force on January 1, 1995 of the WTO Agreement started the clock running on this built-in agenda. The numerous specific issues are scattered throughout the many WTO Agreements, including many of the Multilateral Agreements on Trade in Goods, the *General Agreement on Trade in Services*, the *Agreement on Trade-Related Aspects of Intellectual Property Rights*, the *Understanding on Rules and*

Procedures Governing the Settlement of Disputes, the *Trade Policy Review Mechanism* and the plurilateral *Agreement on Government Procurement*. A survey of these issues and their negotiating timetables follows.

(i) Agenda Items under the Multilateral Agreements on Trade in Goods

(1) Subsidies and countervailing measures. Under Article 8.2(a) of the *Agreement on Subsidies and Countervailing Measures*, on June 30, 1996, the Committee on Subsidies and Countervailing Measures began a review of the operation of the provisions that treat research subsidies as non-actionable. In addition, under Article 30, by June 30, 1999, the Committee is to begin a review of the provisions of Articles 6.1, 8 and 9 concerning serious prejudice and non-actionable subsidies, to determine whether those provisions should be extended beyond their January 2000 termination date, or revised.

(2) Pre-shipment inspection. Article 6 of the *Agreement on Pre-shipment Inspection* called for the first biennial Ministerial Conference to review the implementation and operation of this Agreement. This first review was conducted at the Singapore Ministerial Meeting in December 1996, and subsequent reviews are to be conducted every three years thereafter.

(3) Anti-dumping. The *Ministerial Decision on Review of Article 17.6 of the Agreement on Implementation of Article VI of the General Agreement on Tariffs and Trade 1994*, accepted by Ministers as part of the final Uruguay Round package, calls for a review to take place after January 1, 1998 of the standard of review for disputes arising under that Agreement with the view towards considering the general applicability of that standard of review in the future. (This is generally considered to mean deciding whether the anti-dumping standard of review should be extended to the subsidies and countervailing duty area, and perhaps more generally.) In addition, the *Ministerial Decision on Anti-Circumvention*, also accepted as part of the final package, charges the Committee on Anti-dumping Practices with the goal of developing, as soon as possible, uniform rules relating to anti-circumvention of anti-dumping measures. No fixed deadline for developing these new rules is provided in the Decision.

(4) Technical barriers to trade. Under Article 15.4 of the *Agreement on Technical Barriers to Trade*, no later than January 1, 1998, and at the end of every three years thereafter, the Committee on Technical Barriers to Trade is to review the implementation of that Agreement with a view towards recommending, if necessary, an adjustment of the rights and obligations so as to ensure mutual economic advantage and a balance of rights and obligations.

(5) Agriculture. Under Article 20 of the *Agreement on Agriculture*, commencing January 1, 2000, Members are to commence further negotiations aimed at continuing progress towards the long-term objective under the

Agreement of substantial progressive reductions in support and protection for agriculture.

(6) Sanitary and phytosanitary measures. Under Article 12.7 of the *Agreement on the Application of Sanitary and Phytosanitary Measures,* after December 31, 1997, the Committee on Sanitary and Phytosanitary Measures is to conduct a review of the operation and implementation of that Agreement. Further reviews are to be conducted in the future, as the need arises.

(7) Trade-Related investment measures. Under Article 9 of the *Agreement on Trade-Related Investment Measures,* no later than January 1, 2000, the Council for Trade in Goods is to review the operation of that Agreement and propose amendments, as appropriate. In particular, the Council is to consider whether the Agreement should be complemented with provisions addressing investment and competition policies (discussed further below).

(8) Modification and withdrawal of tariff concessions. Paragraph 1 of the *Understanding on the Interpretation of Article XXVIII of the General Agreement on Tariffs and Trade* provides that after December 31, 1999, the Council for Trade in Goods is to review certain provisions of the Understanding relating to principal supplying interests (which are relevant when a Member proposes to modify or withdraw a tariff concession under GATT Article XXVIII) to determine if those provisions have been effective in securing a redistribution of negotiating rights in Article XXVIII negotiations.

(9) Reservations respecting foreign-built vessels. Article 3(a) of the GATT 1994 provides a relatively broad exemption from GATT 1994 for measures relating to certain foreign-built commercial vessels. The application of this exception is limited primarily to the so-called *Jones Act* of the United States. Article 3(b) of the Agreement provides that this exemption is to be reviewed by the Ministerial Conference no later than January 1, 2000, and every two years thereafter until eliminated.

(ii) Agenda Items under the General Agreement on Trade in Services

(1) Financial services. Because participants were not able to complete the sectoral negotiations on financial services by the formal end of the Uruguay Round, the GATS *Annex on Financial Services* and the *Ministerial Decision on Financial Services,* concluded as part of the Uruguay Round final package, called for the completion of the financial services negotiations by June 30, 1995. These further negotiations (which were then concluded at the end of July 1995) resulted in improved commitments by 29 Members relating to insurance, banking, securities and other financial services. Eight Members eliminated or reduced the scope of their MFN exemptions, while three Members expanded the scope of their MFN exemptions. More importantly, participating Members agreed that further negotiations on financial services would

take place, and that during a 60-day period beginning on 1 November 1997, Members will have the opportunity once again to improve or modify their financial services offers.[1] At the Singapore Ministerial Conference in December 1996, Members agreed to begin these financial services negotiations in April 1997.[2] Negotiations were commenced as planned in April and are expected to conclude by the end of 1997.[3]

(2) Movement of natural persons. The deadline for further negotiations on the movement of natural persons under the *Decision on Negotiations on Movement of Natural Persons* was June 30, 1995. These negotiations (which, like those on financial services did not conclude until July 1995) resulted in additional commitments that, in many cases, will allow qualified professionals, computer specialists, and certain other experts to work in many WTO countries without the requirement that they be linked to a commercial presence in that host country.[4]

(3) Telecommunications. The negotiations on telecommunications services also failed to reach a satisfactory conclusion by the end of the Round. Therefore, the GATS *Annex on Negotiations on Basic Telecommunications* and the *Ministerial Decision on Negotiations on Basic Telecommunications* established a deadline of April 30, 1996 to complete negotiations on basic telecommunications services. The Members failed to reach agreement by this date, and, rather than terminate the negotiations, the deadline was further extended to February 15, 1997. The negotiations were then successfully concluded by this new deadline. The resulting Agreement covers 95 percent of world telecommunications revenues and has been joined by 70 Members. The Agreement has three parts—market access, investment, and procompetitive regulatory principles—and covers local, long distance and international service. It is estimated that the $600 billion telecommunications industry could double over the next 10 years as a result of the Agreement.[5]

(4) Maritime services. Maritime services was another sector where negotiations were extended after the formal conclusion of the Round, in this case to June 30, 1996. Those talks collapsed on June 28, 1996 without success and are not expected to resume again until 2000, when, as discussed below, the first

---

[1] See pages 234-240 for a discussion of issues relating to financial services.

[2] See paragraph 17 of the *Singapore Ministerial Declaration.* The Declaration is attached as an Annex to this chapter.

[3] In order to facilitate these further negotiations, in late September of 1997, the WTO Secretariat published a special study on the positive effects of open financial services markets (*Opening Markets in Financial Services and the Role of the GATS* (Geneva: WTO Secretariat, 1997)).

[4] See pages 232-233 for a discussion of this Agreement.

[5] See pages 243-248 for a discussion of this Agreement.

comprehensive round of GATS market access negotiations is scheduled to begin.[6]

(5) *Government procurement of services.* Although government procurement of services is included within the scope of the *Agreement on Government Procurement*, that Agreement is one of the Plurilateral Trade Agreements and is therefore not subject to the single undertaking approach to WTO accession. Consequently, not all WTO Members are signatories to it. As a result, GATS Article XIII called for separate negotiations on government procurement of services to take place within the context of the GATS commencing no later than January 1, 1997. These negotiations, still at the issue-definition stage, have commenced within the Working Party on GATS Rules.

(6) *Emergency safeguard measures.* Article X of the GATS sets December 31, 1997 as the deadline for the entry into force of provisions concerning emergency safeguards relating to trade in services that are to be negotiated within the context of the GATS. These negotiations are also underway within the Working Party on GATS Rules.

(7) *Trade in services and the environment.* Under the *Decision on Trade in Services and the Environment*, by January 1998, the WTO's Committee on Trade and Environment is to complete a report, with recommendations, if any, on the relationship between trade in services and the environment.

(8) *Subsidies to services.* GATS Article XV provides that Members are to enter into further negotiations to develop multilateral disciplines on the granting of subsidies to services and service-providers with a view to avoiding the distortive effects that such subsidies can sometimes cause. These negotiations, still at the issue-definition stage, have commenced within the Working Group on GATS Rules, although there is no date specified for the conclusion of these negotiations.

(9) *Professional services.* Under the *Ministerial Decision on Professional Services*, and a subsequent decision of the Council for Trade in Services, a Working Party on Professional Services was established to develop further rules relating to trade in professional services, with a first priority being given to the accountancy sector. This Working Party began its work in late 1995 and is expected to finalize additional GATS rules for the accountancy sector by the end of 1997. Work on other professional sectors will then be undertaken. The Working Party has already concluded a set of non-binding guidelines concerning mutual recognition in the accountancy sector.

(10) *Comprehensive market access negotiations.* Under GATS Article XIX, beginning in January 2000, Members are to launch the first in a series of negotiating rounds aimed at further liberalizing trade in services. These

---

[6] See pages 240-243 for a discussion of issues relating to maritime services.

negotiations are to focus on reducing and eliminating adverse effects on trade in services and on opening new sectors. The Council on Trade in Services is also to conduct a review of all MFN exemptions taken under the GATS at this time.

(iii) Agenda Items under the Agreement on Trade-Related Aspects of Intellectual Property Rights

(1) Geographical indications. Article 23.4 of the *Agreement on Trade-Related Aspects of Intellectual Property Rights* requires the TRIPS Council to undertake negotiations concerning the establishment of a multilateral registration system for geographical indications. Preparations for these negotiations commenced on February 8, 1997. Article 24.2 of the TRIPS Agreement further requires the TRIPS Council to periodically review the application of the provisions of Article 24. The first such review was conducted in the fall of 1996. Among other things, Article 24 also requires Members to continue negotiations with the aim of further increasing the protection of individual geographical indications. A commencement or completion date for these negotiations has not been specified.

(2) Patentability of plants and animals. Subject to certain limitations, Article 27.3(b) of the TRIPS Agreement permits Members to exclude plants and animals from patentability. By January 1, 1999, and every four years thereafter, Members are to review the continued applicability of this exclusion.

(3) Overall review of the TRIPS Agreement. The TRIPS Council is to undertake its first review of the overall implementation of the TRIPS Agreement after January 1, 2000. A similar review is to be conducted every two years thereafter.

(iv) Agenda Item Under the Agreement on Government Procurement

Article XXIV:7 of the *Agreement on Government Procurement* establishes January 1999 as the starting date for further government procurement negotiations with the goal of further expanding the coverage of the Agreement.

(v) Agenda Item Under the Understanding on Rules and Procedures Governing the Settlement of Disputes

Under the *Decision on the Application and Review of the Understanding on Rules and Procedures Governing the Settlement of Disputes*, accepted as part of the final results of Uruguay Round, the Ministerial Conference is to complete, by January 1, 1999, a full review of the WTO's new rules and procedures governing the settlement of disputes to determine if they should continue, modify or terminate these rules and procedures.

(vi) Agenda Item under the Trade Policy Review Mechanism

The *Trade Policy Review Mechanism* ("TPRM") provides an ongoing mandate for regular WTO review of Members' trade policies. Under paragraph F of Annex 3 to the WTO Agreement, the Trade Policy Review Body is to undertake an appraisal of the operation of the TPRM by January 1, 2000, to then be presented to the Ministerial Conference. Future appraisals may then be conducted as requested by the Ministerial Conference.

(b) Implementation and Transparency

Full implementation of the WTO Agreement required significant changes to the domestic laws of all WTO Members. Questions and issues relating to implementation continue to arise. In addition, in some areas implementation still continues as many of the WTO Agreements provided longer phase-in periods for developing country Members. Thus, issues relating to implementation are likely to continue to arise for some time. Moreover, the obligation of full implementation has been made even more complex for many Members by the extensive notification and related transparency obligations found in almost all the WTO Agreements. These obligations require regular reporting by WTO Members on developments in many areas regulated by WTO obligations. Lacking the appropriate resources, some Members are already finding it difficult to meet their notification obligations on a regular and timely basis. The various councils and other WTO bodies will have to work to ensure that Members' notification obligations are being sufficiently met so as to protect the important WTO goal of improved overall transparency.

(c) Regionalism

The continued expansion of regional trading arrangements, such as NAFTA, the EC, MERCOSUR and others, continues to be of concern to some Members, particularly those that are not parties to any such regional arrangements. The concern in this area is related primarily to a perceived lack of sufficient WTO rules governing the establishment, expansion and overseeing of these arrangements. While some improvement to the previous GATT rules was introduced through the WTO's *Understanding on Interpretation of Article XXIV of the General Agreement on Tariffs and Trade 1994*, some Members consider that further work in the area is still required. Much analytical background work relating to possible improvements has already been undertaken, including the recent publication of an important study on regionalism by the WTO Secretariat.[7] The study noted that concerns over regional arrange-

---

[7] WTO Secretariat, *Regionalism and the World Trading System* (WTO: Geneva, April 1995).

ments and their consistency with the new WTO rules have taken on a new urgency with the adoption of the much-improved WTO dispute settlement system. The Secretariat suggested that three areas in particular be considered for improvement: the working party process which had been used to review notified regional arrangements; clarification and strengthening of the existing WTO rules which govern such arrangements, including those of GATT Article XXIV; and introducing improved overall transparency and surveillance of these arrangements.

Building on this analytical work, in February 1996, the General Council established a permanent Committee on Regional Trade Agreements. This Committee not only replaced the over 20 *ad hoc* working parties that were then in the process of reviewing notified regional arrangements, but the Committee has also been charged with developing proposals for improved review procedures and other possible amendments to the applicable WTO rules.

(d) Accessions

Work on the accession of new countries was always an important on-going function within the GATT. This work became increasingly important in recent years as the pace of growth in GATT membership accelerated significantly. For example, there were 94 GATT contracting parties at the time the Uruguay Round commenced and, as of September 6, 1997, there were 132 WTO Members. More importantly, 29 countries are now in the process of negotiating accession to the WTO, including the People's Republic of China, Taiwan and Russia.[8] While most accession negotiations are relatively straightforward and conclude quickly, others, such as those involving China and Russia, are taking considerably longer because of questions and concerns over the applicant's existing trade policies and ability to fully implement all the WTO obligations.

While expansion of the WTO to all countries of the world is a desirable goal, this expansion of membership can also carry with it added difficulties and increased work. For example, with increasing membership, consensus on some issues has become more difficult to attain. In addition, many of the countries now negotiating accession are developing countries, thus potentially introducing further issues relating to, amongst others, full implementation of the applicable obligations and the ability to meet the required notification obligations.

(e) Biennial Ministerial Meetings

In order to improve the overall functioning of the world trading system, facilitate continuous trade negotiations, and improve communication at the

---

[8] See the Annexes to chapter 2 for the lists of 132 WTO Members and 29 countries negotiating accession as of May 1, 1997.

highest political level amongst Member countries, Article IV:1 of the WTO Agreement provides that a Conference, comprised of Ministerial-level representatives of all Members, is to meet at least once every two years. The first such meeting of the WTO's Ministerial Conference took place in Singapore from December 9 to 13, 1996. As noted in the Singapore Ministerial Declaration,[9] the purpose of these biennial meetings is to further strengthen the WTO as a forum for negotiations, continue the liberalization of trade within a rules-based system, and provide for a regular multilateral review and assessment of trade policies.

The Singapore Ministerial Conference confirmed much of the ongoing work that is taking place within the WTO. The Conference also directed that work be commenced in a number of additional areas. By way of summary, the Conference:

- *Confirmed*, amongst other items, the role of the WTO, work underway on regionalism, accession negotiations, the new dispute settlement process, implementation, the role of developing countries in the world trading system, full implementation of the *Agreement on Textiles and Clothing*, services negotiations, and other ongoing work on the WTO's built-in agenda.

- *Commented* on the work done to date by the WTO's Committee on Trade and the Environment, and directed this Committee to continue to carry out its work under its existing terms of reference.

- *Established* three new working groups to examine issues relating to the trade and investment, trade and competition policy and transparency in government procurement practices.

- *Concluded* a new Agreement amongst many Members providing for tariff elimination, on an MFN basis, on trade in information technology products.

- *Rejected* the use of labour standards for protectionist purposes and renewed a commitment to observe internationally recognized labour standards, noting that it is for the International Labour Organization (and, by implication, not the WTO) to establish and deal with such standards.

This first Ministerial Conference appears to have been relatively successful, achieving many of the goals originally envisaged for such regular Ministerial meetings. It served to increase the political importance and visibility of trade issues. It proved useful in further fleshing out the WTO's existing agenda, particularly concerning the "trade and" issues, discussed below. And

---

[9] The *Singapore Ministerial Declaration* (18 December 1996) is attached as an Annex to this chapter.

it served as a useful catalyst to conclude an important tariff-elimination agreement on information technology products. The next Ministerial Conference is to be held on May 18 to 20, 1998 in Geneva.

3. THE NEW "TRADE AND" AGENDA ITEMS

In addition to the numerous agenda items relating to the WTO Agreement itself, the WTO has also discussed or commenced work in a number of the so-called "trade and" areas. These include trade and the environment, trade and labour, trade and investment, and trade and competition policy.

(a) Trade and the Environment

One of the most ambitious "trade and" areas is the consideration of the relationship between trade and the environment. This inter-relationship has seen substantial discussion, and analytical work in the trade policy field has been ongoing now for over 10 years. Largely at the insistence of the United States, which sent Vice-President Gore, a committed environmentalist, as its representative to the Marrakesh Meeting, Members brought environmental concerns into the WTO bailiwick through the *Ministerial Decision on Trade and the Environment*. The inclusion of environmental issues within the WTO framework was, and will continue to be, a very contentious issue. While Members generally have reached the consensus that unbridled trade can have deleterious effects on the environment, many Members still fear that environmental measures may easily be used for protectionist purposes, as disguised barriers to trade.

The *Decision on Trade and the Environment* directed the General Council at its first meeting to establish a Committee on Trade and the Environment. This Committee was so established and is open to all Members. It has been charged with considering seven major issues involving the inter-relationship between trade and environmental concerns:

- the relationship between the provisions of the multilateral trading system and trade measures for environmental purposes, including measures pursuant to multilateral environmental Agreements;
- the relationship between the multilateral trading system and environmental policies relevant to trade and environmental measures with significant trade effects;
- the relationship between the provisions of the multilateral trading system and charges and taxes for environmental purposes, and standards, technical regulations, packaging, labelling and recycling requirements for environmental purposes;
- the provisions of the multilateral trading system related to the transparency of trade measures used for environmental purposes and environmental measures that have significant trade effects;

- the relationship between the dispute settlement provisions of the multilateral trading system and those found in multilateral environmental Agreements;
- the effect of environmental provisions on market access; and
- the issue of exports of domestically prohibited goods.

In addition, the Decision also directed the Committee to undertake the Work Programme envisaged in the *Decision on Trade in Services and the Environment*, and the relevant provisions of the *Agreement on Trade-Related Aspects of Intellectual Property Rights*. Since the entry into force of the WTO Agreement, the Committee on Trade and the Environment has met regularly and extensively discussed all of the issues under its mandate. At the end of 1995, the Committee established a schedule of discussions to be reported to the Singapore Ministerial Conference. This schedule clearly narrowed the Committee's focus to three areas where it was believed that recommendations might be reached by December 1996: trade measures taken to enforce environmental agreements; domestically prohibited goods; and ecolabeling.

By September 1996, when the Committee began to draft its report for the Ministerial Conference, the negotiators had become frustrated with the lack of consensus on almost all issues and finally acknowledged that they would not be able to formulate any substantive recommendations for presentation to the Ministerial Conference. As expected, the Committee's report to the Ministers provided no substantive recommendations on trade and the environment, but stressed the consensus of the Members that the issue was serious. The report also discussed the issues that remained under consideration by the Committee and the various proposals that had been advanced by various Members on those issues. The report also set out the Committee's post-Singapore Work Programme.

Ministers reviewed the Committee's report during the Singapore meeting and instructed the Committee to continue to work under the authority of its existing mandate in a continued attempt to develop consensus recommendations on proposed rules to deal with the inter-relationship between trade and the environment.

(b) Trade and Labour

The future inclusion of labour issues under the WTO framework likely will be the most controversial issue before Members for many years to come. The United States has led the call for negotiations on trade and labour within the WTO, with the United States Trade Representative publicly stating that trade and labour is the United States' priority new issue.

By way of summary, issues in the trade and labour area relate to minimum core labour standards and their enforcement. Some Members are of the view that lax labour standards unfairly reduce labour costs and therefore constitute a form of unfair trade. Their position is that the WTO should play a leading role in establishing certain minimum core labour standards and then trade sanctions should be made available within the WTO framework to remedy any failures of Members to properly enforce those minimum standards.

The United States, in particular, urged the creation of a WTO working party which would have focused on five core labour standards: freedom of association; collective organization and bargaining; the elimination of the exploitation of child labour; a prohibition against forced labour; and non-discrimination. The United States found allies in Japan and some members of the EC. However, even within the EC itself, and especially among most developing country Members, there is high suspicion of the United States on the issue and strong disagreement that labour standards should be discussed in the WTO.

The primary argument against the discussion of labour standards within the WTO has been the fear of many developing countries that such talks will result in the elimination of their competitive advantage in labour wages. Because wages in most developing countries are significantly lower than wages in developed countries, the United States and other developed countries have charged that the developing countries maintain low wages by denying worker rights. The developing countries argue that they cannot sustain, and therefore should not be held to, the labour standards of the developed world until their level of economic development is equal to that of developed countries.

The lack of consensus on this issue was apparent in an October 1995 speech by WTO Director-General Renato Ruggiero. Mr. Ruggiero commented that the trade and labour area remains highly contentious, and, in the absence of any consensus on the issue, there is little likelihood that it can be brought onto the WTO's agenda. He also noted two pre-conditions for bringing labour issues into the WTO. First, a consensus must be reached on a narrower set of issues by eliminating those concerned with the comparative advantage of developing countries that result from their lower wages and focusing only on those that involve basic human rights. Second, assuming that consensus can be reached on this first point, the Members must then identify the core labour issues that are related to trade. Only then can the issue be brought within the WTO.

The issue of labour standards figured prominently in the lead-up to the Singapore meeting as the United States strongly pressed its desire for a WTO working group on the issue. It was not successful in the end. While Members generally renewed their commitment to the observance of internationally recognized core labour standards in the Singapore Ministerial Declaration, the

Declaration also stresses that the UN's International Labour Organization (the "ILO") remains the competent body in the field. Members also agreed that the comparative advantage of developing countries resulting from lower wages must, in no way, be put into question. Thus, any WTO work on the trade and labour issue is, for the near future at least, on hold. However, because of the strong interest in the area held by some important WTO Members, the issue of trade and labour standards still promises to remain constant and controversial within the WTO over the immediate term.

(c) Trade and Investment

Trade and investment has been described as the leading candidate for future work within the WTO. Under the GATT 1947, trade and investment were generally considered separate issues, even though trade barriers were often erected as a means of attracting foreign investment. As a result of the Uruguay Round, Members have taken a broader view of market access, and trade and investment are now being seen more as complements rather than alternatives. In a global economy, both trade policy and investment policy affect the ability of companies to trade abroad and the contestibility of domestic markets.

While it was the clear desire of some participants that the Uruguay Round address investment issues in some depth, in the end the WTO Agreement only made some initial attempts at adopting new disciplines, both in the *General Agreement on Trade in Services* and in the *Agreement on Trade-Related Investment Measures*. With respect to the TRIMs Agreement, while some participants had proposed an expansive Agreement that would have included significant new disciplines on the use of investment measures, in the end, the resulting Agreement is considered to have done little more than confirm a number of pre-existing GATT obligations.

However, as discussed above, the TRIMs Agreement does provide that, beginning in January 2000, the Council on Trade in Goods is to consider whether the Agreement should be complemented with additional provisions relating to investment policy. Thus, consideration of the inclusion of investment issues under the WTO framework can be considered to already be part of the WTO's built-in agenda. Preliminary work on this issue within the WTO has already commenced. In October 1996, the WTO Secretariat produced a lengthy report, which introduces and briefly analyzes many of the background issues relating to trade and investment.[10] The Report concludes with a subtle call for negotiations within the WTO.

In addition to work within the WTO, and of more immediate importance, the 27 member countries of the Organization for Economic Development and

---

[10] WTO Secretariat, "Trade and Foreign Direct Investment", 16 October 1996.

Co-operation ("OECD") are currently in the process of negotiating a comprehensive international treaty on investment issues, the *Multilateral Agreement on Investment*. This new Agreement is likely to establish significant new disciplines relating to investment. In an attempt to ensure broad coverage, once the Agreement is complete, accession is likely to be open to all non-OECD countries.

Regardless of this progress on other fronts, many WTO Members still wish to accelerate the process on investment issues within the WTO. These Members are seeking broad international investment rules built upon the WTO principles of non-discrimination that will encourage and protect foreign investment. In 1996, Canada proposed that a WTO Work Programme be established to analyze the possibility of a WTO investment agreement. The Canadian proposal was supported by all of the major industrialized nations, as well as many developing countries. Japan submitted a further proposal that took Canada's one step further, suggesting that the Work Programme develop international investment rules for possible inclusion in the WTO.

At the Singapore Meeting, Ministers did agreed to establish a working group to examine the relationship between trade and investment. In this regard, the Ministerial Declaration encourages cooperation with other organizations in conducting the study to make the best use of available resources. The Declaration cautions, however, that WTO negotiations, if any, regarding multilateral rules on trade and investment will take place only after an explicit consensus decision of Members is taken regarding such negotiations. The General Council will review the work of the working group and will determine in late 1999 how the group's work should proceed. In this regard, the possibility does exist that the working group may recommend that OECD's *Multilateral Agreement on Investment* (which is likely to be in force by then) should be used as the basis for a WTO Agreement on the subject, or alternatively, the OECD Agreement might be brought within or "docked" onto the WTO Agreement in some fashion, such as inclusion as one of the WTO's Plurilateral Agreements.

(d) Trade and Competition Policy

Competition laws, or a lack thereof, and the resulting effects on trade, is a longstanding issue within the global trading system. For example, the 1948 Havana Charter contained a comprehensive scheme for controlling restrictive business practices, whereby signatories would have cooperated with the International Trade Organization to prevent "business practices affecting international trade which restrain competition, limit access to markets, or foster monopolistic control." This lead was then followed in the GATT context by a 1960 Decision of the Contracting Parties that provided for consultations on restrictive business practices that were seen to be affecting trade.[11] However,

---

[11] GATT, BISD 9S/170.

somewhat surprisingly, no consultations were ever requested under this GATT Decision. And, following on this rather schizophrenic history of the issue, the inclusion of competition policy issues in the WTO, although frequently discussed, has, so far at least, received little support.

In the early 1990s, Sir Leon Brittan, then EC Competition Minister, began calling for an expanded GATT role in developing minimum international competition rules that would be enforced by GATT contracting parties. Although such rules never materialized out of the Uruguay Round, the OECD has held serious discussions on the subject, and, in 1993, the International Antitrust Code Working Group (an international independent group of competition law experts) released a draft international antitrust Code designed to be adopted as a WTO Agreement. Again, however, no true international consensus has yet developed around these developments.

The primary difficulty in reaching a consensus has been the inability to define the scope of international competition rules. While such rules likely would cover issues such as merger policy and restrictive business practices, several Members have also urged the inclusion of anti-dumping and subsidies practices within the scope of any negotiations. This suggestion has been met with strong opposition by the United States, which also expresses an additional concern over any international rules that would limit prosecutorial discretion in the competition law area.

The WTO Agreement does, however, already include competition policy-related provisions, such as those in the *General Agreement on Trade in Services*, the *Agreement on Trade-Related Aspects of Intellectual Property Rights* and the *Agreement on Trade-Related Investment Measures*. The TRIMS Agreement, for example, calls on the Council on Trade in Goods, beginning in January 2000, to consider whether that Agreement should be complemented with additional provisions dealing with competition policy.

At the Singapore Meeting, Ministers decided to establish a working group to study issues related to the interaction between trade and competition policy, including anti-competitive practices, in order to identify areas that may merit further consideration in the WTO framework. As with the study of trade and investment, the Declaration cautions that any negotiations on multilateral rules on trade and competition policy will only take place after an explicit consensus of the Members exists to commence such negotiations. The General Council is to review the work of the working group in late 1999 and then decide how the group's work should proceed.

4. CONCLUSION

1998 will mark the fiftieth anniversary of the multilateral trading system, and most commentators would have to agree that the system has been, and continues to be, a success. Since 1948, tariffs and non-tariff barriers have been reduced, and trade in goods has increased substantially. With the birth of the WTO, Member nations extended the multilateral trading system well beyond trade in goods to cover trade in services and intellectual property as well. The WTO now has 132 Members, with a further 29 nations seeking accession. The likely accession of China, Taiwan and the countries of the former USSR means that the WTO will truly become the "World" Trade Organization.

The Singapore Ministerial Declaration best summarizes the success of the multilateral trading system to date and a forecast for its future:

> For nearly 50 years Members have sought to fulfill, first in the GATT and now in the WTO, the objectives reflected in the preamble of the WTO Agreement of conducting our trade relations with a view to raising standards of living worldwide. The rise in global trade facilitated by trade liberalization within the rules-based system has created more and better-paid jobs in many countries. The achievements of the WTO during its first two years bear witness to our desire to work together to make the most of the possibilities that the multilateral system provides to promote sustainable growth and development while contributing to a more stable and secure climate in international relations.

Although the WTO's future agenda is ambitious, the Members have demonstrated that over time, consensus can be reached, even in the most controversial areas. This consensus-building approach has served the multilateral trading system well for the past 50 years, and has established a strong foundation for its future success.

5. ANNEX: SINGAPORE MINISTERIAL DECLARATION

WORLD TRADE ORGANIZATION

WT/MIN(96)/DEC
18 December 1996

(96-5316)

MINISTERIAL CONFERENCE
Singapore, 9-13 December 1996

SINGAPORE MINISTERIAL DECLARATION

Adopted on 13 December 1996

Purpose

1. We, the Ministers, have met in Singapore from 9 to 13 December 1996 for the first regular biennial meeting of the WTO at Ministerial level, as called for in Article IV of the Agreement Establishing the World Trade Organization, to further strengthen the WTO as a forum for negotiation, the continuing liberalization of trade within a rule-based system, and the multilateral review and assessment of trade policies, and in particular to:

- assess the implementation of our commitments under the WTO Agreements and decisions;
- review the ongoing negotiations and Work Programme;
- examine developments in world trade; and
- address the challenges of an evolving world economy.

Trade and Economic Growth

2. For nearly 50 years Members have sought to fulfil, first in the GATT and now in the WTO, the objectives reflected in the preamble to the WTO Agreement of conducting our trade relations with a view to raising standards of living worldwide. The rise in global trade facilitated by trade liberalization within the rules-based system has created more and better-paid jobs in many countries. The achievements of the WTO during its first two years bear witness to our desire to work together to make the most of the possibilities that the multilateral system provides to promote sustainable growth and development while contributing to a more stable and secure climate in international relations.

Integration of Economies; Opportunities and Challenges

3. We believe that the scope and pace of change in the international economy, including the growth in trade in services and direct investment, and the increasing integration of economies offer unprecedented opportunities for improved growth, job creation, and development. These developments require adjustment by economies and societies. They also pose challenges to the trading system. We commit ourselves to address these challenges.

Core Labour Standards

4. We renew our commitment to the observance of internationally recognized core labour standards. The International Labour Organization (ILO) is the competent body to set and deal with these standards, and we affirm our support for its work in promoting them. We believe that economic growth and development fostered by increased trade and further trade liberalization contribute to the promotion of these standards. We reject the use of labour standards for protectionist purposes, and agree that the comparative advantage of countries, particularly low-wage developing countries, must in no way be put into question. In this regard, we note that the WTO and ILO Secretariats will continue their existing collaboration.

Marginalization

5. We commit ourselves to address the problem of marginalization for least-developed countries, and the risk of it for certain developing countries.

We will also continue to work for greater coherence in international economic policy-making and for improved coordination between the WTO and other agencies in providing technical assistance.

Role of WTO

6. In pursuit of the goal of sustainable growth and development for the common good, we envisage a world where trade flows freely. To this end we renew our commitment to:

- a fair, equitable and more open rule-based system;
- progressive liberalization and elimination of tariff and non-tariff barriers to trade in goods;
- progressive liberalization of trade in services;
- rejection of all forms of protectionism;
- elimination of discriminatory treatment in international trade relations;
- integration of developing and least-developed countries and economies in transition into the multilateral system; and
- the maximum possible level of transparency.

Regional Agreements

7. We note that trade relations of WTO Members are being increasingly influenced by regional trade agreements, which have expanded vastly in number, scope and coverage. Such initiatives can promote further liberalization and may assist least-developed, developing and transition economies in integrating into the international trading system. In this context, we note the importance of existing regional arrangements involving developing and least-developed countries. The expansion and extent of regional trade agreements make it important to analyse whether the system of WTO rights and obligations as it relates to regional trade agreements needs to be further clarified. We reaffirm the primacy of the multilateral trading system, which includes a framework for the development of regional trade agreements, and we renew our commitment to ensure that regional trade agreements are complementary to it and consistent with its rules. In this regard, we welcome the establishment and endorse the work of the new Committee on Regional Trade Agreements. We shall continue to work through progressive liberalization in the WTO as we are committed in the WTO Agreement and Decisions adopted at Marrakesh, and in so doing facilitate mutually supportive processes of global and regional trade liberalization.

Accessions

8. It is important that the 28 applicants now negotiating accession contribute to completing the accession process by accepting the WTO rules and

by offering meaningful market access commitments. We will work to bring these applicants expeditiously into the WTO system.

Dispute Settlement

9. The Dispute Settlement Understanding (DSU) offers a means for the settlement of disputes among Members that is unique in international agreements. We consider its impartial and transparent operation to be of fundamental importance in assuring the resolution of trade disputes, and in fostering the implementation and application of the WTO agreements. The Understanding, with its predictable procedures, including the possibility of appeal of panel decisions to an Appellate Body and provisions on implementation of recommendations, has improved Members' means of resolving their differences. We believe that the DSU has worked effectively during its first two years. We also note the role that several WTO bodies have played in helping to avoid disputes. We renew our determination to abide by the rules and procedures of the DSU and other WTO agreements in the conduct of our trade relations and the settlement of disputes. We are confident that longer experience with the DSU, including the implementation of panel and appellate recommendations, will further enhance the effectiveness and credibility of the dispute settlement system.

Implementation

10. We attach high priority to full and effective implementation of the WTO Agreement in a manner consistent with the goal of trade liberalization. Implementation thus far has been generally satisfactory, although some Members have expressed dissatisfaction with certain aspects. It is clear that further effort in this area is required, as indicated by the relevant WTO bodies in their reports. Implementation of the specific commitments scheduled by Members with respect to market access in industrial goods and trade in services appears to be proceeding smoothly. With respect to industrial market access, monitoring of implementation would be enhanced by the timely availability of trade and tariff data. Progress has been made also in advancing the WTO reform programme in agriculture, including in implementation of agreed market access concessions and domestic subsidy and export subsidy commitments.

Notifications and Legislation

11. Compliance with notification requirements has not been fully satisfactory. Because the WTO system relies on mutual monitoring as a means to assess implementation, those Members which have not submitted notifications in a timely manner, or whose notifications are not complete, should renew their efforts. At the same time, the relevant bodies should take appropriate

steps to promote full compliance while considering practical proposals for simplifying the notification process.

12. Where legislation is needed to implement WTO rules, Members are mindful of their obligations to complete their domestic legislative process without further delay. Those Members entitled to transition periods are urged to take steps as they deem necessary to ensure timely implementation of obligations as they come into effect. Each Member should carefully review all its existing or proposed legislation, programmes and measures to ensure their full compatibility with the WTO obligations, and should carefully consider points made during review in the relevant WTO bodies regarding the WTO consistency of legislation, programmes and measures, and make appropriate changes where necessary.

Developing Countries

13. The integration of developing countries in the multilateral trading system is important for their economic development and for global trade expansion. In this connection, we recall that the WTO Agreement embodies provisions conferring differential and more favourable treatment for developing countries, including special attention to the particular situation of least-developed countries. We acknowledge the fact that developing country Members have undertaken significant new commitments, both substantive and procedural, and we recognize the range and complexity of the efforts that they are making to comply with them. In order to assist them in these efforts, including those with respect to notification and legislative requirements, we will improve the availability of technical assistance under the agreed guidelines. We have also agreed to recommendations relative to the decision we took at Marrakesh concerning the possible negative effects of the agricultural reform programme on least-developed and net food-importing developing countries.

Least-Developed Countries

14. We remain concerned by the problems of the least-developed countries and have agreed to:

- a Plan of Action, including provision for taking positive measures, for example duty-free access, on an autonomous basis, aimed at improving their overall capacity to respond to the opportunities offered by the trading system;

- seek to give operational content to the Plan of Action, for example, by enhancing conditions for investment and providing predictable and favourable market access conditions for LLDCs' products, to foster the expansion and diversification of their exports to the markets of all developed countries; and in the case of relevant developing countries in the context of the Global System of Trade Preferences; and

• organize a meeting with UNCTAD and the International Trade Centre as soon as possible in 1997, with the participation of aid agencies, multilateral financial institutions and least-developed countries to foster an integrated approach to assisting these countries in enhancing their trading opportunities.

Textiles and Clothing

15. We confirm our commitment to full and faithful implementation of the provisions of the Agreement on Textiles and Clothing (ATC). We stress the importance of the integration of textile products, as provided for in the ATC, into GATT 1994 under its strengthened rules and disciplines because of its systemic significance for the rule-based, non-discriminatory trading system and its contribution to the increase in export earnings of developing countries. We attach importance to the implementation of this Agreement so as to ensure an effective transition to GATT 1994 by way of integration which is progressive in character. The use of safeguard measures in accordance with ATC provisions should be as sparing as possible. We note concerns regarding the use of other trade distortive measures and circumvention. We reiterate the importance of fully implementing the provisions of the ATC relating to small suppliers, new entrants and least-developed country Members, as well as those relating to cotton-producing exporting Members. We recognize the importance of wool products for some developing country Members. We reaffirm that as part of the integration process and with reference to the specific commitments undertaken by the Members as a result of the Uruguay Round, all Members shall take such action as may be necessary to abide by GATT 1994 rules and disciplines so as to achieve improved market access for textiles and clothing products. We agree that, keeping in view its quasi-judicial nature, the Textiles Monitoring Body (TMB) should achieve transparency in providing rationale for its findings and recommendations. We expect that the TMB shall make findings and recommendations whenever called upon to do so under the Agreement. We emphasize the responsibility of the Goods Council in overseeing, in accordance with Article IV:5 of the WTO Agreement and Article 8 of the ATC, the functioning of the ATC, whose implementation is being supervised by the TMB.

Trade and Environment

16. The Committee on Trade and Environment has made an important contribution towards fulfilling its Work Programme. The Committee has been examining and will continue to examine, *inter alia*, the scope of the comple-

mentarities between trade liberalization, economic development and environmental protection. Full implementation of the WTO Agreements will make an important contribution to achieving the objectives of sustainable development. The work of the Committee has underlined the importance of policy coordination at the national level in the area of trade and environment. In this connection, the work of the Committee has been enriched by the participation of environmental as well as trade experts from Member governments and the further participation of such experts in the Committee's deliberations would be welcomed. The breadth and complexity of the issues covered by the Committee's Work Programme shows that further work needs to be undertaken on all items of its agenda, as contained in its report. We intend to build on the work accomplished thus far, and therefore direct the Committee to carry out its work, reporting to the General Council, under its existing terms of reference.

Services Negotiations

17. The fulfilment of the objectives agreed at Marrakesh for negotiations on the improvement of market access in services — in financial services, movement of natural persons, maritime transport services and basic telecommunications — has proved to be difficult. The results have been below expectations. In three areas, it has been necessary to prolong negotiations beyond the original deadlines. We are determined to obtain a progressively higher level of liberalization in services on a mutually advantageous basis with appropriate flexibility for individual developing country Members, as envisaged in the Agreement, in the continuing negotiations and those scheduled to begin no later than 1 January 2000. In this context, we look forward to full MFN agreements based on improved market access commitments and national treatment. Accordingly, we will:

- achieve a successful conclusion to the negotiations on basic telecommunications in February 1997; and

- resume financial services negotiations in April 1997 with the aim of achieving significantly improved market access commitments with a broader level of participation in the agreed time frame.

With the same broad objectives in mind, we also look forward to a successful conclusion of the negotiations on Maritime Transport Services in the next round of negotiations on services liberalization.

In professional services, we shall aim at completing the work on the accountancy sector by the end of 1997, and will continue to develop multilateral disciplines and guidelines. In this connection, we encourage the successful completion of international standards in the accountancy sector by IFAC, IASC, and IOSCO. With respect to GATS rules, we shall undertake the necessary work with a view to completing the negotiations on safeguards by the end of 1997. We also note that more analytical work will be needed on emergency safeguards measures, government procurement in services and subsidies.

ITA and Pharmaceuticals

18. Taking note that a number of Members have agreed on a Declaration on Trade in Information Technology Products, we welcome the initiative taken by a number of WTO Members and other States or separate customs territories which have applied to accede to the WTO, who have agreed to tariff elimination for trade in information technology products on an MFN basis as well as the addition by a number of Members of over 400 products to their lists of tariff-free products in pharmaceuticals.

Work Programme and Built-in Agenda

19. Bearing in mind that an important aspect of WTO activities is a continuous overseeing of the implementation of various agreements, a periodic examination and updating of the WTO Work Programme is a key to enable the WTO to fulfil its objectives. In this context, we endorse the reports of the various WTO bodies. A major share of the Work Programme stems from the WTO Agreement and decisions adopted at Marrakesh. As part of these Agreements and decisions we agreed to a number of provisions calling for future negotiations on Agriculture, Services and aspects of TRIPS, or reviews and other work on Anti-Dumping, Customs Valuation, Dispute Settlement Understanding, Import Licensing, Preshipment Inspection, Rules of Origin, Sanitary and Phyto-Sanitary Measures, Safeguards, Subsidies and Countervailing Measures, Technical Barriers to Trade, Textiles and Clothing, Trade Policy Review Mechanism, Trade-Related Aspects of Intellectual Property Rights and Trade-Related Investment Measures. We agree to a process of analysis and exchange of information, where provided for in the conclusions and recommendations of the relevant WTO bodies, on the Built-in Agenda issues, to allow Members to better understand the issues involved and identify their interests before undertaking the agreed negotiations and reviews. We agree that:

- the time frames established in the Agreements will be respected in each case;
- the work undertaken shall not prejudge the scope of future negotiations where such negotiations are called for; and
- the work undertaken shall not prejudice the nature of the activity agreed upon (i.e. negotiation or review).

Investment and Competition

20. Having regard to the existing WTO provisions on matters related to investment and competition policy and the built-in agenda in these areas,

including under the TRIMs Agreement, and on the understanding that the work undertaken shall not prejudge whether negotiations will be initiated in the future, we also agree to:

- establish a working group to examine the relationship between trade and investment; and
- establish a working group to study issues raised by Members relating to the interaction between trade and competition policy, including anti-competitive practices, in order to identify any areas that may merit further consideration in the WTO framework.

These groups shall draw upon each other's work if necessary and also draw upon and be without prejudice to the work in UNCTAD and other appropriate intergovernmental fora. As regards UNCTAD, we welcome the work under way as provided for in the Midrand Declaration and the contribution it can make to the understanding of issues. In the conduct of the work of the working groups, we encourage cooperation with the above organizations to make the best use of available resources and to ensure that the development dimension is taken fully into account. The General Council will keep the work of each body under review, and will determine after two years how the work of each body should proceed. It is clearly understood that future negotiations, if any, regarding multilateral disciplines in these areas, will take place only after an explicit consensus decision is taken among WTO Members regarding such negotiations.

21. We further agree to:

Transparency in Government Procurement

- establish a working group to conduct a study on transparency in government procurement practices, taking into account national policies, and, based on this study, to develop elements for inclusion in anppropriate agreement; and

Trade Facilitation

- direct the Council for Trade in Goods to undertake exploratory and analytical work, drawing on the work of other relevant international organizations, on the simplification of trade procedures in order to assess the scope for WTO rules in this area.

22. In the organization of the work referred to in paragraphs 20 and 21, careful attention will be given to minimizing the burdens on delegations, especially those with more limited resources, and to coordinating meetings with those of relevant UNCTAD bodies. The technical cooperation programme of the Secretariat will be available to developing and, in particular, least-developed country Members to facilitate their participation in this work.

23. Noting that the 50th anniversary of the multilateral trading system will occur early in 1998, we instruct the General Council to consider how this historic event can best be commemorated.

* * * * *

Finally, we express our warmest thanks to the Chairman of the Ministerial Conference, Mr. Yeo Cheow Tong, for his personal contribution to the success of this Ministerial Conference. We also want to express our sincere gratitude to Prime Minister Goh Chok Tong, his colleagues in the Government of Singapore and the people of Singapore for their warm hospitality and the excellent organization they have provided. The fact that this first Ministerial Conference of the WTO has been held at Singapore is an additional manifestation of Singapore's commitment to an open world trading system.

Selected Bibliography

Adamantopoulos, Konstantinos. "Towards a Multilateral Investment Regime: Results in the Uruguay Round and Prospects in the OECD", a 1995 Supplement to *International Banking and Financial Law*.

Bello, Judith and Alan Homer. "U.S. Trade Law and Policy Series No. 19: The Uruguay Round: Where Are We Now?" in 25 *The International Law* (Fall 1991) at 723-732.

Buchanan, Mark A. *The Asia-Pacific Region and the Expanding Borders of the WTO: Implications, Challenges and Opportunities*. Victoria, B.C.: Centre for Asia-Pacific Initiatives, 1996.

Cadsby, Charles B. and Kenneth Woodside. *Canada and the New Subsidies Code*. C.D. Howe Commentary No. 75. Toronto: C.D. Howe Institute, 1996.

Canada. "Agreement Establishing the World Trade Organization: Canadian Statement on Implementation" in *Canada Gazette, Part I*, 31 December 1994, at 4845-4953.

Croome, John. *Reshaping the World Trading System: A History of the Uruguay Round*. Geneva: World Trade Organization, 1995.

Curzon, Gerald. *Multilateral Commercial Diplomacy*. London: Michael Joseph, 1965.

Dam, Kenneth W. *The GATT: Law and International Economic Organization*. Chicago: University of Chicago Press, 1970.

Finger, J. Michael and A. Olechowski (eds.). *The Uruguay Round: A Handbook for the Multilateral Trade Negotiations*. Washington, DC: World Bank, 1987.

Footer, Mary E. "GATT and the Multilateral Regulation of Banking Services" in 27 *The International Law* (Summer 1993) 343-367.

GATT. *Basic Instruments and Selected Documents*. Geneva: GATT Secretariat, Supplements published 1953 to 1994.

GATT. *Analytical Index: Guide to GATT Law and Practice* (6th ed.). Geneva: GATT Secretariat, 1994.

GATT. *GATT Focus Newsletter*. Geneva: GATT Secretariat, various issues.

GATT. *News of the Uruguay Round of Multilateral Trade Negotiations*. Geneva: GATT Secretariat, various issues.

GATT. *Trade Policies for a Better Future: Proposals for Action.* Geneva: GATT Secretariat, 1985.

GATT. *Trends in International Trade: Report by a Panel of Experts.* Geneva: GATT, 1958.

Geller, Paul E. "Intellectual Property in the Global Marketplace: Impact of TRIPS Dispute Settlement" in 29 *The International Lawyer* (Spring 1995) 99-115.

Hart, Michael (ed.). *Also Present at the Creation: Dana Wilgress and the United Nations Conference on Trade and Employment at Havana.* Ottawa: Centre for Trade Policy and Law, 1995.

Hoekman, Bernard M. *Trade Laws and Institutions: Good Practices and the World Trade Organization.* (World Bank Discussion Paper 282) Washington, DC: World Bank, 1995.

Horlick, G.N. and Peggy A. Clarke. "The 1994 WTO Subsidies Agreement" in 17 *World Competition* (June 1994) 41-54.

Horlick, G.N. and Eleanor Shea. "The World Trade Organization Antidumping Agreement" in 29 *Journal of World Trade* (1995) 5-13.

Hudec, Robert E. *Enforcing International Trade Law.* Salem, N.H.: Butterworth Legal Publishers, 1993.

Hudec, Robert E. *The GATT Legal System and World Trade Diplomacy* (2nd ed.). Salem N.H.: Butterworth Legal Publishers, 1990.

Hufbauer, G.C., J. Shelton Erb and H.P. Starr. "The GATT Codes and the Unconditional Most-Favored-Nation Principle" in 12:59 *Law & Policy in International Business* (1980) 59-93.

Jackson, John H. "The Birth of the GATT — MTN System: A Constitutional Appraisal" in 12:21 *Law & Policy in International Business* (1980) 21-58.

Jackson, John H. *World Trade and the Law of GATT.* Indianapolis: Bobbs-Merrill, 1969.

Jackson, John H. *The World Trading System.* Cambridge, Mass.: MIT Press, 1989.

Jackson, John H. *Restructuring the GATT System.* London: Printer for the Royal Institute of International Affairs, 1990.

Long, Olivier. *Law and Its Limitations in the GATT Multilateral Trade System.* Dordrecht: Martinus Nijhoff Publishers, 1985.

Miner, W.M. *The GATT Negotiations and Canadian Agriculture: Preparing for the Brussels Ministerial Meeting.* A Discussion Paper prepared for a workshop on the GATT Agricultural Trade Negotiations, Centre for Trade Policy and Law, Carlton University, Ottawa, November 1990.

Organisation for Economic Co-operation and Development (OECD). *The New World Trading System: Readings.* Paris: OECD, 1994.

Organisation for Economic Co-operation and Development (OECD). *Assessing the Effects of the Uruguay Round.* Paris: OECD, 1993.

Quinn, J. and Philip Slayton (eds.). *Non-Tariff Barriers After the Tokyo Round.* Montreal: Institute for Research on Public Policy, 1982.

Sauvé, P. "Assessing the General Agreement on Trade in Services: Half-Full or Half-Empty?" in 29 *Journal of World Trade* (1995), 125-145.

Schott, Jeffrey J. and Johanna Buurman. *The Uruguay Round: An Assessment.* Washington, DC: Institute for International Economics, 1994.

Stewart, T.P. (ed). *The GATT Uruguay Round: A Negotiating History.* Boston: Kluwer Law and Taxation Publishers, 1993.

Stewart, T.P. (ed). *The World Trade Organization: Multilateral Trade Framework for the 21st Century.* Washington, DC: American Bar Association, Section of International Law and Practice, 1996.

Stone, Frank. *Canada, the GATT and the International Trade System.* Montreal: Institute for Research on Public Policy, 1992.

United States. "The Uruguay Round Agreements Act: Statement of Administrative Action" in *Uruguay Round Trade Agreements, Texts of Agreements, Implementing Bill, Statement of Administrative Action, and Required Supporting Documents,* 103d Congress, 2d Session, House Document 103-316, at 656-1162. Washington, DC: U.S. Government Printing Office, 1994.

United States Department of Agriculture. *Agricultural Provisions of the Uruguay Round.* Washington, DC: U.S. Department of Agriculture, 1994.

Whalley, John and Colleen Hamilton. *The Trading System After the Uruguay Round.* Washington, DC: Institute for International Economics, 1996.

Wilcox, Clair. *A Charter for World Trade.* New York: Macmillan, 1949.

World Trade Organization. *WTO Annual Report, 1996.* Geneva: WTO Secretariat, 1997.

World Trade Organization. *Regionalism and the World Trading System.* Geneva: WTO Secretariat, 1995.

World Trade Organization. *WTO Focus Newsletter.* Geneva: WTO Secretariat, ongoing.

Index